MAJOR BIBLE THEMES

An Outline Course in Biblical Teaching
and Christian Living

PAUL E. SNUFFER

WestBow Press books may be ordered through booksellers or by contacting:

WestBow Press
A Division of Thomas Nelson & Zondervan
1663 Liberty Drive
Bloomington, IN 47403
www.westbowpress.com
844-714-3454

Illustrations by Alena Glad

ISBN: 978-1-6642-6311-6 (sc)
ISBN: 978-1-6642-6310-9 (e)

Library of Congress Control Number: 2022906599

Print information available on the last page.

WestBow Press rev. date: 9/30/2022

I wish to acknowledge Rev. John Miles, who has provided much of the outline for this book. John Miles had a major impact on my spiritual life and Biblical training, and I wish to dedicate this book to his memory.

L. John Miles
1916-2009

CONTENTS

INTRODUCTION

This is an outline course in Christian doctrine. It is not intended to be an exhaustive study of Christian teaching or theology but rather has been prepared as a teaching resource for pastors, teachers, or parents to instruct students in the foundational truths of the Christian faith and life.

Acquiring a panoramic understanding of the Bible prepares students to draw a more accurate understanding when reading or studying individual passages. All biblical truth should be understood from the context of God's full revelation. This broader understanding of the Word of God also provides a foundation for identifying heretical teaching.

The appalling fact is that many of our young people are abandoning their Christian faith when they enter the university environment and are faced with new social and intellectual challenges. Unless our youth are well grounded in biblical truth, they may be easily swayed by false teaching. It is not enough to simply know the Sunday School Bible stories, encounter Christian camp experiences, or listen to church youth group devotionals. These activities are not likely to sustain one's faith when separated from family and placed in an academic environment that is increasingly intimidating and often hostile towards genuine Christianity. We can no longer risk "building our house on the sand" (Matthew 7:25–27).

It is important for our young people to know ***what*** **they believe** and ***why*** **they believe it,** as they face the challenges of a godless and secular world. Unless we provide them with a solid biblical foundation, they are apt to accept destructive philosophies and succumb to social pressures.

I am retired now, but I have taught this curriculum in each of the five churches I have served during my pastoral career. Of course, there is no guarantee, but as I look back over my ministry, most of the young people who went through this course are still serving the Lord and walking with Him today.

God bless and guide you as you undertake this teaching commitment.

SUGGESTED USES OF THIS BOOK

This Bible doctrine curriculum will be a benefit to both students and teachers in the following settings:

Note: It is recommended that each student have his or her own personal copy of this book.

1. Pastor's Bible Instruction Class (Pastor's Confirmation Class) – This teaching tool is ideal for youth ages fourteen and older. Preferably, the class calls for a commitment of 1–1½ hours weekly for 2–4 school semesters. This teaching approach calls for a significant teacher/student commitment and can be followed by a formal graduation service before the entire church family.

2. Teen/Adult Home Bible Studies – This book is an effective guide for a small group Bible study.

3. Home School Curriculum – This Bible doctrine course is a valuable asset for any home school or home school cooperative.

4. Christian High School or Bible College Curriculum – This material offers a solid foundation for upper high school students or entry level Bible college students.

5. Sunday School Class – This book gives a clear understanding of Bible doctrine and helps individuals know what the Bible teaches.

CHAPTER 1

Essentials for a Thematic Approach to a Study of the Bible

I. The Definition of Theology

Theology: This word *theology* is used to describe a systematic study of the Bible. The word has two uses: the narrow and broad meanings.

A. The narrow meaning

The doctrine of God (who God is and what God has done, is doing, and will do). The word *theology* comes from two Greek words: *Theos*, which means "God" and *logos*, which means "a word." The narrow meaning therefore is "a word about God or a study of God."

B. The broad meaning

The broad meaning of the word *theology* is a study of the entire scope of Christian teaching drawn from the Bible and arranged in a systematic form. We might call it the "skeleton" of the Bible's teaching. This broader position of theology is not always seen on the surface, nor do we always display it out front, but it gives shape and design to our Christian faith and practice.

II. The Benefits of a Systematic Study of the Bible

A. Efficiency is developed where material is systematically arranged.

It is impossible for scientists, historians, or researchers to make progress unless they can catalog and organize their findings and materials as they proceed in their studies. The human mind seeks a system.

B. Theology, when properly understood, combats false conclusions.

When all scripture passages on a given subject are carefully considered and weighed in the light of their local context, and the context of the message of the entire Bible, accurate conclusions can be drawn. One of the huge failures of false religions and cults is that they do not take into consideration the entirety of scripture. They take an isolated verse here and there, lift it out of context, and are led to false conclusions.

C. A thorough knowledge of theology will help the child of God serve the Lord more effectively with his or her efforts.

Children of God will understand which doctrines are major and important. If people understand God's purpose and aim their lives and ministry efforts in keeping with that purpose, they will make the best use of their time and labors. If they understand God's methods for serving and living, they will focus their time and energy on that which is important and in keeping with the instruction of God's Word.

Note: A builder who seeks to build without a blueprint or plan will produce a monstrosity without design, beauty, or usefulness. He or she must have a master plan to follow. Likewise, we must have an overview of who God is, who we are, and what God's plan is before we can begin building our lives with His beauty and design.

III. Five Requirements for a Serious Study of the Bible

A. The presence of the indwelling Holy Spirit

As we shall learn, the Holy Spirit lives in every true believer. The true believer is a person who is trusting in the shed blood of Christ for the forgiveness of sin and, therefore, is a child of God. One of the ministries of the Holy Spirit to the believer, is that He is our teacher and helps us understand the truth of the Bible. He dwells *only* in the believer; therefore, the student of the Bible must be a true believer and must be in complete submission to the Holy Spirit as his or her teacher. Note the following scripture:

John 16:13–14

> [13] But when He, the Spirit of truth, comes, He will guide you into all the truth; for He will not speak on His own initiative, but whatever He hears, He will speak; and He will disclose to you what is to come. [14] He will glorify Me, for He will take of Mine and will disclose *it* to you.

1 Corinthians 2:6–13

> [6] Yet we do speak wisdom among those who are mature; a wisdom, however, not of this age nor of the rulers of this age, who are passing away; [7] but we speak God's wisdom in a mystery, the hidden *wisdom* which God predestined before the ages to our glory; [8] *the wisdom* which none of the rulers of this age has understood; for if they had understood it they would not have crucified the Lord of glory; [9] but just as it is written,
>
> "THINGS WHICH EYE HAS NOT SEEN AND EAR HAS NOT HEARD, AND *which* HAVE NOT ENTERED THE HEART OF MAN, ALL THAT GOD HAS PREPARED FOR THOSE WHO LOVE HIM."
>
> [10] For to us God revealed *them* through the Spirit; for the Spirit searches all things, even the depths of God. [11] For who among men knows the *thoughts* of a man except the spirit of the man which is in him? Even so the *thoughts* of God no one knows except the Spirit of God. [12] Now we have received, not the spirit of the world, but the Spirit who is from God, so that we may know the things freely given to us by God, [13] which things we also speak, not in words taught by human wisdom, but in those taught by the Spirit, combining spiritual *thoughts* with spiritual *words*.

B. A sincere faith

The Bible is not to be judged by our thinking, but our thinking is to be guided by the Bible. We have all formed certain opinions through the years. Some of our opinions are formed through our own reasoning, some are formed through our experiences, and some through the teaching of well-meaning friends. All these things must be submitted to the teaching of the Word of God. We must approach the Bible as the Word of God and believe what we read is God's truth. We cannot come to the Bible with our own ideas and seek to judge it by what we think or feel. We must come with the attitude that the Bible will teach us the absolute truth.

Hebrews 4:12

> For the word of God is living and active and sharper than any two-edged sword, and piercing as far as the division of soul and spirit, of both joints and marrow, and able to judge the thoughts and intentions of the heart.

1 Thessalonians 2:13

> For this reason we also constantly thank God that when you received the word of God which you heard from us, you accepted *it* not *as* the word of men, but *for* what it really is, the word of God, which also performs its work in you who believe.

Romans 12:2

> And do not be conformed to this world, but be transformed by the renewing of your mind, so that you may prove what the will of God is, that which is good and acceptable and perfect.

C. A genuine desire to know the truth

A sincere desire to know the truth can only be cultivated by a close walk with God. We often have a desire to learn much about politics, sports, hobbies, or career objectives, and we pursue this desire with great enthusiasm and diligence. God desires to bless people who have a desire to know Him and to love His Word. The effectiveness of this study will be measured by your diligence to seek Him.

2 Timothy 2:15

> Be diligent to present yourself approved to God as a workman who does not need to be ashamed, accurately handling the word of truth.

D. A commitment to know Jesus Christ in a personal way

Knowing Christ as your personal Savior is the beginning of a personal relationship with Him. That relationship must grow along with your knowledge of Him. This can only be accomplished through a daily walk in fellowship with the Lord Jesus.

E. A keen sense of the value of organization and system

This study is a systematic approach to Bible study. We will study the Bible topic by topic. This means we will look at many portions of scripture and draw our conclusions from them to form a biblical foundation for our conclusions.

IV. Precautions to Keep in Mind with a Study of Bible Doctrine

A. We must approach such a study of the Bible with a sense of humility.

If we have a prideful attitude as we study the Bible, we might study just so we may win an argument or display our knowledge. Our highest motive should be to study the Bible for our own spiritual growth. Our desire should be to know Him and to please Him.

B. Our spiritual lives must be kept abreast of our biblical knowledge.

We are to "grow in the grace and knowledge of our Lord and Savior Jesus Christ" (2 Peter 3:18). Too many people have tried to study and understand the Bible with no interest in obeying it and have grown cold and callused in their Christian lives. We cannot put too much emphasis on the necessity of obeying scripture truth.

2 Peter 3:17–18

> [17] You therefore, beloved, knowing this beforehand, be on your guard so that you are not carried away by the error of unprincipled men and fall from your own steadfastness, [18] but grow in the grace and knowledge of our Lord and Savior Jesus Christ. To Him *be* the glory, both now and to the day of eternity. Amen.

1 Peter 2:1–3

> [1] Therefore, putting aside all malice and all deceit and hypocrisy and envy and all slander, [2] like newborn babies, long for the pure milk of the word, so that by it you may grow in respect to salvation, [3] if you have tasted the kindness of the Lord.

V. Two Sources of Revelation to Help Us Know God

A. Creation (often referred to as general revelation)

There is much we can learn about the Creator as we look at His work in creation. We can discern His power, His nature, and His glory.

Romans 1:18–20

> [18] For the wrath of God is revealed from heaven against all ungodliness and unrighteousness of men who suppress the truth in unrighteousness, [19] because that which is known about God is evident within them; for God made it evident to them. [20] For since the creation of the world His invisible attributes, His eternal power and divine nature, have been clearly seen, being understood through what has been made, so that they are without excuse.

Psalms 19:1–4

> [1]The heavens are telling of the glory of God;
> And their expanse is declaring the work of His hands.
> [2] Day to day pours forth speech,
> And night to night reveals knowledge.
> [3] There is no speech, nor are there words;
> Their voice is not heard.
> [4] Their line has gone out through all the earth,
> And their utterances to the end of the world.
> In them He has placed a tent for the sun,

B. The Bible (often referred to as specific revelation or written revelation)

The *complete* revelation of God is only through His written Word. These things are revealed to us in the Bible. The Word of God tells us all about the person of God, and His provision of salvation. These truths are not found in nature but are only revealed to us in the Bible. There is relatively little about God revealed in nature, but the Bible provides the complete revelation of the Creator.

2 Timothy 3:16–17

> [16]All Scripture is inspired by God and profitable for teaching, for reproof, for correction, for training in righteousness; [17] so that the man of God may be adequate, equipped for every good work.

VI. False Sources of Information about God

Before we proceed to the study of the Bible, it is essential that we determine in our minds what is the only reliable source of information about God. It is equally important to exclude any false sources that have been devised in the minds of individuals. If this is firmly established, we will have little difficulty in establishing a working basis for our study and for our faith.

A. Human reasoning (rationalism)

This is a source many use in their study of theology. It is born in the mind of men and women and rejects the idea of a supernatural revelation. It is described in the Bible as "the wisdom of this world" (the wisdom of men). This concept is thoroughly flawed. The human mind is a fabricated source of information about God.

1 Corinthians 1:19–21

> [19] For it is written,
>
> "I WILL DESTROY THE WISDOM OF THE WISE,
> AND THE CLEVERNESS OF THE CLEVER I WILL SET ASIDE."
>
> [20] Where is the wise man? Where is the scribe? Where is the debater of this age? Has not God made foolish the wisdom of the world? [21] For since in the wisdom of God the world through its wisdom did not *come to* know God, God was well-pleased through the foolishness of the message preached to save those who believe.

Proverbs 14:12

> There is a way *which seems* right to a man, But its end is the way of death.

B. Mysticism

Mysticism claims additional revelation can be given beyond the Bible to those whom God chooses. This revelation claims to be given through Christian experience or direct revelation. Mary Baker Eddy, founder of Christian Science, and Joseph Smith, founder of Mormonism, are examples of those who claim such an experience and revelation. A particular Christian experience may seem very real to us, but it must never form the basis of any doctrine or teaching concerning God or His dealings with individuals. All such experiences must be measured by the written Word of God.

C. Ecclesiastical supremacy

Ecclesiastical supremacy claims that the church declarations and the writings of the church leaders are equal to the authority of the Bible and, as such, can be used to form Christian doctrine. This elevates the church and its leaders to a place of being equal with the Word of God. It is a dangerous position to take and leads to much spiritual blindness.

Conclusion:

If we are to have any authoritative voice of revelation at all, it must be the Bible. Certainly, if there is a God, and we know there is, He would make Himself and His will known to us. God has revealed Himself, but *not* by a spoken message to individuals and *not* by automatically implanting the truth in the minds of individuals. Neither has He revealed Himself through traditions handed down from generation to generation. All these methods would be subject to much personal distortion and confusion. However, God has revealed Himself through the living Word of God. The best and most accurate way for God to communicate with us is through a book, delivered and preserved by Him to every generation down through the ages. That book, well established as authentic, is the Bible. God has obviously chosen the best and perfect way to reveal Himself to us. If our minds dictate what is truth, there are millions of opinions and ideas. If our experiences are the source of truth, they will be many and varied. If the church is our source of truth, there is a vast array of views. The Bible, the Word of God, is a sure foundation that will never change or pass away. Jesus said, "Heaven and earth will pass away, but my words will never pass away." (Matthew 24:35)

VII. Some of the Requirements of This Class

A. Attendance

If you enroll in this class, you will be expected to make a sincere commitment to faithfully attend every session and complete the entire course.

B. Review questions

After each session, you will be assigned to answer in writing some of the review questions located at the end of each chapter. This assignment must be completed before the next class convenes.

C. A written paper

If this is a formal class, you will be expected to write a paper (1–2 page minimum) on one of the subjects covered during this course.

Suggestions of subjects on which you may to choose to write:

- The principle of lines-of-authority
- Evolution vs. Creation
- The inspiration of the Bible
- The imputation of Christ's righteousness to the believer
- The three covenants given in the Old Testament and how they relate to biblical prophecy
- How archaeology confirms the history covered in the Bible
- A focus on any one of the chapter themes in this book
- Any other topic approved by the teacher

REVIEW QUESTIONS

1. Give the narrow and broad meanings of the word *theology*.
2. Name five requirements for an effective study of the Bible.
3. Learn to quote from memory 2 Timothy 2:15.
4. If a person studies theology, does it mean he or she is a spiritual person? Explain.
5. Give three reasons why a systematic understanding of major Bible themes is valuable.
6. Explain the importance of the Holy Spirit in the process of studying biblical truth as taught in 1 Corinthians 2:7–14.
7. Of what value is Christian experience to a study of Bible doctrine?
8. What are good motives for studying the Bible?
9. Name and give the biblical foundation for two valid sources of information about God.
10. Name and explain three unreliable or false sources of information about God.
11. Name, spell correctly, and define the ten divisions of doctrine that we will study in this class. (See Chapters 2–12.)
12. PROJECT**:** One who is to be successful in any endeavor must be disciplined to excel. This is true in athletics, politics, business, or in any other area of life. This is also true in spiritual growth. Memorize and study 1 Corinthians 9:24–27. Commit yourself to spending some time in Bible study and in prayer every day. You might want to keep a journal of your study and prayer time.

    Your journal should include:

    - The date and time
    - The passage studied
    - Your personal observations from the Bible text
    - The amount of time spent in Bible study that day
    - The amount of time spent in prayer that day
    - A column recording the date and your prayer concerns
    - A column recording the date and answers to your prayer

CHAPTER 2

Bibliology
(What the Bible Teaches About Itself)

I. The Bible is the Inspired Word of God

A. God is the author of the Bible.

2 Timothy 3:16–17

> [16] All Scripture is inspired by God and profitable for teaching, for reproof, for correction, for training in righteousness; [17] so that the man of God may be adequate, equipped for every good work.

1. All scripture means every book, every verse, every line, and every word.

2. "Is Inspired" literally means God breathed (accurate, from the very breath of God).

3. The Bible is useful for:

- Teaching – instruction which cannot be learned from other sources
- Reproof – to convict, to reprimand, to admonish, to reprove
- Correction – to set straight that which is in error
  (The Bible is the final court of appeals for faith and practice.)
- Training in righteousness – training in the character of God's righteousness
  (This training is in harmony with God's standards of right and wrong or good and evil.)

B. The Bible is a work of the Holy Spirit.

2 Peter 1:21

> for no prophecy was ever made by an act of human will, but men moved by the Holy Spirit spoke from God.

1. The Word of God never had its origin in the will of humankind, nor was it penned by an act of the human will. It is not the product of individuals. People did not decide to write the Bible, nor did they generate its production.

2. Men spoke from God. Specially chosen men were the vehicles through whom the Bible was given.

3. The Greek word *moved* literally means "carried along." The human authors were moved along by the Holy Spirit, as a sailboat is moved by the wind. Without the wind, there is no movement. Without the Holy Spirit, there is no authorship of God.

4. The Word of God is a special work of the Spirit of God, who is the ultimate agent and author.

C. The "Law" is the Word of God.

John 10:34–36

> [34] Jesus answered them, "Has it not been written in your Law, 'I SAID, YOU ARE GODS'? [35] If he called them gods, to whom the word of God came (and the Scripture cannot be broken), [36] do you say of Him, whom the Father sanctified and sent into the world, 'You are blaspheming,' because I said, 'I am the Son of God'?"

1. In these verses, Jesus identifies the Law as the Word of God and scripture.

2. The Law (scripture) cannot be broken. It is settled and established.

3. This is an example of Christ giving honor to the Old Testament scriptures, as the authoritative Word of God. In many other passages in the gospels, Christ quotes scripture as the authority by which He speaks. We must remember that Jesus Christ is God, and God is the author of scripture.

D. The Bible is living and active.

Hebrews 4:12

> For the Word of God is living and active and sharper than any two-edged sword and piercing as far as the division of soul and spirit, of both joints and marrow, and able to judge the thoughts and intentions of the heart.

1. The Bible is truly the Word of God.

2. The Bible is "living and active." It is not just the lifeless and idle words of men. It is unlike any other book in the world.

3. Scripture is "sharper than any double-edged sword." It is not merely effective on the outward behavior of people, nor only in the minds of individuals, but it penetrates deep into the heart (into the spirit and soul). It reaches into the mind, the will (attitudes and intentions), and the heart (emotions) of individuals.

Isaiah 55:9–11

> [9] "For *as* the heavens are higher than the earth,
> So are My ways higher than your ways
> And My thoughts than your thoughts.
> [10] "For as the rain and the snow come down from heaven,
> And do not return there without watering the earth
> And making it bear and sprout,
> And furnishing seed to the sower and bread to the eater;
> [11] So will My word be which goes forth from My mouth;
> It will not return to Me empty,
> Without accomplishing what I desire,
> And without succeeding *in the matter* for which I sent it."

4. God's word (the Word of God) goes out of His very mouth (v.11). It is owned by God.

5. Just as the rain and snow accomplishes its purpose, so the reading and teaching of the Word of God will be used by God in achieving His purposes in the lives of those who hear or read it.

1 Corinthians 2:12–13

> [12] Now we have received, not the spirit of the world, but the Spirit who is from God, so that we may know the things freely given to us by God, [13] which things we also speak, not in words taught by human wisdom, but in those taught by the Spirit, combining spiritual *thoughts* with spiritual *words*.

6. The Holy Spirit indwells the believer.

7. The Holy Spirit teaches the Bible, which has been given to us by God.

8. These words are not taught by human wisdom but are taught by the Holy Spirit, expressing spiritual truth in spiritual words.

II. Terms and Definitions Used to Describe the Bible

A. Revelation

God has revealed certain truths to us. Revelation is the act of God, by which He reveals himself to humankind. This includes things we understand through creation and the written Word of God.

B. Inspiration

These truths have been recorded in a book through human authors whereby the end product is the Word of God, not the product of those human authors. This is the procedure by which the Holy Spirit chose certain men and moved upon these human authors in such a way that He guided in the selection of words, content, and subject matter. The human author's style, vocabulary, and personal characteristics were used to create a perfect Bible without error, contradiction, or discrepancy.

C. Infallible

Infallible means to be without error or contradiction in the original language.

D. Authoritative

The Bible is conclusive and the final court of appeal for what is right and true.

E. Perfect

The Bible is complete and without flaw.

F. Illumination

The Holy Spirit is the author of the Bible. He lives in every believer and, as our teacher, sheds light on scriptures which have already been written. Illumination does <u>not</u> mean the Holy Spirit is producing new truth or adding to the Bible.

1 Corinthians 2:10–16

> [10] For to us God revealed *them* through the Spirit; for the Spirit searches all things, even the depths of God. [11] For who among men knows the *thoughts* of a man except the spirit of the man which is in him? Even so the *thoughts* of God no one knows except the Spirit of God. [12] Now we have received, not the spirit of the world, but the Spirit who is from God, so that we may know the things freely given to us by God, [13] which things we also speak, not in words taught by human wisdom, but in those taught by the Spirit, combining spiritual *thoughts* with spiritual *words*.

> [14] But a natural man does not accept the things of the Spirit of God, for they are foolishness to him; and he cannot understand them, because they are spiritually appraised. [15] But he who is spiritual appraises all things, yet he himself is appraised by no one. [16] For WHO HAS KNOWN THE MIND OF THE LORD, THAT HE WILL INSTRUCT HIM? But we have the mind of Christ.

G. Verbal plenary inspiration

The Bible clearly teaches verbal plenary inspiration.

1. Verbal – Every word is inspired by God. (This is called verbal inspiration.)

2. Plenary – Every word is equally inspired by God. Every word in the original manuscripts of the Bible is the Word of God. (This is called plenary inspiration.)

3. Some Bibles show the words of Jesus in red. This does not mean that Jesus' words were more inspired than the rest of the Bible.

4. Inspiration covers the entire scope of the Bible.

5. The Bible is the combined production of God and the individual authors. It is a dual authorship, yet as the product of God, it is infallible (without error).

Matthew 24:35 (Jesus said)

> Heaven and earth will pass away, but My words will not pass away.

III. The Scriptures Do Not Support the Following Theories

A. The concept theory

This is the theory that the Bible *contains* the Word of God but is not in fact the Word of God. This theory teaches that only the thoughts and concepts are inspired by God, but not the very words. Of course, we know that there can be no concepts presented without words; words are of the utmost importance in arriving at concepts. This theory does not support verbal plenary inspiration.

B. The mechanical or dictation theory

This is the theory that the human authors were mere robots (or secretaries), and God dictated His message to them word for word as they wrote it down. This theory does not account for the differences in style of writing and vocabulary. If the human authors were nothing more than secretaries, then the text of every book in the Bible would be in the same style, personality, and vocabulary.

C. Degrees of inspiration theory

This is the theory that some parts of the Bible are more inspired than others. Those who hold to this theory set themselves up as judges who decide which parts of the Bible are inspired and which parts are not inspired. This ignores 2 Timothy 3:16, which says that "all Scripture is inspired by God." It is evident that the Bible stands or falls as a whole book. If it cannot all be accepted as authoritative, then none of it can be accepted.

D. Natural inspiration theory

This theory holds that the Bible is inspired in the same way that men have been inspired to produce great masterpieces of art, literature, and other fields. This theory claims that the human authors were given a great natural ability and were able to write the scriptures. It removes the idea of God's authorship altogether, except perhaps as the Giver of gifts to men. It makes the Bible merely a product of human authorship.

E. Mystical inspiration theory

This theory bases its claims on the idea that the Christian is empowered by God for various responsibilities (or spiritual gifts). Using these gifts, the scriptures were written. If this is true, then we might be looking for more scripture to be authored at any time. This theory makes the Bible something less than a special revelation, which was produced by the Holy Spirit once for all.

IV. Warnings Regarding the Inspiration of the Bible

Deuteronomy 4:2

> "You shall not add to the word which I am commanding you, nor take away from it, that you may keep the commandments of the Lord your God which I command you."

Revelation 22:18–19

> [18] I testify to everyone who hears the words of the prophecy of this book: if anyone adds to them, God will add to him the plagues which are written in this book; [19] and if anyone takes away from the words of the book of this prophecy, God will take away his part from the tree of life and from the holy city, which are written in this book.

V. Reasons Why We Believe the Bible is Inspired by God

A. The claims that the Bible makes to be the Word of God

The Bible claims to be the Word of God in both the Old Testament and the New Testament.

B. The attitude of Christ toward the Old Testament

Jesus quoted the Old Testament with respect and honor.

C. The uniqueness of the Bible

Humankind has produced other books that claim to be from God, but they present information and concepts that are nothing like the unique message of the Bible.

D. The exposing of our sinful condition

The Bible exposes our sinful condition. Apart from God, we tend to justify our sin.

E. The central theme of the Bible

God is the central theme of the Bible. It is a revelation of Himself. No other book presents God in the same way. Concepts of God originating from a human perspective inevitably reflect God in a distorted way. This is evident in our imaginations and idol images.

F. The unique teachings in the Bible about God

These teaching could not come from our own human reasoning.

G. The teaching of the Trinity (one God, and yet, three persons)

H. The teaching of salvation as a gift

Biblical salvation is contrary to every other religious system.

I. The person of Jesus Christ

Jesus Christ, the God-Man, is one person, yet with two natures.

J. The wonderful knowledge of the Bible

The Bible was not written to be a scientific book, but as it touches on science, medicine, astronomy, and many other subjects, it is accurate, though it was written many years before modern scientific technology.

K. The biblical teachings of the creation of all things

It speaks about heaven and about hell. Its reach moves from the physical world to the spiritual world without hesitation.

L. The ethics of the Bible

The Bible presents a complete code of ethics. It presents a code of ethics different from anything humankind has produced through its best philosophers, religious leaders, and governments. Those who have no contact with the Bible are seldom disturbed about morals. Godless education, arts, and science tend to ignore morality; yet the Bible teaches from cover to cover the highest code of ethics and morality.

M. The continuity of the scriptures

The Bible carries the same message from cover to cover.

- It contains 66 books.
- It was written by about 40 different authors.
- Its human authors include farmers, fishermen, kings, priests, and scholars.
- It covers hundreds of years of history, written by men from many generations.

Continuity would be impossible in any other book under these conditions, yet the Bible is a marvelous harmonious whole. The only answer to this phenomenon is that the Holy Spirit is the author behind every human author.

N. The one central theme of the Bible

The theme of the Bible is someone!

- In the Old Testament, someone is coming.
- In the gospels, someone is here.
- In Acts and the epistles, someone has come and is coming again.
- This someone is Jesus Christ.

O. The eternal character of the Bible

People have devised philosophies, religions, governments, and civilizations, which have flourished and then faded into history. However, the Word of God continues to bring the truth and meet the deepest needs of those who will take time to read it, to study it, and to obey it.

P. The prophetic message of the Bible and its fulfillment

As you compare prophecies with the events that follow, you get the impression that these prophecies were written after the events happened, however, it is well documented that these passages were written hundreds of years before the events took place.

- Psalm 22 is an excellent example. This passage was written about one thousand years before Christ, yet it tells of His crucifixion in much detail hundreds of years before the Romans ever invented crucifixion.
- Isaiah 53 describes the suffering servant, which foretells the substitutionary death of Jesus Christ.
- Ezekiel 37 foretells the establishment of the sovereignty of Israel as a nation. This was fulfilled on May 14, 1948, over twenty-five hundred years after God gave this vision to Ezekiel.
- Ezekiel 26:1–5 describes the destruction of the great city of Tyre and how the debris of the city would be scraped into the sea. This is another example of the graphic way in which prophecy was fulfilled. (See also Daniel, Micah 5:2, Isaiah 7:14, Isaiah 9:6–7.)

Q. The literary excellence of the Bible

This is the ability of the Bible to say so much in so few words; it makes an appeal to all types of people from all walks of life.

Note: The story is told of Benjamin Franklin reading a story to the British Parliament during a filibuster. Members of Parliament were so impressed at the literary quality of the piece that they crowded around him to determine the source of the writing. Benjamin Franklin was happy to tell them, "It is the Book of Ruth from the Bible."

R. The freshness of the Bible

The Bible appeals to people down through the ages and never grows old to anyone who will take the time to study it.

S. The power of the Bible

The Bible sets forth a message that can transform lives. No other book has changed the course of people's lives and human history as much as the Bible. Individuals are changed daily by its glorious message.

T. The agreement of archaeology and the Bible

1. Archaeology has wonderfully supported the Bible. There has never been an archeological discovery that has contradicted the narrative of the Bible.

2. Modern science, when honestly considered, has found agreement with the Bible. We do not test the Bible by science; we test science by the Bible.

3. The Bible's narrative was unlike the conglomeration of theories that existed in the days when certain books of the Bible were written.

Note: Moses was educated in all the ways of the Egyptians, yet notice the contrast between what they wrote and what he wrote:

The Egyptians believed the earth had hatched from a winged egg, which flew around in space until finally the earth emerged.	Moses wrote, "In the beginning God created the heavens and the earth." (Genesis 1:1)
The Egyptians believed that men originally hatched from certain white worms that were found in the slime of the Nile.	Moses wrote, "And the Lord God formed man of the dust of the ground..." (Genesis 2:7)

VI. Exhortations of the Bible

Matthew 28:18–20

> [18] And Jesus came up and spoke to them, saying, "All authority has been given to Me in heaven and on earth. [19] Go therefore and make disciples of all the nations, baptizing them in the name of the Father and the Son and the Holy Spirit, [20] teaching them to observe all that I commanded you; and lo, I am with you always, even to the end of the age."

2 Timothy 4:2

> preach the word; be ready in season *and* out of season; reprove, rebuke, exhort, with great patience and instruction.

These passages teach us to:

- Proclaim the message of the Bible and not keep it to ourselves.
- Be ready to share it and look for opportunities to do so.
- Correct the wrong thinking of those who are in error, rebuke those who would distort it, and exhort those who are using the Bible with authority.
- Proclaim with great patience, not using the Bible as a "club." (2 Timothy 4:2)

VII. The Potential of the Word of God

Psalm 119

Verse 9 – The Bible has a moral cleansing effect on us.
Verse 11 – The Bible keeps our heart from sin.
Verse 15,16 – We are encouraged to meditate and delight in the Word of God.
Verse 17 – We should obey the Word of God.
Verse 89 – The Word of God is eternal.
Verse 103 – The Word of God is sweet to our spiritual taste.
Verse 105 – We are guided by the Word of God.
Verse 130 – The Word of God is our light in life.
Verse 140 – The Word of God is pure.

VIII. The Best Way for God to Communicate with Humankind

A. Two methods might be possible

1. Immediate revelation to each person – This method would require the process to be repeated each time to each person. The difficulty with this method would be that people could easily disagree or misunderstand their personal communication. This system would invite contradiction, misrepresentation, and false claims.

2. Written revelation – This method is more reasonable in that the truth is well authenticated, accurate, permanent, and easily well documented.

B. God has chosen to communicate with us through written revelation (the Bible)

God has revealed the truth as His written Word. Through the Bible, God has clearly imparted the truth about:

1. Who we are

2. How we got here

3. The purpose of life

4. The person and work of Jesus Christ

5. The way of salvation

6. The description and reality of heaven and hell

7. God's design for living lives pleasing to Him

IX. The Right Attitude Towards the Word of God

A. Reverence – When someone important speaks, we should give respect.

B. Faith – Every work and promise that comes out of the mouth of God is truth.

C. Obedience – Because God is love, any direction He gives is best and good for us.

D. Attention – God's message is important, and we should listen carefully.

X. How we Acquired Our English Bible of Today

A. Except for parts of Jeremiah, Daniel, and Ezra, the Old Testament was written in the Hebrew language.

B. The entire New Testament was written in the common Greek language of the apostles' day.

C. None of the original manuscripts of the books of the Bible have ever been found.

D. It is *incorrect* to believe that down through the ages many mistakes were made by those who were producing hand-written copies, and that we cannot trust the accuracy of today's Bible.

E. There are three sources of information that are meticulously compared, studied, and used in the preparation and formation of an accurate text in the original languages.

1. Manuscripts – These are early copies of the text of scriptures, which were copied word for word by scribes or penman especially trained for such work. Obviously, the earlier the date on the manuscript the more accurate. Some are dated BC.

2. Versions – These are early translations of the Bible from one language to another. Some of them are dated very early. They are compared with other versions, etc.

3. The writings of the early church fathers – Many of the early church leaders wrote letters and books that date back to the first century. In these books and letters, many passages of scripture were quoted. These are carefully compared with the other sources to determine accuracy. Almost the entire New Testament is quoted in various writings of the church fathers, dated from 96 AD to 600 AD.

Note: These three sources are meticulously classified (by date), studied, and compared to formulate an accurate manuscript in the original language. This manuscript is then translated into the English (or another language) very carefully, so we can be confident that our Bible is reliable in our own language. This process stands in contrast to the notion by some that the Bible has been translated from one language to another, and when it finally reached us in our generation, we cannot trust that it is at all what the original authors intended.

XI. The Addition of Chapter and Verse Divisions

A. The first divisions were instituted in 586 BC.

This happened when the Pentateuch was divided into 154 segments. These segments were modified and expanded about fifty years later.

B. The oldest system of chapter divisions is from 350 AD.

These chapter divisions held until Stephen Langton, a professor at the University of Paris, divided the Bible into the modern chapter divisions.

C. The first standard verse divisions were used about 900 AD.

Verse indicators were in existence earlier than 900 AD.

D. The Latin Vulgate was translated by Jerome in the 4th century AD.

This was the first translation to use both chapter and verse divisions.

XII. The Canon

The word *canon* comes from the root word *reed*. The Hebrew word is *ganah*, and the Greek word is *kanon*. The reed was used as a measuring rod and the expression came to mean "standard." The word canon is used in connection with the Bible in reference to the standard by which a book is measured (or evaluated), to be included in our Bible.

Five tests applied to a book for it to be included in our Bible:

Note: We do not know these were the exact tests used in a formal way. We are also not aware of any formal council that was called to determine which books were to be included in the canon. Remember, the Holy Spirit is the author and, as such, is the superintendent of the canonicity of the Bible. However, these are the kinds of tests a book would have had to meet to be included in the canon of scripture.

1. Does the book come with a "thus saith the Lord?" format. Does it carry the authoritative "Word of God" testimony?

2. Was the human author recognized as a prophet or a "man of God" by the fathers of our faith?

3. Is the text accurate and authentic? The fathers of our faith seemed to employ the policy of "when in doubt, throw it out."

4. Does the book carry the life-changing power of God in its message?

5. Was it received, collected, read, and used by the people of God? (For example, Peter recognized the writings of Paul.)

2 Peter 3:14–16

> [14] Therefore, beloved, since you look for these things, be diligent to be found by Him in peace, spotless and blameless, [15] and regard the patience of our Lord *as* salvation; just as also our beloved brother Paul, according to the wisdom given him, wrote to you, [16] as also in all *his* letters, speaking in them of these things, in which are some things hard to understand, which the untaught and unstable distort, as *they do* also the rest of the scriptures, to their own destruction.

XIII. Apocryphal Literature

A. Some Bibles include a series of books called the Apocryphal books.

These books were added about fourteen hundred years after the books of the Bible were established as authentic books inspired by God. These books are:

1. The First Book of Esdras (also known as Third Esdras)

2. The Second Book of Esdras (also known as Fourth Esdras)

3. Tobit

4. Judith

5. The Additions to the Book of Esther

6. The Wisdom of Solomon

7. Ecclesiasticus, or the Wisdom of Jesus the Son of Sirach

8. Baruch

9. The Letter of Jeremiah (This letter is sometimes incorporated as the last chapter of Baruch. When this is done the number of books is fourteen instead of fifteen.)

10. The Prayer of Azariah and the Song of the Three Young Men

11. Susanna
12. Bel and the Dragon
13. The Prayer of Manasseh
14. The First Book of Maccabees
15. The Second Book of Maccabees

B. Reasons why many Bible scholars exclude apocryphal literature from the canon of scripture.

Here we highlight those conclusions:

1. The apocryphal books are filled with historical and geographical inaccuracies.
2. The apocryphal books teach doctrines which are false and foster practices which are at variance with the inspired scripture.
3. The apocryphal books present subject matter and styling that is not in keeping with inspired scripture.
4. The apocryphal books lack the distinctive elements which are characteristic of genuine scripture, such as the power and the feeling that this is indeed the Word of God.
5. Although Jesus quoted from many of the Old Testament books, He never quoted from any of the apocryphal literature.
6. Not one of the New Testament writers ever quoted from any of the Apocryphal books.
7. Neither the Jewish scholars, nor the secular historians, recognized these books as part of scripture.
8. The early Christian church rejected the Apocryphal books as part of the canon.
9. Martin Luther and the other reformers rejected the canonicity of these books.
10. It was not until 1546 AD when the Roman Catholic Church granted canonical status to the Apocryphal books.

XIV. Terms Used to Describe Types of Bibles

A. Translation

This term describes a Bible that simply has been translated from one language to another.

B. Version

This term describes a translation of the Bible which is specifically translated from the original languages of Greek and Hebrew.

C. Revision or revised version

These terms are used to describe versions of the Bible that have been reviewed in light of the original languages of Greek and Hebrew. This is done to correct any errors in the original version or more accurately translate faulty or unclear words in some verses or passages.

D. A paraphrase

This describes a Bible that is not necessarily a direct translation from the original languages. Instead, taking the original languages into consideration, it is a restatement of the text in the translator's own words to give the *sense* of the passage rather than to translate it word for word.

XV. Some Simple Helps Available for Personal Bible Study

A. A good study Bible

Scofield Reference Bible or the Ryre Study Bible are two excellent study Bibles.

B. A good complete concordance

There are many fine concordances available in your local Christian bookstore.

C. A good Bible study computer program

One of the best and most reasonably priced computer Bible programs is PC Study Bible available from Biblesoft. It can be found at http://www.biblesoft.com/new/ or http://www.amazon.com.

XVI. Three Step by Step Bible Study Methods for Personal Bible Study

A. The textual approach

The textual approach to Bible study involves studying a passage of a particular text. The goal of this approach is to draw from the text its true meaning and determine what application this truth has for your daily life.

1. Begin with prayer, asking God the Holy Spirit to open your eyes to the truth.
2. Choose your text.
3. Examine and compare your chosen passage to different Bible versions.
4. List and define every important word in your text, even if you think you know the meaning.
5. Examine the context of the passage and discover the main subject matter. A text without a context is a pretext.
6. Discover through repeated readings the one unifying subject of this passage.
7. Examine each phrase in light of the unifying subject.
8. Make an outline of your text.
9. Write out the text in your own words.
10. Write out the things that were personally challenging to you as you studied this passage.
11. List the things you have learned, clarified, or acquired.
12. Ask yourself the question, "What do these truths have to do with my life?" Write out your answer.
13. Spend some time in prayer, asking God to use what you have learned and give you an opportunity to share this truth with someone else.

B. The biographical approach

The biographical approach to Bible study focuses on the life and character of a biblical personality.

1. In prayer ask God to open your eyes to the truths of His Word.

2. Choose your Bible character.

3. List all the Bible references that include information about this Bible character.

4. Carefully read each of the passages you have listed in Step 3.

5. Arrange this material using the following outline:

    - Birth and early life
    - Conversion experience or call to a specific task or ministry
    - Record his or her ministry for the Lord

6. List those things that refer to his or her character.

7. Record any relationships he or she had with others.

8. Record any information given about his or her death.

9. Find out as much as you can about this Bible character's environments.

10. Examine what other scripture passages say about this Bible character.

11. Insert this new information into your outline and record your personal observations in connection with each item.

12. From the data gathered, ask the following questions:

    - What were the things that were important to your Bible character?
    - Who were your Bible character's closest friends and how might they have influenced your Bible character?
    - Who were his or her enemies and how might they have influenced your Bible character?
    - What effect did his or her family, environment, government, and culture have on your Bible character's life and ministry?
    - What might have influenced your Bible character's failures or successes?
    - Add any other questions to this list that you think might be important.

13. Go over the outline and data you have gathered and ask yourself the following questions:

    - What weaknesses are there in my Bible character's life that are similar to mine?
    - How might I learn from my Bible character's successes or failures?
    - What are the pitfalls I should avoid?
    - What examples in my Bible character's life can teach me God's lessons?
    - What strengths might my Bible character have that need to be built into my life?

14. Spend some time in prayer asking God to teach you the lessons from this Bible character's life.

C. The topical approach

The topical approach to a study of the Bible is designed to follow a particular subject through the Bible. In this approach certain conclusions are drawn from various passages of scripture. This study is perhaps more difficult than other approaches but can be very helpful in getting answers to your doctrinal questions.

Note: A word of warning is expedient here. It is important to draw your conclusions from the entire biblical truth without violating the context of any single passage. Many false conclusions have been drawn by those who do not use care in this kind of study.

2 Timothy 2:15

> Be diligent to present yourself approved to God as a workman who does not need to be ashamed, accurately handling the word of truth.

1. Begin by inviting the Holy Spirit to open your eyes to the truth of God's Word.
2. Choose your topic. Be sure your topic is not too broad.
3. Make a list of all the terms, verses, or phrases you can call to remembrance that might have something to do with the subject.
4. With your concordance and study helps, begin to look through your Bible for passages that shed light on your subject. As you work through this project step by step, be looking for a major and central passage on your subject.
5. It is extremely important that you keep in mind the context, historical setting, and the disposition of each text you examine.
6. Use the cross-references in the margins of your study Bible to lead you to parallel passages.
7. Keep a list of all the facts and conclusions you have gathered from your study.
8. Arrange your list in an outline form as best you can.
9. Go over your list and outline, asking yourself the following questions in connection to each conclusion:
    - What difference do these truths make to me in the way I ought to live and the attitudes I should maintain?

- What priorities in my life should change if I obey the truths I have discovered?

10. Spend some time in prayer using your answers to the previous two questions as your prayer guide.

XVII. Promises for Those Who Will Meditate in God's Word

Joshua 1:8	Meditate and obey God's Word	Make your way prosperous / have success
Psalms 1:1–3	Delight in & meditate on God's Word	Whatever he does will prosper
Psalms 104:34	Meditate on God's Word	Happiness in the Lord
Psalms 119:9–11	Obey and treasure God's Word	Purity of life
Psalms 119:97–100	Love and meditate on God's Word	Wiser than my enemies
Psalms 119:165	Love God's Word	Peace and confidence
Proverbs 4:4	Hold fast and obey God's Word	Full life
Proverbs 3:1–6	Remember and keep God's Word	Favor and good reputation with God and others
Romans 10:17	Hear the Word of God	Increased faith
1 Timothy 4:15–16	Take God's Word seriously	All will notice your success

REVIEW QUESTIONS

1. Quote from memory 2 Timothy 3:16–17. Be able to explain.
2. Quote from memory 2 Peter 1:21. Be able to explain this verse.
3. Explain the significance of John 10:34–35.
4. What characteristics are mentioned in Hebrews 4:12 concerning the Word of God?
5. Define revelation.
6. Define inspiration.
7. Define illumination.
8. What do we mean by the term verbal plenary inspiration?
9. What is the *concept* theory?
10. Does the Bible have any contradictions or errors? Explain your answer.
11. Explain the *mechanical* (or dictation) theory.
12. What is the *Degrees of Inspiration* theory?
13. What is the *Mystical Inspiration* theory?
14. Explain why we are not looking for any other books to be written and added to the Bible as the Word of God?
15. What warning is given in Revelation 22:18–19?
16. Is the Bible accurate when it speaks on scientific matters?
17. What is the pastor of a church required to preach according to 2 Timothy 4:2?
18. Explain why written revelation is better than an oral revelation to each individual.
19. Name and explain four attitudes we should have towards the Bible.
20. What is the difference between a version of the Bible and a paraphrase edition?

21. Name three sources used in arriving at an accurate version of the Bible.

22. Which would be more accurate generally speaking, a paraphrase or a version?

23. According to Joshua 1:8, what is a sure way to be successful?

24. Quote from memory Psalms 1:1–3.

25. List 5 promises for those who will meditate on God's Word.

CHAPTER 3

Theology
(What the Bible Teaches About the Triune God)

I. The Existence of God

A. A biblical basis for the existence of God

Genesis 1:1

> In the beginning God created the heavens and the earth.

1. This verse is cited as typical of many. The existence of God is everywhere *assumed* in the Bible.

2. No attempt is made in the scriptures to prove what is an evident fact. It is merely assumed.

3. He exists and is the creator and source of all things outside of Himself.

Romans 1:19–21

> [19] because that which is known about God is evident within them; for God made it evident to them. [20] For since the creation of the world His invisible attributes, His eternal power and divine nature, have been clearly seen, being understood through what has been made, so that they are without excuse. [21] For even though they knew God, they did not honor Him as God or give thanks, but they became futile in their speculations, and their foolish heart was darkened.

4. People are aware of God's existence because of the innate consciousness of Him. People are by nature religious creatures. God's existence is evident within them.

5. Creation displays certain attributes of the invisible God. (His wisdom, His power, His great knowledge, His love, His kindness, His caring provision)

6. Creation shows His eternal character. (His divine nature)

7. People may know God by following the light they have been given through His creation. There is no excuse for not knowing God.

8. It is natural for a man to believe in God. If he denies the existence of God, it is because he has not glorified God, believed God, or acknowledged Him with thanksgiving.

9. A general principle of biblical truth here applies. Light *followed* brings more light and ultimately the light of the gospel of Christ. Light *rejected* causes us to wander deeper into spiritual darkness. Failure to follow the light brings darkness.

   Note: If you were lost and wandering in the wilderness of total darkness, and you saw a small flickering light in the distance, that light would represent your only hope of finding your way to civilization and help. A wise person would move in the direction of the light.

   Romans 1:28

   > And just as they did not see fit to acknowledge God any longer, God gave them over to a depraved mind, to do those things which are not proper,

   John 3:19–20

   > [19] This is the judgment, that the Light has come into the world, and men loved the darkness rather than the Light, for their deeds were evil. [20] For everyone who does evil hates the Light and does not come to the Light for fear that his deeds will be exposed.

10. From birth each person has had God in his or her knowledge.

11. Most people willingly cast Him out of their knowledge. They have turned away from the spiritual light, and consequently, God has given them up to their own sinful minds.

12. The reason many reject the light is that they love their sin more than the truth.

Conclusion:

A knowledge of God's existence is intuitively a part of every person. This is the inborn knowledge of God's existence that precedes what every person sees in nature and concludes by his or her own reasoning. The passages quoted above show the individual experience of people who begin life with an inborn knowledge of God. Many reject this inborn knowledge in unbelief. In such cases, the individual is turned over to his own sinful desires and unclean practices.

The existence of God should be obvious to any rational person seeking the truth who is able to observe creation. (See also Psalms 19:1–2 and Romans 1:20.)

B. Logical evidence for the existence of God

Psalms 14:1

> The fool has said in his heart, "There is no God."
> They are corrupt, they have committed abominable deeds;
> There is no one who does good.

God's existence is evidenced by human logic. This human logic is in harmony with the law of cause and effect. The intricate design of nature and the supernatural character of Jesus Christ must also be addressed and explained by human logic. This extra-biblical evidence gives great credence to the scripture passages quoted above. However, many who reject the existence of God, reject Him because they walk away from the truth and love their sin. It is not usually an intellectual problem but a moral problem.

Logical arguments are valid and helpful as we present the gospel, but we must always remember that logic and argument will not usually win people to Christ. We will win people to Christ by showing the love of Christ and sharing the gospel in the power of the Holy Spirit. It is the Word of God that is the "sword of the Spirit."

C. Key terms in connection with the existence of God

1. Theism – A belief in the existence of a personal God (We believe in theism.)

2. Deism – A belief in God, but it denies that He has anything to do with the universe, world, or humankind

3. Atheism – A denial of God's existence

4. Agnosticism – A belief that God exists but cannot be personally known

Note: The Bible does not leave us without information about God. In the scriptures, we find not only His existence, but also much information concerning His personality, His works, and His plan for our lives. Furthermore, this information is not sketchy or vague. It is complete and satisfying to the individual who will accept and obey what God has said.

II. God Is a Personal Being

God is not just a power or force. He is not like the idols of our imagination. He is a person with personality. He has the make-up of a person:

- A Mind – the ability to reason
- Feelings – emotions, sensitivity
- A Will – the ability to make decisions and carry out plans

A. The mind of God

Proverbs 15:3

> The eyes of the Lord are in every place,
> Watching the evil and the good.

Romans 11:33–36

> [33] Oh, the depth of the riches both of the wisdom and knowledge of God! How unsearchable are His judgments and unfathomable His ways! [34] For WHO HAS KNOWN THE MIND OF THE LORD, OR WHO BECAME HIS COUNSELOR? [35] OR WHO HAS FIRST GIVEN TO HIM THAT IT MIGHT BE PAID BACK TO HIM AGAIN? [36] For from Him and through Him and to Him are all things. To Him *be* the glory forever. Amen.

1. God sees everything. God comprehends what He sees. He has intelligence.

2. His mind is so superior to ours that we cannot fathom it.

3. His mind is perfect. He depends on no one else to teach Him. He is the source of all wisdom and knowledge.

B. The emotions of God

John 3:16

> "For God so loved the world, that He gave His only begotten Son, that whoever believes in Him shall not perish, but have eternal life." (See also Psalms 33:5; 103:8–13.)

Deuteronomy 12:31

> You shall not behave thus toward the LORD your God, for every abominable act which the LORD hates they have done for their gods; for they even burn their sons and daughters in the fire to their gods.

Ephesians 4:30

> Do not grieve the Holy Spirit of God, by whom you were sealed for the day of redemption.

1. God loves. He has the emotion of love.

2. God hates. He despises evil.

3. God the Holy Spirit is grieved when we sin.

4. God has feelings or emotional responses.

C. The will of God

Isaiah 46:10–11

> [10]Declaring the end from the beginning,
> And from ancient times things which have not been done,
> Saying, 'My purpose will be established,
> And I will accomplish all My good pleasure';
> [11]Calling a bird of prey from the east,
> The man of My purpose from a far country.
> Truly I have spoken; truly I will bring it to pass.
> I have planned *it, surely* I will do it.

Daniel 4:35

> "All the inhabitants of the earth are accounted as nothing,
> But He does according to His will in the host of heaven
> And *among* the inhabitants of earth;
> And no one can ward off His hand
> Or say to Him, 'What have You done?'"

1. God knows the end from the beginning.

2. God makes His own decisions. He fulfills His own pleasure. He exercises His will.

3. No one has the power to change His plan.

4. He puts into effect all that He has planned.

Psalms 115:2–8

[2] Why should the nations say,
"Where, now, is their God?"
[3] But our God is in the heavens;
He does whatever He pleases.
[4] Their idols are silver and gold,
The work of man's hands.
[5] They have mouths, but they cannot speak;
They have eyes, but they cannot see;
[6] They have ears, but they cannot hear;
They have noses, but they cannot smell;
[7] They have hands, but they cannot feel;
They have feet, but they cannot walk;
They cannot make a sound with their throat.
[8] Those who make them will become like them,
Everyone who trusts in them.

Conclusion:

1. These verses contrast the true God with the idol gods. (Idols have no mind, no feelings, and cannot make or carry out decisions.)

2. God is not the same as the fabrications and idols of humankind.

3. From the scriptures we note that God possesses all three characteristics that define a person (intellect, feelings, and a will).

4. These three elements make up a personality or a person.

5. God is a person, not merely an influence or blind force. We are often prone to believe that only something with a physical body could be a person, but this is a false concept. God is a person.

III. A Biblical Definition of God

How does the Bible describe God?

John 4:24

"God is spirit, and those who worship Him must worship in spirit and truth."

1 John 1:5

> This is the message we have heard from Him and announce to you, that God is Light, and in Him there is no darkness at all.

1 John 4:16

> We have come to know and have believed the love which God has for us. God is love, and the one who abides in love abides in God, and God abides in him.

Hebrews 12:29

> for our God is a consuming fire.

Isaiah 6:1–3

> [1] In the year of King Uzziah's death I saw the Lord sitting on a throne, lofty and exalted, with the train of His robe filling the temple. [2] Seraphim stood above Him, each having six wings: with two he covered his face, and with two he covered his feet, and with two he flew. [3] And one called out to another and said,
>
> "Holy, Holy, Holy, is the Lord of hosts,
> The whole earth is full of His glory."

A. God is a spiritual being.

B. God is truth. (But truth is not God.)

C. God is transparent in righteousness (light) and cannot sin or tolerate sin.

D. God is love. (But love is not God.)

E. God is a God of judgment and true justice.

F. God is holy.

The word *holy* is repeated three times by the angel to describe God (Isaiah 6:3). The word *holy* means that God is so unique and unlike all other beings that He is in a category by Himself. He created all things, and there is nothing to which He can be compared.

G. God is not defined in any one statement of scripture.

These and many other passages must be taken as a whole to define the character of God.

Conclusion:

Though it is impossible to fully define God in a simple statement with all His complexity and infinite attributes, from these verses (and others too numerous to mention), we can form this simple definition of God: *God is the only infinite, eternal being, creator of all things, preserver, and ruler over all His creation, who is spirit, love, light, and in whom all things have their source and end.*

IV. The Trinity (The unity and plurality of God)

A. The unity of the Godhead (one God)

Deuteronomy 6:4

"Hear, O Israel! The Lord *(Jehovah – singular form of His name) is our God (*Elohim* –plural form of His name), the Lord (Jehovah) is one."

*Note: The parenthetical words have been added by author.

1. The name here translated *LORD* is the name Jehovah – singular form.
2. The name here translated *Elohim* is the plural name for God.
3. The words that are used here teach us that God, though plural, is one.

Isaiah 45:22

"Turn to Me and be saved, all the ends of the earth;
For I am God, and there is no other."

4. Though people on earth may look to what they may call "their god," there is only one God in existence.
5. The only true God is the God of the Bible.
6. Everyone everywhere is to look to this *one* God for salvation and *only* He deserves our worship.

Genesis 1:1

In the beginning God *(Hebrew = *Elohim* – plural form of His name) created (Hebrew = *bara* – singular verb form) the heavens and the earth.

*Note: The parenthetical words have been added by author.

7. The word *Elohim* is plural, and it is used here with a singular verb *bara*.

8. In this first mention of God, His plurality and singleness are evident. This is a clear reference to the fact that all the members of the Trinity had a part in creation, a fact that is substantiated in the New Testament.

Genesis 1:26

> Then God said, "Let Us make man in Our image, according to Our likeness; and let them rule over the fish of the sea and over the birds of the sky and over the cattle and over all the earth, and over every creeping thing that creeps on the earth."

9. The words *Us* and *Our* are obviously plural pronouns used in reference to the Godhead.

10. It is a clear reference to the plurality of the Godhead and draws attention to the Trinity.

11. This does not tell us that we physically look like God. We are like God in that we are created with a mind, emotions (feelings), and the power to make decisions (a will).

12. God declared that people are the only creatures created in His image.

13. We may describe our pet animals as having thoughts, having feelings, or making decisions, but that is only a man-made description. Animals are creatures of natural instinct.

Isaiah 6:8

> Then I heard the voice of the Lord, saying, "Whom shall I send, and who will go for Us?" Then I said, "Here am I. Send me!"

14. Notice the pronoun "I" and the pronoun "Us." God is a singular God but exists in plurality. This obviously refers to the three-in-one triune God.

B. The plurality of the Godhead (the Father, the Son, and the Holy Spirit)

Matthew 3:16–17

> [16] After being baptized, Jesus came up immediately from the water; and behold, the heavens were opened, and he saw the Spirit of God descending as a dove *and* lighting on Him, [17] and behold, a voice out of the heavens said, "This is My beloved Son, in whom I am well-pleased."

1. This passage is significant in that at Christ's baptism all three members of the Godhead were present at the same place and at the same time.

    - The Son – Jesus was being baptized by John.
    - The Father – The voice of the Father came from heaven.
    - The Holy Spirit – The Spirit appeared by descending like a dove and rested on Jesus.

Matthew 28:18–19

> [18] And Jesus came up and spoke to them, saying, "All authority has been given to Me in heaven and on earth. [19] Go therefore and make disciples of all the nations, baptizing them in the name of the Father and the Son and the Holy Spirit,"

2 Corinthians 13:14

> The grace of the Lord Jesus Christ, and the love of God, and the fellowship of the Holy Spirit, be with you all.

2. All three members of the Godhead are mentioned in these passages.

3. At the baptism of Jesus, all three members of the Godhead are distinctive and present at the same time.

4. Each member of the Trinity is given the same honor and authority here.

5. The Holy Spirit was *not* a dove but descended *like* a dove.

V. The Deity of Each Member of the Godhead (The unity of the Godhead)

A. The deity of the Father

The deity of the Father is unquestioned by the preceding scriptures in this chapter. These passages clearly testify as to the deity of the Father.

B. The deity of the Son – Jesus

(We will look at the deity of Christ and the deity of the Holy Spirit in more detail when we study chapter 4 on Christology and chapter 6 on Pneumatology. Therefore, we will not go into great detail of these issues at this time.)

John 1:1–3

> [1] In the beginning was the Word, and the Word was with God, and the Word was God. [2] He was in the beginning with God. [3] All things came into being through Him, and apart from Him nothing came into being that has come into being.

1 John 5:20

> And we know that the Son of God has come, and has given us understanding so that we may know Him who is true; and we are in Him who is true, in His Son Jesus Christ. This is the true God and eternal life.

Romans 9:5

> whose are the fathers, and from whom is the Christ according to the flesh, who is over all, God blessed forever. Amen.

Colossians 1:13–17 (His beloved Son)

> [13] For He rescued us from the domain of darkness, and transferred us to the kingdom of His beloved Son, [14] in whom we have redemption, the forgiveness of sins.
>
> [15] He is the image of the invisible God, the firstborn of all creation. [16] For by Him all things were created, *both* in the heavens and on earth, visible and invisible, whether thrones or dominions or rulers or authorities—all things have been created through Him and for Him. [17] He is before all things, and in Him all things hold together.

Hebrews 1:1–3

> [1] God, after He spoke long ago to the fathers in the prophets in many portions and in many ways, [2] in these last days has spoken to us in His Son, whom He appointed heir of all things, through whom also He made the world. [3] And He is the radiance of His glory and the exact representation of His nature, and upholds all things by the word of His power. When He had made purification of sins, He sat down at the right hand of the Majesty on high,

C. The deity of the Holy Spirit

Acts 5:2–3 (The devious plot of Ananias and his wife.)

> [2] and kept back *some* of the price for himself, with his wife's full knowledge, and bringing a portion of it, he laid it at the apostles' feet. [3] But Peter said, "Ananias, why has Satan filled your heart to lie to the Holy Spirit and to keep back *some* of the price of the land?"

Matthew 28:18–19

> [18] And Jesus came up and spoke to them, saying, "All authority has been given to Me in heaven and on earth. [19] Go therefore and make disciples of all the nations, baptizing them in the name of the Father and the Son and the Holy Spirit,"

2 Corinthians 13:13–14

> [13] All the saints greet you.
>
> [14] The grace of the Lord Jesus Christ, and the love of God, and the fellowship of the Holy Spirit, be with you all.

The Athanasian Creed was one of the earliest statements of the Christian faith and first published in the 3rd century AD. It states, *"We worship one God in Trinity and Trinity in neither confounding the persons nor dividing the substance."*

Conclusion:

1. The God of the Bible is one God, existing in three persons (not three gods).
2. There is a distinction of persons in the Godhead, and yet there is perfect unity in the Godhead.
3. The deity of each person of the Godhead is clearly taught in the Bible.
4. The three persons of the Godhead are not three manifestations of the same person.
5. Members of the Trinity speak to one another. (John 17:1–26)
6. The Bible uses personal pronouns in connection with each member of the Godhead. (John 16:7)
7. The word *Trinity* is not found in scripture but is a theological term that is used to describe a biblical teaching.

8. The Trinity is not a whole composed of three parts (one plus one plus one equals three), but one which is three, each of which is equal in essence and attributes to the others.

9. The Bible teaches one God yet existing in three persons. It is not possible for the human mind, finite as it is, to fully comprehend the concept of the Trinity.

10. Theologians have often tried, but never perfectly, to illustrate the Trinity in human terms.

11. The Trinity is clearly taught in the Bible, and we need only to accept it by faith. It is not necessary for us to fully understand something to believe it.

D. Two important truths which must always be maintained in a biblical understanding of the Trinity

1. The unity of God refers to one God, not three gods.

2. The Father, the Son, and the Holy Spirit are not three manifestations of God but three distinct individual persons of the Godhead.

VI. Biblical Names of God

The Bible uses many names for God. These names tell us much about the person and nature of God. Your Bible should have an explanation in it that indicates which word for God is used and how it is designated in your translation. There are three main Old Testament Hebrew words that, when translated, refer to God. In most English Bibles we can distinguish which name for God is used by the spelling and capitalization. This section is not meant to be an exhaustive list of the names that are attributed to God. The names defined below will give you an idea of how truly awesome the God of the Bible is. He is the only true God and there is none other.

A. **Lord** (capital *L* with lower case *ord*)

'Adon – This word, translated in many places throughout the Old Testament, is *'adon* or *'adonay*, meaning "lord; master; Lord." Basically, 'adon means lord or master. *'Adon* describes the one who occupies the position of a master or lord over a slave or servant. This word denotes God's position as the one who has authority (like a master) over His people to reward the obedient and punish the disobedient.

B. **LORD** (All capital letters)

Jehovah Yahweh – One of the most important names for God in the Old Testament is Yahweh or Jehovah from the verb "to be," meaning, simply, but profoundly, "I am who I am" and "I will be who I will be." The four-letter Hebrew word *YHWH* was the name by which God revealed Himself to Moses in the burning bush, as recorded in Exodus 3:14.

The following names are combined with Jehovah in the Old Testament. They give a deeper meaning to the name, when combined with the basic name of Yahweh.

- *Jehovah-jireh* – This name is translated as "The LORD Will Provide." (Genesis 22:14)
- *Jehovah-shammah* – This phrase expresses the presence of the LORD and means "The LORD Is There." (Ezekiel 48:35)
- *Jehovah-nissi* – This name means "The LORD Is My Banner." (Exodus 17:15)
- *Jehovah-shalom* – This phrase means "The LORD Is Peace." (Judges 6:24)
- *Jehovah Elohe Israel* – This name means "LORD God of Israel," and it appears in Isaiah, Jeremiah, and the Psalms. Other names similar to this are Netsah Israel, "The Strength of Israel" (1 Samuel 15:29) and Abir Yisrael, "The Mighty One of Israel" (Isaiah 1:24).
- *Jehovah-tsebaoth* – This name is translated "The LORD of Hosts." (1 Samuel 1:3)

C. God (capital *G* with lower case *od*)

Elohim – Elohim is the plural form of El, but it is usually translated in the singular. Elohim conveys the sense of the one Supreme Being who is the only true God.

D. Other names that describe the person and character of God

1. Glory – God is described as Glory (Shekinah) in Exodus 16:7, Psalm 104:31, and Isaiah 60:1. In the New Testament, Jesus shares the glory of God in Matthew 25:31, 1 Corinthians 2:8, and Hebrews 1:3.

2. Wisdom – Paul describes Christ in these terms in Colossians 1:13–19; 2:1–3. Wisdom also appears in Proverbs 8:1–36, as the speaker who always says and does what is righteous. Wisdom here is personified and is equal to the voice of God. Wisdom is implemented in the creation of the universe.

3. Servant – The name of Servant also identifies this divine person and His saving ministry on behalf of His people. God's Servant is described in terms that apply to Jesus. He is upheld and chosen by God. He delights in God. He receives God's Spirit. Like Wisdom in Proverbs 8, He is holy, just, and righteous. The Servant will bring Jacob back to God and will be a light to the nations since He is seen as an offering for sin in Isaiah 42:1–4; 49:1–7; 53:1–12.

4. Shepherd – God is also described in prophecy as the Shepherd who will feed His flock, gather the lambs in His arms, carry them in His bosom, and gently lead those with young. (Isaiah 40:11; Ezekiel 34:11–16) Jesus applied this name to Himself in Luke 15:4–7 and John 10:11–16, making Himself equal to God, which infuriated the Jewish leaders of His day. Jesus Christ is also named Shepherd by His followers in 1 Peter 5:4, Hebrews 13:20, and Revelation 7:17.

5. Branch of Righteousness – Jeremiah 23:5–6 names the coming messianic figure, the Branch of Righteousness, who will be a descendent of David. He will be raised up to reign as King and to execute judgment and righteousness on the earth.

6. King – This descendant of David will have several divine qualities. He will be a Branch of Righteousness and King.

7. Word – The expression *Word* refers to Jesus Christ as the eternal God. Everything that defines God is found in Jesus. The eternal Son of God took on human form. (John 1:1, 14)

8. Father – Psalms 89:26

9. Rock – Psalms 89:26

10. Almighty – Exodus 6:3

11. Redeemer – Jeremiah 50:34

12. Ancient of Days – Daniel 7:9

E. The names for the three persons of the Trinity

With the birth of Jesus Christ, the names of the three persons of the Trinity are made more explicit.

1. God the Father – In the New Testament, God is known as *Father* in Matthew 5:16 and 28:19. The Father is called *Abba* in Mark 14:36 and Galatians 4:6.

2. God the Son – Jesus is named as:

   - Son – Matthew 11:27
   - Son of God – John 3:16–18
   - Son of Man – Matthew 8:20
   - Messiah – John 1:41
   - Lord – Romans 14:8
   - Word – John 1:1
   - Wisdom – 1 Corinthians 1:30
   - Bridegroom – Mark 2:19-20
   - Good Shepherd – John 10:11
   - Vine – John 15:1
   - Light – John 1:9
   - I AM – John 8:58

3. God the Holy Spirit – The Holy Spirit is called the Helper (Comforter in some translations) in John 14:16. The Greek word here literally means "One called alongside to help."

VII. The Attributes of God

The following attributes are those qualities of God which are essential, basic, and unique. These characteristics distinguish Him as the only true God. If you want to refer to all these qualities in one word, use the word *holy.*

A. Omniscience

God is all-knowing. God knows all and possesses all true knowledge.

Psalms 139:1–6

[1] O LORD, You have searched me and known *me.*
[2] You know when I sit down and when I rise up;
You understand my thought from afar.
[3] You scrutinize my path and my lying down,
And are intimately acquainted with all my ways.
[4] Even before there is a word on my tongue,
Behold, O LORD, You know it all.
[5] You have enclosed me behind and before,
And laid Your hand upon me.
[6] *Such* knowledge is too wonderful for me;
It is *too* high, I cannot attain to it.

B. Omnipotent

God is all powerful. He is limitless in power within the framework of His character, and He is the source of all power.

Psalms 115:3

But our God is in the heavens;
He does whatever He pleases.

Job 42:2

"I know that You can do all things,
And that no purpose of Yours can be thwarted."

Jeremiah 32:17

> 'Ah Lord God! Behold, You have made the heavens and the earth by Your great power and by Your outstretched arm! Nothing is too difficult for You,'

Jeremiah 32:27

> "Behold, I am the Lord, the God of all flesh; is anything too difficult for Me?"

Isaiah 14:27

> "For the Lord of hosts has planned, and who can frustrate *it*? And as for His stretched-out hand, who can turn it back?"

Isaiah 43:13

> "Even from eternity I am He,
> And there is none who can deliver out of My hand;
> I act and who can reverse it?"

C. Omnipresent

God is everywhere present. He is not limited by time or space.

Psalms 139:7–12

> [7] Where can I go from Your Spirit?
> Or where can I flee from Your presence?
> [8] If I ascend to heaven, You are there;
> If I make my bed in Sheol, behold, You are there.
> [9] If I take the wings of the dawn,
> If I dwell in the remotest part of the sea,
> [10] Even there Your hand will lead me,
> And Your right hand will lay hold of me.
> [11] If I say, "Surely the darkness will overwhelm me,
> And the light around me will be night,"
>
> [12] Even the darkness is not dark to You,
> And the night is as bright as the day.
> Darkness and light are alike *to You*.

D. Holy

God is set apart from all other beings and there is none like Him.

Isaiah 40:18

To whom then will you liken God?
Or what likeness will you compare with Him?

Exodus 15:11

"Who is like You among the gods, O Lord?
Who is like You, majestic in holiness,
Awesome in praises, working wonders?"

Leviticus 19:2

"Speak to all the congregation of the sons of Israel and say to them,
'You shall be holy, for I the Lord your God am holy.'"

Deuteronomy 32:4

"The Rock! His work is perfect,
For all His ways are just;
A God of faithfulness and without injustice,
Righteous and upright is He."

1 Samuel 2:2

"There is no one holy like the Lord,
Indeed, there is no one besides You,
Nor is there any rock like our God."

Isaiah 6:1–3

[1] In the year of King Uzziah's death I saw the Lord sitting on a throne, lofty and exalted, with the train of His robe filling the temple. [2] Seraphim stood above Him, each having six wings: with two he covered his face, and with two he covered his feet, and with two he flew. [3] And one called out to another and said,

"Holy, Holy, Holy, is the Lord of hosts,
The whole earth is full of His glory."

E. Immutable

God is unchanging.

Numbers 23:19–20

[19] "God is not a man, that He should lie,
Nor a son of man, that He should repent;
Has He said, and will He not do it?
Or has He spoken, and will He not make it good?
[20] "Behold, I have received *a command* to bless;
When He has blessed, then I cannot revoke it."

Psalms 33:11

The counsel of the LORD stands forever,
The plans of His heart from generation to generation.

Malachi 3:6

"For I, the LORD, do not change; therefore you, O sons of Jacob, are not consumed."

Hebrews 13:8

Jesus Christ *is* the same yesterday and today and forever.

F. Just

God's judgments are always true and righteous.

Psalms 89:14

Righteousness and justice are the foundation of Your throne;
Lovingkindness and truth go before You.

Deuteronomy 32:3–4

[3] "For I proclaim the name of the LORD;
Ascribe greatness to our God!
[4] "The Rock! His work is perfect,
For all His ways are just;
A God of faithfulness and without injustice,
Righteous and upright is He."

Revelation 15:3

And they sang the song of Moses, the bond-servant of God, and the song of the Lamb, saying,

"Great and marvelous are Your works,
O Lord God, the Almighty;
Righteous and true are Your ways,
King of the nations!"

Romans 3:24–26

[24] being justified as a gift by His grace through the redemption which is in Christ Jesus; [25] whom God displayed publicly as a propitiation in His blood through faith. *This was* to demonstrate His righteousness, because in the forbearance of God He passed over the sins previously committed; [26] for the demonstration, *I say,* of His righteousness at the present time, so that He would be just and the justifier of the one who has faith in Jesus.

G. Impartial

God has no favorites. He treats everyone the same.

Deuteronomy 10:17

For the LORD your God is the God of gods and the Lord of lords, the great, the mighty, and the awesome God who does not show partiality nor take a bribe.

Colossians 3:25

For he who does wrong will receive the consequences of the wrong which he has done, and that without partiality.

Acts 10:34–35

[34] Opening his mouth, Peter said:

"I most certainly understand *now* that God is not one to show partiality, [35] but in every nation the man who fears Him and does what is right is welcome to Him."

H. Love

God's love is unconditional and is well defined in 1 Corinthians 13.

Psalms 103:13–17

[13] Just as a father has compassion on *his* children,
So the LORD has compassion on those who fear Him.
[14] For He Himself knows our frame;
He is mindful that we are *but* dust.

[15] As for man, his days are like grass;
As a flower of the field, so he flourishes.
[16] When the wind has passed over it, it is no more,
And its place acknowledges it no longer.
[17] But the lovingkindness of the LORD is from everlasting to everlasting on those who fear Him,
And His righteousness to children's children,

Jeremiah 31:3

The LORD appeared to him from afar, *saying*,
"I have loved you with an everlasting love;
Therefore I have drawn you with lovingkindness."

John 3:16

"For God so loved the world, that He gave His only begotten Son, that whoever believes in Him shall not perish, but have eternal life."

1 John 4:8–10

[8] The one who does not love does not know God, for God is love. [9] By this the love of God was manifested in us, that God has sent His only begotten Son into the world so that we might live through Him. [10] In this is love, not that we loved God, but that He loved us and sent His Son *to be* the propitiation for our sins.

1 John 4:16

We have come to know and have believed the love which God has for us. God is love, and the one who abides in love abides in God, and God abides in him.

I. Goodness

God's basic character is good.

Exodus 34:6

> Then the LORD passed by in front of him and proclaimed, "The LORD, the LORD God, compassionate and gracious, slow to anger, and abounding in lovingkindness and truth;"

1 Chronicles 16:34

> O give thanks to the LORD, for *He is* good;
> For His lovingkindness is everlasting.

Psalms 100:5

> For the LORD is good;
> His lovingkindness is everlasting
> And His faithfulness to all generations.

Nahum 1:7

> The LORD is good,
> A stronghold in the day of trouble,
> And He knows those who take refuge in Him.

James 1:17

> Every good thing given and every perfect gift is from above, coming down from the Father of lights, with whom there is no variation or shifting shadow.

J. Eternal

God's existence is without beginning and without end.

Exodus 15:18

> "The LORD shall reign forever and ever."

Psalms 9:7

> But the LORD abides forever;
> He has established His throne for judgment,

Psalms 41:13

> Blessed be the LORD, the God of Israel,
> From everlasting to everlasting.
> Amen and Amen.

Psalms 90:2

> Before the mountains were born
> Or You gave birth to the earth and the world,
> Even from everlasting to everlasting, You are God.

Isaiah 44:6

> "Thus says the LORD, the King of Israel and his Redeemer, the LORD of hosts:
>
> 'I am the first and I am the last,
> And there is no God besides Me.'"

Revelation 4:8–11

> [8] And the four living creatures, each one of them having six wings, are full of eyes around and within; and day and night they do not cease to say,
>
> "HOLY, HOLY, HOLY *is* THE LORD GOD, THE ALMIGHTY, WHO WAS AND WHO IS AND WHO IS TO COME."
>
> [9] And when the living creatures give glory and honor and thanks to Him who sits on the throne, to Him who lives forever and ever, [10] the twenty-four elders will fall down before Him who sits on the throne, and will worship Him who lives forever and ever, and will cast their crowns before the throne, saying,
>
> [11] "Worthy are You, our Lord and our God, to receive glory and honor and power; for You created all things, and because of Your will they existed, and were created."

K. Sovereign

God reigns over all. He makes His own decisions and carries out His own eternal plan.

Psalms 22:28

For the kingdom is the LORD's
And He rules over the nations.

Daniel 4:34–35

[34] "But at the end of that period, I, Nebuchadnezzar, raised my eyes toward heaven and my reason returned to me, and I blessed the Most High and praised and honored Him who lives forever;

For His dominion is an everlasting dominion,
And His kingdom *endures* from generation to generation.
[35] "All the inhabitants of the earth are accounted as nothing,
But He does according to His will in the host of heaven
And *among* the inhabitants of earth;
And no one can ward off His hand
Or say to Him, 'What have You done?'"

Psalms 47:7–8

[7] For God is the King of all the earth;
Sing praises with a skillful psalm.
[8] God reigns over the nations,
God sits on His holy throne.

Daniel 7:14

"And to Him was given dominion,
Glory and a kingdom,
That all the peoples, nations and *men of every* language
Might serve Him.
His dominion is an everlasting dominion
Which will not pass away;
And His kingdom is one
Which will not be destroyed."

Revelation 11:15

> Then the seventh angel sounded; and there were loud voices in heaven, saying,
>
> "The kingdom of the world has become *the kingdom* of our Lord and of His Christ; and He will reign forever and ever."

Psalms 103:19

> The LORD has established His throne in the heavens,
> And His sovereignty rules over all.

VIII. The Sovereignty of God and Our Free Will

We are tempted to elevate one of these views over the other. If we do this, we either become robots controlled by a sovereign God with no responsibility for our actions and decisions, or we alone are fully in charge and able to manipulate God. Both the sovereignty of God and our free will are clearly taught in scripture, and we must accept the reality of both and maintain the balance the Bible affirms. The key word is *balance.*

A. The free will of individuals

John 3:16

> "For God so loved the world, that He gave His only begotten Son, that whoever believes in Him shall not perish, but have eternal life."

Revelation 22:17

> The Spirit and the bride say, "Come." And let the one who hears say, "Come." And let the one who is thirsty come; let the one who wishes take the water of life without cost.

Joshua 24:15

> "If it is disagreeable in your sight to serve the LORD, choose for yourselves today whom you will serve: whether the gods which your fathers served which were beyond the River, or the gods of the Amorites in whose land you are living; but as for me and my house, we will serve the LORD."

1. These passages above are typical of thousands of references in which God calls upon human beings to make choices.

2. The “whoever,” “choose for yourselves,” and “who wishes” would reflect that it is *our* choice.

3. Alongside of the sovereignty of God stands the free will of humanity.

4. The gospel invitation is addressed to individuals who have the capability to accept it or reject it.

5. People are held responsible for their decisions concerning Christ, which implies the freedom of the will.

B. The sovereignty of God

1. God does whatever He pleases.

Psalm 115:3

> But our God is in the heavens;
> He does whatever He pleases.

Psalm 135:5–7

> [5] For I know that the Lord is great
> And that our Lord is above all gods.
> [6] Whatever the Lord pleases, He does,
> In heaven and in earth, in the seas and in all deeps.
> [7] He causes the vapors to ascend from the ends of the earth;
> Who makes lightnings for the rain,
> Who brings forth the wind from His treasuries.

2. The sovereignty of God is clearly taught in scripture.

Psalms 103:19

> The Lord has established His throne in the heavens,
> And His sovereignty rules over all.

Romans 9:19–21

> [19] You will say to me then, “Why does He still find fault? For who resists His will?” [20] On the contrary, who are you, O man, who answers back to God? The thing molded will not say to the molder, “Why did you make me like this,” will it? [21] Or does not the potter have a right over the clay, to make from the same lump one vessel for honorable use and another for common use?

Conclusion:

The sovereignty of God is clearly taught in scripture, but within the framework of His sovereignty, He has made room for us to make choices. When God created us in His own image, He created us with a mind, emotions, and a will. He did not create pre-programmed robots.

The sovereignty of God and the free will of humankind may seem to be opposites which cannot be reconciled. God in His Word declares the reality of both. Therefore, both are true even though it seems impossible to the reasoning of the human mind. These truths we accept by faith, though we may not completely comprehend them.

IX. The Works of God

A. Creation

All members of the Godhead were involved in creation.

Genesis 1:1

> In the beginning God created the heavens and the earth.

The word *created* is the Hebrew word *bara* and means "to make a thing without the use of pre-existing material." Bara is used three times in Genesis 1.

- Referring to matter (v. 1)
- Referring to animal life (v. 21)
- Referring to human life (v. 26–27)

Hebrews 11:3

> By faith we understand that the worlds were prepared by the word of God, so that what is seen was not made out of things which are visible.

God spoke and it was so. God made the world and all that appears to the eye without the use of pre-existing material. God is responsible for creating everything outside of Himself.

1. Creation and God the Father

1 Corinthians 8:6

> yet for us there is *but* one God, the Father, from whom are all things and we *exist* for Him; and one Lord, Jesus Christ, by whom are all things, and we *exist* through Him.

2. Creation and God the Son

John 1:3

All things came into being through Him, and apart from Him nothing came into being that has come into being.

Colossians 1:16

For by Him all things were created, *both* in the heavens and on earth, visible and invisible, whether thrones or dominions or rulers or authorities—all things have been created through Him and for Him.

Hebrews 1:2

in these last days has spoken to us in His Son, whom He appointed heir of all things, through whom also He made the world.

3. Creation and God the Holy Spirit

Job 33:4

"The Spirit of God has made me,
And the breath of the Almighty gives me life."

Each member of the Godhead (Father, Son, and the Holy Spirit) had a part in creation. Creation was the work of the Triune God.

B. Preservation

God not only created all things, but He preserves all He created.

Colossians 1:17

He is before all things, and in Him all things hold together.

Psalms 75:3

"The earth and all who dwell in it melt;
It is I who have firmly set its pillars." *Selah.*

Acts 17:28

for in Him we live and move and exist, as even some of your own poets have said, 'For we also are His children.'

Psalms 104:14

> He causes the grass to grow for the cattle,
> And vegetation for the labor of man,
> So that he may bring forth food from the earth,

1. God existed before all things.

2. God maintains all things. He keeps all things which He has created in operation.

3. God preserves His creation. He preserves the earth, and all created things are under His control.

C. Providence

God has a plan and the capability to carry that plan out to conclusion.

Psalms 103:19

> The LORD has established His throne in the heavens,
> And His sovereignty rules over all.

Ephesians 1:18–23

> [18] *I pray that* the eyes of your heart may be enlightened, so that you will know what is the hope of His calling, what are the riches of the glory of His inheritance in the saints, [19] and what is the surpassing greatness of His power toward us who believe. *These are* in accordance with the working of the strength of His might [20] which He brought about in Christ, when He raised Him from the dead and seated Him at His right hand in the heavenly *places*, [21] far above all rule and authority and power and dominion, and every name that is named, not only in this age but also in the one to come. [22] And He put all things in subjection under His feet, and gave Him as head over all things to the church, [23] which is His body, the fullness of Him who fills all in all.

Psalms 47:2

> For the LORD Most High is to be feared,
> A great King over all the earth.

1. God continuously makes all the events of the physical and spiritual universe fulfill the original plan for which He created it. This process is called the providence of God.

2. Providence is different from preservation. Preservation has to do with the continuance of creation; providence has to do with the plan of God for the universe through all the ages.

3. This providence reaches even to the actions of individuals, as well. God can bring good out of evil in this regard.

4. Read Joseph's statement (below) made to his evil brothers, who had sold him into slavery.

Genesis 50:18–20

> [18] Then his brothers also came and fell down before him and said, "Behold, we are your servants." [19] But Joseph said to them, "Do not be afraid, for am I in God's place? [20] As for you, you meant evil against me, *but* God meant it for good in order to bring about this present result, to preserve many people alive."

X. God's Providence with Respect to People's Evil – Accomplished in Four Ways

A. By preventing people from sinning

Genesis 20:2–10

> [2] Abraham said of Sarah his wife, "She is my sister." So Abimelech king of Gerar sent and took Sarah. [3] But God came to Abimelech in a dream of the night, and said to him, "Behold, you are a dead man because of the woman whom you have taken, for she is married." [4] Now Abimelech had not come near her; and he said, "Lord, will You slay a nation, even *though* blameless? [5] Did he not himself say to me, 'She is my sister'? And she herself said, 'He is my brother.' In the integrity of my heart and the innocence of my hands I have done this." [6] Then God said to him in the dream, "Yes, I know that in the integrity of your heart you have done this, and I also kept you from sinning against Me; therefore I did not let you touch her. [7] Now therefore, restore the man's wife, for he is a prophet, and he will pray for you and you will live. But if you do not restore *her*, know that you shall surely die, you and all who are yours."
>
> [8] So Abimelech arose early in the morning and called all his servants and told all these things in their hearing; and the men were greatly frightened. [9] Then Abimelech called Abraham and said to him, "What have you done to us? And how have I sinned against you, that you have brought on me and on my kingdom a great sin? You have done to me things that ought not to be done." [10] And Abimelech said to Abraham, "What have you encountered, that you have done this thing?"

B. By allowing people to sin and not preventing it

Acts 14:16–17

> [16] "In the generations gone by He permitted all the nations to go their own ways; [17] and yet He did not leave Himself without witness, in that He did good and gave you rains from heaven and fruitful seasons, satisfying your hearts with food and gladness."

C. By overruling evil and bringing good from it

Genesis 50:19–20

> [19] But Joseph said to them, "Do not be afraid, for am I in God's place? [20] As for you, you meant evil against me, *but* God meant it for good in order to bring about this present result, to preserve many people alive.

Romans 8:28

> And we know that God causes all things to work together for good to those who love God, to those who are called according to *His* purpose.

D. By prescribing the bounds of sin and its effects

Satan could go only so far and no further with Job.

Job 1:12

> Then the LORD said to Satan, "Behold, all that he has is in your power, only do not put forth your hand on him." So Satan departed from the presence of the LORD.

Job 2:6

> So the LORD said to Satan, "Behold, he is in your power, only spare his life."

XI. The Administration of God's Love, Care, and Protection

The works of God include His sovereignty, His creation, His preservation, and His providence. God created us, and in His providence, He created certain *lines of authority* to bring order to our lives. Through these lines of authority, He carries out His will for us by using the four ways previously mentioned regarding God's providence. (See Roman numeral X.) God uses this line of authority to help guide our lives. The way we respond to authority determines the track our lives will take.

Proverbs 1:8–10

> [8] Hear, my son, your father's instruction
> And do not forsake your mother's teaching;
> [9] Indeed, they are a graceful wreath to your head
> And ornaments about your neck.
> [10] My son, if sinners entice you,
> Do not consent.

Ephesians 6:1–3

> [1] Children, obey your parents in the Lord, for this is right. [2] HONOR YOUR FATHER AND MOTHER (which is the first commandment with a promise), [3] SO THAT IT MAY BE WELL WITH YOU, AND THAT YOU MAY LIVE LONG ON THE EARTH.

Everyone is under authority except God. God has designed our lives so that our first experience with this authority structure is the relationship we have with our parents. If we learn how to respond to our father and mother, we are positioning ourselves for success.

A. God sets the standard of righteousness.

If we honor Him and obey His Word, it will keep us from making destructive, personal choices that can ruin our lives.

Leviticus 19:2

> "Speak to all the congregation of the sons of Israel and say to them, 'You shall be holy, for I the LORD your God am holy."

1 Corinthians 11:1

> Be imitators of me, just as I also am of Christ.

1 John 2:6

> the one who says he abides in Him ought himself to walk in the same manner as He walked.

B. The Bible is to be our guide and standard for faith and life.

2 Timothy 3:16–17

> [16] All Scripture is inspired by God and profitable for teaching, for reproof, for correction, for training in righteousness; [17] so that the man of God may be adequate, equipped for every good work.

C. Human authority is ordained by God to maintain order and direct our lives.

1 Peter 2:13–17

> [13] Submit yourselves for the Lord's sake to every human institution, whether to a king as the one in authority, [14] or to governors as sent by him for the punishment of evildoers and the praise of those who do right. [15] For such is the will of God that by doing right you may silence the ignorance of foolish men. [16] *Act* as free men, and do not use your freedom as a covering for evil, but *use it* as bondslaves of God. [17] Honor all people, love the brotherhood, fear God, honor the king.

Romans 13:1–7

> [1] Every person is to be in subjection to the governing authorities. For there is no authority except from God, and those which exist are established by God. [2] Therefore whoever resists authority has opposed the ordinance of God; and they who have opposed will receive condemnation upon themselves. [3] For rulers are not a cause of fear for good behavior, but for evil. Do you want to have no fear of authority? Do what is good and you will have praise from the same; [4] for it is a minister of God to you for good. But if you do what is evil, be afraid; for it does not bear the sword for nothing; for it is a minister of God, an avenger who brings wrath on the one who practices evil. [5] Therefore it is necessary to be in subjection, not only because of wrath, but also for conscience' sake. [6] For because of this you also pay taxes, for *rulers* are servants of God, devoting themselves to this very thing. [7] Render to all what is due them: tax to whom tax *is due*; custom to whom custom; fear to whom fear; honor to whom honor.

1. Husband / wife relationships

Ephesians 5:22–33

> [22] Wives, *be subject* to your own husbands, as to the Lord. [23] For the husband is the head of the wife, as Christ also is the head of the church, He Himself *being* the Savior of the body. [24] But as the church is subject to Christ, so also the wives *ought to be* to their husbands in everything.
>
> [25] Husbands, love your wives, just as Christ also loved the church and gave Himself up for her, [26] so that He might sanctify her, having cleansed her by the washing of water with the word, [27] that He might present to Himself the church in all her glory, having no spot or wrinkle or any such thing; but that she would be holy and blameless. [28] So husbands ought also to love their own wives as their own bodies. He who loves his own wife loves himself; [29] for no one ever hated his own flesh, but nourishes and cherishes it, just as Christ also *does* the church, [30] because we are members of His body. [31] FOR THIS REASON A MAN SHALL LEAVE HIS FATHER AND MOTHER AND SHALL BE JOINED TO HIS WIFE, AND THE TWO SHALL BECOME ONE FLESH. [32] This mystery is great; but I am speaking with reference to Christ and the church. [33] Nevertheless, each individual among you also is to love his own wife even as himself, and the wife must *see to it* that she respects her husband.

1 Peter 3:1–7

> [1] In the same way, you wives, be submissive to your own husbands so that even if any *of them* are disobedient to the word, they may be won without a word by the behavior of their wives, [2] as they observe your chaste and respectful behavior. [3] Your adornment must not be *merely* external—braiding the hair, and wearing gold jewelry, or putting on dresses; [4] but *let it be* the hidden person of the heart, with the imperishable quality of a gentle and quiet spirit, which is precious in the sight of God. [5] For in this way in former times the holy women also, who hoped in God, used to adorn themselves, being submissive to their own husbands; [6] just as Sarah obeyed Abraham, calling him lord, and you have become her children if you do what is right without being frightened by any fear.
>
> [7] You husbands in the same way, live with *your wives* in an understanding way, as with someone weaker, since she is a woman; and show her honor as a fellow heir of the grace of life, so that your prayers will not be hindered.

2. Parent / child relationships

Exodus 20:12

"Honor your father and your mother, that your days may be prolonged in the land which the LORD your God gives you."

Ephesians 6:1–3

[1] Children, obey your parents in the Lord, for this is right. [2] HONOR YOUR FATHER AND MOTHER (which is the first commandment with a promise), [3] SO THAT IT MAY BE WELL WITH YOU, AND THAT YOU MAY LIVE LONG ON THE EARTH.

Colossians 3:20

Children, be obedient to your parents in all things, for this is well-pleasing to the Lord.

Proverbs 6:20–23

[20] My son, observe the commandment of your father
And do not forsake the teaching of your mother;
[21] Bind them continually on your heart;
Tie them around your neck.
[22] When you walk about, they will guide you;
When you sleep, they will watch over you;
And when you awake, they will talk to you.
[23] For the commandment is a lamp and the teaching is light;
And reproofs for discipline are the way of life

3. Employer / employee relationships

1 Peter 2:18–20

[18] Servants, be submissive to your masters with all respect, not only to those who are good and gentle, but also to those who are unreasonable. [19] For this *finds* favor, if for the sake of conscience toward God a person bears up under sorrows when suffering unjustly. [20] For what credit is there if, when you sin and are harshly treated, you endure it with patience? But if when you do what is right and suffer *for it* you patiently endure it, this *finds* favor with God.

Ephesians 6:5–9

> [5] Slaves, be obedient to those who are your masters according to the flesh, with fear and trembling, in the sincerity of your heart, as to Christ; [6] not by way of eyeservice, as men-pleasers, but as slaves of Christ, doing the will of God from the heart. [7] With good will render service, as to the Lord, and not to men, [8] knowing that whatever good thing each one does, this he will receive back from the Lord, whether slave or free.
>
> [9] And masters, do the same things to them, and give up threatening, knowing that both their Master and yours is in heaven, and there is no partiality with Him.

Colossians 3:22–25

> [22] Slaves, in all things obey those who are your masters on earth, not with external service, as those who *merely* please men, but with sincerity of heart, fearing the Lord. [23] Whatever you do, do your work heartily, as for the Lord rather than for men, [24] knowing that from the Lord you will receive the reward of the inheritance. It is the Lord Christ whom you serve. [25] For he who does wrong will receive the consequences of the wrong which he has done, and that without partiality.

4. The underlying principle in all authority and responsibility relationships: If the authority in my life orders me to do something that is dishonest, immoral, evil, or illegal, I must obey the higher authority, which is ultimately the Word of God.

Note the following examples:

Acts 4:17–20

> [17] "But so that it will not spread any further among the people, let us warn them to speak no longer to any man in this name." [18] And when they had summoned them, they commanded them not to speak or teach at all in the name of Jesus. [19] But Peter and John answered and said to them, "Whether it is right in the sight of God to give heed to you rather than to God, you be the judge; [20] for we cannot stop speaking about what we have seen and heard."

Acts 5:27–29

> [27] When they had brought them, they stood them before the Council. The high priest questioned them, [28] saying, "We gave you strict orders not to continue teaching in this name, and yet, you have filled Jerusalem with your teaching and intend to bring this man's blood upon us." [29] But Peter and the apostles answered, "We must obey God rather than men."

Conclusions and principles:

1. God is the ultimate source of all authority.
2. This *line of authority* is not meant to manipulate others; it is God's plan of love, guidance, and care.
3. We are instructed to obey the authority over us as an obedience to God and His Word.
4. If we are asked to do something evil or illegal, we are to obey the higher authority, which is ultimately God and His Word. (Acts 4:19–20; Acts 5:27–29)
5. Apart from the exceptions in Acts 4:19–20 and Acts 5:27–29, disobeying the authority over us is the same as disobeying God.
6. Even when we must decline to obey an evil assignment, we should do so graciously and with respect.
7. Understand that everyone in our lives must answer to those in authority over them. Even those in authority are accountable to someone else.
8. Because we are born with a sinful and selfish nature, it is often more difficult to honor and obey those closest to us. We *must* learn to see all authority as chosen by God.
9. There are two aspects of our responsibility toward the authority over us: <u>honor</u> (respect) and <u>obedience</u> (to do as you are told).
10. This line of authority is not designed to imprison or manipulate us but to guide our lives in the will of God.
11. If we apply this principle at home in relationship to our parents, we will have success in all authoritative relationships.

Please note the following illustration:

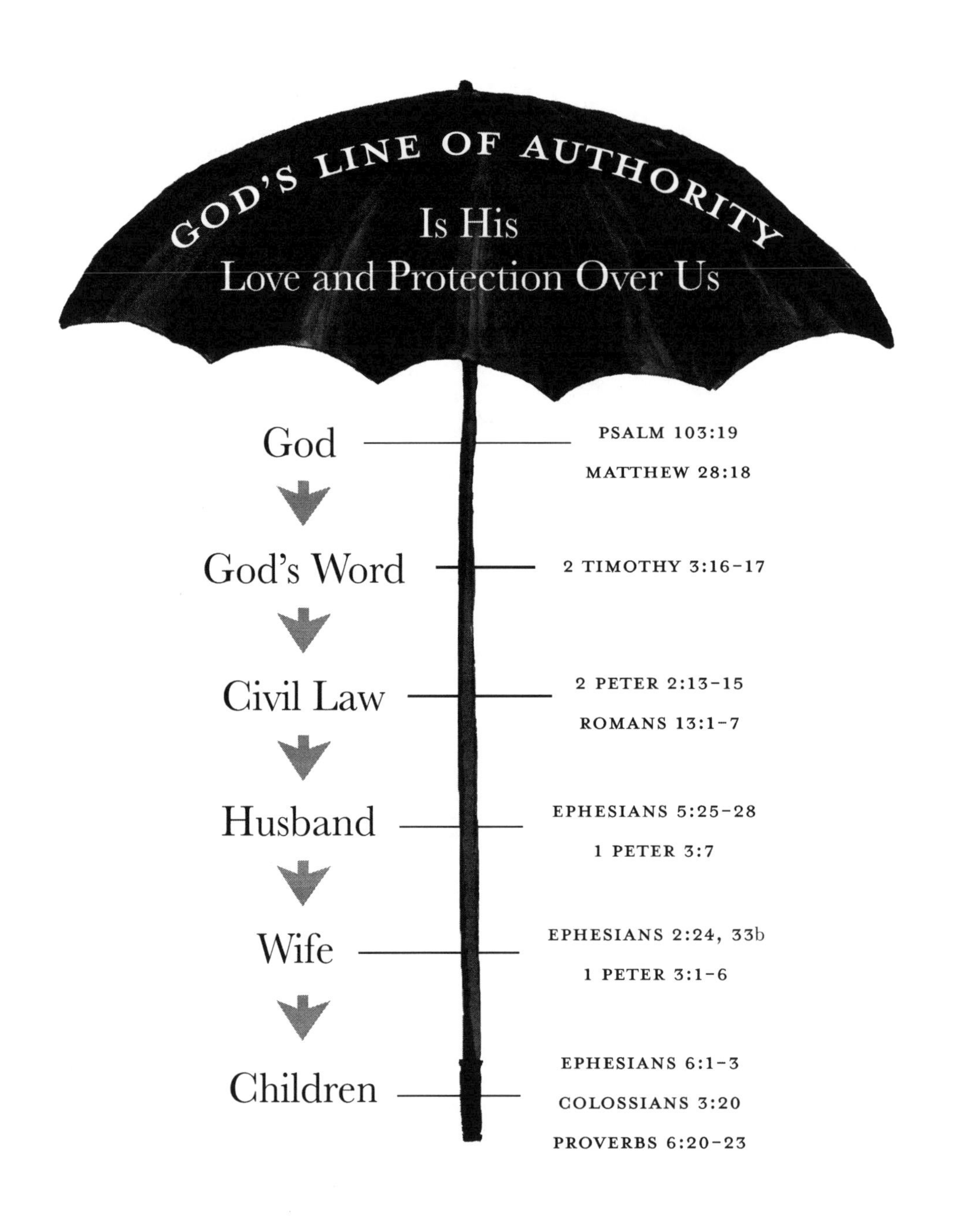

REVIEW QUESTIONS

1. Explain the significance of Romans 1:19–21 in the light of a belief in God.
2. Are we born with a knowledge of God?
3. Should the existence of God be obvious to all people? Why?
4. Define Theism. Do we believe in Theism?
5. Define Atheism.
6. Define Agnosticism.
7. What three things must be present in a definition of personality?
8. Give four descriptions of God found in the Bible. Give a reference for each.
9. Prove from scripture that God is <u>one God</u>.
10. Is God three manifestations of one person or one God in three persons?
11. Is each member of the Trinity fully God?
12. Explain the significance of Matthew 3:16–17 in the light of the Trinity.
13. We believe in three gods. True or false?
14. What are the two truths that must be maintained in connection with the Trinity?
15. Name the three primary names for God. Give the meaning of each and tell how they are distinguished in the English Bible.
16. Define omniscience.
17. Define sensibility.
18. Define omnipotence.
19. Define omnipresence.
20. Define eternity.
21. Define sovereignty.

22. Do we believe people have the capacity to choose to follow or reject God?

23. Define preservation.

24. Define providence.

25. List four ways in which God works His providence in spite of our sin.

26. List in order God's line of authority. (Refer to umbrella graphic titled "GOD'S LINE OF AUTHORITY Is His Love and Protection Over Us.")

27. If there is a conflict of commands between two authorities in our lives, which authority should we obey?

28. What does it mean to honor those in authority over us?

29. What does it mean to submit to those in authority over us?

30. Why should I honor the authority over me, even if I see much wrong in their lives and attitudes?

31. What promise is given to those who obey and honor their parents?

32. Memorize the books of the New Testament and be ready to quote them in order at our next class.

CHAPTER 4

Christology
(What the Bible Teaches About the Person of Jesus Christ)

Under the subject of the Trinity in chapter three, we were confronted with truths that are beyond our human comprehension, limited as we are with finite minds. We will face this issue again as we study the person of Jesus Christ. Jesus Christ is 100 percent God and 100 percent man, and yet, one person. This concept has been an enigma to many. Jesus is not half God and half man. Only a strong adherence to the Word of God and a solid faith will keep us from error in this regard. Christianity and Jesus Christ are inseparably linked together. Without a clear understanding of the person and work of Jesus Christ, there can be no true Christianity.

I. The Eternal Nature of Jesus Christ

A. Christ existed with God in the beginning. (John 1:1–3 and Genesis 1:1)

John 1:1–3

> [1] In the beginning was the Word, and the Word was with God, and the Word was God. [2] He was in the beginning with God. [3] All things came into being through Him, and apart from Him nothing came into being that has come into being.

B. He existed from eternity past. He had no beginning. (Micah 5:2)

Micah 5:2

> "But as for you, Bethlehem Ephrathah,
> *Too* little to be among the clans of Judah,
> From you One will go forth for Me to be ruler in Israel.
> His goings forth are from long ago,
> From the days of eternity."

John 8:58–59

> [58] Jesus said to them, "Truly, truly, I say to you, before Abraham was born, I am." [59] Therefore they picked up stones to throw at Him, but Jesus hid Himself and went out of the temple."

C. He is eternal in His existence. He had no beginning and will have no end.

Revelation 22:13

> "I am the Alpha and the Omega, the first and the last, the beginning and the end."

D. Christ's eternal character is defined in Melchizedek's appearance.

Whether we see Melchizedek as a pre-incarnate appearance of Christ or simply a picture of Christ is a matter of opinion. In either case, Hebrews 7 defines Jesus Christ as an eternal being.

Hebrews 6:20–7:6

> [20] where Jesus has entered as a forerunner for us, having become a high priest forever according to the order of Melchizedek.
>
> [1] For this Melchizedek, king of Salem, priest of the Most High God, who met Abraham as he was returning from the slaughter of the kings and blessed him, [2] to whom also Abraham apportioned a tenth part of all *the spoils*, was first of all, by the translation *of his name*, king of righteousness, and then also king of Salem, which is king of peace. [3] Without father, without mother, without genealogy, having neither beginning of days nor end of life, but made like the Son of God, he remains a priest perpetually.
>
> [4] Now observe how great this man was to whom Abraham, the patriarch, gave a tenth of the choicest spoils. [5] And those indeed of the sons of Levi who receive the priest's office have commandment in the Law to collect a tenth from the people, that is, from their brethren, although these are descended from Abraham. [6] But the one whose genealogy is not traced from them collected a tenth from Abraham and blessed the one who had the promises.

Psalms 110:4

> The LORD has sworn and will not change His mind,
> "You are a priest forever
> According to the order of Melchizedek."

Genesis 14:18–20

> [18] And Melchizedek king of Salem brought out bread and wine; now he was a priest of God Most High. [19] He blessed him and said,
>
> "Blessed be Abram of God Most High,
> Possessor of heaven and earth;
> [20] And blessed be God Most High,
> Who has delivered your enemies into your hand."
>
> He gave him a tenth of all.

Note: The term *pre-existence* does not merely mean that Jesus Christ existed before His incarnation. The Jehovah's Witnesses teach this. But along with this teaching, they add that Jesus was created by God the Father before Jesus came to earth. When we use the term pre–existence, we refer to the fact that Christ is eternal in that He never had a beginning.

II. The Incarnation of Jesus Christ

The eternal Son of God took on humanity and became flesh.

A. Pre-incarnate appearances of Christ

The message of the Old Testament fully anticipated the Jewish Messiah would come. The Old Testament prophets understood the Messiah would be God and would become the God-Man. The prophets made it truly clear that God would so identify Himself with humanity, and as such, would provide for the redemption for all.

The eternal Son of God had appeared in several ways throughout the Old Testament. Many times, He appeared as the Angel of the Lord or manifested Himself in human form. These manifestations are called *theophanies.* In our study of angels (chapter 9), we will learn the Angel of the Lord is none other than the pre-incarnate appearance of Christ. Below are five accounts that are typical theophanies.

Judges 13:8–24

[8] Then Manoah entreated the LORD and said, "O Lord, please let the man of God whom You have sent come to us again that he may teach us what to do for the boy who is to be born." [9] God listened to the voice of Manoah; and the angel of God came again to the woman as she was sitting in the field, but Manoah her husband was not with her. [10] So the woman ran quickly and told her husband, "Behold, the man who came the *other* day has appeared to me." [11] Then Manoah arose and followed his wife, and when he came to the man he said to him, "Are you the man who spoke to the woman?" And he said, "I am." [12] Manoah said, "Now when your words come *to pass*, what shall be the boy's mode of life and his vocation?" [13] So the angel of the LORD said to Manoah, "Let the woman pay attention to all that I said. [14] She should not eat anything that comes from the vine nor drink wine or strong drink, nor eat any unclean thing; let her observe all that I commanded."

[15] Then Manoah said to the angel of the LORD, "Please let us detain you so that we may prepare a young goat for you." [16] The angel of the LORD said to Manoah, "Though you detain me, I will not eat your food, but if you prepare a burnt offering, *then* offer it to the LORD." For Manoah did not know that he was the angel of the LORD. [17] Manoah said to the angel of the LORD, "What is your name, so that when your words come *to pass*, we may honor you?" [18] But the angel of the LORD said to him, "Why do you ask my name, seeing it is wonderful?" [19] So Manoah took the young goat with the grain offering and offered it on the rock to the LORD, and He performed wonders while Manoah and his wife looked on. [20] For it came about when the flame went up from the altar toward heaven, that the angel of the LORD ascended in the flame of the altar. When Manoah and his wife saw *this*, they fell on their faces to the ground.

[21] Now the angel of the LORD did not appear to Manoah or his wife again. Then Manoah knew that he was the angel of the LORD. [22] So Manoah said to his wife, "We will surely die, for we have seen God." [23] But his wife said to him, "If the LORD had desired to kill us, He would not have accepted a burnt offering and a grain offering from our hands, nor would He have shown us all these things, nor would He have let us hear *things* like this at this time."

[24] Then the woman gave birth to a son and named him Samson; and the child grew up and the LORD blessed him.

Genesis 16:11–13

> [11] The angel of the LORD said to her further,
>
> "Behold, you are with child,
> And you will bear a son;
> And you shall call his name Ishmael,
> Because the LORD has given heed to your affliction.
> [12] "He will be a wild donkey of a man,
> His hand *will be* against everyone,
> And everyone's hand *will be* against him;
> And he will live to the east of all his brothers."
>
> [13] Then she called the name of the LORD who spoke to her, "You are a God who sees"; for she said, "Have I even remained alive here after seeing Him?"

Genesis 22:11–13

> [11] But the angel of the LORD called to him from heaven and said, "Abraham, Abraham!" And he said, "Here I am." [12] He said, "Do not stretch out your hand against the lad, and do nothing to him; for now I know that you fear God, since you have not withheld your son, your only son, from Me." [13] Then Abraham raised his eyes and looked, and behold, behind *him* a ram caught in the thicket by his horns; and Abraham went and took the ram and offered him up for a burnt offering in the place of his son.

Genesis 32:24–30

> [24] Then Jacob was left alone, and a man wrestled with him until daybreak. [25] When he saw that he had not prevailed against him, he touched the socket of his thigh; so the socket of Jacob's thigh was dislocated while he wrestled with him. [26] Then he said, "Let me go, for the dawn is breaking." But he said, "I will not let you go unless you bless me." [27] So he said to him, "What is your name?" And he said, "Jacob." [28] He said, "Your name shall no longer be Jacob, but Israel; for you have striven with God and with men and have prevailed." [29] Then Jacob asked him and said, "Please tell me your name." But he said, "Why is it that you ask my name?" And he blessed him there. [30] So Jacob named the place Peniel, for *he said*, "I have seen God face to face, yet my life has been preserved."

Exodus 3:5–6

> [5]Then He said, "Do not come near here; remove your sandals from your feet, for the place on which you are standing is holy ground." [6]He said also, "I am the God of your father, the God of Abraham, the God of Isaac, and the God of Jacob." Then Moses hid his face, for he was afraid to look at God.

B. There are many Old Testament prophetic pictures of the coming of Jesus Christ and His work of redemption.

Some of these examples are:

1. The Lamb slain (Exodus 12; John 1:29)

2. The Servant (Psalm 40:6–8)

3. The Son (Psalm 2)

4. The Branch (Isaiah 4:2; 11:1; Zechariah 3:8; 6:12)

C. The Old Testament clearly anticipates the incarnation of the Savior.

Genesis 3:15

> "And I will put enmity
> Between you and the woman,
> And between your seed and her seed;
> He shall bruise you on the head,
> And you shall bruise him on the heel."

1. A battle is predicted between the offspring of the woman (the one born of a virgin) and Satan.

2. Satan will inflict a wounding blow to Christ (the heel of the offspring of the woman).

3. At the same time Christ will deal a deadly blow to Satan (the head of Satan).

4. When Christ died and rose again, He paved the way for the believer to be free from the grip of Satan.

5. At the death and resurrection of Jesus, the battle was won, and Christ is the Victor. The believing sinner can now be free from the control of Satan.

Isaiah 7:14

> Therefore the Lord Himself will give you a sign: Behold, a virgin will be with child and bear a son, and she will call His name Immanuel.

6. The Lord will give a special sign to all the world that will designate the identity of Immanuel.

7. That sign is the virgin birth. Christ is the only one ever born to a virgin.

8. The Son of the virgin birth was to be called Immanuel, which means "God with us."

Isaiah 9:6–7

> 6 For a child will be born to us, a son will be given to us;
> And the government will rest on His shoulders;
> And His name will be called Wonderful Counselor, Mighty God,
> Eternal Father, Prince of Peace.
> 7 There will be no end to the increase of *His* government or of peace,
> On the throne of David and over his kingdom,
> To establish it and to uphold it with justice and righteousness
> From then on and forevermore.
> The zeal of the LORD of hosts will accomplish this.

9. "The child born" is a reference to the humanity of Jesus Christ. The eternal Son of God took on human form when He was conceived by the Holy Spirit in the womb of Mary. At that point in time, He became the God-Man.

10. "The Son given" is a reference to the eternal Son of God, who existed before His human birth and was given to all of us to become our Savior.

11. The names that would be given to Him are the names of God Himself.

12. He will be a direct descendent of King David and the eternal fulfillment of the Davidic Covenant. (2 Samuel 7)

13. He will one day sit on David's throne and reign with true justice and righteousness.

14. His kingdom will never end.

D. The New Testament reports the literal fulfillment of the incarnation in Jesus Christ.

Matthew 1:18–25

> [18] Now the birth of Jesus Christ was as follows: when His mother Mary had been betrothed to Joseph, before they came together she was found to be with child by the Holy Spirit. [19] And Joseph her husband, being a righteous man and not wanting to disgrace her, planned to send her away secretly. [20] But when he had considered this, behold, an angel of the Lord appeared to him in a dream, saying, "Joseph, son of David, do not be afraid to take Mary as your wife; for the Child who has been conceived in her is of the Holy Spirit. [21] She will bear a Son; and you shall call His name Jesus, for He will save His people from their sins." [22] Now all this took place to fulfill what was spoken by the Lord through the prophet: [23] "BEHOLD, THE VIRGIN SHALL BE WITH CHILD AND SHALL BEAR A SON, AND THEY SHALL CALL HIS NAME IMMANUEL," which translated means, "GOD WITH US." [24] And Joseph awoke from his sleep and did as the angel of the Lord commanded him, and took *Mary* as his wife, [25] but kept her a virgin until she gave birth to a Son; and he called His name Jesus.

1. Matthew's account of the life of Christ establishes the reality of the virgin birth of Jesus.

2. Notice Matthew quotes from Isaiah 7:14 to link the birth of Christ to Isaiah's prophecy.

3. A careful and honest study of Matthew's account leaves no doubt in the mind of the student as to Matthew's intention to affirm that Jesus was indeed born of a virgin.

Luke 1:26–36

> [26] Now in the sixth month the angel Gabriel was sent from God to a city in Galilee called Nazareth, [27] to a virgin engaged to a man whose name was Joseph, of the descendants of David; and the virgin's name was Mary. [28] And coming in, he said to her, "Greetings, favored one! The Lord *is* with you." [29] But she was very perplexed at *this* statement, and kept pondering what kind of salutation this was. [30] The angel said to her, "Do not be afraid, Mary; for you have found favor with God. [31] And behold, you will conceive in your womb and bear a son, and you shall name Him Jesus. [32] He will be great and will be called the Son of the Most High; and the Lord God will give Him the throne of His father David; [33] and He will reign over the house of Jacob forever, and

His kingdom will have no end." [34] Mary said to the angel, "How can this be, since I am a virgin?" [35] The angel answered and said to her, "The Holy Spirit will come upon you, and the power of the Most High will overshadow you; and for that reason the holy Child shall be called the Son of God. [36] And behold, even your relative Elizabeth has also conceived a son in her old age; and she who was called barren is now in her sixth month."

4. The context of Luke 1:26–36 will show that the "sixth month" refers to the pregnancy of Elizabeth when she was carrying John the Baptist in her womb.

5. The name *Jesus* means Savior and refers to His humanity. (v. 31)

6. The name *Son of the Most High* refers to His deity. (v. 32)

7. This account by Luke looks back to the promises God made to David and to all Israel that the Messiah will come, and He will be their King forever.

8. This is all clearly promised in the following passages: 2 Samuel 7:12–13; Isaiah 9:6–7; Isaiah 16:5; Jeremiah 23:5–6; and Jeremiah 33:14–17.

9. Mary's pregnancy is to come about, not because of Joseph and Mary's marriage, but as the result of the supernatural work of God the Holy Spirit.

John 1:1–3

[1] In the beginning was the Word, and the Word was with God, and the Word was God. [2] He was in the beginning with God. [3] All things came into being through Him, and apart from Him nothing came into being that has come into being.

John 1:14

And the Word became flesh, and dwelt among us, and we saw His glory, glory as of the only begotten from the Father, full of grace and truth.

John 14:7–9

[7] "If you had known Me, you would have known My Father also; from now on you know Him, and have seen Him."

[8] Philip said to Him, "Lord, show us the Father, and it is enough for us." [9] Jesus said to him, "Have I been so long with you, and *yet* you have not come to know Me, Philip? He who has seen Me has seen the Father; how *can* you say, 'Show us the Father'?"

10. The term *Word* here refers to the "exact expression" of the Godhead. This is why Jesus said, "He who has seen Me has seen the Father."

11. The term *Word* is a reference to Jesus Christ.

12. In the beginning of time, Christ already existed.

    - Christ existed as co-equal with God the Father and God the Holy Spirit.
    - Jesus Christ is God.
    - Christ was involved in every act of creation.
    - This "Word" came down to earth as a man (flesh) and lived among men on earth. (John 1:14)
    - Those who contemplate Him (in John's generation and all generations) clearly see the glory of the Father.

Romans 8:3

> For what the Law could not do, weak as it was through the flesh, God *did*: sending His own Son in the likeness of sinful flesh and *as an offering* for sin, He condemned sin in the flesh,

13. Jesus Christ existed as the eternal Son of God before He became a man.

14. Jesus' humanity began at conception.

15. God sent His Son in the likeness of sinful people. Paul uses the word *likeness*, because He was in every respect a man, yet without sin.

16. As a man, Jesus represented the human race before the Father, making full payment for our sin when He suffered and died on Calvary.

Galatians 4:4

> But when the fullness of the time came, God sent forth His Son, born of a woman, born under the Law,

17. In God's timing, when all the "players" had arrived and the "stage" was set, God sent His Son into the world.

18. As you research things like language, the Roman road system, spiritual hunger, and the Roman invention of crucifixion, it is clear that Jesus' death and resurrection were both in God's timing.

19. He was born of a woman (a reference to the virgin birth).

III. Jesus Christ – The God-Man

A. His humanity

The scriptures, quoted in the previous section, clearly state that the eternal Son of God, at a point in time, became a man. To deny the humanity of Jesus Christ is to deny the bulk of the biblical text of the four gospels. While down through history there have been many attacks on the deity of Christ, reducing Him to only a man, there have been very few attacks on His humanity. This holds true in our generation.

Romans 8:3

> For what the Law could not do, weak as it was through the flesh, God *did*: sending His own Son in the likeness of sinful flesh and *as an offering* for sin, He condemned sin in the flesh,

Galatians 4:4

> But when the fullness of the time came, God sent forth His Son, born of a woman, born under the Law,

Luke 2:6–7

> While they were there, the days were completed for her to give birth. [7] And she gave birth to her firstborn son; and she wrapped Him in cloths, and laid Him in a manger, because there was no room for them in the inn.

Luke 2:40

> The Child continued to grow and become strong, increasing in wisdom; and the grace of God was upon Him.

1 Timothy 2:5

> For there is one God, *and* one mediator also between God and men, *the* man Christ Jesus,

John 4:9

> Therefore the Samaritan woman said to Him, “How is it that You, being a Jew, ask me for a drink since I am a Samaritan woman?” (For Jews have no dealings with Samaritans.)

1. He had human characteristics. We have no evidence that there was anything different about His appearance. (John 4:9)

   a. As He grew, He became stronger, just like any other healthy human being.

   b. He grew in wisdom and in size as He grew older, just like any normal human being.

   c. John 4:9 is typical of the observations of those who met Jesus face to face. The Samaritan woman never questioned Jesus' humanity or His nationality as a Jew.

   d. The humanity of Jesus was necessary for Him to mediate between the human race and God. As our High Priest, Jesus presented Himself as a blood sacrifice in full payment for our sins. (1 Timothy 2:5)

      Isaiah 53:2

      > For He grew up before Him like a tender shoot,
      > And like a root out of parched ground;
      > He has no *stately* form or majesty
      > That we should look upon Him,
      > Nor appearance that we should be attracted to Him.

   e. Isaiah's prophecy of Christ's birth and human development states that His outward appearance was not anything special.

   f. He had no halo over His head, as is pictured by popular artists' conceptions of Jesus. It was His inner qualities, His teachings, and His miraculous deeds of love that attracted others to Him.

   g. He was in every way a normal looking man.

   h. These passages clearly point out that Jesus Christ was the eternal Son of God, and that He humbled Himself to become a man.

      Ephesians 2:4-8

      > [4] But God, being rich in mercy, because of His great love with which He loved us, [5] even when we were dead in our transgressions, made us alive together with Christ (by grace you have been saved), [6] and raised us up with Him, and seated us with Him in the heavenly *places* in Christ Jesus, [7] so that in the ages to come He might show the surpassing riches of His grace in kindness toward us in Christ Jesus.

[8] For by grace you have been saved through faith; and that not of yourselves, *it is* the gift of God

John 1:14

And the Word became flesh, and dwelt among us, and we saw His glory, glory as of the only begotten from the Father, full of grace and truth.

i. Jesus did not cease to be God when He became a man, any more than a servant ceases to become a man when he takes the position of servanthood.

j. One of the first attacks that was made in the early church against the person of Christ was against His humanity. The opening verses of the first epistle of John carefully declares the reality of His humanity.

k. In his gospel, after John establishes the deity of the Word (Jesus Christ), he points out that this "Word" became flesh (human) and lived among us.

l. Jesus experienced normal human behavior. The body of Jesus had needs and responses, just like other men.

- He grew hungry (Matthew 4:2)
- He experienced thirst (John 19:28)
- He became weary (John 4:6)
- He needed rest and sleep (Matthew 8:24)
- He mourned (Matthew 23:37)
- He cried (John 11:35)

2. Human titles were assigned to Him.

a. Son of Man (Luke 19:10)

b. The man Christ Jesus (1 Timothy 2:5)

3. His suffering and death were normal human responses.

B. His deity

Here we establish the fact that Jesus Christ is God.

1. The names of God are ascribed to Jesus Christ.

John 1:1

> In the beginning was the Word, and the Word was with God, and the Word was God.

Hebrews 1:8

> But of the Son *He says,*
>
> "YOUR THRONE, O GOD, IS FOREVER AND EVER,
> AND THE RIGHTEOUS SCEPTER IS THE SCEPTER OF HIS KINGDOM."

John 20:27–28

> 27 Then He said to Thomas, "Reach here with your finger, and see My hands; and reach here your hand and put it into My side; and do not be unbelieving, but believing." 28 Thomas answered and said to Him, "My Lord and my God!"

1 John 5:20

> And we know that the Son of God has come, and has given us understanding so that we may know Him who is true; and we are in Him who is true, in His Son Jesus Christ. This is the true God and eternal life.

Isaiah 9:6

> For a child will be born to us, a son will be given to us;
> And the government will rest on His shoulders;
> And His name will be called Wonderful Counselor, Mighty God,
> Eternal Father, Prince of Peace.

Isaiah 7:14

> Therefore the Lord Himself will give you a sign: Behold, a virgin will be with child and bear a son, and she will call His name Immanuel.

a. These passages refer to Jesus Christ, not only as the Son of God, but as God.

b. Note the names given to Christ in these passages all refer to Him as God.

2. The attributes of deity are ascribed to Him.

    a. He is eternal.

Isaiah 9:6

For a child will be born to us, a son will be given to us;
And the government will rest on His shoulders;
And His name will be called Wonderful Counselor, Mighty God,
Eternal Father, Prince of Peace.

Hebrews 1:8

But of the Son *He says,*

"YOUR THRONE, O GOD, IS FOREVER AND EVER,
AND THE RIGHTEOUS SCEPTER IS THE SCEPTER OF HIS KINGDOM."

b. He is omnipresent.

Matthew 18:20

"For where two or three have gathered together in My name, I am there in their midst."

c. He is omniscient.

John 4:28–29

[28] So the woman left her waterpot, and went into the city and said to the men, [29] "Come, see a man who told me all the things that I *have* done; this is not the Christ, is it?"

John 1:47–49

[47] Jesus saw Nathanael coming to Him, and said of him, "Behold, an Israelite indeed, in whom there is no deceit!" [48] Nathanael said to Him, "How do You know me?" Jesus answered and said to him, "Before Philip called you, when you were under the fig tree, I saw you." [49] Nathanael answered Him, "Rabbi, You are the Son of God; You are the King of Israel."

d. He is omnipotent.

Revelation 1:8

"I am the Alpha and the Omega," says the Lord God, "who is and who was and who is to come, the Almighty."

Hebrews 1:1–3

> [1] God, after He spoke long ago to the fathers in the prophets in many portions and in many ways, [2] in these last days has spoken to us in His Son, whom He appointed heir of all things, through whom also He made the world. [3] And He is the radiance of His glory and the exact representation of His nature, and upholds all things by the word of His power. When He had made purification of sins, He sat down at the right hand of the Majesty on high,

Mark 4:39–41

> [39] And He got up and rebuked the wind and said to the sea, "Hush, be still." And the wind died down and it became perfectly calm. [40] And He said to them, "Why are you afraid? Do you still have no faith?" [41] They became very much afraid and said to one another, "Who then is this, that even the wind and the sea obey Him?"

e. He is immutable (unchangeable).

Hebrews 1:12

> "And like a mantle You will roll them up;
> Like a garment they will also be changed.
> But You are the same,
> And Your years will not come to an end."

Hebrews 13:8

> Jesus Christ *is* the same yesterday and today and forever.

Hebrews 1:3

> And He is the radiance of His glory and the exact representation of His nature, and upholds all things by the word of His power. When He had made purification of sins, He sat down at the right hand of the Majesty on high,

3. The offices of deity are ascribed to Him.

a. He is the creator.

John 1:3

> All things came into being through Him, and apart from Him nothing came into being that has come into being.

Hebrews 1:1–2

> [1] God, after He spoke long ago to the fathers in the prophets in many portions and in many ways, [2] in these last days has spoken to us in His Son, whom He appointed heir of all things, through whom also He made the world.

Colossians 1:16

> For by Him all things were created, *both* in the heavens and on earth, visible and invisible, whether thrones or dominions or rulers or authorities—all things have been created through Him and for Him.

Colossians 1:17

> He is before all things, and in Him all things hold together.

b. He forgives sin.

Matthew 9:2

> And they brought to Him a paralytic lying on a bed. Seeing their faith, Jesus said to the paralytic, "Take courage, son; your sins are forgiven."

Matthew 9:6

> But so that you may know that the Son of Man has authority on earth to forgive sins"—then He said to the paralytic, "Get up, pick up your bed and go home."

Luke 7:47–49

> [47] "For this reason I say to you, her sins, which are many, have been forgiven, for she loved much; but he who is forgiven little, loves little." [48] Then He said to her, "Your sins have been forgiven." [49] Those who were reclining *at the table* with Him began to say to themselves, "Who is this *man* who even forgives sins?"

c. He executes judgment.

John 5:22

> For not even the Father judges anyone, but He has given all judgment to the Son,

2 Corinthians 5:10

> For we must all appear before the judgment seat of Christ, so that each one may be recompensed for his deeds in the body, according to what he has done, whether good or bad.

Acts 17:31

> "because He has fixed a day in which He will judge the world in righteousness through a Man whom He has appointed, having furnished proof to all men by raising Him from the dead."

d. He has life-giving power.

John 5:21

> For just as the Father raises the dead and gives them life, even so the Son also gives life to whom He wishes.

John 5:26

> For just as the Father has life in Himself, even so He gave to the Son also to have life in Himself;

John 14:6

> Jesus said to him, "I am the way, and the truth, and the life; no one comes to the Father but through Me."

John 11:25–26

> [25] Jesus said to her, "I am the resurrection and the life; he who believes in Me will live even if he dies, [26] and everyone who lives and believes in Me will never die. Do you believe this?"

4. He is associated with the Father and the Holy Spirit.

Matthew 28:19

> Go therefore and make disciples of all the nations, baptizing them in the name of the Father and the Son and the Holy Spirit,

2 Corinthians 13:14

> The grace of the Lord Jesus Christ, and the love of God, and the fellowship of the Holy Spirit, be with you all.

John 10:30

> "I and the Father are one."

5. Divine worship is bestowed upon Him and accepted by Him.

Matthew 4:10

> Then Jesus said to him, "Go, Satan! For it is written, 'YOU SHALL WORSHIP THE LORD YOUR GOD, AND SERVE HIM ONLY.'"

Exodus 34:14

> —for you shall not worship any other god, for the LORD, whose name is Jealous, is a jealous God—

Isaiah 42:8

> "I am the LORD, that is My name;
> I will not give My glory to another,
> Nor My praise to graven images."

Hebrews 1:6

> And when He again brings the firstborn into the world, He says,
>
> "AND LET ALL THE ANGELS OF GOD WORSHIP HIM."

6. Other people and the angels rejected worship and rightly so. The Bible lists the consequences of people accepting praise as though they were God (Acts 12:20–23).

Acts 10:25–26

> [25] When Peter entered, Cornelius met him, and fell at his feet and worshiped *him*. [26] But Peter raised him up, saying, "Stand up; I too am *just* a man."

Acts 14:12–15

> [12] And they *began* calling Barnabas, Zeus, and Paul, Hermes, because he was the chief speaker. [13] The priest of Zeus, whose *temple* was just outside the city, brought oxen and garlands to the gates, and wanted to offer sacrifice with the crowds. [14] But when the apostles Barnabas and Paul heard of it, they tore their robes and rushed out into the crowd, crying out [15] and saying, "Men, why are you doing these things? We are also men of the same nature as you, and preach the gospel to you that you should turn from these vain things to a living God, WHO MADE THE HEAVEN AND THE EARTH AND THE SEA AND ALL THAT IS IN THEM."

Revelation 19:10

> Then I fell at his feet to worship him. But he said to me, "Do not do that; I am a fellow servant of yours and your brethren who hold the testimony of Jesus; worship God. For the testimony of Jesus is the spirit of prophecy."

Revelation 22:8–9

> [8] I, John, am the one who heard and saw these things. And when I heard and saw, I fell down to worship at the feet of the angel who showed me these things. [9] But he said to me, "Do not do that. I am a fellow servant of yours and of your brethren the prophets and of those who heed the words of this book. Worship God."

Acts 12:20–23

> [20] Now he was very angry with the people of Tyre and Sidon; and with one accord they came to him, and having won over Blastus the king's chamberlain, they were asking for peace, because their country was fed by the king's country. [21] On an appointed day Herod, having put on his royal apparel, took his seat on the rostrum and *began* delivering an address to them. [22] The people kept crying out, "The voice of a god and not of a man!" [23] And immediately an angel of the Lord struck him because he did not give God the glory, and he was eaten by worms and died.

IV. The Purpose of the Incarnation

The purpose of the coming of the Son of God is primarily to fulfill three offices: Prophet, Priest, and King.

A. To fill the office of Prophet

A prophet in biblical times not only foretold future events, but he also told forth God's message. A prophet taught and delivered God's truth. A prophet often did miracles by God's power and prophesied future events by God's revelation.

1. Christ's teaching ministry was evident throughout His earthly ministry.

2. Matthew 5:2–7:29 records what we refer to as *The Sermon on the Mount.* Jesus is seen teaching in this passage.

   John 7:46

   > The officers answered, "Never has a man spoken the way this man speaks."

3. Christ performed miracles on many occasions.

   - Healing the sick
   - Giving sight to the blind
   - Causing the deaf to hear
   - Making the lame to walk
   - Feeding the hungry
   - Causing the dumb to speak
   - Restoring life to the dead

4. Christ predicted future events with accuracy.

   - He predicted the fall of Jerusalem that took place in 70 AD.
   - He predicted His betrayal by Judas.
   - He predicted Peter's denial.
   - He predicted His own death and resurrection.
   - Many of His prophesies have yet to be fulfilled, and we have every assurance that they will be fulfilled just as Jesus Christ predicted.

5. Moses prophesied the coming of a great Prophet that would come out of the nation of Israel.

Deuteronomy 18:15

> "The LORD your God will raise up for you a prophet like me from among you, from your countrymen, you shall listen to him."

John 1:45

> Philip found Nathanael and said to him, "We have found Him of whom Moses in the Law and *also* the Prophets wrote—Jesus of Nazareth, the son of Joseph."

Acts 7:37

> This is the Moses who said to the sons of Israel, 'GOD WILL RAISE UP FOR YOU A PROPHET LIKE ME FROM YOUR BRETHREN.'

Hebrews 1:1–3

> [1] God, after He spoke long ago to the fathers in the prophets in many portions and in many ways, [2] in these last days has spoken to us in His Son, whom He appointed heir of all things, through whom also He made the world. [3] And He is the radiance of His glory and the exact representation of His nature, and upholds all things by the word of His power. When He had made purification of sins, He sat down at the right hand of the Majesty on high,

6. There were many prophets among the Jews, but the nation of Israel was looking for the greatest of all Prophets of whom Moses wrote.
7. All the other prophets brought the message of God to the people and prophesied of the coming of the Messiah.
8. Jesus was the greatest Teacher of the truth. He revealed the Word of God not just by His words, but by His person.
9. Jesus Christ is described by John as the Word of God. (John 1:1–3)
10. Jesus Christ is that Prophet.

B. To fill the office of Priest

Isaiah 53:4–8

[4] Surely our griefs He Himself bore,
And our sorrows He carried;
Yet we ourselves esteemed Him stricken,
Smitten of God, and afflicted.
[5] But He was pierced through for our transgressions,
He was crushed for our iniquities;
The chastening for our well-being *fell* upon Him,
And by His scourging we are healed.
[6] All of us like sheep have gone astray,
Each of us has turned to his own way;
But the LORD has caused the iniquity of us all To fall on Him.

[7] He was oppressed and He was afflicted,
Yet He did not open His mouth;
Like a lamb that is led to slaughter,
And like a sheep that is silent before its shearers,
So He did not open His mouth.
[8] By oppression and judgment He was taken away;
And as for His generation, who considered
That He was cut off out of the land of the living
For the transgression of my people, to whom the stroke *was due.*

Matthew 1:23

"BEHOLD, THE VIRGIN SHALL BE WITH CHILD AND SHALL BEAR A SON, AND THEY SHALL CALL HIS NAME IMMANUEL," which translated means, "GOD WITH US."

John 1:29

The next day he saw Jesus coming to him and said, "Behold, the Lamb of God who takes away the sin of the world!"

John 3:16–17

[16] "For God so loved the world, that He gave His only begotten Son, that whoever believes in Him shall not perish, but have eternal life. [17] For God did not send the Son into the world to judge the world, but that the world might be saved through Him."

Hebrews 7:17

> For it is attested *of Him*,
>
> "YOU ARE A PRIEST FOREVER
> ACCORDING TO THE ORDER OF MELCHIZEDEK."

Hebrews 7:23–27

> [23] The *former* priests, on the one hand, existed in greater numbers because they were prevented by death from continuing, [24] but Jesus, on the other hand, because He continues forever, holds His priesthood permanently. [25] Therefore He is able also to save forever those who draw near to God through Him, since He always lives to make intercession for them.
>
> [26] For it was fitting for us to have such a high priest, holy, innocent, undefiled, separated from sinners and exalted above the heavens; [27] who does not need daily, like those high priests, to offer up sacrifices, first for His own sins and then for the *sins* of the people, because this He did once for all when He offered up Himself.

1 Timothy 2:5–6

> [5] For there is one God, *and* one mediator also between God and men, *the* man Christ Jesus, [6] who gave Himself as a ransom for all, the testimony *given* at the proper time.

Hebrews 4:14–16

> [14] Therefore, since we have a great high priest who has passed through the heavens, Jesus the Son of God, let us hold fast our confession. [15] For we do not have a high priest who cannot sympathize with our weaknesses, but One who has been tempted in all things as *we are, yet* without sin. [16] Therefore let us draw near with confidence to the throne of grace, so that we may receive mercy and find grace to help in time of need.

1. Jesus Christ provided Himself as "The Lamb of God that takes away the sin of the world." Jesus was an offering for the sin of the world.

2. This is the good news that is at the heart of the message of the Bible.

3. Because Jesus was the pure Lamb of God, without moral spot or blemish, He could offer Himself as a sacrifice for the sin of the world.

4. Both Jesus' humanity and His deity are important in this regard. Since Jesus is God, He is without sin. Since Jesus is a man, He qualifies to represent the human race to the Father.

5. For those of us who are trusting in Christ for the forgiveness of sin, Jesus continues to be our High Priest and our representative before the throne of God.

   Note: We will go into more detail concerning this in chapter 5, as we discuss the work of Christ in connection with salvation (Soteriology).

C. To fill the office of King of the Jews

Matthew chapter 1 records the genealogy of Jesus back to Abraham and King David.

2 Samuel 7:12–16

> [12] "When your days are complete and you lie down with your fathers, I will raise up your descendant after you, who will come forth from you, and I will establish his kingdom. [13] He shall build a house for My name, and I will establish the throne of his kingdom forever. [14] I will be a father to him and he will be a son to Me; when he commits iniquity, I will correct him with the rod of men and the strokes of the sons of men, [15] but My lovingkindness shall not depart from him, as I took *it* away from Saul, whom I removed from before you. [16] Your house and your kingdom shall endure before Me forever; your throne shall be established forever."

Luke 1:31–33

> [31] "And behold, you will conceive in your womb and bear a son, and you shall name Him Jesus. [32] He will be great and will be called the Son of the Most High; and the Lord God will give Him the throne of His father David; [33] and He will reign over the house of Jacob forever, and His kingdom will have no end."

Matthew 27:11

> Now Jesus stood before the governor, and the governor questioned Him, saying, "Are You the King of the Jews?" And Jesus said to him, "*It is as* you say."

Matthew 27:29

> And after twisting together a crown of thorns, they put it on His head, and a reed in His right hand; and they knelt down before Him and mocked Him, saying, "Hail, King of the Jews!"

Matthew 27:37

> And above His head they put up the charge against Him which read, "THIS IS JESUS THE KING OF THE JEWS."

Philippians 2:9–11

> [9] For this reason also, God highly exalted Him, and bestowed on Him the name which is above every name, [10] so that at the name of Jesus EVERY KNEE WILL BOW, of those who are in heaven and on earth and under the earth, [11] and that every tongue will confess that Jesus Christ is Lord, to the glory of God the Father.

John 19:13–14

> [13] Therefore when Pilate heard these words, he brought Jesus out, and sat down on the judgment seat at a place called The Pavement, but in Hebrew, Gabbatha. [14] Now it was the day of preparation for the Passover; it was about the sixth hour. And he said to the Jews, "Behold, your King!"

1. God established the house of David and the throne of David as an eternal institution.
2. As you follow the family line of Jesus Christ given in Matthew 1, Matthew clearly shows that Jesus was born of the line of David.
3. It is noteworthy that once Jesus Christ appears on the scene, the Bible ceases to trace David's family tree.
4. Jesus Christ is the fulfillment of 2 Samuel 7:16.
5. Matthew's whole purpose in writing about the birth and life of Jesus Christ is to present Him as "King of the Jews."
6. Though the Jews rejected their King and crucified Him, Jesus Christ will one day return and rule on the throne of David throughout all of eternity.

V. The Condescension and Humility of Jesus

A. Jesus took on the role of a servant

It was an act of condescension (humiliation) for Christ to leave heaven's glory, come to earth, and take on human form. In human form, he allowed himself to die on the cross as a common criminal. Philippians 2:5–8 describes this process. It is called the *kenosis* (the self-emptying of Christ).

Philippians 2:5–8

> [5] Have this attitude in yourselves which was also in Christ Jesus, [6] who, although He existed in the form of God, did not regard equality with God a thing to be grasped, [7] but emptied Himself, taking the form of a bond-servant, *and* being made in the likeness of men. [8] Being found in appearance as a man, He humbled Himself by becoming obedient to the point of death, even death on a cross.

1. The big question is this: Of what did Christ empty Himself?
2. Christ did not *and could not* empty Himself of His deity. He remained God while taking on human flesh.
3. Jesus did not *and could not* empty Himself of his attributes and still remain God.
4. As a servant, Christ emptied Himself of the independent use of His attributes.
5. Jesus emptied Himself of His visible glory with the Father when He willingly came to earth and became the God-Man.
6. Just as a servant does not cease to be a person when he takes the position as a servant, so Christ did not cease to be God when He became a man.
7. Jesus submitted His attributes to the leadership of the Father and only exercised them in the power of the Holy Spirit.
8. Christ came to do the Father's will. Some of the features of Christ's humility are as follows:
   - He became a servant of God.
   - He became a servant of humankind.
   - He became obedient to death.
   - He allowed Himself to endure the cruel suffering and death of the cross.
   - He allowed Himself to die as a common criminal.
   - He was willing to go to the depths for us.

Matthew 11:29–30

> [29] "Take My yoke upon you and learn from Me, for I am gentle and humble in heart, and YOU WILL FIND REST FOR YOUR SOULS. [30] For My yoke is easy and My burden is light."

Mark 10:45

> "For even the Son of Man did not come to be served, but to serve, and to give His life a ransom for many."

9. Jesus' teaching reflects His humility.

10. Jesus' interest was not in serving His own glory but in serving others.

11. Christ ministered to people regardless of their position.

12. Christ often served those who did not deserve to be served.

13. The truly humble person is characterized by the following qualities:

    - He seeks not his own interest but puts God's will before his own plans.
    - He demonstrates sincere love for others.
    - He serves without thought as to whether he is humble.
    - He views his talents and abilities as gifts from God.
    - He gives God the credit and glory for all he accomplishes.

B. Peter's response in contrast to Jesus' humility

1 Peter 2:23

> and while being reviled, He did not revile in return; while suffering, He uttered no threats, but kept entrusting *Himself* to Him who judges righteously;

1. Peter became angry, defensive, and violent when Jesus was arrested in the garden (John 18:1–11).

2. A true servant submits all His rights to the Father.

3. Jesus refused to display anger towards those abusing Him, because He had already submitted His rights to the Father.

4. Jesus did not give up His deity when He came to earth. He submitted himself to the leadership of the Father.

5. As followers of Jesus, we also are urged to do the same. In other words, when someone offends or insults us, since we have already given up our rights, there is no logical or emotional reason to become angry.

C. Overcoming anger by embracing the attitude of Jesus

Philippians 2:5

> Have this attitude in yourselves which was also in Christ Jesus,

1. It is a staggering thought to realize that the Creator of the universe was willing to come to this earth and become a man. He endured the scorn, ridicule, and physical suffering heaped upon Him by His enemies. In ignorance and spiritual darkness the world failed to recognize who Jesus was, and therefore, He was despised and rejected.

2. His perfect attitude of servanthood, humility, and grace demonstrated His great love for us and is another validation that He was God. In Philippians 2:5–8, Paul states that our attitude is to be like Jesus' attitude (that of a servant).

Isaiah 53:3

> He was despised and forsaken of men,
> A man of sorrows and acquainted with grief;
> And like one from whom men hide their face
> He was despised, and we did not esteem Him.

Isaiah 53:7

> He was oppressed and He was afflicted,
> Yet He did not open His mouth;
> Like a lamb that is led to slaughter,
> And like a sheep that is silent before its shearers,
> So He did not open His mouth.

Luke 15:1–2

> [1] Now all the tax collectors and the sinners were coming near Him to listen to Him. [2] Both the Pharisees and the scribes *began* to grumble, saying, "This man receives sinners and eats with them."

Luke 7:36–39

> [36] Now one of the Pharisees was requesting Him to dine with him, and He entered the Pharisee's house and reclined *at the table.* [37] And there was a woman in the city who was a sinner; and when she learned that He was reclining *at the table* in the Pharisee's house, she brought an alabaster vial of perfume, [38] and standing behind *Him* at His feet, weeping, she began to wet His feet with her tears, and kept wiping them with the hair of her head, and kissing His feet and anointing them with the perfume. [39] Now when the Pharisee who had invited Him saw this, he said to himself, "If this man were a prophet He would know who and what sort of person this woman is who is touching Him, that she is a sinner."

Matthew 26:60–63

> [60] They did not find *any,* even though many false witnesses came forward. But later on two came forward, [61] and said, "This man stated, 'I am able to destroy the temple of God and to rebuild it in three days.'" [62] The high priest stood up and said to Him, "Do You not answer? What is it that these men are testifying against You?" [63] But Jesus kept silent. And the high priest said to Him, "I adjure You by the living God, that You tell us whether You are the Christ, the Son of God."

Luke 22:23–27

> [23] And they began to discuss among themselves which one of them it might be who was going to do this thing.[24] And there arose also a dispute among them *as to* which one of them was regarded to be greatest. [25] And He said to them, "The kings of the Gentiles lord it over them; and those who have authority over them are called 'Benefactors.' [26] But *it is* not this way with you, but the one who is the greatest among you must become like the youngest, and the leader like the servant. [27] For who is greater, the one who reclines *at the table* or the one who serves? Is it not the one who reclines *at the table*? But I am among you as the one who serves."

3. Christ shows us by example that the only road to true greatness is by becoming a servant to others.

4. We have the notion that we achieve greatness by using and abusing people to get to the top.

5. Jesus taught the opposite view. He told his disciples that becoming a meek servant is the path to real leadership.

VI. The Perpetuity of the Incarnation

By *perpetuity* we mean that Christ became a man forever. Various theories in the past have claimed that Jesus Christ became man for a period and then ceased to be a man and returned to His original state, the state He had before the incarnation. This theory is not taught in the Bible. The Bible makes it clear that Jesus Christ became the *God-Man* forever. The following is a list of 6 reasons why this issue is so important:

A. The perpetuity of the incarnation is fundamental to the integrity of Jesus Christ's humanity.

If Jesus is not a man forever, the question is raised as to whether He was ever really a man. At the incarnation Christ did not become two persons. He is one person with two natures. To say that He one day ceased to be man, invalidates the value of His suffering and death on the cross.

B. His post resurrection appearances demonstrate that He is still a man.

Matthew 28:9

> And behold, Jesus met them and greeted them. And they came up and took hold of His feet and worshiped Him.

Luke 24:2–3

> [2] And they found the stone rolled away from the tomb, [3] but when they entered, they did not find the body of the Lord Jesus.

Luke 24:30–31

> [30] When He had reclined *at the table* with them, He took the bread and blessed *it*, and breaking *it*, He *began* giving *it* to them. [31] Then their eyes were opened and they recognized Him; and He vanished from their sight.

Luke 24:40–42

> [40] And when He had said this, He showed them His hands and His feet. [41] While they still could not believe *it* because of their joy and amazement, He said to them, "Have you anything here to eat?" [42] They gave Him a piece of a broiled fish;

Luke 24:50

> And He led them out as far as Bethany, and He lifted up His hands and blessed them.

John 20:16–17

> [16] Jesus said to her, "Mary!" She turned and said to Him in Hebrew, "Rabboni!" (which means, Teacher). [17] Jesus said to her, "Stop clinging to Me, for I have not yet ascended to the Father; but go to My brethren and say to them, 'I ascend to My Father and your Father, and My God and your God.'"

John 20:20–28

> [20] And when He had said this, He showed them both His hands and His side. The disciples then rejoiced when they saw the Lord. [21] So Jesus said to them again, "Peace *be* with you; as the Father has sent Me, I also send you." [22] And when He had said this, He breathed on them and said to them, "Receive the Holy Spirit. [23] If you forgive the sins of any, *their sins* have been forgiven them; if you retain the *sins* of any, they have been retained."
>
> [24] But Thomas, one of the twelve, called Didymus, was not with them when Jesus came. [25] So the other disciples were saying to him, "We have seen the Lord!" But he said to them, "Unless I see in His hands the imprint of the nails, and put my finger into the place of the nails, and put my hand into His side, I will not believe."
>
> [26] After eight days His disciples were again inside, and Thomas with them. Jesus came, the doors having been shut, and stood in their midst and said, "Peace *be* with you." [27] Then He said to Thomas, "Reach here with your finger, and see My hands; and reach here your hand and put it into My side; and do not be unbelieving, but believing." [28] Thomas answered and said to Him, "My Lord and my God!"

John 21:12–13

> [12] Jesus said to them, "Come *and* have breakfast." None of the disciples ventured to question Him, "Who are You?" knowing that it was the Lord. [13] Jesus came and took the bread and gave *it* to them, and the fish likewise.

C. Jesus' ascension shows no change in His existing as a man.

Acts 1:9

> And after He had said these things, He was lifted up while they were looking on, and a cloud received Him out of their sight.

D. He appeared as a man to some people after His ascension.

1. Stephen

Acts 7:55–56

> [55] But being full of the Holy Spirit, he gazed intently into heaven and saw the glory of God, and Jesus standing at the right hand of God; [56] and he said, "Behold, I see the heavens opened up and the Son of Man standing at the right hand of God."

2. Saul/Paul

1 Corinthians 15:7–8

> [7] then He appeared to James, then to all the apostles; [8] and last of all, as to one untimely born, He appeared to me also.

3. John

Revelation 1:17–18

> [17] When I saw Him, I fell at His feet like a dead man. And He placed His right hand on me, saying, "Do not be afraid; I am the first and the last, [18] and the living One; and I was dead, and behold, I am alive forevermore, and I have the keys of death and of Hades."

E. The perpetuity of the incarnation is essential for Christ's high-priestly intercession today.

1 Timothy 2:5–6

> [5] For there is one God, *and* one mediator also between God and men, *the* man Christ Jesus, [6] who gave Himself as a ransom for all, the testimony *given* at the proper time.

Romans 8:34

> who is the one who condemns? Christ Jesus is He who died, yes, rather who was raised, who is at the right hand of God, who also intercedes for us.

Hebrews 2:17–18

> [17] Therefore, He had to be made like His brethren in all things, so that He might become a merciful and faithful high priest in things pertaining to God, to make propitiation for the sins of the people. [18] For since He Himself was tempted in that which He has suffered, He is able to come to the aid of those who are tempted.

Hebrews 4:14–15

> [14] Therefore, since we have a great high priest who has passed through the heavens, Jesus the Son of God, let us hold fast our confession. [15] For we do not have a high priest who cannot sympathize with our weaknesses, but One who has been tempted in all things as *we are, yet* without sin.

Hebrews 9:24

> For Christ did not enter a holy place made with hands, a *mere* copy of the true one, but into heaven itself, now to appear in the presence of God for us;

F. The perpetuity of the incarnation is necessary for Christ's return as King.

2 Samuel 7:12–16

> [12] "When your days are complete and you lie down with your fathers, I will raise up your descendant after you, who will come forth from you, and I will establish his kingdom. [13] He shall build a house for My name, and I will establish the throne of his kingdom forever. [14] I will be a father to him and he will be a son to Me; when he commits iniquity, I will correct him with the rod of men and the strokes of the sons of men, [15] but My lovingkindness shall not depart from him, as I took *it* away from Saul, whom I removed from before you. [16] Your house and your kingdom shall endure before Me forever; your throne shall be established forever."

Zechariah 12:9–10

> [9] And in that day I will set about to destroy all the nations that come against Jerusalem.

> [10] "I will pour out on the house of David and on the inhabitants of Jerusalem, the Spirit of grace and of supplication, so that they will look on Me whom they have pierced; and they will mourn for Him, as one mourns for an only son, and they will weep bitterly over Him like the bitter weeping over a firstborn."

Acts 1:10–11

> [10] And as they were gazing intently into the sky while He was going, behold, two men in white clothing stood beside them. [11] They also said, "Men of Galilee, why do you stand looking into the sky? This Jesus, who has been taken up from you into heaven, will come in just the same way as you have watched Him go into heaven."

VII. The Hypostatic Union

John 1:14

> And the Word became flesh, and dwelt among us, and we saw His glory, glory as of the only begotten from the Father, full of grace and truth.

A. Definition of the hypostatic union

The term *hypostatic union* is the theological term to describe the miracle of the merging of the deity of the eternal Son of God, with the humanity of Mary's baby. Jesus Christ is truly man and truly God.

1. Jesus is 100 percent God and 100 percent man and yet these two natures were wonderfully merged into one person. That person is Jesus Christ. With our finite minds, it is difficult for us to comprehend such a person.

2. If we try to explain this phenomenon with human reasoning, our conclusions will not reflect the teaching of the scriptures. We will find ourselves stressing Jesus' humanity to the demise of His deity, or we will stress Jesus' deity to the impairment of His humanity.

B. We must keep these two truths in proper biblical balance.

1. The rule to describe the person of Christ is: We cannot divide Jesus into two persons or confuse the natures of Jesus Christ. He is fully man and fully God.

2. Many errors have arisen through the centuries in connection with the person of Christ, and they usually originate from a failure to follow the rule quoted above.

3. Once again, we are faced with a truth that does not fit into our human reasoning but is clearly taught in the Bible. We must realize that just because we, with our finite minds, cannot fathom the person of the infinite God, does not mean that the teachings of the Word of God are untrue or contradictive. For this reason, we must exercise faith and simply trust the Author of the Bible.

    1 Timothy 2:5

    > For there is one God, *and* one mediator also between God and men, *the* man Christ Jesus,

C. Jesus Christ is one person.

1. Jesus Christ possesses two natures.

2. Jesus Christ is not half God and half man, but He is the God-Man.

3. We never observe in scripture one nature speaking to the other nature, as there is sometimes seen between the persons of the Trinity.

4. The divine and human natures of Christ do not act independently of one another.

    - It is the one Person, the God-Man, who acts.
    - It is the God-Man who willingly went to Calvary and died.
    - As the Son of Man, He can be the perfect sacrifice for our sin.
    - As the Son of God, His death is of infinite value.

5. Some false teachers affirm that Christ's deity left His humanity at the cross. This false teaching would destroy the reality of Christ's incarnation and would dissolve the immeasurable value of His sacrifice for our sin.

Conclusion:

1. No one is comparable to the person of Christ. He is unique. In His incarnation He represents the Godhead to humankind; for He is God.

2. He represents the human race before God; for He is man.

3. John writes, "The Word became flesh and made his dwelling among us. We have seen his glory, the glory of the One and Only, who came from the Father, full of grace and truth." (John 1:14)

    - *Grace* includes qualities like His love, His mercy, His compassion, His gentleness, His patience, and His meekness.

- *Truth* includes the character of every word He spoke. It also includes His righteousness, His justice, His self-control, His honesty, and His goodness.
- An example of these two aspects of His person is found in John's account of the woman caught in adultery. (John 8:1–11) Truth can be stern and rigid without grace. Grace can be permissive and accommodating in the absence of truth.
- Jesus had the perfect balance between grace and truth.

REVIEW QUESTIONS

1. What do we mean by pre-existence?

2. Christ, the Son of God, had no beginning. True or false?

3. Who was the Angel of the Lord?

4. Jesus Christ is two persons: God and man. True or false?

5. Jesus Christ is fully human like we are. True or false?

6. Jesus grew and developed like any other child. True or false?

7. Prove with scripture that Jesus Christ is God.

8. Name and explain two purposes for the incarnation of Christ.

9. Explain thoroughly Philippians 2:5–8. Of what did Christ empty Himself?

10. What attitude is emphasized in Philippians 2:5–8?

11. What is meant by the term *hypostatic union*?

12. Christ's deity left His humanity at the cross. True or false?

13. Jesus Christ possessed two natures. Name them.

14. Name and explain three offices (or titles) Christ fulfilled that were anticipated in the Old Testament for the Messiah.

15. Which one of the three, mentioned in question #14, did the Jews of Jesus' day place the most emphasis upon and why?

CHAPTER 5

Soteriology
(What the Bible Teaches About the Work of Christ in Providing Salvation)

The Lord Jesus Christ came to this earth for a specific purpose. The work that He accomplished is one of the broadest themes in the Word of God. We learned from our study of Bibliology (chapter 2) that Jesus Christ is the theme and central message of the entire Bible. The truths concerning His person (who He is) and His work (what He accomplished) is essential to the salvation of any individual. Every false teaching that attacks the gospel strikes at either the person of Christ or the work of Christ.

1 Corinthians 2:2

> For I determined to know nothing among you except Jesus Christ, **(His person)* and Him crucified. *(His work)*

*Note: The parenthetical words have been added by author.

I. The Work of Christ Anticipated

Because of Israel's political and national problems, the Jews were primarily expecting a King. In their mind, they wanted and needed someone to free them from the cruel Roman "yoke." They looked for someone to help them out of their political problems. That "a mighty King was coming" was predicted in the Old Testament, and this was the Jewish leaders' expectation and focus. But it was also predicted that this King would be a humble servant, who would give His life in payment for their sins (Isaiah 53). The "humble servant and savior" features were somewhat neglected in Jewish minds. This is one of the reasons why they did not recognize Jesus as their Messiah and rejected Him as their King. However, Jesus Christ, the Prophet, Priest, and King, is also their Messiah. He is presented, as such, in the Old Testament, both by direct predictions (prophecies) and by types (descriptive pictures). The New Testament records the fulfillment of those Old Testament prophecies and pictures.

We have already looked at Jesus' offices of Prophet, Priest, and King (chapter 4). In this chapter we will focus our attention in more detail on the priesthood of Christ in connection with our salvation.

A. Here are some of the Old Testament types that picture Jesus Christ and His work.

A *type* is an Old Testament picture or figure that finds its counterpart in a New Testament truth.

1. King David – King David is a picture of the Eternal King, who was to come after him.

2. Old Testament prophets – The Old Testament prophets foreshadow the One who was to come and speak gracious and prophetic words.

3. The Levitical system – The whole Levitical system is a portrayal of Christ and His work.

4. Adam and Eve's coverings – Adam and Eve's fig leaves illustrate the futility of man-made efforts in providing a righteous covering before the holiness of God. The coats of skins illustrate the shedding of blood to provide forgiveness and a righteous covering before God. (Genesis 3:7; 3:21)

5. Cain's fruit of the ground – Cain's fruit of the ground represents human effort, while Abel's lamb represents the blood sacrifice of Christ. (Genesis 4:3–5)

6. The sacrificial lamb without blemish – The sacrificial lamb without blemish pictures the perfect Lamb of God, who shed his own blood on the cross as He offered Himself a sacrifice for our sin. This is the reason John the Baptist introduced Jesus as the Lamb of God that takes away the sin of the world.

7. Abraham's offering of Isaac – The offering of Isaac and the substitute sacrifice of the ram, provided by God, pictures Jesus as a substitute offering for sin. (Genesis 22)

8. The Passover lamb – The Passover lamb depicts Christ's shed blood. The application of the blood on the door post illustrates the application of the blood of Christ that saves us from God's judgment. (Exodus 12)

9. The bronze serpent – The bronze serpent of Numbers 21:4–9 is explained in the gospel of John. (John 3:14–15)

B. Most Old Testament types find their fulfillment in Jesus Christ.

Hebrews 9:22

And according to the Law, *one may* almost *say*, all things are cleansed with blood, and without shedding of blood there is no forgiveness.

1 Peter 1:18–19

[18] knowing that you were not redeemed with perishable things like silver or gold from your futile way of life inherited from your forefathers, [19] but with precious blood, as of a lamb unblemished and spotless, *the blood* of Christ.

John 1:29

The next day he saw Jesus coming to him and said, "Behold, the Lamb of God who takes away the sin of the world!"

John 3:14–15

[14] As Moses lifted up the serpent in the wilderness, even so must the Son of Man be lifted up; [15] so that whoever believes will in Him have eternal life.

Note: This is not an exhaustive list of types. There are many other types, and their fulfillments in the Bible are too numerous to mention here.

II. The Work of Christ During His Earthly Ministry

Salvation is not provided by Jesus' life, earthly ministry, or teaching, but His life and earthly ministry are important. Throughout His ministry, Jesus taught and performed miracles, as He met the needs of those around Him. This attested to His identity as the Son of God. He made an impact upon this world in a few short years that will never be forgotten and cannot be denied. Jesus lived life as an example to us who believe. His life was faultless, pure, and gracious. He demonstrated a life of perfection amid a wicked and rebellious world.

A. Jesus announced the kingdom and taught the principles of the kingdom.

Jesus Christ lived under the law and kept the law in every detail. (Matthew 5–7 and Matthew 10)

Galatians 4:4–5

[4] But when the fullness of the time came, God sent forth His Son, born of a woman, born under the Law, [5] so that He might redeem those who were under the Law, that we might receive the adoption as sons.

Matthew 5:17

"Do not think that I came to abolish the Law or the Prophets; I did not come to abolish but to fulfill."

B. Jesus knowingly and willingly moved toward Calvary.

1. He predicted He would die for the sins of the world.

Matthew 20:17–19

[17] As Jesus was about to go up to Jerusalem, He took the twelve *disciples* aside by themselves, and on the way He said to them, [18] "Behold, we are going up to Jerusalem; and the Son of Man will be delivered to the chief priests and scribes, and they will condemn Him to death, [19] and will hand Him over to the Gentiles to mock and scourge and crucify *Him*, and on the third day He will be raised up."

2. He foresaw the church as His saved ones, who would spread the message of the good news of salvation.

3. John 13–17 sets forth teachings that would afterward be amplified and defined in the epistles.

C. Jesus predicted His death throughout His earthly ministry as He willingly moved toward what would face Him in Jerusalem.

Jerusalem was the place of His suffering and death. It was for this purpose that He came into the world. (Matthew 12:40; 16:21)

Matthew 16:21

From that time Jesus began to show His disciples that He must go to Jerusalem, and suffer many things from the elders and chief priests and scribes, and be killed, and be raised up on the third day.

Matthew 12:40

for just as JONAH WAS THREE DAYS AND THREE NIGHTS IN THE BELLY OF THE SEA MONSTER, so will the Son of Man be three days and three nights in the heart of the earth.

D. Jesus taught, healed, rebuked, warned, predicted, and urged the nation of Israel to repent.

Luke 13:34

> O Jerusalem, Jerusalem, *the city* that kills the prophets and stones those sent to her! How often I wanted to gather your children together, just as a hen *gathers* her brood under her wings, and you would not *have it*!

III. The Work of Jesus Christ on the Cross

When we consider most people, we think of their lives as being far more important than their deaths. In considering Christ, however, it is His death and resurrection that are of supreme importance. His death did not come upon Him as a surprise. It was planned from eternity past. During His life, Jesus set His sights on His death on the cross. Christ was not the victim of circumstances, nor was He mistakenly crucified as a misunderstood casualty of His generation. He voluntarily offered Himself as a sacrifice for sin. His death was a definite choice on His part to accomplish the goal of our salvation, which could not be achieved in any other way. Jesus clearly stated the following:

John 10:17–18

> [17] "For this reason the Father loves Me, because I lay down My life so that I may take it again. [18] No one has taken it away from Me, but I lay it down on My own initiative. I have authority to lay it down, and I have authority to take it up again. This commandment I received from My Father."

A. False theories concerning Christ's death

People have misunderstood the death of Christ from the beginning. Those who participated in putting Christ to death felt they had scored a triumph. Some believed His death was nothing more than the end of another life and the end of His claims. Some asked Him to come down from the cross and prove that He was the Son of God. These people did not understand *why* He died. Many today still do not understand.

1. The Accident Theory: This theory claims Christ was merely a man and, as such, subject to death. The people of His day opposed His teachings and His principles, so they killed Him. This theory asserts there was no special significance in His death.

   This theory overlooks the fact that His death was predicted in the Old Testament, and that Christ predicted His own death. This theory ignores all the biblical teaching on the cross, such as the blood, the forgiveness of sin, etc.

2. The Martyr Theory: This theory is also referred to as the Example Theory. It maintains that Christ's death was the death of a martyr. He died because He was faithful to a set of principles. This theory merely challenges us to be willing to give our life, if need be, for what we believe. Jesus' death was no more than an example to us.

   This theory completely bypasses the issue of sin, salvation, and eternal life and assumes salvation is purely achieved by human merit. It defines Jesus' death simply as an example to stand up for your beliefs, regardless of the consequences. It does not deal at all with the issue of sin.

3. The Moral Influence Theory: This theory asserts Christ's death is the natural result of possessing human nature. He merely suffered by identifying with the sins of His creatures. His death manifests the love of God, not by bearing our sin and penalty, but by suffering the difficulties, which is a normal part of life. It teaches that the purpose of Jesus' death is to soften human hearts and bring them to God.

   Much like the Martyr Theory, this theory also ignores the sin of humankind and the fact that God's righteousness must be vindicated. The suffering and death of Christ met all the just demands of God against the sinner.

B. Biblical terms that clarify the true meaning of Christ's death

1. Redemption – Redemption means the releasing liberation from captivity, slavery, etc., by the payment of a price (a ransom). The death of Christ is represented as the payment of a price or ransom.

   Matthew 20:28

   > "just as the Son of Man did not come to be served, but to serve, and to give His life a ransom for many."

   1 Peter 1:18–19

   > [18] knowing that you were not redeemed with perishable things like silver or gold from your futile way of life inherited from your forefathers, [19] but with precious blood, as of a lamb unblemished and spotless, *the blood* of Christ.

   1 Timothy 2:5–6

   > [5] For there is one God, *and* one mediator also between God and men, *the* man Christ Jesus, [6] who gave Himself as a ransom for all, the testimony *given* at the proper time.

The New Testament uses three Greek words for redemption:

- *agorazo* – to purchase in the market
- *exagorazo* – to buy out of the market
- *lutroo* – to set free by paying a price

Note: Some teach that the ransom price was paid to Satan. This is not logical nor is it taught in the Bible. The purchase price for our redemption was paid only to God. He is the Judge and the one whose righteousness must be vindicated.

2. Reconciliation – *Reconciliation* means "the adjustment of a difference." In the case of our salvation, we are reconciled to God by the death of Christ. In this reconciliation, the believer is transformed the moment he or she trusts Jesus as Savior. God cannot lower His standards of righteousness. We must understand that it is the *believer* who is reconciled to God. God is not reconciled to us, because God cannot compromise His perfect righteousness. God has given Christ's own righteousness to the believer, and the believer is thereby reconciled to God.

2 Corinthians 5:16–21

> [16] Therefore from now on we recognize no one according to the flesh; even though we have known Christ according to the flesh, yet now we know *Him in this way* no longer. [17] Therefore if anyone is in Christ, *he is* a new creature; the old things passed away; behold, new things have come. [18] Now all *these* things are from God, who reconciled us to Himself through Christ and gave us the ministry of reconciliation, [19] namely, that God was in Christ reconciling the world to Himself, not counting their trespasses against them, and He has committed to us the word of reconciliation.
>
> [20] Therefore, we are ambassadors for Christ, as though God were making an appeal through us; we beg you on behalf of Christ, be reconciled to God. [21] He made Him who knew no sin *to be* sin on our behalf, so that we might become the righteousness of God in Him.

Romans 5:10

> For if while we were enemies we were reconciled to God through the death of His Son, much more, having been reconciled, we shall be saved by His life.

Ephesians 2:16

> and might reconcile them both in one body to God through the cross, by it having put to death the enmity.

3. Propitiation – *Propitiation* means "an appeasing, placating, being kindly disposed toward another." In reference to the cross, propitiation means that the death of Christ satisfied all the righteous and just demands of God against the sinner. The death of Christ is the only ground whereby God is favorably disposed toward the sinner. This involves God's righteous nature. God cannot accept a sinner apart from the sacrifice of Christ. It was the suffering and death of Jesus Christ that satisfied God's just demands against the sinner, and His resurrection is proof that God's justice was fully satisfied. The following passages refer to this propitiation:

    Romans 3:25–26

    [25] whom God displayed publicly as a propitiation in His blood through faith. *This was* to demonstrate His righteousness, because in the forbearance of God He passed over the sins previously committed; [26] for the demonstration, *I say*, of His righteousness at the present time, so that He would be just and the justifier of the one who has faith in Jesus.

    1 John 2:2

    and He Himself is the propitiation for our sins; and not for ours only, but also for *those of* the whole world.

    Romans 4:25

    He who was delivered over because of our transgressions, and was raised because of our justification.

4. Substitution – Substitution refers to the truth that Christ's sacrificial death on the cross paid the punishment for our sin. By this, we mean that Christ took our place. He suffered the penalty for sin that rightly belonged to us. When Jesus died on Calvary, He was dying on our behalf, so all who trust in Him for salvation might be free from the penalty we deserve.

    Isaiah 53:5–6

    [5] But He was pierced through for our transgressions,
    He was crushed for our iniquities;
    The chastening for our well-being *fell* upon Him,
    And by His scourging we are healed.
    [6] All of us like sheep have gone astray,
    Each of us has turned to his own way;
    But the LORD has caused the iniquity of us all
    To fall on Him.

Romans 8:1

> Therefore there is now no condemnation for those who are in Christ Jesus.

2 Corinthians 5:21

> He made Him who knew no sin *to be* sin on our behalf, so that we might become the righteousness of God in Him.

1 Peter 2:24

> and He Himself bore our sins in His body on the cross, so that we might die to sin and live to righteousness; for by His wounds you were healed.

1 Peter 3:18

> For Christ also died for sins once for all, *the* just for *the* unjust, so that He might bring us to God, having been put to death in the flesh, but made alive in the spirit;

C. Terms that refer to the substitutionary death of Christ

1. <u>Vicarious</u> – *Vicarious* describes the suffering and agony endured by one person in the place of another as a substitute. Essential to its meaning is the dismissal of the charge against the person in whose place the suffering is endured. The root word *vicar* means "a substitute" (one who takes the place of another and acts in his capacity).

2. <u>Voluntary</u> – The substitutionary work of Christ was voluntary on His part. He willingly offered Himself to die in our place.

   John 10:17–18

   > [17] "For this reason the Father loves Me, because I lay down My life so that I may take it again. [18] No one has taken it away from Me, but I lay it down on My own initiative. I have authority to lay it down, and I have authority to take it up again. This commandment I received from My Father."

3. <u>Satisfaction</u> – Related to this term is the word *propitiation*. The substitutionary work of Christ satisfied the justice of God. God cannot free the sinner until the demands of justice are satisfied. God is just in forgiving because those demands were satisfied by Christ's death. (Notice the last part of Romans 3:26.)

Romans 3:25–26

> [25] whom God displayed publicly as a propitiation in His blood through faith. *This was* to demonstrate His righteousness, because in the forbearance of God He passed over the sins previously committed; [26] for the demonstration, *I say*, of His righteousness at the present time, so that He would be just and the justifier of the one who has faith in Jesus.

4. Substitution and the demands of Old Testament law of God – In Christ, all the demands of the Law were met so that when the sinner trusts Christ as Savior, it is as though he has kept every demand of God's righteousness.

5. Atonement – The word *atone* (or atonement) is an Old Testament word which means "to cover." Though some English translations of the New Testament use the term "atonement," it is translated from a different Greek word. In the Old Testament, the term atonement means that the atoning sacrifices under the law only *covered* sin, but the perfect sacrifice of Christ has the power to *take away* sin.

Leviticus 6:2–7

> [2] "When a person sins and acts unfaithfully against the LORD, and deceives his companion in regard to a deposit or a security entrusted *to him*, or through robbery, or *if* he has extorted from his companion, [3] or has found what was lost and lied about it and sworn falsely, so that he sins in regard to any one of the things a man may do; [4] then it shall be, when he sins and becomes guilty, that he shall restore what he took by robbery or what he got by extortion, or the deposit which was entrusted to him or the lost thing which he found, [5] or anything about which he swore falsely; he shall make restitution for it in full and add to it one-fifth more. He shall give it to the one to whom it belongs on the day *he presents* his guilt offering. [6] Then he shall bring to the priest his guilt offering to the LORD, a ram without defect from the flock, according to your valuation, for a guilt offering, [7] and the priest shall make atonement for him before the LORD, and he will be forgiven for any one of the things which he may have done to incur guilt."

Leviticus 4:13–20

> [13] 'Now if the whole congregation of Israel commits error and the matter escapes the notice of the assembly, and they commit any of the things which the LORD has commanded not to be done, and they become guilty; [14] when the sin which they have committed becomes known, then the assembly shall offer a bull of the herd for a sin offering and bring it

> before the tent of meeting. [15] Then the elders of the congregation shall lay their hands on the head of the bull before the LORD, and the bull shall be slain before the LORD. [16] Then the anointed priest is to bring some of the blood of the bull to the tent of meeting; [17] and the priest shall dip his finger in the blood and sprinkle *it* seven times before the LORD, in front of the veil. [18] He shall put some of the blood on the horns of the altar which is before the LORD in the tent of meeting; and all the blood he shall pour out at the base of the altar of burnt offering which is at the doorway of the tent of meeting. [19] He shall remove all its fat from it and offer it up in smoke on the altar. [20] He shall also do with the bull just as he did with the bull of the sin offering; thus he shall do with it. So the priest shall make atonement for them, and they will be forgiven.'

At the baptism of Jesus, John introduced Jesus with these words, "Behold the Lamb of God who takes away the sin of the world" (John 1:29). Only Jesus can remove sin completely. God covered the sin of the Old Testament saints with the atoning sacrifice until the time when Jesus completely took away their sin with His death on the cross.

D. The extent of Christ's death and resurrection

For whom did Christ die? Did He die for all men? Did He die for the elect only? The Bible teaches Christ died for the entire world. His death was sufficient for every person. While salvation is available for everyone and the effectiveness of the cross of Christ is available to the worst of sinners, its effect is limited to those who believe.

1 John 2:2

> and He Himself is the propitiation for our sins; and not for ours only, but also for *those of* the whole world.

John 1:12 (John the Baptist introduces Jesus before Jesus' baptism.)

> But as many as received Him, to them He gave the right to become children of God, *even* to those who believe in His name,

2 Corinthians 5:18–19

> [18] Now all *these* things are from God, who reconciled us to Himself through Christ and gave us the ministry of reconciliation, [19] namely, that God was in Christ reconciling the world to Himself, not counting their trespasses against them, and He has committed to us the word of reconciliation.

1 Timothy 1:15

It is a trustworthy statement, deserving full acceptance, that Christ Jesus came into the world to save sinners, among whom I am foremost *of all.*

E. Reasonings which lead to false conclusions

1. Christ died for all; therefore, all are saved. This is the false teaching of Universalism. However, the Bible makes it clear that the application of what Christ has done is conditional, in that the work of Christ on the cross applies only to the individual believing sinner.

2. Only the elect is saved; therefore, Christ died for the elect only. This teaching is one of the 5 points of Calvinism. However, Jesus' work on the cross was for all people. The scriptures plainly teach us that Christ died for the entire world.

1 Timothy 4:9–10

[9] It is a trustworthy statement deserving full acceptance. [10] For it is for this we labor and strive, because we have fixed our hope on the living God, who is the Savior of all men, especially of believers.

F. Our responsibility regarding Christ's death and resurrection

Because Christ died in our place, paying the full penalty for our sin, salvation is now an available gift to all who believe. Salvation is a free gift to be received by faith, not earned by good deeds. The key word is *believe.*

Romans 6:23

For the wages of sin is death, but the free gift of God is eternal life in Christ Jesus our Lord.

Ephesians 2:8–9

[8] For by grace you have been saved through faith; and that not of yourselves, *it is* the gift of God; [9] not as a result of works, so that no one may boast.

Acts 16:30–31 (the Philippian jailer)

[30] and after he brought them out, he said, "Sirs, what must I do to be saved?"

[31] They said, "Believe in the Lord Jesus, and you will be saved, you and your household."

John 1:12

> But as many as received Him, to them He gave the right to become children of God, *even* to those who believe in His name,

IV. The Resurrection of Christ

A. Here are six biblical reasons why Christ's resurrection is so important.

1. He arose because He is the eternal Son of God, and it was not possible for death to hold Him in the grave.

   Acts 2:24

   > But God raised Him up again, putting an end to the agony of death, since it was impossible for Him to be held in its power.

2. He arose because, as the Messiah (the Son of David), He must one day rule upon the throne of David.

   Acts 2:30–32

   > [30] And so, because he was a prophet and knew that GOD HAD SWORN TO HIM WITH AN OATH TO SEAT *one* OF HIS DESCENDANTS ON HIS THRONE, [31] he looked ahead and spoke of the resurrection of the Christ, that HE WAS NEITHER ABANDONED TO HADES, NOR DID His flesh SUFFER DECAY. [32] This Jesus God raised up again, to which we are all witnesses.

3. He arose because He was to become Head of all things to the church, which is His body.

   Ephesians 1:20–23

   > [20] which He brought about in Christ, when He raised Him from the dead and seated Him at His right hand in the heavenly *places*, [21] far above all rule and authority and power and dominion, and every name that is named, not only in this age but also in the one to come. [22] And He put all things in subjection under His feet, and gave Him as head over all things to the church, [23] which is His body, the fullness of Him who fills all in all.

4. He arose because He is the giver of resurrection life.

   John 11:25

   > Jesus said to her, "I am the resurrection and the life; he who believes in Me will live even if he dies,"

5. He arose because He must impart His resurrection power to those who believe.

Ephesians 1:18–21

> [18] *I pray that* the eyes of your heart may be enlightened, so that you will know what is the hope of His calling, what are the riches of the glory of His inheritance in the saints, [19] and what is the surpassing greatness of His power toward us who believe. *These are* in accordance with the working of the strength of His might [20] which He brought about in Christ, when He raised Him from the dead and seated Him at His right hand in the heavenly *places*, [21] far above all rule and authority and power and dominion, and every name that is named, not only in this age but also in the one to come.

6. He arose because believing sinners are justified and there is no reason for Him to remain in the grave.

Romans 4:25

> *He* who was delivered over because of our transgressions, and was raised because of our justification.

B. Jesus' resurrection was a new kind of resurrection.

The Resurrection of Christ is of primary importance. Never had anyone been raised to a resurrection life before Christ's resurrection. There is a difference between restoration to life and resurrection. For example, Lazarus (John 11), the widow's son (1 Kings 17), and the synagogue ruler's daughter (Mark 5) had all been restored to life, only to experience physical death again at a later date. The Resurrection of Jesus Christ and the future resurrection of the believer include receiving a new glorified and immortal body that will last for all for eternity. Christ's resurrection body was immortal and is indicative of the kind of resurrected body that the believer will possess when the dead in Christ are resurrected. Even believers who are still alive at the Rapture will receive a body fit for eternity. Note the following teaching of scripture:

1 Corinthians 15:20–23

> [20] But now Christ has been raised from the dead, the first fruits of those who are asleep. [21] For since by a man *came* death, by a man also *came* the resurrection of the dead. [22] For as in Adam all die, so also in Christ all will be made alive. [23] But each in his own order: Christ the first fruits, after that those who are Christ's at His coming,

1 Corinthians 15:50–54

[50] Now I say this, brethren, that flesh and blood cannot inherit the kingdom of God; nor does the perishable inherit the imperishable. [51] Behold, I tell you a mystery; we will not all sleep, but we will all be changed, [52] in a moment, in the twinkling of an eye, at the last trumpet; for the trumpet will sound, and the dead will be raised imperishable, and we will be changed. [53] For this perishable must put on the imperishable, and this mortal must put on immortality. [54] But when this perishable will have put on the imperishable, and this mortal will have put on immortality, then will come about the saying that is written, "DEATH IS SWALLOWED UP in victory."

C. The Resurrection of Christ is one of the best-substantiated facts of ancient history.

1. The synagogue officials did all they could to prevent Jesus' resurrection.
2. The empty tomb shouted out the fact the Jesus had conquered the grave.
3. Both Jesus' friends and enemies testified as to Jesus' bodily resurrection.
4. The soldiers guarding the tomb acknowledged His resurrection.
5. The Jewish leaders paid off the soldiers to lie about Jesus' resurrection.
6. Thomas actually examined the resurrected body of Jesus and was convinced.
7. Many of Jesus' disciples died as martyrs because they were totally convinced that Jesus was alive.

1 Corinthians 15:4–7

[4] and that He was buried, and that He was raised on the third day according to the Scriptures, [5] and that He appeared to Cephas, then to the twelve. [6] After that He appeared to more than five hundred brethren at one time, most of whom remain until now, but some have fallen asleep; [7] then He appeared to James, then to all the apostles;

Additional reading:

- *Evidence That Demands a Verdict*, Josh McDowell and Sean McDowell. (2017). Nashville: Thomas Nelson.
- *The Case for Christ,* Lee Strobel. (1998). Grand Rapids: Zondervan Publishers.

D. The Resurrection of Christ proves that our justification was secured by the death of Christ.

Romans 4:25

> *He* who was delivered over because of our transgressions, and was raised because of our justification.

V. The Ascension of Christ

Forty days after His resurrection, Jesus Christ ascended back to heaven and is now seated at the right hand of God.

Acts 1:3

> To these He also presented Himself alive after His suffering, by many convincing proofs, appearing to them over *a period of* forty days and speaking of the things concerning the kingdom of God.

Acts 1:9

> And after He had said these things, He was lifted up while they were looking on, and a cloud received Him out of their sight.

Acts 7:55–56

> [55] But being full of the Holy Spirit, he gazed intently into heaven and saw the glory of God, and Jesus standing at the right hand of God; [56] and he said, "Behold, I see the heavens opened up and the Son of Man standing at the right hand of God."

VI. The Present Three-Fold Ministry of Christ

A. Jesus Christ is the head of the church.

Ephesians 1:22–23

> [22] And He put all things in subjection under His feet, and gave Him as head over all things to the church, [23] which is His body, the fullness of Him who fills all in all.

B. Jesus Christ is our Intercessor.

Hebrews 7:25

> Therefore He is able also to save forever those who draw near to God through Him, since He always lives to make intercession for them.

1. His intercessory prayer began before He was arrested and crucified. (John 17:1–26)
2. His intercessory prayer is focused on Christians. (John 17:9)
3. His intercessory prayer addresses the weakness and helplessness of the saints.

Romans 8:34

> who is the one who condemns? Christ Jesus is He who died, yes, rather who was raised, who is at the right hand of God, who also intercedes for us.

C. Christ is our Advocate.

1 John 2:1–3

> [1] My little children, I am writing these things to you so that you may not sin. And if anyone sins, we have an Advocate with the Father, Jesus Christ the righteous; [2] and He Himself is the propitiation for our sins; and not for ours only, but also for *those of* the whole world.
>
> [3] By this we know that we have come to know Him, if we keep His commandments.

This ministry addresses the Christian's sin. Christ is our advocate. He pleads our case and pleads His own blood before the Father. Satan is the accuser of the believer (Revelation 12:10), but Christ represents us as our advocate.

VII. The Coming Again of Christ

We will consider these events in more detail in our study of chapters 11 and 12 (Eschatology). Here we will briefly list the two phases to Christ's coming:

A. Jesus is coming *for* his saints.

This is called the Rapture of the church. Jesus will not come all the way to earth but will, in an instant, meet believers in the air and take them to be with Him forever. This event will include all believers who died in Christ and all believers who are still alive when He comes.

1 Thessalonians 4:13–18

> [13] But we do not want you to be uninformed, brethren, about those who are asleep, so that you will not grieve as do the rest who have no hope. [14] For if we believe that Jesus died and rose again, even so God will bring with Him those who have fallen asleep in Jesus. [15] For this we say to you by the word of the Lord, that we who are alive and remain until the coming of the Lord, will not precede those who have fallen asleep. [16] For the Lord Himself will descend from heaven with a shout, with the voice of *the* archangel and with the trumpet of God, and the dead in Christ will rise first. [17] Then we who are alive and remain will be caught up together with them in the clouds to meet the Lord in the air, and so we shall always be with the Lord. [18] Therefore comfort one another with these words.

1 Corinthians 15:50–58

> [50] Now I say this, brethren, that flesh and blood cannot inherit the kingdom of God; nor does the perishable inherit the imperishable. [51] Behold, I tell you a mystery; we will not all sleep, but we will all be changed, [52] in a moment, in the twinkling of an eye, at the last trumpet; for the trumpet will sound, and the dead will be raised imperishable, and we will be changed. [53] For this perishable must put on the imperishable, and this mortal must put on immortality. [54] But when this perishable will have put on the imperishable, and this mortal will have put on immortality, then will come about the saying that is written, "Death is swallowed up in victory. [55] O death, where is your victory? O death, where is your sting?" [56] The sting of death is sin, and the power of sin is the law; [57] but thanks be to God, who gives us the victory through our Lord Jesus Christ.
>
> [58] Therefore, my beloved brethren, be steadfast, immovable, always abounding in the work of the Lord, knowing that your toil is not *in* vain in the Lord.

B. Jesus is coming *with* His saints.

This is referring to His Second Advent. This will take place at the end of the seven-year tribulation period at the Battle of Armageddon when Christ will come again to earth, where He will sit on the throne of David to rule for one thousand years.

Matthew 24:42–44

> [42] "Therefore be on the alert, for you do not know which day your Lord is coming. [43] But be sure of this, that if the head of the house had known at what time of the night the thief was coming, he would have been on the alert and would not have allowed his house to be broken into. [44] For this reason you also must be ready; for the Son of Man is coming at an hour when you do not think *He will*."

1 Thessalonians 5:1–5

> [1] Now as to the times and the epochs, brethren, you have no need of anything to be written to you. [2] For you yourselves know full well that the day of the Lord will come just like a thief in the night. [3] While they are saying, "Peace and safety!" then destruction will come upon them suddenly like labor pains upon a woman with child, and they will not escape. [4] But you, brethren, are not in darkness, that the day would overtake you like a thief; [5] for you are all sons of light and sons of day. We are not of night nor of darkness;

Revelation 19:11–16

> [11] And I saw heaven opened, and behold, a white horse, and He who sat on it *is* called Faithful and True, and in righteousness He judges and wages war. [12] His eyes *are* a flame of fire, and on His head *are* many diadems; and He has a name written *on Him* which no one knows except Himself. [13] *He is* clothed with a robe dipped in blood, and His name is called The Word of God. [14] And the armies which are in heaven, clothed in fine linen, white *and* clean, were following Him on white horses. [15] From His mouth comes a sharp sword, so that with it He may strike down the nations, and He will rule them with a rod of iron; and He treads the wine press of the fierce wrath of God, the Almighty. [16] And on His robe and on His thigh He has a name written, "KING OF KINGS, AND LORD OF LORDS."

REVIEW QUESTIONS

1. Name and describe the first three false theories concerning the death of Christ.
2. Explain the term redemption.
3. Explain the term reconciliation.
4. Explain the term propitiation.
5. Explain the doctrine of substitution.
6. Explain the word *vicarious.*
7. Did Jesus willingly offer Himself to die on the cross?
8. What did the death of Christ satisfy?
9. Explain the word *atonement.*
10. How does the sinner appropriate the value of what Christ has done for him or her on Calvary? (In other words, what must we do to be saved?)
11. What is the difference between a restoration to life (like Lazarus) and a resurrection to life?
12. Explain why the resurrection of Christ is so important.
13. Name and explain the present three-fold ministry of Christ.
14. Name the two phases of the Second Advent of Christ.

CHAPTER 6

Pneumatology
(What the Bible Teaches About the Holy Spirit)

Part 1: The Person of the Holy Spirit

I. The Holy Spirit is a Person

The Holy Spirit is a distinct person. He is not simply a power, a figment of our imagination, or a mere force or influence. Neither is He simply a manifestation of the Father or of the Son. He is one of the three persons of the Godhead and is co-equal with the Father and the Son. God the Holy Spirit is a distinct person with a personality. He has *feelings* (emotions). He has *a mind* (the ability to think). He has a *will* (the power to make decisions, make choices, and carry out plans).

A. The Holy Spirit has characteristics of a person.

1. The Holy Spirit has a mind, intelligence, understanding, and thoughts.

1 Corinthians 2:11

> For who among men knows the *thoughts* of a man except the spirit of the man which is in him? Even so the *thoughts* of God no one knows except the Spirit of God.

Romans 8:27

> and He who searches the hearts knows what the mind of the Spirit is, because He intercedes for the saints according to *the will of* God.

Isaiah 11:2

> The Spirit of the LORD will rest on Him,
> The spirit of wisdom and understanding,
> The spirit of counsel and strength,
> The spirit of knowledge and the fear of the LORD.

a. The Holy Spirit has knowledge and intelligence.

b. The Holy Spirit owns and understands God's truth.

c. The Holy Spirit takes the truth of God's Word and reveals it to us.

d. He is called the Spirit of wisdom, understanding, counsel, and knowledge.

2. The Holy Spirit has feelings, sensibility, and emotions.

Ephesians 4:30

> Do not grieve the Holy Spirit of God, by whom you were sealed for the day of redemption.

Isaiah 63:10

> But they rebelled
> And grieved His Holy Spirit;
> Therefore He turned Himself to become their enemy,
> He fought against them.

Galatians 5:22–23

> But the fruit of the Spirit is love, joy, peace, patience, kindness, goodness, faithfulness, [23] gentleness, self-control; against such things there is no law.

a. When we sin the Holy Spirit has the emotion of grief.

b. The fruit of the Spirit includes the emotions of love, joy, and peace (lack of worry).

c. God the Holy Spirit definitely has feelings and emotions.

3. The Holy Spirit has a will, the ability to make and carry out plans and decisions.

1 Corinthians 12:11

> But one and the same Spirit works all these things, distributing to each one individually just as He wills.

Acts 13:2

> While they were ministering to the Lord and fasting, the Holy Spirit said, "Set apart for Me Barnabas and Saul for the work to which I have called them."

Acts 16:6

> They passed through the Phrygian and Galatian region, having been forbidden by the Holy Spirit to speak the word in Asia;

a. The Holy Spirit decides who among Christians will receive which spiritual gifts.

b. The Holy Spirit had a plan in connection with the ministry of Barnabas and Saul.

c. God the Holy Spirit revealed a plan for Paul and his companions concerning their travels and ministry in Asia.

Conclusions:

1. From the above scripture we note that God the Holy Spirit possesses intellect (a mind), sensibility (emotions or feelings), and a will (power to say yes or no).

2. These three elements make up a personality; therefore, we conclude that the Holy Spirit is a person, not merely an influence or a power.

3. We are often prone to believe that only someone with a physical body could be a person, but this is not true. You will still be a person after your physical body dies.

4. The Holy Spirit is a person.

B. Personal pronouns are used to describe the Holy Spirit.

John 15:26

> "When the Helper comes, whom I will send to you from the Father, *that is* the Spirit of truth who proceeds from the Father, He will testify about Me,"

John 16:7–8

> [7] But I tell you the truth, it is to your advantage that I go away; for if I do not go away, the Helper will not come to you; but if I go, I will send Him to you. [8] And He, when He comes, will convict the world concerning sin and righteousness and judgment.

C. Personal accomplishments are attributed to the Holy Spirit.

1. The Holy Spirit teaches.

John 14:26

> But the Helper, the Holy Spirit, whom the Father will send in My name, He will teach you all things, and bring to your remembrance all that I said to you.

2. The Holy Spirit speaks.

Galatians 4:6

> Because you are sons, God has sent forth the Spirit of His Son into our hearts, crying, "Abba! Father!"

3. The Holy Spirit reproves.

John 16:7–11

> [7] But I tell you the truth, it is to your advantage that I go away; for if I do not go away, the Helper will not come to you; but if I go, I will send Him to you. [8] And He, when He comes, will convict the world concerning sin and righteousness and judgment; [9] concerning sin, because they do not believe in Me; [10] and concerning righteousness, because I go to the Father and you no longer see Me; [11] and concerning judgment, because the ruler of this world has been judged.

4. The Holy Spirit prays (intercedes).

Romans 8:26–27

> [26] In the same way the Spirit also helps our weakness; for we do not know how to pray as we should, but the Spirit Himself intercedes for *us* with groanings too deep for words; [27] and He who searches the hearts knows what the mind of the Spirit is, because He intercedes for the saints according to *the will of* God.

5. The Holy Spirit regenerates (the new birth is attributed to the Holy Spirit).

John 3:6–7

> [6] That which is born of the flesh is flesh, and that which is born of the Spirit is spirit. [7] Do not be amazed that I said to you, 'You must be born again.'

6. The Holy Spirit commands and appoints.

   Acts 20:28

   > Be on guard for yourselves and for all the flock, among which the Holy Spirit has made you overseers, to shepherd the church of God which He purchased with His own blood.

7. The Bible refers to the Holy Spirit as a person.

   a. We may grieve the Holy Spirit.

   Ephesians 4:30

   > Do not grieve the Holy Spirit of God, by whom you were sealed for the day of redemption.

   b. We may lie to the Holy Spirit.

   Acts 5:3

   > But Peter said, "Ananias, why has Satan filled your heart to lie to the Holy Spirit and to keep back *some* of the price of the land?"

   c. We may quench or resist the Holy Spirit.

   1 Thessalonians 5:19

   > Do not quench the Spirit;

   d. We may blaspheme the Holy Spirit.

   Matthew 12:31

   > "Therefore I say to you, any sin and blasphemy shall be forgiven people, but blasphemy against the Spirit shall not be forgiven."

II. The Deity of the Holy Spirit

A. The Holy Spirit possesses divine attributes.

1. His eternal character – The Holy Spirit is called *the eternal Spirit.* He is without a beginning and without an end.

Hebrews 9:14

> how much more will the blood of Christ, who through the eternal Spirit offered Himself without blemish to God, cleanse your conscience from dead works to serve the living God?

2. His omnipresence (everywhere present, not limited by time or space) – We cannot remove ourselves from His presence.

Psalms 139:7–10

> [7] Where can I go from Your Spirit?
> Or where can I flee from Your presence?
> [8] If I ascend to heaven, You are there;
> If I make my bed in Sheol, behold, You are there.
> [9] If I take the wings of the dawn,
> If I dwell in the remotest part of the sea,
> [10] Even there Your hand will lead me,
> And Your right hand will lay hold of me.

B. The Holy Spirit performs divine works.

1. The Holy Spirit participated in creation.

Genesis 1:2

> The earth was formless and void, and darkness was over the surface of the deep, and the Spirit of God was moving over the surface of the waters.

Job 33:4

> "The Spirit of God has made me,
> And the breath of the Almighty gives me life."

2. The Holy Spirit regenerates by giving the believer new life.

Titus 3:5

> He saved us, not on the basis of deeds which we have done in righteousness, but according to His mercy, by the washing of regeneration and renewing by the Holy Spirit,

3. The Holy Spirit is the source of inspiration. (He is the true author of the Word of God.)

2 Peter 1:21

for no prophecy was ever made by an act of human will, but men moved by the Holy Spirit spoke from God.

C. The Holy Spirit is linked with the other members of the Godhead.

Matthew 28:19

Go therefore and make disciples of all the nations, baptizing them in the name of the Father and the Son and the Holy Spirit,

2 Corinthians 13:14

The grace of the Lord Jesus Christ, and the love of God, and the fellowship of the Holy Spirit, be with you all.

D. The Holy Spirit may be blasphemed.

Matthew 12:31

"Therefore I say to you, any sin and blasphemy shall be forgiven people, but blasphemy against the Spirit shall not be forgiven."

E. The Holy Spirit holds the titles of deity.

1. The Holy Spirit is called *the Spirit of God.*

Genesis 1:2

The earth was formless and void, and darkness was over the surface of the deep, and the Spirit of God was moving over the surface of the waters.

2. The Holy Spirit is called *the Spirit of the Lord.*

Luke 4:18

"The Spirit of the Lord is upon Me,
Because He anointed Me to preach the gospel to the poor.
He has sent Me to proclaim release to the captives,
And recovery of sight to the blind,
To set free those who are oppressed,"

3. The Holy Spirit is called *the Spirit of our God.*

    1 Corinthians 6:11

    > Such were some of you; but you were washed, but you were sanctified, but you were justified in the name of the Lord Jesus Christ and in the Spirit of our God.

4. The Holy Spirit is called *His Spirit.*

    Numbers 11:29

    > But Moses said to him, "Are you jealous for my sake? Would that all the LORD's people were prophets, that the LORD would put His Spirit upon them!"

5. The Holy Spirit is called *the Spirit of Jehovah.*

    Judges 3:10

    > The Spirit of the LORD came upon him, and he judged Israel. When he went out to war, the LORD gave Cushan-rishathaim king of Mesopotamia into his hand, so that he prevailed over Cushan-rishathaim.

Remember: LORD spelled with all capital letters is a translation of the name "Jehovah."

6. The Holy Spirit is called the *Spirit of your Father.*

    Matthew 10:20

    > For it is not you who speak, but *it is* the Spirit of your Father who speaks in you.

7. The Holy Spirit is called the *Spirit of the Living God.*

    2 Corinthians 3:3

    > being manifested that you are a letter of Christ, cared for by us, written not with ink but with the Spirit of the living God, not on tablets of stone but on tablets of human hearts.

III. Biblical Symbols of the Holy Spirit

A. Dove

The Holy Spirit is not a dove but descended like a dove.

Matthew 3:16

> After being baptized, Jesus came up immediately from the water; and behold, the heavens were opened, and he saw the Spirit of God descending as a dove *and* lighting on Him,

B. Water

The Holy Spirit is not water but is symbolized sometimes as water.

John 7:37–39

> [37] Now on the last day, the great *day* of the feast, Jesus stood and cried out, saying, "If anyone is thirsty, let him come to Me and drink. [38] He who believes in Me, as the Scripture said, 'From his innermost being will flow rivers of living water.'" [39] But this He spoke of the Spirit, whom those who believed in Him were to receive; for the Spirit was not yet *given*, because Jesus was not yet glorified.

C. Fire

The Holy Spirit is not a fire but is symbolized sometimes as fire.

Acts 2:2–4

> [2] And suddenly there came from heaven a noise like a violent rushing wind, and it filled the whole house where they were sitting. [3] And there appeared to them tongues as of fire distributing themselves, and they rested on each one of them. [4] And they were all filled with the Holy Spirit and began to speak with other tongues, as the Spirit was giving them utterance.

D. Wind

The Holy Spirit is not the wind but is symbolized sometimes as wind.

John 3:7–8

> [7] "Do not be amazed that I said to you, 'You must be born again.' [8] The wind blows where it wishes and you hear the sound of it, but do not know where it comes from and where it is going; so is everyone who is born of the Spirit."

E. Oil

The Holy Spirit is not oil but sometimes is symbolized as oil.

1 Samuel 16:12–13

> [12] So he sent and brought him in. Now he was ruddy, with beautiful eyes and a handsome appearance. And the LORD said, "Arise, anoint him; for this is he." [13] Then Samuel took the horn of oil and anointed him in the midst of his brothers; and the Spirit of the LORD came mightily upon David from that day forward. And Samuel arose and went to Ramah.

Since we know that the Holy Spirit is a person, we ought to live our lives with an awareness and realization that He is dwelling inside us. He is very much aware of what is going on in our lives, and when we sin, He is grieved. When God gives us an opportunity to fulfill a spiritual ministry or physical activity, we can call upon the Holy Spirit, who resides within us to supply the power and the ability to carry it out.

Ephesians 4:30

> Do not grieve the Holy Spirit of God, by whom you were sealed for the day of redemption.

Acts 1:8

> "but you will receive power when the Holy Spirit has come upon you; and you shall be My witnesses both in Jerusalem, and in all Judea and Samaria, and even to the remotest part of the earth."

Part 2: The Work of the Holy Spirit

What does the Holy Spirit do in the believer and through the believer?

I. General Factors to Keep in Mind as We Consider the Work of the Spirit

In previous chapters, we have considered each member of the Godhead, and we have discovered that each member had a part in various activities attributed to God. In Chapter 2 (Bibliology), we learned the Holy Spirit was active in the production of the Bible. In

Chapter 4 (Christology), we were taught the Holy Spirit was responsible for the virgin birth of Jesus. In Genesis 1:1–2, we find the Holy Spirit moving over the surface of the waters at Creation.

A. The work of the Holy Spirit in the Old Testament and today (Acts 2)

The work of the Holy Spirit in the Old Testament era differed from His work after the Day of Pentecost (recorded in Acts 2) and continues to the present time. Failure to understand this fact causes much confusion about the work of the Holy Spirit. This difference is seen in at least three ways:

1. Who could receive the Holy Spirit?

Old Testament Era	Pentecost and Present Time
In the Old Testament the Bible records the Holy Spirit "coming in or coming upon" *certain people* to accomplish a specific task.	In the New Testament and today, the Holy Spirit takes up "permanent residence" in *every believer.*

2. How often could they receive the Holy Spirit?

Old Testament Era	Pentecost and Present Time
In the Old Testament, the Holy Spirit often "came upon" certain people *to accomplish a specific task.* When the task was completed, the Holy Spirit no longer remained with them.	In the New Testament and today, the Holy Spirit takes up "permanent residence" in every believer. The power of the Holy Spirit is *continually available* for victory over sin and daily ministry.

3. How permanent was the availability of the Holy Spirit?

Old Testament Era	Pentecost and Present Time
In the Old Testament, the Bible records the Holy Spirit "coming upon" certain people and *then leaving.*	After Pentecost (Acts 2), the Holy Spirit takes up "permanent residence" and *never leaves.*

B. Old Testament examples of the work of the Holy Spirit

1. Samson

Judges 14:6

The Spirit of the LORD came upon him mightily, so that he tore him as one tears a young goat though he had nothing in his hand; but he did not tell his father or mother what he had done.

Judges 14:19

Then the Spirit of the LORD came upon him mightily, and he went down to Ashkelon and killed thirty of them and took their spoil and gave the changes *of clothes* to those who told the riddle. And his anger burned, and he went up to his father's house.

Judges 15:14

When he came to Lehi, the Philistines shouted as they met him. And the Spirit of the LORD came upon him mightily so that the ropes that were on his arms were as flax that is burned with fire, and his bonds dropped from his hands.

Judges 16:19–20

[19] he made him sleep on her knees, and called for a man and had him shave off the seven locks of his hair. Then she began to afflict him, and his strength left him. [20] She said, "The Philistines are upon you, Samson!" And he awoke from his sleep and said, "I will go out as at other times and shake myself free." But he did not know that the LORD had departed from him.

2. King Saul

1 Samuel 10:6

Then the Spirit of the Lord will come upon you mightily, and you shall prophesy with them and be changed into another man.

1 Samuel 16:13–14

[13] Then Samuel took the horn of oil and anointed him in the midst of his brothers; and the Spirit of the LORD came mightily upon David from that day forward. And Samuel arose and went to Ramah.

[14] Now the Spirit of the LORD departed from Saul, and an evil spirit from the LORD terrorized him.

1 Samuel 28:16

> Samuel said, "Why then do you ask me, since the LORD has departed from you and has become your adversary?"

3. King David

Psalms 51:11 (David's prayer)

> Do not cast me away from Your presence
> And do not take Your Holy Spirit from me.

4. Gideon

Judges 6:34

> So the Spirit of the LORD came upon Gideon; and he blew a trumpet, and the Abiezrites were called together to follow him.

5. Balaam

Numbers 24:2

> And Balaam lifted up his eyes and saw Israel camping tribe by tribe; and the Spirit of God came upon him.

6. Othniel

Judges 3:9–10

> [9] When the sons of Israel cried to the LORD, the LORD raised up a deliverer for the sons of Israel to deliver them, Othniel the son of Kenaz, Caleb's younger brother. [10] The Spirit of the LORD came upon him, and he judged Israel. When he went out to war, the LORD gave Cushan-rishathaim king of Mesopotamia into his hand, so that he prevailed over Cushan-rishathaim.

7. Azariah

2 Chronicles 15:1

> Now the Spirit of God came on Azariah the son of Oded,

8. Zechariah

2 Chronicles 24:20

> Then the Spirit of God came on Zechariah the son of Jehoiada the priest; and he stood above the people and said to them, "Thus God has said, 'Why do you transgress the commandments of the LORD and do not prosper? Because you have forsaken the LORD, He has also forsaken you.'"

II. The Ministry of the Holy Spirit During this Present Age

By *this present age* we mean the work of the Holy Spirit during what some theologians refer to as the "age of the church" or the "age of the Holy Spirit." This age began when the Holy Spirit first came to baptize and indwell the believers on the Day of Pentecost (Acts 2). This work will continue until Christ returns in the clouds to meet His bride (the church) in the air. As we will learn in our study of the future (Eschatology), this event is called "the Rapture of the church." The word *rapture* is not found in the Bible but is a theological term that means "a taking up" or the transporting of all believers to heaven.

It is of the utmost importance that we understand the unique working of the Holy Spirit as recorded in the book of Acts. We do not draw our conclusions about the work of the Holy Spirit from Old Testament examples. Our conclusions should be drawn from the record of Christ's earthly ministry and the entire New Testament. As Christ clearly taught (John 14–16 and Acts 1:1–8), a new relationship and ministry of the Holy Spirit was to begin after His ascension. The Bible student who does not recognize this will be confused concerning the work of the Holy Spirit.

Key passages in Acts:

To understand the work of the Holy Spirit in the book of Acts, we must recognize that the book of Acts is a transitional book. Much confusion and frustration would have existed in the days of the apostles if God would have abruptly moved from the culture of the law (found in the Old Testament) to the new culture of the church (established in the New Testament gospels and taught in the epistles). During the time recorded in the book of Acts, God was shifting from the Old Testament system of the law and His work with Israel, to the New Testament culture of grace and His work with the church. The book of Acts records the slow and careful transitional interval, and it also introduces the New Testament era of the church and the removal of the wall between the Jews and the Gentiles. God wisely did not decide to suddenly begin a new phase. His work during this transitional period is unique. If we draw our conclusions about the work of the Holy Spirit based only on the book of Acts, we can easily become puzzled and be found in error.

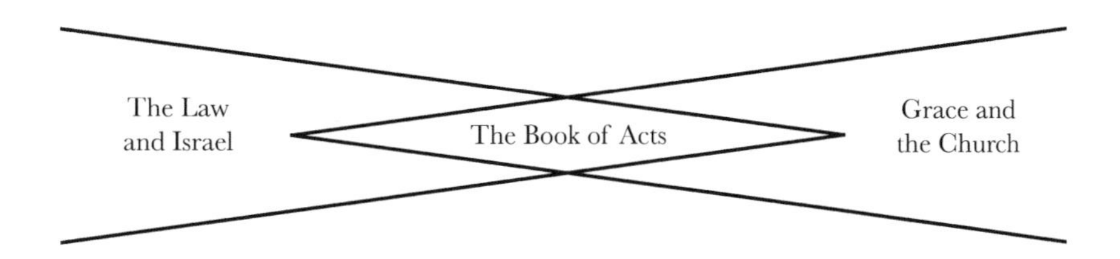

III. Three Major Works of the Holy Spirit

Many times, the student of the Word of God will be confused either by lumping these three things together or by confusing them regarding the timing in the Christian life. It is important to understand that each of these works are individual events. We must also determine from the Bible as to when these events take place in the life of the believer.

A. The indwelling of the Holy Spirit

The word *indwell* means "to take up a permanent residency."

1. The promise of the Holy Spirit that was given to Christ's disciples was to be fulfilled after Christ would return to the Father.

    John 7:38–39

    > [38] "He who believes in Me, as the Scripture said, 'From his innermost being will flow rivers of living water.'" [39] But this He spoke of the Spirit, whom those who believed in Him were to receive; for the Spirit was not yet *given*, because Jesus was not yet glorified.

2. Jesus promises his disciples that, though the Holy Spirit was *with them*, he would one day be *in them.*

    John 14:16–17

    > [16] I will ask the Father, and He will give you another Helper, that He may be with you forever; [17] *that is* the Spirit of truth, whom the world cannot receive, because it does not see Him or know Him, *but* you know Him because He abides with you and will be in you.

3. All believers have the Holy Spirit dwelling in them. Romans 8:9 makes it clear that if the Holy Spirit is not residing in a believer, he or she is not truly born again.

Romans 5:5

> and hope does not disappoint, because the love of God has been poured out within our hearts through the Holy Spirit who was given to us.

Romans 8:9–11

> [9] However, you are not in the flesh but in the Spirit, if indeed the Spirit of God dwells in you. But if anyone does not have the Spirit of Christ, he does not belong to Him. [10] If Christ is in you, though the body is dead because of sin, yet the spirit is alive because of righteousness. [11] But if the Spirit of Him who raised Jesus from the dead dwells in you, He who raised Christ Jesus from the dead will also give life to your mortal bodies through His Spirit who dwells in you.

4. The carnal believers in Corinth were indwelled by the Spirit of God. Even though these believers were sinning, the Holy Spirit did not leave them.

1 Corinthians 3:16

> Don't you know that you yourselves are God's temple and that God's Spirit dwells in your midst?

1 Corinthians 2:12

> Now we have received, not the spirit of the world, but the Spirit who is from God, so that we may know the things freely given to us by God,

Romans 8:9–11

> [9] However, you are not in the flesh but in the Spirit, if indeed the Spirit of God dwells in you. But if anyone does not have the Spirit of Christ, he does not belong to Him. [10] If Christ is in you, though the body is dead because of sin, yet the spirit is alive because of righteousness. [11] But if the Spirit of Him who raised Jesus from the dead dwells in you, He who raised Christ Jesus from the dead will also give life to your mortal bodies through His Spirit who dwells in you.

5. The picture of the body being the "temple of the Holy Spirit" is best understood as a permanent dwelling place of God. The temporary tabernacle (tent) was used in the wilderness travels of Israel, but Solomon built the permanent temple of God once they possessed the land. Our bodies are pictured as the temple of the Holy Spirit, not the tent of the Holy Spirit.

1 Corinthians 6:19

> Or do you not know that your body is a temple of the Holy Spirit who is in you, whom you have from God, and that you are not your own?

6. The Holy Spirit indwells us because we have put our faith in Christ and that makes us His own children.

Galatians 4:6

> Because you are sons, God has sent forth the Spirit of His Son into our hearts, crying, "Abba! Father!"

1 John 4:13

> By this we know that we abide in Him and He in us, because He has given us of His Spirit.

Some scriptures (especially in the book of Acts) seem to indicate that the indwelling of the Holy Spirit comes sometime *after* salvation. Some would cite that the disciples believed on Jesus before Pentecost and therefore the Holy Spirit came upon them after salvation. This, of course, ignores the differences in the work of the Holy Spirit under the Old Testament law (including Jesus' earthly ministry) and what Jesus predicted would happen after his ascension in Acts 1:1–8. It also ignores the transitional character of the book of Acts. (We will study more about this later in the chapter. There are several passages of scripture we will consider separately to aid in our understanding of this issue.)

B. The baptism of the Holy Spirit

1. John the Baptist speaks of the baptism of the Holy Spirit when he introduces Jesus, who is about to be baptized with water.

Luke 3:16

> John answered and said to them all, "As for me, I baptize you with water; but One is coming who is mightier than I, and I am not fit to untie the thong of His sandals; He will baptize you with the Holy Spirit and fire."

2. Just before His ascension, Jesus refers to John's statement when He instructs His disciples concerning the baptism of the Holy Spirit that would soon take place. Jesus' words were fulfilled on the Day of Pentecost.

Acts 1:4–5

> [4] Gathering them together, He commanded them not to leave Jerusalem, but to wait for what the Father had promised, "Which," *He said*, "you heard of from Me; [5] for John baptized with water, but you will be baptized with the Holy Spirit not many days from now."

Acts 11:15–17

> [15] "And as I began to speak, the Holy Spirit fell upon them just as *He did* upon us at the beginning. [16] And I remembered the word of the Lord, how He used to say, 'John baptized with water, but you will be baptized with the Holy Spirit.' [17] Therefore if God gave to them the same gift as *He gave* to us also after believing in the Lord Jesus Christ, who was I that I could stand in God's way?"

(In this passage Peter reports to a doubting church his experience in leading Cornelius to Christ and the work of the Holy Spirit on that occasion.)

3. There are two major results of the baptism of the Holy Spirit:

   a. The Holy Spirit unites the new believer with all other believers into one body, the Body of Christ.

   1 Corinthians 12:12–13

   > [12] For even as the body is one and *yet* has many members, and all the members of the body, though they are many, are one body, so also is Christ. [13] For by one Spirit we were all baptized into one body, whether Jews or Greeks, whether slaves or free, and we were all made to drink of one Spirit.

   Galatians 3:26–28

   > [26] For you are all sons of God through faith in Christ Jesus. [27] For all of you who were baptized into Christ have clothed yourselves with Christ. [28] There is neither Jew nor Greek, there is neither slave nor free man, there is neither male nor female; for you are all one in Christ Jesus.

   b. The new believer is united with Christ, who is the Head of the church. Romans 6:3–5 sets forth our identification and unification with Christ.

Romans 6:3–5

> [3] Or do you not know that all of us who have been baptized into Christ Jesus have been baptized into His death? [4] Therefore we have been buried with Him through baptism into death, so that as Christ was raised from the dead through the glory of the Father, so we too might walk in newness of life. [5] For if we have become united with *Him* in the likeness of His death, certainly we shall also be *in the likeness* of His resurrection,

Nowhere in scripture are we commanded, or even encouraged, to be baptized by the Holy Spirit. This baptism takes place automatically and immediately at the time of our salvation.

Many pastors and teachers read this passage at water baptism services, and I, as author of this book, have no major problem with this. However, a closer look at the things accomplished according to this passage are primarily accomplished by the baptism of the Holy Spirit, not by water baptism. This unification comes about as a result of the baptism of the Holy Spirit.

Being "baptized into Christ," the believer is united with Him in His crucifixion, death, burial, and resurrection. This becomes the basis for the godly lifestyle of the believer. There is no reference to water anywhere in Romans 6:3–5.

4. John 17:20–22 are the words of Christ in His prayer for believers (the church).

5. Christ always received from the Father whatever He asked because, being God, He always prayed according to the will of God.

6. This prayer looks forward to the baptism of the Holy Spirit, uniting believers into one body and joining them to Christ.

7. Sometimes there is division in the local church, and often the apostle Paul addresses this issue in his letters to various churches. The primary application here is the baptism of the Holy Spirit. This is the answer to Christ's prayer for unity.

John 17:20–22 (Jesus' intercessory prayer)

> [20] "I do not ask on behalf of these alone, but for those also who believe in Me through their word; [21] that they may all be one; even as You, Father, *are* in Me and I in You, that they also may be in Us, so that the world may believe that You sent Me.
>
> [22] The glory which You have given Me I have given to them, that they may be one, just as We are one;"

8. Acts 1:4–5 records Jesus' teaching concerning the baptism of the Holy Spirit. This passage bridges John the Baptist's prophecy to the baptism of the Holy Spirit.

    Acts 1:4–5

    > [4] Gathering them together, He commanded them not to leave Jerusalem, but to wait for what the Father had promised, "Which," *He said*, "you heard of from Me; [5] for John baptized with water, but you will be baptized with the Holy Spirit not many days from now."

9. Acts 2:1–4 records the events on the Day of Pentecost (the fulfillment of the prophecy of John the Baptist and Jesus).

    Acts 2:1–4

    > [1] When the day of Pentecost had come, they were all together in one place. [2] And suddenly there came from heaven a noise like a violent rushing wind, and it filled the whole house where they were sitting. [3] And there appeared to them tongues as of fire distributing themselves, and they rested on each one of them. [4] And they were all filled with the Holy Spirit and began to speak with other tongues, as the Spirit was giving them utterance.

10. The Spirit united all the believers into one body on that day. This was the beginning of the church (the Body of Christ).

11. Colossians 2:12 stresses union with Christ by means of the baptism of the Holy Spirit. Though a reference to the Spirit in connection with this baptism is not found, the results of the baptism (union with Christ) can only be accomplished through the baptism of the Holy Spirit.

12. Note the strong references to union with Christ.

    Colossians 2:12

    > having been buried with Him in baptism, in which you were also raised up with Him through faith in the working of God, who raised Him from the dead.

Romans 6:3–6

> [3] Or do you not know that all of us who have been baptized into Christ Jesus have been baptized into His death? [4] Therefore we have been buried with Him through baptism into death, so that as Christ was raised from the dead through the glory of the Father, so we too might walk in newness of life. [5] For if we have become united with *Him* in the likeness of His death, certainly we shall also be *in the likeness* of His resurrection, [6] knowing this, that our old self was crucified with *Him*, in order that our body of sin might be done away with, so that we would no longer be slaves to sin;

13. In Ephesians 4:3–6, the apostle Paul is stressing practical unity among believers. In so doing, he stresses that all believers are already unified by the baptism of the Holy Spirit because of our position in Christ.

Ephesians 4:3–6

> [3] being diligent to preserve the unity of the Spirit in the bond of peace. [4] *There is* one body and one Spirit, just as also you were called in one hope of your calling; [5] one Lord, one faith, one baptism, [6] one God and Father of all who is over all and through all and in all.

14. Paul names seven spiritual truths in Ephesians 4:

- one body (the church)
- one Spirit (the Holy Spirit)
- one hope (the blessed hope)
- one Lord (Jesus Christ)
- one faith (faith in Jesus for salvation)
- one baptism (the baptism of the Holy Spirit)
- one God (the only true God)

15. This is a reference to the baptism of the Holy Spirit, not water baptism.

16. Paul points out in Ephesians 4 that when we properly understand the concept of the baptism of the Holy Spirit and the oneness of the Body of Christ, it produces a powerful incentive among believers to practice unity.

Conclusion:

Except for those who trusted Christ before the Day of Pentecost, every believer is baptized by the Holy Spirit at the moment of salvation. The baptism of the Holy Spirit is the work by which the believer is placed into the Body of Christ (the true church) and is also joined to the Head of the body (Jesus Christ). Although the baptism of the Holy Spirit takes place at the same time as regeneration, sealing, and indwelling, it must not be confused with regeneration, sealing, and indwelling.

C. The filling of the Holy Spirit.

The filling of the Holy Spirit does not mean possessing *more* of the Holy Spirit. As we have already seen, the Holy Spirit, in all His fullness, lives inside every believer. The filling of the Holy Spirit is not an emotional feeling or an outburst. The filling of the Holy Spirit means that the Holy Spirit takes full control of the individual in whom He dwells. The filling of the Holy Spirit is not a matter of how much of the Holy Spirit you possess, it is how much of you is under the full control of Holy Spirit.

Unlike the indwelling and baptism of the Holy Spirit, which are ours when we trust Christ as Savior and is a once-for-all work, the filling of the Spirit is a re-occurring work. There are certain conditions that must be met for the filling of the Holy Spirit. If these conditions are met, the result will be the filling of the Holy Spirit. Likewise, it is possible for a believer to be filled with the Holy Spirit one day and not the next.

Ephesians 5:18

> And do not get drunk with wine, for that is dissipation, but be filled with the Spirit,

1. Some have read Ephesians 5:18 and have used it as a justification for emotional or out-of-control behavior, but the opposite is the thrust of this verse.

2. The Greek word *dissipation* refers to out-of-control behavior, which is the result of being under the influence of wine.

3. To be filled with the Holy Spirit refers to being controlled by the Spirit of God.

4. When we are controlled by the Spirit of God, He will produce the fruit of the Spirit in us. This fruit is listed in Galatians 5:22–23, part of which is self-control.

Galatians 5:22–23

> [22] But the fruit of the Spirit is love, joy, peace, patience, kindness, goodness, faithfulness, [23] gentleness, self-control; against such things there is no law.

IV. The Three Conditions for the Filling of the Holy Spirit

A. Do not resist the Holy Spirit.

1 Thessalonians 5:19

> Do not quench the Spirit;

1. The word *quench* means "to put out a fire" or "to extinguish a fire."
2. The Greek word *quench* is in the present imperative tense and could be translated "stop putting out the fire."
3. The quenching of the Holy Spirit is done by saying "no" when we are prompted by the Holy Spirit. It means to resist His prompting and His will.
4. We can never become a Spirit-filled Christian if we resist the Holy Spirit, say no to His guidance, or refuse to yield to the Word of God, as He applies it to us personally.
5. There must be a constant attitude of surrender to the Holy Spirit, rather than rebellion.
6. The leading of the Holy Spirit is not only crucial in connection with the major issues of God's plan for our lives, but it applies to all the decisions we make every day. The Holy Spirit will always encourage us to make decisions that are in harmony with the Word of God.
7. Saying "no" to the Holy Spirit is sin.

B. Deal with sin through confession.

Ephesians 4:30–31

> [30] Do not grieve the Holy Spirit of God, by whom you were sealed for the day of redemption. [31] Let all bitterness and wrath and anger and clamor and slander be put away from you, along with all malice.

1. The word *grieve* means "to sadden." It would be a word we might use to describe our emotions at the death of a loved one.
2. We grieve the Holy Spirit when there are things in our lives that are contrary to God's Word.

3. Our fellowship is with a person, the person of the Holy Spirit. Our relationship to God can never be satisfactory, as long as we continue in unconfessed and unforsaken sin.

4. All believers have the sin nature.

Romans 5:12

> Therefore, just as through one man sin entered into the world, and death through sin, and so death spread to all men, because all sinned—

5. All believers commit sinful acts. The key word for believers who have sinned is *confess*.

1 John 1:9–2:1

> [9] If we confess our sins, He is faithful and righteous to forgive us our sins and to cleanse us from all unrighteousness. [10] If we say that we have not sinned, we make Him a liar and His word is not in us.
>
> [1] My little children, I am writing these things to you so that you may not sin. And if anyone sins, we have an Advocate with the Father, Jesus Christ the righteous;

C. Live in the power of the Holy Spirit.

Galatians 5:16

> But I say, walk by the Spirit, and you will not carry out the desire of the flesh.

Romans 8:4–5

> [4] so that the requirement of the Law might be fulfilled in us, who do not walk according to the flesh but according to the Spirit. [5] For those who are according to the flesh set their minds on the things of the flesh, but those who are according to the Spirit, the things of the Spirit.

Galatians 5:25

> If we live by the Spirit, let us also walk by the Spirit.

Colossians 2:6

> Therefore as you have received Christ Jesus the Lord, *so* walk in Him,

1. Because the Holy Spirit indwells the believer, the believer is exhorted to live in harmony with His holiness and by His power.

2. Walking by the Holy Spirit implies a moment-by-moment, step-by-step relationship.

3. We received Christ by a total dependence on Him (by faith), and our victory in the Christian life is obtained only by a moment-by-moment dependence on the Holy Spirit.

V. The Benefits of the Filling of the Spirit

Being filled with the Holy Spirit is not something to be feared but pursued. The Holy Spirit is not interested in controlling us to produce some strange and extreme behavior. He wants to control us to bring about the following results in our lives:

A. Being filled with the Holy Spirit allows Him to produce the fruit of the Spirit in the believer.

Galatians 5:22–23

> [22] But the fruit of the Spirit is love, joy, peace, patience, kindness, goodness, faithfulness, [23] gentleness, self-control; against such things there is no law.

B. Being filled with the Holy Spirit gives an increased victory over sin.

Galatians 5:16

> But I say, walk by the Spirit, and you will not carry out the desire of the flesh.

C. Being filled with the Holy Spirit produces a clearer understanding of the Word of God.

John 16:12–13

> [12] "I have many more things to say to you, but you cannot bear *them* now. [13] But when He, the Spirit of truth, comes, He will guide you into all the truth; for He will not speak on His own initiative, but whatever He hears, He will speak; and He will disclose to you what is to come."

1 Corinthians 2:15

> But he who is spiritual appraises all things, yet he himself is appraised by no one.

D. Being filled with the Holy Spirit gives greater assurance of salvation.

Romans 8:16

> The Spirit Himself testifies with our spirit that we are children of God,

E. Being filled with the Holy Spirit will give greater confidence before God.

1 John 3:21–22

> [21] Beloved, if our heart does not condemn us, we have confidence before God; [22] and whatever we ask we receive from Him, because we keep His commandments and do the things that are pleasing in His sight.

F. Being filled with the Holy Spirit will give the believer power and confidence in sharing the gospel.

Acts 1:8

> "but you will receive power when the Holy Spirit has come upon you; and you shall be My witnesses both in Jerusalem, and in all Judea and Samaria, and even to the remotest part of the earth."

Acts 4:13

> Now as they observed the confidence of Peter and John and understood that they were uneducated and untrained men, they were amazed, and *began* to recognize them as having been with Jesus.

Acts 4:29

> And now, Lord, take note of their threats, and grant that Your bond-servants may speak Your word with all confidence,

1 Corinthians 2:1–5

> [1] And when I came to you, brethren, I did not come with superiority of speech or of wisdom, proclaiming to you the testimony of God. [2] For I determined to know nothing among you except Jesus Christ, and Him crucified. [3] I was with you in weakness and in fear and in much trembling, [4] and my message and my preaching were not in persuasive words of wisdom, but in demonstration of the Spirit and of power, [5] so that your faith would not rest on the wisdom of men, but on the power of God.

2 Timothy 1:7

> For God has not given us a spirit of timidity, but of power and love and discipline.

G. Being filled with the Holy Spirit produces honest fellowship with God.

1 John 1:4–2:2

> [4] These things we write, so that our joy may be made complete.
>
> [5] This is the message we have heard from Him and announce to you, that God is Light, and in Him there is no darkness at all. [6] If we say that we have fellowship with Him and *yet* walk in the darkness, we lie and do not practice the truth; [7] but if we walk in the Light as He Himself is in the Light, we have fellowship with one another, and the blood of Jesus His Son cleanses us from all sin. [8] If we say that we have no sin, we are deceiving ourselves and the truth is not in us. [9] If we confess our sins, He is faithful and righteous to forgive us our sins and to cleanse us from all unrighteousness. [10] If we say that we have not sinned, we make Him a liar and His word is not in us.
>
> [1] My little children, I am writing these things to you so that you may not sin. And if anyone sins, we have an Advocate with the Father, Jesus Christ the righteous; [2] and He Himself is the propitiation for our sins; and not for ours only, but also for *those of* the whole world.

1. God is transparent (truthful) with us and wants us to be transparent with Him.

2. Walking in the light does not mean living a sinless life. It means being honest with God about our sin.

3. The Greek word here translated "confess" could be translated "to agree with."

4. God fully knows we have sinned. When we confess, we are just agreeing with Him.

5. Jesus (our Advocate) represents us before the Father and pleads His blood on our behalf.

Dealing with Sin in the Life of the Believer

1 Corinthians 10:13
No temptation has overtaken you but such as is common to man; and God is faithful, who will not allow you to be tempted beyond what you are able, but with the temptation will provide the way of escape also, so that you will be able to endure it.

1 John 2:1–2
My little children, I am writing these things to you so that you may not sin. And if anyone sins, we have an Advocate with the Father, Jesus Christ the righteous; and He Himself is the propitiation for our sins; and not for ours only, but also for those of the whole world.

1 John 1:6
If we say that we have fellowship with Him and yet walk in the darkness, we lie and do not practice the truth.

1 John 1:9
If we confess our sins, He is faithful and righteous to forgive us our sins and to cleanse us from all unrighteousness.

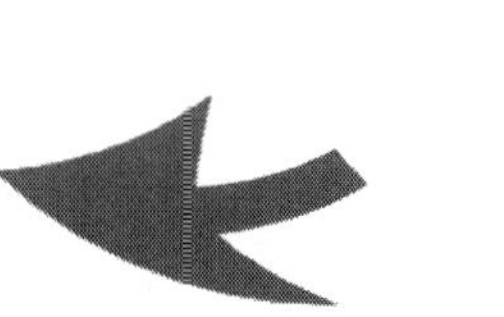

1 John 1:7
But if we walk in the Light as He himself is in the Light, we have fellowship with one another, and the blood of Jesus his Son cleanses us from all sin.

Reminder: Temptation is not sin. It only becomes sin when we act upon it.

VI. Spiritual Maturity and the Filling of the Holy Spirit

It is a distinct advantage to know the truth of God's Word concerning these important issues and to be able to identify the failures and discrepancies of various teachings that fall into error on this subject.

A. The Bible distinguishes three spiritual classifications of people.

1. The natural person

1 Corinthians 2:14–15

> [14] But a natural man does not accept the things of the Spirit of God, for they are foolishness to him; and he cannot understand them, because they are spiritually appraised. [15] But he who is spiritual appraises all things, yet he himself is appraised by no one.

Romans 8:9

> However, you are not in the flesh but in the Spirit, if indeed the Spirit of God dwells in you. But if anyone does not have the Spirit of Christ, he does not belong to Him.

a. The natural person is one who *does not* have the Holy Spirit. This person is not a Christian.

b. The natural person does not understand spiritual things because he or she does not have the Holy Spirit (the Teacher).

2. The worldly (fleshly) person

1 Corinthians 3:3

> for you are still fleshly. For since there is jealousy and strife among you, are you not fleshly, and are you not walking like mere men?

Romans 8:5–8

> [5] For those who are according to the flesh set their minds on the things of the flesh, but those who are according to the Spirit, the things of the Spirit. [6] For the mind set on the flesh is death, but the mind set on the Spirit is life and peace, [7] because the mind set on the flesh is hostile toward God; for it does not subject itself to the law of God, for it is not even able *to do so,* [8] and those who are in the flesh cannot please God.

a. The worldly person is a Christian, in whom the Holy Spirit dwells, but this person is controlled by fleshly desires and walks in sin.

b. The worldly person is addressed as a babe in Christ, not because this person is a new Christian, but because he or she is walking in the power of the flesh and has not experienced spiritual growth. The worldly person may have been a Christian for a long time, but with very little spiritual growth.

c. The worldly person is a Christian who is a "backslider" or a Christian who is not obedient to the Word of God.

d. The worldly person is hard to distinguish from the non-Christian because this person is acting "like mere men" or is conducting his or her life like someone without the Holy Spirit.

e. This kind of Christian very often causes great division in the church because he or she is self-centered rather than Christ-centered.

3. The spiritual person

Galatians 5:22–25

> [22] But the fruit of the Spirit is love, joy, peace, patience, kindness, goodness, faithfulness, [23] gentleness, self-control; against such things there is no law. [24] Now those who belong to Christ Jesus have crucified the flesh with its passions and desires.
>
> [25] If we live by the Spirit, let us also walk by the Spirit.

a. The spiritual person is the Christian who walks in the power of the Holy Spirit, and, though he or she is not sinless, he or she regularly experiences victory over sin.

b. The spiritual person is the obedient Christian who walks in harmony with the Spirit of God and allows the Holy Spirit to produce the "fruit of the Spirit" in and through his or her life.

c. This Christian daily seeks to meet the three conditions of the filling of the Holy Spirit, and his or her life is conducted in obedience to the Word of God.

- Do not resist the Holy Spirit.
- Deal with sin through confession.
- Live in the power of the Holy Spirit.

God's ideal is that we all might be spiritual Christians. It is one thing to know the right scriptural principles pertaining to the filling of the Holy Spirit and quite another thing to implement these principles and build them into our lives. While we are never commanded, or even encouraged, to seek the indwelling or the baptism of the Holy Spirit (because these are the results of our salvation), we are encouraged to "keep on being filled with the Spirit."

B. Spiritual maturity is a process.

It is possible for the believer to be filled with the Holy Spirit at any stage of his or her Christian experience, for God specifically exhorts us to be filled with the Spirit. There is another issue, however, that must not be neglected, which is spiritual growth. Spiritual growth is God's development of the Christian life and character by walking with God. This could also be called Christian maturity. Just as there is a physical, mental, and emotional growth process of a baby as it moves toward adulthood, there is also a spiritual growth process that takes place in the life of the obedient Christian. This process cannot be accomplished through a "quick-fix" spiritual experience. It is the result of healthy nourishment in the Word of God, the development of a personal love relationship with Christ through prayer, and the encouragement of the Body of Christ.

In Ephesians 5:18, the Greek word translated *be filled* is in the present imperative tense. It could be translated "keep on being filled." Instead of being constantly under the domination and influence of wine, be constantly dominated and obedient to the Spirit of God, as He empowers us to live godly lives and opens our hearts to God's Word. These verses refute the theory of a so-called "second blessing" that supposedly solves all the problems of the Christian life in one grand spiritual experience. Spiritual growth is the result of a moment-by-moment walk with the Spirit of God.

1. Peter encourages us to leave sinful practices and, as new Christians, to begin growing by studying simple truths (milk) in the Word of God. These simple truths will give us a greater understanding of our salvation.

1 Peter 2:1–2

> [1] Therefore, putting aside all malice and all deceit and hypocrisy and envy and all slander, [2] like newborn babies, long for the pure milk of the word, so that by it you may grow in respect to salvation,

2. We are encouraged to grow in the grace and knowledge of our Lord to become more like Jesus.

2 Peter 3:18

> but grow in the grace and knowledge of our Lord and Savior Jesus Christ. To Him *be* the glory, both now and to the day of eternity. Amen.

3. Paul adds in Ephesians that the purpose of those gifted as spiritual leaders and teachers is that they may become stronger in faith and knowledge and be able to avoid false teaching.

Ephesians 4:11–15

> [11] And He gave some *as* apostles, and some *as* prophets, and some *as* evangelists, and some *as* pastors and teachers, [12] for the equipping of the saints for the work of service, to the building up of the body of Christ; [13] until we all attain to the unity of the faith, and of the knowledge of the Son of God, to a mature man, to the measure of the stature which belongs to the fullness of Christ. [14] As a result, we are no longer to be children, tossed here and there by waves and carried about by every wind of doctrine, by the trickery of men, by craftiness in deceitful scheming; [15] but speaking the truth in love, we are to grow up in all *aspects* into Him who is the head, *even* Christ,

VII. The Erroneous Theory of Eradication of the Old Sinful Nature Has No Basis in Scripture

Some people erroneously teach that spiritual maturity is reached by an immediate sanctification or "second blessing." They teach that the old sinful nature is rooted out, or eradicated, and a state of sinless perfection is attained. There is no biblical support for such teaching. This thinking is a result of failure to discern biblical truth.

- A failure to accurately define sin. (See Chapter 7 – Hamartiology)
- A failure to distinguish between 1) positional truth that is a result of our relationship in Christ and 2) experiential truth that is the reality in our daily walk with Christ.

The following passages refute this theory:

Galatians 5:16–18

> [16] But I say, walk by the Spirit, and you will not carry out the desire of the flesh. [17] For the flesh sets its desire against the Spirit, and the Spirit against the flesh; for these are in opposition to one another, so that you may not do the things that you please. [18] But if you are led by the Spirit, you are not under the Law.

Romans 7:14–25

> [14] For we know that the Law is spiritual, but I am of flesh, sold into bondage to sin. [15] For what I am doing, I do not understand; for I am not practicing what I *would* like to *do*, but I am doing the very thing I hate. [16] But if I do the very thing I do not want *to do*, I agree with the Law, *confessing* that the Law is good. [17] So now, no longer am I the one doing it, but sin which dwells in me. [18] For I know that nothing good dwells in me, that is, in my flesh; for the willing is present in me, but the doing of the good *is* not. [19] For the good that I want, I do not do, but I practice the very evil that I do not want. [20] But if I am doing the very thing I do not want, I am no longer the one doing it, but sin which dwells in me.
>
> [21] I find then the principle that evil is present in me, the one who wants to do good. [22] For I joyfully concur with the law of God in the inner man, [23] but I see a different law in the members of my body, waging war against the law of my mind and making me a prisoner of the law of sin which is in my members. [24] Wretched man that I am! Who will set me free from the body of this death? [25] Thanks be to God through Jesus Christ our Lord! So then, on the one hand I myself with my mind am serving the law of God, but on the other, with my flesh the law of sin.

1 John 1:8–10

> [8] If we say that we have no sin, we are deceiving ourselves and the truth is not in us. [9] If we confess our sins, He is faithful and righteous to forgive us our sins and to cleanse us from all unrighteousness. [10] If we say that we have not sinned, we make Him a liar and His word is not in us.

The New Testament uses such terms as *righteousness* and *sanctification* sometimes with reference to our position in Christ and sometimes with reference to our daily lives. If we fail to discern from the contextual use of these terms, we will reach the wrong conclusions.

For example, our position before God is a result of having received Christ. Christ's own righteousness is accredited to us. Thus, we stand before God as righteous, even though from a practical standpoint, we may commit sin in our daily lives. Christ's righteousness is eternal and can never change.

A. The biblical meaning of *perfect or complete*

There are five Greek root words that are translated *perfect* in the New Testament. Of the five, only two have relevance to the doctrine of perfection, as related to sin.

1. Biblical meaning of the word *perfection*

    a. *Katartizo* has the idea of being complete in all details and ready for service. It refers to perfection in the sense of completeness. This word is used in classical writings of completing the installation of the intricate rigging of a sailing ship of that day. Once the hull was built, many months went into completing the ship so that it was ready for service. The Holy Spirit obviously uses this term to refer to the process of spiritual growth, which prepares the Christian for effective service.

    b. *Teleios* focuses on "having reached its end or being finished, completed, and perfected." This term is often used of persons, referring primarily to their physical development. It is also used in a moral or character sense, referring to a person who is fully mature.

1 Corinthians 2:6

> Yet we do speak wisdom among those who are mature *(teleios); a wisdom, however, not of this age nor of the rulers of this age, who are passing away;

2 Corinthians 13:9

> For we rejoice when we ourselves are weak but you are strong; this we also pray for, that you be made complete (katartizo).

2 Corinthians 13:11

> Finally, brethren, rejoice, be made complete (katartizo), be comforted, be like-minded, live in peace; and the God of love and peace will be with you.

Ephesians 4:12–13

> [12] for the equipping (katartizo) of the saints for the work of service, to the building up of the body of Christ; [13] until we all attain to the unity of the faith, and of the knowledge of the Son of God, to a mature (teleios) man, to the measure of the stature which belongs to the fullness of Christ.

2 Timothy 3:16–17

> [16] All Scripture is inspired by God and profitable for teaching, for reproof, for correction, for training in righteousness; [17] so that the man of God may be adequate (katartizo), equipped for every good work.

Philippians 3:15–16

> [15] Let us therefore, as many as are perfect (teleios), have this attitude; and if in anything you have a different attitude, God will reveal that also to you; [16] however, let us keep living by that same *standard* to which we have attained.

Colossians 3:14

> Beyond all these things *put on* love, which is the perfect (teleios) bond of unity.

Colossians 4:12

> Epaphras, who is one of your number, a bondslave of Jesus Christ, sends you his greetings, always laboring earnestly for you in his prayers, that you may stand perfect (teleios) and fully assured in all the will of God.

*Note: The parenthetical words have been added by author.

2. Biblical aspects of *perfection*

    a. Positional perfection – This belongs to all believers because they are accredited with the righteousness of Christ.

    b. Relative perfection – This must be indicated by the context of the scripture passage. Sometimes spiritual maturity is referred to as perfection.

    c. Ultimate perfection – This is referring to the eternal state of the godly, when the believer will be perfect in body, soul, and spirit.

B. The words *sanctify, sanctification*, or *holy*

The word *sanctify* comes from the Greek word *hagiazo* which means "to set apart for special treatment or purpose." The words *holy, sanctification, sanctuary*, and *saint* all come from the same root word. When these words are used to define God, it describes Him as unique and incomparable. (See chapter 3 of this book.)

The Hebrew word *qodesh* in its general use throughout the Old Testament means "to set apart for special use or the state of being set apart" and is generally translated "consecrate, sanctify, or holy."

Leviticus 21:8

> You shall consecrate him, therefore, for he offers the food of your God; he shall be holy to you; for I the LORD, who sanctifies you, am holy.

The New American Standard Bible gives a good example of the various ways the Hebrew word *godesh* can be translated. The same root word is used four times. It is translated once as "consecrate," it is translated twice as "holy," and it is translated once as "sanctifies." Sinless perfection is not implied in this word.

Note the following examples: *holy men, holy nation, holy things,* etc.

- These are holy according to a particular standard, which set them apart from other men, other nations, and other things. The Corinthian Christians were sanctified, and yet, Paul severely censored them for fleshly living and sinful practices. Paul used the Greek term *hagiazo* to define the Corinthians' positional sanctification. (1 Corinthians)
- Inanimate objects were often described as sanctified in scripture, especially in the Old Testament. We are not to conclude that these objects once had a sinful nature and, as a result of being sanctified, had that sinful nature removed.
- Many people who were said to be sanctified were called to higher degrees of righteous living, but there is no indication in scripture that these people had attained perfection.

An accurate understanding of the following words will help us clear up the teaching of scripture on this matter of the eradication of the sinful nature:

- Holy – the state of being set apart
- Sanctify – to set apart
- Saint – one who is set apart

These terms are used when referring to Israel as God's chosen people. These terms are sometimes used to refer to believers, but this does not necessarily refer to their character, walk, and daily life, but rather to their position in Christ.

VIII. Four Types of Sanctification Referred to in the Bible

A. General sanctification

This refers to someone or something that is set aside by God for special purposes.

Genesis 2:3

> Then God blessed the seventh day and sanctified it, because in it He rested from all His work which God had created and made.

1 Corinthians 7:13–14

> [13] And a woman who has an unbelieving husband, and he consents to live with her, she must not send her husband away. [14] For the unbelieving husband is sanctified through his wife, and the unbelieving wife is sanctified through her believing husband; for otherwise your children are unclean, but now they are holy.

B. Positional sanctification

In 1 Corinthians, Paul refers to all Christians at Corinth as "saints" even though some of them were not living up to the biblical standard of the Christian life. In Ephesians, Paul refers to the church (Christians) as being sanctified, not because everyone in the church was living a sinless life, but because each member was born again into the family of God.

1 Corinthians 1:2

> To the church of God which is at Corinth, to those who have been sanctified in Christ Jesus, saints by calling, with all who in every place call on the name of our Lord Jesus Christ, their *Lord* and ours:

Ephesians 5:25–27

> [25] Husbands, love your wives, just as Christ also loved the church and gave Himself up for her, [26] so that He might sanctify her, having cleansed her by the washing of water with the word, [27] that He might present to Himself the church in all her glory, having no spot or wrinkle or any such thing; but that she would be holy and blameless.

All believers are sanctified because of their position in Christ. Therefore, everyone in Christ is a *saint* before God. This bears no relationship to our daily life, except it is held before us as an incentive for godly living. Sanctification is ours by virtue of our having accepted Christ and by virtue of our position as a child of God. Perhaps the simplest explanation of this is that when we trust Christ as Savior, we are set aside as members of His own family.

1 John 3:2–3

> [2] Beloved, now we are children of God, and it has not appeared as yet what we will be. We know that when He appears, we will be like Him, because we will see Him just as He is. [3] And everyone who has this hope *fixed* on Him purifies himself, just as He is pure.

C. Ongoing (developing) sanctification

This refers to the believer's dedication to God and obedience to the Word of God. As the believer grows in Christ and yields himself or herself fully to God, he or she is set apart unto God by his or her own choice.

1 Peter 2:2

> like newborn babies, long for the pure milk of the word, so that by it you may grow in respect to salvation,

Ephesians 4:14–15

> [14] As a result, we are no longer to be children, tossed here and there by waves and carried about by every wind of doctrine, by the trickery of men, by craftiness in deceitful scheming; [15] but speaking the truth in love, we are to grow up in all *aspects* into Him who is the head, *even* Christ,

Romans 12:1–2

> [1] Therefore I urge you, brethren, by the mercies of God, to present your bodies a living and holy sacrifice, acceptable to God, *which is* your spiritual service of worship. [2] And do not be conformed to this world, but be transformed by the renewing of your mind, so that you may prove what the will of God is, that which is good and acceptable and perfect.

Ongoing sanctification is the process of turning away from sin and experiencing victory. Every time we have victory over sin, it is a *setting apart* of ourselves unto God and is, therefore, a personal sanctification.

D. Ultimate sanctification

This refers to our final perfection in heaven. We will finally be like Him.

1 John 3:1–3

> [1] See how great a love the Father has bestowed on us, that we would be called children of God; and *such* we are. For this reason the world does not know us, because it did not know Him. [2] Beloved, now we are children of God, and it has not appeared as yet what we will be. We know that when He appears, we will be like Him, because we will see Him just as He is. [3] And everyone who has this hope *fixed* on Him purifies himself, just as He is pure.

Ephesians 5:27

> that He might present to Himself the church in all her glory, having no spot or wrinkle or any such thing; but that she would be holy and blameless.

IX. Four Things God Has Provided to Make This Spiritual Growth Possible

God wants the new believer to pursue spiritual growth and spiritual maturity. New Christians are immature in a wisdom which comes through a knowledge of the Word of God. Spiritual growth comes as we walk in fellowship with Christ and other believers and through a consistent study of His Word. This growth brings the believer to be more and more *set apart* from the standards and practices of the world to living and serving in a way that is pleasing to God.

2 Peter 3:18 (Peter ends his 2nd epistle with this exhortation.)

> but grow in the grace and knowledge of our Lord and Savior Jesus Christ. To Him *be* the glory, both now and to the day of eternity. Amen.

A. The Word of God

1 Peter 2:2

> like newborn babies, long for the pure milk of the word, so that by it you may grow in respect to salvation,

Psalms 119:11

> Your word I have treasured in my heart,
> That I may not sin against You.

B. The intercessory prayer of Christ and the Holy Spirit

Hebrews 7:25

> Therefore He is able also to save forever those who draw near to God through Him, since He always lives to make intercession for them.

Romans 8:26

> In the same way the Spirit also helps our weakness; for we do not know how to pray as we should, but the Spirit Himself intercedes for *us* with groanings too deep for words;

C. The power and presence of the Holy Spirit in our lives

1 John 4:4

> You are from God, little children, and have overcome them; because greater is He who is in you than he who is in the world.

Galatians 5:16

> But I say, walk by the Spirit, and you will not carry out the desire of the flesh.

D. The Church (fellow believers)

1 Thessalonians 5:11

> Therefore encourage one another and build up one another, just as you also are doing.

Ephesians 4:11–16

> [11] And He gave some *as* apostles, and some *as* prophets, and some *as* evangelists, and some *as* pastors and teachers, [12] for the equipping of the saints for the work of service, to the building up of the body of Christ; [13] until we all attain to the unity of the faith, and of the knowledge of the Son of God, to a mature man, to the measure of the stature which belongs to the fullness of Christ. [14] As a result, we are no longer to be children, tossed here and there by waves and carried about by every wind of doctrine, by the trickery of men, by craftiness in deceitful scheming; [15] but speaking the truth in love, we are to grow up in all *aspects* into Him who is the head, *even* Christ, [16] from whom the whole body, being fitted and held together by what every joint supplies, according to the proper working of each individual part, causes the growth of the body for the building up of itself in love.

Hebrews 10:24–25

> [24] and let us consider how to stimulate one another to love and good deeds, [25] not forsaking our own assembling together, as is the habit of some, but encouraging *one another*; and all the more as you see the day drawing near.

X. Additional Works of the Holy Spirit

A. The sealing of the Holy Spirit

The sealing of the Holy Spirit is God's way of putting His seal on the new relationship between the believer and God.

1. Comparing the *sealing* of the Holy Spirit to the Roman seal, used in the first century, gives us a good picture of why this is an important work of the Holy Spirit.

    - A finished transaction – The Roman seal was used in business to signify a finished transaction. The sealing of the Holy Spirit points to the finished work of Christ in redeeming us.
    - Security and safety – The Roman seal was used to ensure security and safety by communicating the power and authority declared by the seal. The sealing of the Holy Spirit points to our security in Christ.
    - Declares ownership – The Roman seal was used to declare ownership. The sealing of the Holy Spirit speaks of God's ownership of the child of God.

    Ephesians 1:13–14

    > [13] In Him, you also, after listening to the message of truth, the gospel of your salvation—having also believed, you were sealed in Him with the Holy Spirit of promise, [14] who is given as a pledge of our inheritance, with a view to the redemption of *God's own* possession, to the praise of His glory.

    Ephesians 4:30

    > Do not grieve the Holy Spirit of God, by whom you were sealed for the day of redemption.

    1 Corinthians 6:19–20

    > [19] Or do you not know that your body is a temple of the Holy Spirit who is in you, whom you have from God, and that you are not your own? [20] For you have been bought with a price: therefore glorify God in your body.

2. These passages speak of both the indwelling of the Holy Spirit and the sealing of the Holy Spirit.

3. The indwelling and sealing of the Holy Spirit are not to be viewed as the same work.

4. The pledge (Ephesians 1:14) is the result of the sealing of the Holy Spirit.

5. The indwelling Holy Spirit is the seal.

6. The sealing of the Holy Spirit is a direct result of hearing the gospel and believing it unto salvation. The believer is sealed by the Holy Spirit at the very moment he or she trusts Christ for salvation.

7. There is a promise (a pledge) connected with the sealing of the Holy Spirit.

8. All believers are sealed by the Holy Spirit in that all believers are indwelt by the Holy Spirit.

9. The seal of the Holy Spirit looks forward to the coming of Christ (the "day of redemption").

10. The indwelling Holy Spirit is the "earnest" (down payment) of our redemption in the same way that earnest money is a pledge that the full purchase price of our redemption is paid. (Ephesians 4:30)

11. The sealing of the Holy Spirit expresses God's promise of full and complete redemption.

12. The "day of redemption" is the time of complete deliverance from all sin. It is the Rapture of the church, and that time when we will receive our new glorified bodies. (1 Corinthians 15:50–58)

B. The restraining work of the Holy Spirit

The restraining work of the Holy Spirit is the process of His opposition to the evil work of humankind and Satan. The believer in whom the Holy Spirit dwells often points out and opposes the evil in the world and, in doing so, restrains the evil one. When the church is raptured, the Holy Spirit leaves along with the church.

2 Thessalonians 2:3–9

> [3] Let no one in any way deceive you, for *it will not come* unless the apostasy comes first, and the man of lawlessness is revealed, the son of destruction, [4] who opposes and exalts himself above every so-called god or object of worship, so that he takes his seat in the temple of God, displaying himself as being God. [5] Do you not remember that while I was still with you, I was telling you these things? [6] And you know what restrains him now, so that in his time he will be revealed. [7] For the mystery of lawlessness is already at work; only he who now restrains *will do so* until he is taken out of the way. [8] Then that lawless one will be revealed whom the Lord will slay with the breath of His mouth and bring to an end by the appearance of His coming; [9] *that is*, the one whose coming is in accord with the activity of Satan, with all power and signs and false wonders,

1. The restraining of the Holy Spirit refers to restricting the evil intentions of man and Satan.

2. The restraining of the Holy Spirit may be carried on through various means but primarily through the influence of the Christian presence in the world.

3. The Holy Spirit indwells *every* believer.

4. The personal pronoun *He* is a reference to the Holy Spirit who will be taken "out of the way" when the church is raptured and taken out of the world.

5. When the Rapture takes place, the restraint of the Holy Spirit will be removed, clearing the way for the evil work of the anti-Christ.

6. When Christians are motivated by the Holy Spirit to speak out on moral issues (such as abortion, pornography, corruption, etc.), the Holy Spirit is working through believers to restrain the world from greater sin and degradation.

C. The convicting work of the Holy Spirit

John 16:7–11

> [7] But I tell you the truth, it is to your advantage that I go away; for if I do not go away, the Helper will not come to you; but if I go, I will send Him to you. [8] And He, when He comes, will convict the world concerning sin and righteousness and judgment; [9] concerning sin, because they do not believe in Me; [10] and concerning righteousness, because I go to the Father and you no longer see Me; [11] and concerning judgment, because the ruler of this world has been judged.

2 Corinthians 5:20

> Therefore, we are ambassadors for Christ, as though God were making an appeal through us; we beg you on behalf of Christ, be reconciled to God.

1. The convicting work of the Holy Spirit extends to everyone in the world.

2. The convicting work of the Holy Spirit is evident in believers who are living out their Christian lives under the control of the Holy Spirit.

3. Jesus came to represent the Father to the world.

4. Jesus spoke of sin, righteousness, and judgment.

5. Jesus promised His disciples that after He returned to His place with the Father, He would send the Holy Spirit to indwell every believer.

6. Since Jesus is no longer here living out the truth of the Father, the Holy Spirit continues to speak the truth through believers.

7. The Holy Spirit convicts the world (2 Corinthians 5:20):

   - of sin and the sinful condition of those without Christ.
   - of the righteousness that God requires, which is only available through the shed blood of Christ.
   - of judgment that rests upon all who reject the gospel of Christ. (John 3:18)

D. The regenerating work of the Holy Spirit

The regenerating work of the Holy Spirit is that process whereby the Holy Spirit gives new life to the believing sinner.

Titus 3:5

> He saved us, not on the basis of deeds which we have done in righteousness, but according to His mercy, by the washing of regeneration and renewing by the Holy Spirit,

John 3:3–8

> [3] Jesus answered and said to him, "Truly, truly, I say to you, unless one is born again he cannot see the kingdom of God."
>
> [4] Nicodemus said to Him, "How can a man be born when he is old? He cannot enter a second time into his mother's womb and be born, can he?" [5] Jesus answered, "Truly, truly, I say to you, unless one is born of water and the Spirit he cannot enter into the kingdom of God. [6] That which is born of the flesh is flesh, and that which is born of the Spirit is spirit. [7] Do not be amazed that I said to you, 'You must be born again.' [8] The wind blows where it wishes and you hear the sound of it, but do not know where it comes from and where it is going; so is everyone who is born of the Spirit."

1. The context here will reveal that Christ was speaking to Nicodemus, who by our standards, was a deeply religious and righteous person. His personal righteousness was not enough to secure eternal life. (John 3:3–8)

2. The "washing" in Titus 3:5 is a symbol of the Holy Spirit. It is not to be interpreted as water baptism.

3. Just as in physical birth, physical life is the result; so, in the second birth, spiritual and eternal life is obtained.

4. The giving of this new life is the regenerating work of the Holy Spirit. (John 3:5–6, 8)

5. The wind and its blowing are given to illustrate this work of regeneration. We *cannot* see the wind.

    - We cannot determine its source nor detect its destination. In the same way, the regeneration of the Holy Spirit is spiritual and unseen. (2 Corinthians 4:18)
    - We *can* see the results of the wind. Just as we can see the leaves blowing and the flag waving in the wind, so, too, we can observe the results of the regeneration of the Holy Spirit, which can be seen in the life of the believer.

6. The regenerating work of the Holy Spirit takes place at the instant a person trusts Christ as Savior.

7. Regeneration is not the result of pleasing God with good deeds and performing acts of righteousness. It is a free gift of grace.

8. Regeneration is the imparting of new life, resulting in eternal life. To the one who was spiritually dead because of sin, the Holy Spirit imparts spiritual life.

9. Regeneration is a reference to the new birth.

    Ephesians 2:5

    > even when we were dead in our transgressions, made us alive together with Christ (by grace you have been saved),

    2 Corinthians 5:17

    > Therefore if anyone is in Christ, *he is* a new creature; the old things passed away; behold, new things have come.

10. "In Christ" is a New Testament expression which refers to one who has trusted Christ for salvation. (Ephesians 1)

11. Regeneration is not simply making a transition in our lives that is more positive, it is actually becoming a new creature (a new creation of God the Holy Spirit).

Galatians 6:15

> For neither is circumcision anything, nor uncircumcision, but a new creation.

Ephesians 4:22–24

> [22] that, in reference to your former manner of life, you lay aside the old self, which is being corrupted in accordance with the lusts of deceit, [23] and that you be renewed in the spirit of your mind, [24] and put on the new self, which in *the likeness of* God has been created in righteousness and holiness of the truth.

12. The appetites in our lives that were displeasing to God are being removed as we grow in this new life.

13. Some of the ways this new life will be demonstrated:

    - Our language
    - Our habits
    - Our close friends
    - Places we frequent
    - Activities in which we participate
    - Our attitudes
    - Our conduct
    - Things we read
    - Movies and television we watch

14. In the same way, the "new creation" should produce new appetites that are introduced into the life of one who has trusted Christ as Savior. Some of these new appetites are:

    - A new appreciation for the Word of God
    - A new sensitivity to sin in our lives
    - A new admiration for what is right, true, and righteous
    - A new love for the people of God
    - A new interest in serving others
    - A desire that others should come to Christ
    - A new desire to please and serve God

Conclusion:

This work of the Holy Spirit is the imparting of new life and a new nature, which seeks to please God. Regeneration is noticeable only as we observe it in the new lifestyle of the Christian. Though it is not sinless perfection, new appetites emerge in the life of the one who is regenerated by the Holy Spirit. It is also the imparting of eternal life for those who were "dead in their trespasses and sins." This eternal life is received by faith and is the possession only of those who believe. Regeneration brings about a new nature. One becomes a child of God by actual regeneration through this work of the Holy Spirit.

Part 3: The Gifts of The Holy Spirit

Spiritual gifts are special aptitudes and abilities given to us by the Holy Spirit when we accept Christ as Savior. These gifts are to be used in ministering to one another in the church and carrying out the work of God.

I. Spiritual Gifts are Unlike our Natural Talents and Strengths

Someone may be gifted with a natural ability in the arts, mathematics, sports, or personality traits. These can be used in any context. People with these kinds of aptitudes may use their talent in the sports stadium, a concert hall, in a night club, or a political arena, but these are only natural talents often used for selfish purposes. After someone accepts Christ, that person might be able to use a natural gift as an avenue through which spiritual gifts may be exercised. However, the gifts of the Holy Spirit are to be used for ministry and for the glory of God.

- Natural talents and strengths were given by God through physical birth and can be developed by usage over time. (Psalms 139:13–16)
- The gifts of the Holy Spirit are given at the time of our second birth (salvation) and can be identified through following the leading of the Holy Spirit in ministry opportunities.
- The gifts of the Holy Spirit are given at the time of our second birth and should be developed through usage and dependance on the Holy Spirit.

Example: A Christian may be given the spiritual gift of teaching, but if he turns down every opportunity to teach, he may never even know he possesses the gift of teaching.

A. Spiritual gifts are given by the sovereign will of the Holy Spirit and cannot be earned or self-generated.

1 Corinthians 12:4–14

> [4] Now there are varieties of gifts, but the same Spirit. [5] And there are varieties of ministries, and the same Lord. [6] There are varieties of effects, but the same God who works all things in all *persons.* [7] But to each one is given the manifestation of the Spirit for the common good. [8] For to one is given the word of wisdom through the Spirit, and to another the word of knowledge according to the same Spirit; [9] to another faith by the same Spirit, and to another gifts of healing by the one Spirit, [10] and to another the effecting of miracles, and to another prophecy, and to another the distinguishing of spirits, to another *various* kinds of tongues, and to another the interpretation of tongues. [11] But one and the same Spirit works all these things, distributing to each one individually just as He wills.
>
> [12] For even as the body is one and *yet* has many members, and all the members of the body, though they are many, are one body, so also is Christ. [13] For by one Spirit we were all baptized into one body, whether Jews or Greeks, whether slaves or free, and we were all made to drink of one Spirit.
>
> [14] For the body is not one member, but many.

Romans 12:3

> For through the grace given to me I say to everyone among you not to think more highly of himself than he ought to think; but to think so as to have sound judgment, as God has allotted to each a measure of faith.

1. There is a diversity of spiritual gifts. (v. 4)
2. There is a variety of ministries in which the spiritual gifts can be used. (v. 5)
3. There are various effects (or results) when the gifts are used. (v. 6)
4. Every believer has at least one spiritual gift. (v. 7)
5. These special abilities are for the common good of every member of the church body. (v. 7)

6. Spiritual gifts are generated by the Spirit of God "just as He wills." (v. 11)

7. The Holy Spirit bestows these gifts as He pleases. They cannot be earned. They are gifts and are not to be a point of pride. (1 Corinthians 12:11, Romans 12:3)

8. These gifts are distributed at the time of salvation and are closely related to the baptism and indwelling of the Holy Spirit. They are given when the believer is installed into the Body of Christ, the church. (v. 12–13)

Romans 12:4–8

> [4] For just as we have many members in one body and all the members do not have the same function, [5] so we, who are many, are one body in Christ, and individually members one of another. [6] Since we have gifts that differ according to the grace given to us, *each of us is to exercise them accordingly*: if prophecy, according to the proportion of his faith; [7] if service, in his serving; or he who teaches, in his teaching; [8] or he who exhorts, in his exhortation; he who gives, with liberality; he who leads, with diligence; he who shows mercy, with cheerfulness.

1 Corinthians 12:7

> But to each one is given the manifestation of the Spirit for the common good.

9. Believers are not necessarily given the same gift or grouping of gifts. (v. 4)

10. All spiritual gifts are meant to complement one another. (Romans 12:5, 1 Corinthians 12:7)

11. When all the members are exercising their gifts, the body functions effectively. (vv. 5–6)

12. Believers are encouraged to exercise their gift(s) in harmony with others. (vv. 6–8)

B. Every believer possesses one or more spiritual gifts.

1. Wisdom of God expressed in the distribution of spiritual gifts

Ephesians 4:11–13

> [11] And He gave some *as* apostles, and some *as* prophets, and some *as* evangelists, and some *as* pastors and teachers, [12] for the equipping of the saints for the work of service, to the building up of the body of Christ; [13] until we all attain to the unity of the faith, and of the knowledge of the Son of God, to a mature man, to the measure of the stature which belongs to the fullness of Christ.

1 Corinthians 12:12

> For even as the body is one and *yet* has many members, and all the members of the body, though they are many, are one body, so also is Christ.

1 Corinthians 12:18

> But now God has placed the members, each one of them, in the body, just as He desired.

a. Every believer possesses at least one, and likely, a combination of spiritual gifts.

b. All believers possess spiritual gifts. (This includes men, women, children, teens, senior citizens.)

c. We tend to think that the only ones with spiritual gifts are:

- Church leaders
- Talented individuals
- Those with public speaking abilities
- Pastors, missionaries, and full-time Christian workers

2. The purpose of spiritual gifts

Spiritual gifts are given for the mutual building up of the spiritual lives of the Body of Christ, the church.

1 Corinthians 12:7

> But to each one is given the manifestation of the Spirit for the common good.

Ephesians 4:11–16

> [11] And He gave some *as* apostles, and some *as* prophets, and some *as* evangelists, and some *as* pastors and teachers, [12] for the equipping of the saints for the work of service, to the building up of the body of Christ; [13] until we all attain to the unity of the faith, and of the knowledge of the Son of God, to a mature man, to the measure of the stature which belongs to the fullness of Christ. [14] As a result, we are no longer to be children, tossed here and there by waves and carried about by every wind of doctrine, by the trickery of men, by craftiness in deceitful scheming; [15] but speaking the truth in love, we are to grow up in all *aspects* into Him who is the head, *even* Christ, [16] from whom the whole body, being fitted and held together by what every joint supplies, according to the proper working of each individual part, causes the growth of the body for the building up of itself in love.

a. Spiritual gifts are imparted for the profit of all in the church.

b. Spiritual gifts are imparted so the church might be built up in the things of God.

c. Spiritual gifts are imparted to prepare the church for effective service.

d. Spiritual gifts are imparted for the carrying out of the mission of the church.

Conclusions:

1. Spiritual gifts are special abilities, given to believers at the time of their conversion to allow them to have a special and unique ministry.

2. Spiritual gifts differ from natural talents in that they are given as a result of spiritual birth.

3. Spiritual gifts are given to us by the Spirit of God and are not the result of spiritual merit.

4. Every believer has at least one spiritual gift, and it is likely that most have more than one.

5. All Christians have a unique ministry in which to use their gift(s) in a distinctive way that cannot be exactly duplicated by any other believer.

6. The purpose of these gifts is for the building up of the Body of Christ for the accomplishment of the ultimate mission of sharing Christ with the world.

II. Two Divisions of Gifts

Sign gifts – These are supernatural gifts given to the early church leaders to signify that the writings and teachings of the apostles were of God. These were necessary until the writing of the New Testament was completed.

Ministry gifts – These are gifts given for the edification of the church.

A. Sign gifts

Certain gifts of the Spirit were given to the apostles and other Christians before the writing of the New Testament was completed. These gifts were given as a sign of God's stamp of approval on the radically new ministry and teaching of the apostles. Once the text of the New Testament and the message of the gospel was clearly established, these sign gifts were no longer necessary. There is a definite pattern in the Book of Acts concerning the frequency of the use of these gifts. As the message was established, the occurrence of these sign gifts tapered off. These sign gifts are referred to many times in the New Testament. Though it is not beyond the power of God to use miracles today, those who claim to possess these gifts seem to be more interested in calling attention to themselves rather than to the glory of God. For example, God may heal anyone at any time from any disease, and we can call upon Him to do so through fervent prayer. The notion that anyone today who claims to have the gift of healing and alleges to be able to exercise that gift at any time, may make for a *great show* but this is just not a reality.

1. The Purpose of Sign Gifts

Hebrews 2:3–4

> [3] how will we escape if we neglect so great a salvation? After it was at the first spoken through the Lord, it was confirmed to us by those who heard, [4] God also testifying with them, both by signs and wonders and by various miracles and by gifts of the Holy Spirit according to His own will.

a. The human author of the book of Hebrews is referring to the great salvation found in Christ Jesus.

b. Salvation was proclaimed through Christ while He taught here on earth.

c. The message of salvation was confirmed again by those who heard Jesus preach and teach.

d. The Spirit of God joined in the establishing of the message by bestowing miraculous gifts to those who were preaching and teaching after Christ returned to heaven.

e. These miraculous gifts were given by the sovereign will of the Holy Spirit.

Mark 16:14–20

> [14] Afterward He appeared to the eleven themselves as they were reclining *at the table*; and He reproached them for their unbelief and hardness of heart, because they had not believed those who had seen Him after He had risen. [15] And He said to them, "Go into all the world and preach the gospel to all creation. [16] He who has believed and has been baptized shall be saved; but he who has disbelieved shall be condemned. [17] These signs will accompany those who have believed: in My name they will cast out demons, they will speak with new tongues; [18] they will pick up serpents, and if they drink any deadly *poison*, it will not hurt them; they will lay hands on the sick, and they will recover."
>
> [19] So then, when the Lord Jesus had spoken to them, He was received up into heaven and sat down at the right hand of God. [20] And they went out and preached everywhere, while the Lord worked with them, and confirmed the word by the signs that followed.

f. The disciples met with Jesus just before His ascension.

g. Jesus teaches concerning miraculous signs that would follow, after He ascended into heaven. (vv. 17–18)

h. Notice how carefully Jesus tied all these miraculous signs to believing the gospel of Christ. (vv. 14–16)

i. Following Jesus' ascension, the disciples did preach the gospel, and it was confirmed with signs and wonders. (v. 20)

j. This supernatural activity was implemented after Jesus' ascension into heaven because:

- The New Testament had not yet been written.
- What God was about to do, through His apostles, needed to be established as God's work and God's message.

John 4:48

So Jesus said to him, "Unless you *people* see signs and wonders, you *simply* will not believe."

Acts 2:21–22

[21] 'AND IT SHALL BE THAT EVERYONE WHO CALLS ON THE NAME OF THE LORD WILL BE SAVED.'

[22] "Men of Israel, listen to these words: Jesus the Nazarene, a man attested to you by God with miracles and wonders and signs which God performed through Him in your midst, just as you yourselves know—"

Acts 2:43

Everyone kept feeling a sense of awe; and many wonders and signs were taking place through the apostles.

Acts 4:30

"while You extend Your hand to heal, and signs and wonders take place through the name of Your holy servant Jesus."

Acts 5:12

At the hands of the apostles many signs and wonders were taking place among the people; and they were all with one accord in Solomon's portico.

Acts 8:9–16

[9] Now there was a man named Simon, who formerly was practicing magic in the city and astonishing the people of Samaria, claiming to be someone great; [10] and they all, from smallest to greatest, were giving attention to him, saying, "This man is what is called the Great Power of God." [11] And they were giving him attention because he had for a long time astonished them with his magic arts. [12] But when they believed Philip preaching the good news about the kingdom of God and the name of Jesus Christ, they were being baptized, men and women alike. [13] Even Simon himself believed; and after being baptized, he continued on with Philip, and as he observed signs and great miracles taking place, he was constantly amazed.

> [14] Now when the apostles in Jerusalem heard that Samaria had received the word of God, they sent them Peter and John, [15] who came down and prayed for them that they might receive the Holy Spirit. [16] For He had not yet fallen upon any of them; they had simply been baptized in the name of the Lord Jesus.

Note: Simon, who was a man who knew the power of signs and wonders to sway people, was amazed at the great miracles that were taking place through the apostles (v. 13). He believed as a result of the signs and wonders. He later erroneously coveted these miraculous gifts and was sternly rebuked by Peter and told that these gifts could not be purchased with money.

Acts 14:3 (Paul preaching at Iconium)

> Therefore they spent a long time *there* speaking boldly *with reliance* upon the Lord, who was testifying to the word of His grace, granting that signs and wonders be done by their hands.

Acts 15:12

> All the people kept silent, and they were listening to Barnabas and Paul as they were relating what signs and wonders God had done through them among the Gentiles.

k. The New Testament speaks much of the purpose of supernatural signs and wonders.

l. As you carefully study the flow of the Book of Acts, you will find a definite pattern concerning the frequency and the use of these gifts of signs and wonders.

m. During this time, the books of the New Testament were being written and accepted by the church as the Word of God.

n. As time went on and the writing of the New Testament was completed, the need for these confirmation miracles was progressively less necessary.

o. With a few exceptions (Stephen, Barnabas, etc.), these gifts of signs and wonders were limited to circumstances surrounding the ministry of the writing apostles.

Romans 15:19

> in the power of signs and wonders, in the power of the Spirit; so that from Jerusalem and round about as far as Illyricum I have fully preached the gospel of Christ.

p. The context of Romans 15:19 will reveal that Paul is giving verification of his ministry to a church he had never visited.

q. It is not surprising that he would write concerning the signs and wonders he had done in the power of the Spirit.

1 Corinthians 14:22

> So then tongues are for a sign, not to those who believe but to unbelievers; but prophecy *is for a sign*, not to unbelievers but to those who believe.

2 Corinthians 12:12

> The signs of a true apostle were performed among you with all perseverance, by signs and wonders and miracles.

r. Paul is writing concerning spiritual gifts in 1 Corinthians 12, 13, and 14.

s. Paul makes it clear that the gift of tongues is a sign gift.

t. Paul uses signs, wonders, and miracles to verify his apostleship and ministry.

2. Signs and wonders were not new to God's methods:

a. Miracles were used in the past to validate the prophet and his message.

- Moses' message to the Jews and Egypt
- Elijah and Elisha's message during the days of spiritual darkness in Israel
- A confirmation of Jesus' true identity in the Gospels

b. Sign gifts were given to establish the validity and authenticity of the apostles' message.

3. The character of these sign gifts:

a. They were miraculous in character.

b. They were designed to draw the attention of people to a messenger and his message.

c. They were designed to show God's blessing and approval upon a messenger and his message.

d. Once the message was established there was no need for the sign to continue.

e. These sign gifts needed to be verified as miraculous in order to be valid signs to the world.

4. New Testament Examples of Sign Gifts

a. The gift of prophecy – A prophet has two functions: the proclamation of God's Word and the revelation of future events.

1) The gift of prophecy is a sign gift in respect to foretelling the future.

Acts 11:27–28 (Agabus predicted the famine in the world.)

> [27] Now at this time some prophets came down from Jerusalem to Antioch. [28] One of them named Agabus stood up and *began* to indicate by the Spirit that there would certainly be a great famine all over the world. And this took place in the *reign* of Claudius.

Acts 21:10–11 (Agabus warned Paul of the sufferings that awaited him in Jerusalem.)

> [10] As we were staying there for some days, a prophet named Agabus came down from Judea. [11] And coming to us, he took Paul's belt and bound his own feet and hands, and said, "This is what the Holy Spirit says: 'In this way the Jews at Jerusalem will bind the man who owns this belt and deliver him into the hands of the Gentiles.'"

2) The gift of prophecy is a sign gift in respect to proclaiming the Word of God.

1 Corinthians 12:28–29

> [28] And God has appointed in the church, first apostles, second prophets, third teachers, then miracles, then gifts of healings, helps, administrations, *various* kinds of tongues. [29] All are not apostles, are they? All are not prophets, are they? All are not teachers, are they? All are not *workers of* miracles, are they?

Romans 12:6

> Since we have gifts that differ according to the grace given to us, *each of us is to exercise them accordingly*: if prophecy, according to the proportion of his faith;

b. The gift of miracles

Miraculous gifts are listed among the lesser gifts. (1 Corinthians 12:28–29)

c. The gift of healing

Acts 3:1–9

> [1] Now Peter and John were going up to the temple at the ninth *hour*, the hour of prayer. [2] And a man who had been lame from his mother's womb was being carried along, whom they used to set down every day at the gate of the temple which is called Beautiful, in order to beg alms of those who were entering the temple. [3] When he saw Peter and John about to go into the temple, he *began* asking to receive alms. [4] But Peter, along with John, fixed his gaze on him and said, "Look at us!" [5] And he *began* to give them his attention, expecting to receive something from them. [6] But Peter said, "I do not possess silver and gold, but what I do have I give to you: In the name of Jesus Christ the Nazarene—walk!" [7] And seizing him by the right hand, he raised him up; and immediately his feet and his ankles were strengthened. [8] With a leap he stood upright and *began* to walk; and he entered the temple with them, walking and leaping and praising God. [9] And all the people saw him walking and praising God;

Acts 19:11–12

> [11] God was performing extraordinary miracles by the hands of Paul, [12] so that handkerchiefs or aprons were even carried from his body to the sick, and the diseases left them and the evil spirits went out.

d. The gift of tongues

Acts 2:1–12

> [1] When the day of Pentecost had come, they were all together in one place. [2] And suddenly there came from heaven a noise like a violent rushing wind, and it filled the whole house where they were sitting. [3] And there appeared to them tongues as of fire distributing themselves, and they rested on each one of them. [4] And they were all filled with the Holy Spirit and began to speak with other tongues, as the Spirit was giving them utterance.

> [5] Now there were Jews living in Jerusalem, devout men from every nation under heaven. [6] And when this sound occurred, the crowd came together, and were bewildered because each one of them was hearing them speak in his own language. [7] They were amazed and astonished, saying, "Why, are not all these who are speaking Galileans? [8] And how is it that we each hear *them* in our own language to which we were born? [9] Parthians and Medes and Elamites, and residents of Mesopotamia, Judea and Cappadocia, Pontus and Asia, [10] Phrygia and Pamphylia, Egypt and the districts of Libya around Cyrene, and visitors from Rome, both Jews and proselytes, [11] Cretans and Arabs—we hear them in our *own* tongues speaking of the mighty deeds of God." [12] And they all continued in amazement and great perplexity, saying to one another, "What does this mean?"

The Greek word translated *tongues* in the New Testament is *glossa* (pronounced – gloce-sah'). The word is used to describe a language, especially a language naturally unacquired. Glossa is particularly evident here in Acts 2 when many were surprised that these unlearned disciples were able to speak in foreign languages. This was obviously a sign gift, which caught the attention of all those present in the crowd. Notice how amazed and confused they were at this phenomenon.

1 Corinthians 14:28 tells us that the gift of tongues was only to be used on limited occasions when an interpreter of the tongue was present. Contrary to the popularity of this gift in some churches today, it was reported only three times in the entire book of Acts. (Acts 2, Acts 10, and Acts 19) It is seen each time God did something new and different in the days of the early church.

B. Ministry gifts

Ministry gifts are found and employed in the church today.

1. The purpose of the ministry gifts

   a. To minister to the needs of fellow believers

   b. To be used in the context of a spiritual ministry

   c. To be used in harmony with the spiritual gifts of others in the church

   d. To encourage spiritual growth of one another in love

   e. To meet the needs of the ministry of the church

   f. To reach out to those in need of the gospel

(Carefully read 1 Corinthians 12 and 13.)

2. General observations concerning the ministry gifts

   a. A partial list of the character and functions of the ministry gifts

      - Faith – An unusual ability to trust God with a strong and unshakeable assurance in His Word and His promises
      - Teaching – An exceptional ability to teach the Word of God and make it come alive to the hearers
      - Giving – A special longing and joy, accompanied by resources, to meet the needs of others and support the work of God
      - Mercy – A special ability to understand and respond to the spiritual, emotional, and physical hurts of others
      - Exhortation – The ability to guide and graciously encourage others to make wise and godly choices in life
      - Leadership/Administration – A special aptitude to sort through the details and render the work of God to be more efficient and effective
      - Helps – An exceptional ability to see and respond to small details, resulting in serving others and the ministry of the church
      - Evangelism – An extraordinary appetite and effectiveness in sharing the gospel and leading others to salvation in Christ
      - Pastor/Teacher – A gifting in leadership, communication, and vision, with a special ability to wisely lead the ministry of the local church

   b. Spiritual gifts do not excuse other believers from exercising their responsibilities in these ministry areas.

      Examples:

      - All believers are instructed to give, even though we may not have the gift of giving.
      - All believers should be sharing the gospel with the lost, even though we may not have the gift of evangelism.
      - All believers are called upon to help, even though we may not have the gift of helps.
      - As believers, we may not have the gift of faith, but we are to trust God in all things.

   c. Satan is often quick to twist these gifts and tempt us to use them for selfish reasons.

Examples:

- Teaching – Using this gift to build ourselves up in pride.
- Giving – Using our wealth to control the church.
- Exhortation – Bullying others for selfish purposes.
- Leadership – Using this gift to manipulate others.
- Evangelism – Becoming critical of others who do not have the same passion.

REVIEW QUESTIONS

1. Is the Holy Spirit a person? Explain your answer.
2. Prove the deity of the Holy Spirit.
3. Name the six symbols of the Holy Spirit and give the characteristics of each.
4. Why is this age sometimes called the age of the Holy Spirit?
5. Name three distinctions between the work of the Holy Spirit in the Old Testament and the work of the Holy Spirit during this age.
6. Name and define five ministries of the Holy Spirit.
7. Are all believers indwelt by the Holy Spirit? Verify your answer with scripture.
8. Name two results of the baptism of the Holy Spirit.
9. When are believers baptized by the Holy Spirit?
10. Name three things the Holy Spirit does the moment an individual is saved.
11. What is the filling of the Holy Spirit?
12. Define the following: the natural person, the worldly (fleshly) person, and the spiritual person.
13. Is there any difference between spirituality and maturity? Explain your answer.
14. Can some believers receive more of the Holy Spirit?
15. Name the three conditions for the Holy Spirit's filling.
16. Write out the text of 1 Thessalonians 5:19.
17. How does someone quench the Holy Spirit?
18. How does someone grieve the Holy Spirit?
19. Can believers rid themselves of the sin nature in this life?
20. What is the key word for restoration of fellowship for those who have sinned?
21. What happens to the believer who does not confess his sin? (See 1 John 1)

22. What is the so-called *second blessing* theory?

23. Name and explain the four types of sanctification.

24. Name three things God gives believers to help them experience victory over sin.

25. What are spiritual gifts?

26. Name the two general classifications of spiritual gifts.

27. Why were some gifts given to the early church?

28. Does God ever heal today?

29. Does the gift of tongues make use of actual languages?

30. How do the tongues in the Book of Acts differ from those mentioned in 1 Corinthians 12–14?

31. What was the purpose of tongues in the New Testament?

32. Can every Spirit filled believer expect to speak in tongues?

33. Is speaking in tongues a test of spirituality?

CHAPTER 7

Hamartiology
(What the Bible Teaches About Sin)

Introduction:

Nothing has brought more sorrow, trouble, and havoc into the world than sin. We find its effects all around us. We see its presence within us. We live in a world that is torn apart by it. Yet it is difficult for us to define it and analyze its effects. Because we are by nature sinful and selfish, we tend to excuse ourselves and fail to see sin as God sees it. We are often so involved in sin ourselves; we tend to see it from a distorted point of view. Criminologists agree that every crime is justified in the mind of the perpetrator before it is committed. We cannot trust ourselves to define sin accurately.

Jeremiah 17:9

"The heart is more deceitful than all else
And is desperately sick;
Who can understand it?"

In any culture where sin is eroding the morals of a nation or a society, there is a grave danger of redefining sin to the extent that it becomes nonexistent. When sin is no longer accurately defined, the whole society suffers. History records the grave results of human conduct in which entire nations have justified unspeakable atrocities. A case closer to home is the tolerance and justification of killing millions of babies in the womb.

Isaiah 5:20

Woe to those who call evil good, and good evil;
Who substitute darkness for light and light for darkness;
Who substitute bitter for sweet and sweet for bitter!

Because we are by nature sinners, we tend to grade our morals by focusing on the actions of others. If we can find others who are more sinful than ourselves, we tend to justify our own wickedness by pointing our finger at them. Often even Christians rationalize away sinful practices by following just one step behind the world's standards.

Ephesians 4:17–24

> [17] So this I say, and affirm together with the Lord, that you walk no longer just as the Gentiles also walk, in the futility of their mind, [18] being darkened in their understanding, excluded from the life of God because of the ignorance that is in them, because of the hardness of their heart; [19] and they, having become callous, have given themselves over to sensuality for the practice of every kind of impurity with greediness. [20] But you did not learn Christ in this way, [21] if indeed you have heard Him and have been taught in Him, just as truth is in Jesus, [22] that, in reference to your former manner of life, you lay aside the old self, which is being corrupted in accordance with the lusts of deceit, [23] and that you be renewed in the spirit of your mind, [24] and put on the new self, which in *the likeness of* God has been created in righteousness and holiness of the truth.

Since God is the only person without sin, and since He is the one who is chiefly offended by it, He is the only one qualified to define it and describe accurately its devastating effects. In this chapter, we will see what God's Word has to say about sin.

There is a great need among the people of God to see sin as God sees it. Then, and only then, will we begin to live lives in direct contrast to those who do not know the reality of salvation in Christ. People without a relationship with Christ should not dictate the standards of our morality. God is our standard. The mandate given to Moses in Leviticus 19:2 is for us also. "You shall be holy, for I the LORD your God am holy." Studying the subject of sin will not change your lifestyle and bring it into harmony with God's righteousness. We must see our sin as God sees it. Here again, we are reminded of the importance of keeping our spiritual growth in agreement with our Bible knowledge.

I. The Origin of Sin

A. Sin began in the heavenly realm with Satan's rebellion against God.

Isaiah 14:12–15

> [12] "How you have fallen from heaven,
> O star of the morning, son of the dawn!
> You have been cut down to the earth,
> You who have weakened the nations!
> [13] "But you said in your heart,
> 'I will ascend to heaven;
> I will raise my throne above the stars of God,
> And I will sit on the mount of assembly
> In the recesses of the north.

> [14] 'I will ascend above the heights of the clouds;
> I will make myself like the Most High.'
> [15] "Nevertheless you will be thrust down to Sheol,
> To the recesses of the pit."

1. Lucifer's plan was to take over control and become the supreme being.
   - By unseating God from His position
   - By replacing God with himself
   - By creating his own set of self-serving rules

2. Lucifer's five-fold "I will" statement recorded here illustrates this very vividly. Our sin follows this same pattern. (Isaiah 14:13-14)

3. Sin is an act of rebellion against God.
   - Sin is an act of the will, not a mistake.
   - We would *like* to think that sin is just a little blunder.
   - Perhaps we see sin as a flaw in judgment or an act of ignorance.
   - We might blame our sin on a personal weakness.
   - In the eyes of God, sin is the willful act of disobedience for which we are accountable to Him.

4. Sin is an act of self-destruction.
   - Lucifer's request for freedom from God was granted.
   - He was eternally separated from God.
   - He wanted independence, and God gave him his independence. (Isaiah 14:12)

5. Sin brings the judgment of God.
   - Satan became the object of the wrath of God.
   - There is a tremendous price to pay for sin. (Isaiah 14:15)

James 1:13–15

> [13] Let no one say when he is tempted, "I am being tempted by God"; for God cannot be tempted by evil, and He Himself does not tempt anyone. [14] But each one is tempted when he is carried away and enticed by his own lust. [15] Then when lust has conceived, it gives birth to sin; and when sin is accomplished, it brings forth death.

Genesis 3:1–6

> [1] Now the serpent was more crafty than any beast of the field which the LORD God had made. And he said to the woman, "Indeed, has God said, 'You shall not eat from any tree of the garden'?" [2] The woman said to the serpent, "From the fruit of the trees of the garden we may eat; [3] but from the fruit of the tree which is in the middle of the garden, God has said, 'You shall not eat from it or touch it, or you will die.'" [4] The serpent said to the woman, "You surely will not die! [5] For God knows that in the day you eat from it your eyes will be opened, and you will be like God, knowing good and evil." [6] When the woman saw that the tree was good for food, and that it was a delight to the eyes, and that the tree was desirable to make *one* wise, she took from its fruit and ate; and she gave also to her husband with her, and he ate.

Titus 1:15–16

> [15] To the pure, all things are pure; but to those who are defiled and unbelieving, nothing is pure, but both their mind and their conscience are defiled. [16] They profess to know God, but by *their* deeds they deny *Him*, being detestable and disobedient and worthless for any good deed.

6. Titus 1:15a – This does not mean that Christians can do anything they want. Sin is sin.
7. Those who choose to live a godly life produce pure and godly behavior.
8. Titus 1:15b–16 – In contrast to the godly person, those who say they know God but do not live according to the truth, deny the Lord by their conduct.
9. By an act of the will, the unbelieving and defiled choose and produce only disobedience.
10. By an act of the will, the ungodly choose evil and are not bothered by a guilty conscience.
11. These disobedient individuals can be identified by their attitude, lifestyle, and behavior.

B. The cost of sin is death.

Romans 6:23

> For the wages of sin is death, but the free gift of God is eternal life in Christ Jesus our Lord.

Ephesians 2:1–2

> [1] And you were dead in your trespasses and sins, [2] in which you formerly walked according to the course of this world, according to the prince of the power of the air, of the spirit that is now working in the sons of disobedience.

1. Sin separates from God. The basic meaning of the word *death* is "separation."

2. Because our sin was placed on Him, Jesus cried out from the cross, "MY GOD, MY GOD, WHY HAVE YOU FORSAKEN ME?" (Matthew 27:46)

3. Jesus knew why He had been separated from the Father. Jesus suffered and died alone on the cross because He took our sin upon Himself and suffered death in full payment for *our* sin.

4. This question was not asked because Jesus was wondering why this was happening to Him. It was to testify to the fact and acknowledge that He was indeed separated from the Father for our sins.

5. The gift of eternal life is free for us who believe because Jesus fully paid for our sin. Therefore, we are pardoned.

II. The Definition of Sin

The Bible does not in any one place give us a complete definition of sin. It is our responsibility to use the Word of God as a whole and to analyze its references to sin. We must formulate a definition of sin that will be broad enough to cover everything but narrow enough not to add things like traditions, cultural taboos, or distasteful things. There are many passages of scripture that declare the various features of sin. The following are some examples:

1 John 3:4

> Everyone who practices sin also practices lawlessness; and sin is lawlessness.

1 John 5:17a

> All unrighteousness is sin

Romans 14:23 (Paul writes concerning meat offered to idols.)

> But he who doubts is condemned if he eats, because *his eating is* not from faith; and whatever is not from faith is sin.

James 4:16–17

> [16] But as it is, you boast in your arrogance; all such boasting is evil. [17] Therefore, to one who knows *the* right thing to do and does not do it, to him it is sin.

Proverbs 20:23

> Differing weights are an abomination to the LORD,
> And a false scale is not good.

Proverbs 21:4

> Haughty eyes and a proud heart,
> The lamp of the wicked, is sin.

Proverbs 6:16–19

> [16] There are six things which the LORD hates,
> Yes, seven which are an abomination to Him:
> [17] Haughty eyes, a lying tongue,
> And hands that shed innocent blood,
> [18] A heart that devises wicked plans,
> Feet that run rapidly to evil,
> [19] A false witness *who* utters lies,
> And one who spreads strife among brothers.

A. Hebrew words that are translated *sin* in the Old Testament

1. There are many Hebrew words in the Old Testament that are translated *sin*. These words vary in their shades of meaning. We will not take time or space to have a lesson in Hebrew, but here are the definitions of some of these Hebrew words:

    - bent
    - twisted
    - rebellion
    - pride
    - a habit of evil
    - apostasy
    - crooked
    - revolt against rightful authority
    - transgression
    - vanity
    - crossing over a line

- wandering astray
- stubbornness
- hardness of heart
- to miss the mark

2. The most used word for *sin* in the Old Testament literally signifies "to miss the mark."

B. Greek words that are translated *sin* in the New Testament

1. There are many expressions of *sin* in our New Testament English translations. Some of these words are:

   - wickedness
   - ungodliness
   - unrighteousness
   - covetousness
   - enmity
   - debt
   - lawlessness
   - failure
   - violation of a precept

2. Many specific sins are listed in the New Testament. (For examples of some specific sins, read Galatians 5:19–21.)

3. There are nine words in the Greek New Testament used to describe sin:

   - *Hamartia* – to miss the mark
   - *Hamartema* – to miss the mark
   - *Parabasis* – overstepping or transgressing of a line or trespassing into a forbidden area
   - *Parakoa* – failing to be attentive to a voice or disobedience to a voice
   - *Paraptoma* – a falling down where one should have stood upright
   - *Paranomia* or *anomia* – non-observance of the law; lawlessness, without law, or anarchy
   - *Attama* – coming short of one's duty; failing to carry out one's duty
   - *Agnoana* – ignorance of what should have been known
   - *Plammeleia* – a discord in the harmonies of God's universe

4. The word for *sin* most used in the New Testament is the word *harmartia*, meaning "to miss the mark." This word includes both the sinful action and nature of sin. This word appears more than 200 times in the New Testament.

5. Judges 20:16 gives an illustration of amazing marksmanship.

Judges 20:16

Out of all these people 700 choice men were left-handed; each one could sling a stone at a hair and not miss.

6. Anything less than that of slinging a stone and hitting the hair is "to miss the mark." Missing the mark can represent a sinful condition, a wicked act, or an evil habit. It is a missing of the divine will or goal; a going beyond, falling short, a turning aside from God's own perfect righteousness.

C. An all-inclusive and biblical definition of sin

1. With the information stated in this chapter and scripture passages as a background, various individuals have attempted to formulate a biblical definition of sin. Here are just a few of those definitions:

    - Sin is the lack of conformity to the law of God.
    - Sin is a willful transgression of the law.
    - Sin is selfishness.
    - Sin is the lack of conformity to the holy character of God.

2. While each of these simple definitions have value, none of them appear to be broad enough to incorporate *all* of what the Bible teaches us about sin.

D. False ideas concerning sin

1. Sin is a sickness.

    Some people like to think of sin as something for which they take no responsibility, like a sickness. Sin may result in sickness, but sin is not sickness. Sickness is used often in the Bible as an illustration of sin, but sin is much more than a sickness. Drunkenness, illicit drug abuse, and gluttony are sinful, which can result in sickness, but it is the sinful practice of these things which are at the heart of the matter.

    Notice what the book of Proverbs has to say about this:

    Proverbs 23:19–34

    [19] Listen, my son, and be wise,
    And direct your heart in the way.
    [20] Do not be with heavy drinkers of wine,
    Or with gluttonous eaters of meat;
    [21] For the heavy drinker and the glutton will come to poverty,
    And drowsiness will clothe *one* with rags.

[22] Listen to your father who begot you,
And do not despise your mother when she is old.
[23] Buy truth, and do not sell *it*,
Get wisdom and instruction and understanding.
[24] The father of the righteous will greatly rejoice,
And he who sires a wise son will be glad in him.
[25] Let your father and your mother be glad,
And let her rejoice who gave birth to you.

[26] Give me your heart, my son,
And let your eyes delight in my ways.
[27] For a harlot is a deep pit
And an adulterous woman is a narrow well.
[28] Surely she lurks as a robber,
And increases the faithless among men.

[29] Who has woe? Who has sorrow?
Who has contentions? Who has complaining?
Who has wounds without cause?
Who has redness of eyes?
[30] Those who linger long over wine,
Those who go to taste mixed wine.
[31] Do not look on the wine when it is red,
When it sparkles in the cup,
When it goes down smoothly;
[32] At the last it bites like a serpent
And stings like a viper.
[33] Your eyes will see strange things
And your mind will utter perverse things.
[34] And you will be like one who lies down in the middle of the sea,
Or like one who lies down on the top of a mast.

2. Sin is an accident.

Some believe sin entered the world as an unfortunate event of chance, consequently bringing little or no guilt upon humankind. The Bible teaches that Adam and Eve willfully disobeyed God's only mandate. The Bible everywhere holds us responsible for our sinful attitudes and deeds. The following verses in the book of Proverbs teaches that we are fully responsible for our sinful actions:

Proverbs 5:21

> For the ways of a man are before the eyes of the LORD,
> And He watches all his paths.

Proverbs 15:3

> The eyes of the LORD are in every place,
> Watching the evil and the good.

Proverbs 16:2

> All the ways of a man are clean in his own sight,
> But the LORD weighs the motives.

Proverbs 21:2

> Every man's way is right in his own eyes,
> But the LORD weighs the hearts.

3. Sin is non-existent.

Much of modern psychology teaches that there is no such thing as right and wrong. Many people blame all our emotional problems on a sense of guilt brought about by the instruction of parents and clergy. With this attitude they seek to eliminate all sense of moral standards.

Romans 3:19

> Now we know that whatever the Law says, it speaks to those who are under the Law, so that every mouth may be closed and all the world may become accountable to God;

Provision was made under the law for the sin of ignorance; even though it was unintentional, the sinner was still held fully responsible for it. Sacrifices were to be offered for this sin like other sins. (See Leviticus 4:1–5:19.)

4. Sin is the absence of righteousness.

This incorrect view is taught by the Christian Science religion. Sin is much more than the absence of righteousness. Sin is a hostile act of rebellion against God's holy character. Sin is an act of the will. Sin is aggressive, not the simple absence of good. Sin's existence is very real. We see the destructive results of sin all around us.

Sin is sometimes personified today as being an impish little old fellow who makes us do naughty things that are not exactly right. Often these sins are not viewed as bad in the eyes of others. This attitude is supported by cartoons, which picture sin as a little elf with horns. These cartoon character prompt us to do sinful things. This kind of evil is regularly joked about rather than abhorred. The mocking of wrongful acts is one of the ways people are blinded concerning sin.

The Bible teaches that we are ultimately accountable for our sin. When we stand before the Judge of all the earth, we will have nothing to say in our own defense. Sin is a serious offense to God, and we must view it as a serious matter. Some seek to avoid facing the consequences of their sin by embracing atheism. (Psalm 14:1)

Psalms 14:1

> The fool has said in his heart, "There is no God."
> They are corrupt, they have committed abominable deeds;
> There is no one who does good.

E. Various characteristics of sin

1. The Ten Commandments have two divisions.

    a. Our obligation toward God (Exodus 20:2–11)

    b. Our obligation toward others (Exodus 20:12–17)

2. Some sins are *sins of commission,* and some are *sins of omission.*

    a. Sins of commission are actions or attitudes which are opposed to God's righteous and holy character. They are selfish acts of rebellion against God.

    1 Samuel 12:25

    > "But if you still do wickedly, both you and your king will be swept away."

    b. Sins of omission are failures to do that which should have been done.

    James 4:17

    > Therefore, to one who knows *the* right thing to do and does not do it, to him it is sin.

3. Sin may take the form of an attitude or an action.

    - Attitude – pride, stubbornness, and hatred
    - Action – drunkenness, murder, lying, and stealing

Psalms 51:4

> Against You, You only, I have sinned
> And done what is evil in Your sight,
> So that You are justified when You speak
> And blameless when You judge.

4. Sin is the result of a sinful nature.

The sinful nature of the human race has been passed on to everyone through Adam and Eve. We are born with a sinful nature. We sin because we possess a sinful nature. It is out of this sinful disposition that all other sins are generated. This sinful nature gives us an innate appeal to sin. In Romans 7, Paul describes the inner war that goes on when the Christian resists the desires of this sinful nature.

Romans 7:14–25

> [14] For we know that the Law is spiritual, but I am of flesh, sold into bondage to sin. [15] For what I am doing, I do not understand; for I am not practicing what I *would* like to *do*, but I am doing the very thing I hate. [16] But if I do the very thing I do not want *to do*, I agree with the Law, *confessing* that the Law is good. [17] So now, no longer am I the one doing it, but sin which dwells in me. [18] For I know that nothing good dwells in me, that is, in my flesh; for the willing is present in me, but the doing of the good *is* not. [19] For the good that I want, I do not do, but I practice the very evil that I do not want. [20] But if I am doing the very thing I do not want, I am no longer the one doing it, but sin which dwells in me.
>
> [21] I find then the principle that evil is present in me, the one who wants to do good. [22] For I joyfully concur with the law of God in the inner man, [23] but I see a different law in the members of my body, waging war against the law of my mind and making me a prisoner of the law of sin which is in my members. [24] Wretched man that I am! Who will set me free from the body of this death? [25] Thanks be to God through Jesus Christ our Lord! So then, on the one hand I myself with my mind am serving the law of God, but on the other, with my flesh the law of sin.

Psalms 51:5

> Behold, I was brought forth in iniquity,
> And in sin my mother conceived me.

1 Corinthians 15:21–22

> [21] For since by a man *came* death, by a man also *came* the resurrection of the dead. [22] For as in Adam all die, so also in Christ all will be made alive.

5. The Bible describes an unpardonable sin.

Matthew 12:31

> "Therefore I say to you, any sin and blasphemy shall be forgiven people, but blasphemy against the Spirit shall not be forgiven."

The sin of unbelief is the only unpardonable sin because it is the sin of rejecting God's only way of forgiveness and salvation. There is a distinction between sins and the sin of unbelief in connection with Christ. The Holy Spirit is convicting people today of the sin of unbelief in connection with Christ.

John 16:8–9

> [8] And He, when He comes, will convict the world concerning sin and righteousness and judgment; [9] concerning sin, because they do not believe in Me;

F. Ultimately, there are only two kingdoms: The kingdom of light and of God and the kingdom of darkness and evil.

1 Thessalonians 5:4–5

> [4] But you, brethren, are not in darkness, that the day would overtake you like a thief; [5] for you are all sons of light and sons of day. We are not of night nor of darkness;

Ephesians 5:8–11

> [8] for you were formerly darkness, but now you are Light in the Lord; walk as children of Light [9] (for the fruit of the Light *consists* in all goodness and righteousness and truth), [10] trying to learn what is pleasing to the Lord. [11] Do not participate in the unfruitful deeds of darkness, but instead even expose them;

Matthew 7:13–14

> [13] "Enter through the narrow gate; for the gate is wide and the way is broad that leads to destruction, and there are many who enter through it. [14] For the gate is small and the way is narrow that leads to life, and there are few who find it."

1. The Narrow Gate – living a life yielded to God. It is a life of obedience and complete dependence on Him. This way of life begins with accepting Jesus Christ as Savior and is profoundly serious about living for Him.

2. The Broad Gate – living in rebellion to God's will and living for self. It is a life separated from God. This life rejects God's free offer of salvation and refuses to recognize the only true God and Sovereign One. It is a life that is unwilling to acknowledge sin before God. It is a life that rejects Christ and fails to submit to His will.

Conclusion:

1. The broad gate is the more popular and populated gate.

2. The narrow gate is less popular and far less populated.

3. The more popular gate leads to ruin and loss.

4. The less popular gate leads to life.

III. The Fact of Sin

The Bible universally acknowledges the fact of sin's existence. In the chapter on Anthropology (Chapter 8) under the section titled *The Disastrous Results of the Fall of the Human Race*, we included a long list of scripture references that declare the existence of sin. Even if we did not possess the scriptures, it would still be obvious that evil exists as a terrible reality. Note several other forms of evidence:

A. Self-examination verifies it.

Romans 2:14–15

> [14] For when Gentiles who do not have the Law do instinctively the things of the Law, these, not having the Law, are a law to themselves, [15] in that they show the work of the Law written in their hearts, their conscience bearing witness and their thoughts alternately accusing or else defending them,

Jeremiah 16:17

> For My eyes are on all their ways; they are not hidden from My face, nor is their iniquity concealed from My eyes.

B. Observation confirms it.

We see it manifested everywhere in our daily lives. It is reported on the pages of our newspapers, magazines, radio, TV news broadcasts, and all over the internet. The presence of our ever-expanding and crowded prisons gives testimony to sin's presence and power over many. All too often sin is exposed in the dealings of our political and business communities. The self-centered and greedy attitude of the nations in international affairs clearly demonstrates the reality of sin. To deny sin's existence and its effects in the world is to live in utter denial of reality.

IV. The Extent of Sin

A. Sin affected the heavens.

Ephesians 6:12

> For our struggle is not against flesh and blood, but against the rulers, against the powers, against the world forces of this darkness, against the spiritual *forces* of wickedness in the heavenly *places.*

Revelation 12:7–8

> [7] And there was war in heaven, Michael and his angels waging war with the dragon. The dragon and his angels waged war, [8] and they were not strong enough, and there was no longer a place found for them in heaven.

(See Isaiah 14 and Ezekiel 28)

B. Sin has dramatically affected nature.

1. The ground is cursed and looks forward to deliverance.

Genesis 3:17

> Then to Adam He said, "Because you have listened to the voice of your wife, and have eaten from the tree about which I commanded you, saying, 'You shall not eat from it';
>
> Cursed is the ground because of you;
> In toil you will eat of it
> All the days of your life."

Romans 8:19–20

> [19] For the anxious longing of the creation waits eagerly for the revealing of the sons of God. [20] For the creation was subjected to futility, not willingly, but because of Him who subjected it, in hope

Isaiah 55:13

> "Instead of the thorn bush the cypress will come up,
> And instead of the nettle the myrtle will come up,
> And it will be a memorial to the LORD,
> For an everlasting sign which will not be cut off."

Isaiah 35:1–7

> [1] The wilderness and the desert will be glad,
> And the Arabah will rejoice and blossom;
> Like the crocus
> [2] It will blossom profusely
> And rejoice with rejoicing and shout of joy.
> The glory of Lebanon will be given to it,
> The majesty of Carmel and Sharon.
> They will see the glory of the LORD,
> The majesty of our God.
> [3] Encourage the exhausted, and strengthen the feeble.
> [4] Say to those with anxious heart,
> "Take courage, fear not.
> Behold, your God will come *with* vengeance;
> The recompense of God will come,
> But He will save you."
> [5] Then the eyes of the blind will be opened
> And the ears of the deaf will be unstopped.
> [6] Then the lame will leap like a deer,
> And the tongue of the mute will shout for joy.
> For waters will break forth in the wilderness
> And streams in the Arabah.
> [7] The scorched land will become a pool
> And the thirsty ground springs of water;
> In the haunt of jackals, its resting place,
> Grass *becomes* reeds and rushes.

2. The animal kingdom is affected by sin and looks forward to deliverance.

Isaiah 11:6–9

> [6] "And the wolf will dwell with the lamb,
> And the leopard will lie down with the young goat,
> And the calf and the young lion and the fatling together;
> And a little boy will lead them.
> [7] Also the cow and the bear will graze,
> Their young will lie down together,
> And the lion will eat straw like the ox.
> [8] The nursing child will play by the hole of the cobra,
> And the weaned child will put his hand on the viper's den.
> [9] They will not hurt or destroy in all My holy mountain,
> For the earth will be full of the knowledge of the LORD
> As the waters cover the sea.

Isaiah 65:25

> "The wolf and the lamb will graze together, and the lion will eat straw like the ox; and dust will be the serpent's food. They will do no evil or harm in all My holy mountain," says the LORD.

3. Humankind has suffered because of sin.

Psalms 51:3–5

> [3] For I know my transgressions,
> And my sin is ever before me.
> [4] Against You, You only, I have sinned
> And done what is evil in Your sight,
> So that You are justified when You speak
> And blameless when You judge.
>
> [5] Behold, I was brought forth in iniquity,
> And in sin my mother conceived me.

Romans 3:9–20

> [9] What then? Are we better than they? Not at all; for we have already charged that both Jews and Greeks are all under sin; [10] as it is written,
>
> "There is none righteous, not even one;
> [11] There is none who understands,
> There is none who seeks for God;
> [12] All have turned aside, together they have become useless;
> There is none who does good,
> There is not even one."
> [13] "Their throat is an open grave,
> With their tongues they keep deceiving,"
> "The poison of asps is under their lips";
> [14] "Whose mouth is full of cursing and bitterness";
> [15] "Their feet are swift to shed blood,
> [16] Destruction and misery are in their paths,
> [17] And the path of peace they have not known."
> [18] "There is no fear of God before their eyes."
>
> [19] Now we know that whatever the Law says, it speaks to those who are under the Law, so that every mouth may be closed and all the world may become accountable to God; [20] because by the works of the Law no flesh will be justified in His sight; for through the Law *comes* the knowledge of sin.

a. The entire nature of humankind has been corrupted.

b. People have been alienated from God.

c. Our bodies and minds have been weakened by sin.

d. Humankind is depraved and, apart from the saving grace of God found in Jesus Christ, we would have no hope.

Jeremiah 17:9

> "The heart is more deceitful than all else
> And is desperately sick;
> Who can understand it?"

V. The Origin and Destiny of Sin (A Panoramic View)

A. Sin began with Satan's rebellion in heaven.

Ezekiel 28:14–15

[14] "You were the anointed cherub who covers,
And I placed you *there.*
You were on the holy mountain of God;
You walked in the midst of the stones of fire.
[15] "You were blameless in your ways
From the day you were created
Until unrighteousness was found in you."

Isaiah 14:12–14

[12] "How you have fallen from heaven,
O star of the morning, son of the dawn!
You have been cut down to the earth,
You who have weakened the nations!
[13] "But you said in your heart,
'I will ascend to heaven;
I will raise my throne above the stars of God,
And I will sit on the mount of assembly
In the recesses of the north.
[14] 'I will ascend above the heights of the clouds;
I will make myself like the Most High.'"

B. Sin entered the human race with the disobedience of Adam and Eve.

Genesis 3:5–7

[5] "For God knows that in the day you eat from it your eyes will be opened, and you will be like God, knowing good and evil." [6] When the woman saw that the tree was good for food, and that it was a delight to the eyes, and that the tree was desirable to make *one* wise, she took from its fruit and ate; and she gave also to her husband with her, and he ate. [7] Then the eyes of both of them were opened, and they knew that they were naked; and they sewed fig leaves together and made themselves loin coverings.

Romans 5:12

> Therefore, just as through one man sin entered into the world, and death through sin, and so death spread to all men, because all sinned—

C. Sin has been passed on from generation to generation by the transmitted sin nature.

Psalms 51:5

> Behold, I was brought forth in iniquity,
> And in sin my mother conceived me.

Ephesians 2:3

> Among them we too all formerly lived in the lusts of our flesh, indulging the desires of the flesh and of the mind, and were by nature children of wrath, even as the rest.

Romans 5:12–19

> [12] Therefore, just as through one man sin entered into the world, and death through sin, and so death spread to all men, because all sinned— [13] for until the Law sin was in the world, but sin is not imputed when there is no law. [14] Nevertheless death reigned from Adam until Moses, even over those who had not sinned in the likeness of the offense of Adam, who is a type of Him who was to come.
>
> [15] But the free gift is not like the transgression. For if by the transgression of the one the many died, much more did the grace of God and the gift by the grace of the one Man, Jesus Christ, abound to the many. [16] The gift is not like *that which came* through the one who sinned; for on the one hand the judgment *arose* from one *transgression* resulting in condemnation, but on the other hand the free gift *arose* from many transgressions resulting in justification. [17] For if by the transgression of the one, death reigned through the one, much more those who receive the abundance of grace and of the gift of righteousness will reign in life through the One, Jesus Christ.
>
> [18] So then as through one transgression there resulted condemnation to all men, even so through one act of righteousness there resulted justification of life to all men. [19] For as through the one man's disobedience the many were made sinners, even so through the obedience of the One the many will be made righteous.

D. Jesus' death and resurrection provides the only escape from the awful penalty of our sin.

1 Timothy 2:5

For there is one God, *and* one mediator also between God and men, *the* man Christ Jesus,

Romans 5:10

For if while we were enemies we were reconciled to God through the death of His Son, much more, having been reconciled, we shall be saved by His life.

2 Corinthians 5:21

He made Him who knew no sin *to be* sin on our behalf, so that we might become the righteousness of God in Him.

Ephesians 1:7

In Him we have redemption through His blood, the forgiveness of our trespasses, according to the riches of His grace

Romans 4:25

He who was delivered over because of our transgressions, and was raised because of our justification.

1. Jesus paid the just penalty for our sin and the sin of the world when He suffered and died on the cross.

2. His burial for three days and three nights was proof of the reality of Jesus' physical death.

3. Jesus' victorious bodily resurrection is proof that sin's penalty was entirely paid, and in Christ we are fully justified before God.

E. All sin and rebellion against God will ultimately come to an end.

1 Corinthians 15:24–25

[24] then *comes* the end, when He hands over the kingdom to the God and Father, when He has abolished all rule and all authority and power. [25] For He must reign until He has put all His enemies under His feet.

F. Death will be ultimately destroyed.

1 Corinthians 15:26

The last enemy that will be abolished is death.

G. Satan, death, and Hades will be cast into the lake of fire.

Revelation 20:10–14

[10] And the devil who deceived them was thrown into the lake of fire and brimstone, where the beast and the false prophet are also; and they will be tormented day and night forever and ever.

[11] Then I saw a great white throne and Him who sat upon it, from whose presence earth and heaven fled away, and no place was found for them. [12] And I saw the dead, the great and the small, standing before the throne, and books were opened; and another book was opened, which is *the book* of life; and the dead were judged from the things which were written in the books, according to their deeds. [13] And the sea gave up the dead which were in it, and death and Hades gave up the dead which were in them; and they were judged, every one *of them* according to their deeds. [14] Then death and Hades were thrown into the lake of fire. This is the second death, the lake of fire.

H. Those who reject Christ's free offer of salvation will experience the second death.

Revelation 21:8

"But for the cowardly and unbelieving and abominable and murderers and immoral persons and sorcerers and idolaters and all liars, their part *will be* in the lake that burns with fire and brimstone, which is the second death."

Revelation 20:15

And if anyone's name was not found written in the book of life, he was thrown into the lake of fire.

VI. The Future Judgment of Sin

Under this section we are primarily concerned with the eternal effects of sin in people's lives, which is the judgment of God on the unrepentant wicked. Those who refused the truth of the gospel and reject Jesus Christ and His free gift of salvation will one day stand before the Judge of all the earth. His judgment of eternal death is final. This is the second death and is an irrevocable separation from God.

A. The Bible teaches the doctrine of eternal punishment.

1. There will be those who are accursed by God.

2. They will be cast into a fire that burns forever.

3. This eternal fire was originally prepared for Satan and his angels (demons).

    Matthew 25:41

    > "Then He will also say to those on His left, 'Depart from Me, accursed ones, into the eternal fire which has been prepared for the devil and his angels;"

4. Both the wicked and righteous will be resurrected.

5. Those who have rejected the gospel will experience the judgment of God.

6. Those who accept Jesus Christ as their Savior will experience eternal life.

7. God's judgment will be a righteous (just) judgment because He knows all and sees all.

8. Jesus' resurrection is the proof that all will one day be raised from the dead.

    John 5:28–29

    > [28] Do not marvel at this; for an hour is coming, in which all who are in the tombs will hear His voice, [29] and will come forth; those who did the good *deeds* to a resurrection of life, those who committed the evil *deeds* to a resurrection of judgment.

    1 John 5:12 makes this very clear and simple.

    > He who has the Son has the life; he who does not have the Son of God does not have the life.

9. The day of judgment is fixed and Acts 17:31 implies that this day cannot be changed.

10. Jesus Christ is the "Man" who will judge.

    Acts 17:31

    > because He has fixed a day in which He will judge the world in righteousness through a Man whom He has appointed, having furnished proof to all men by raising Him from the dead.

11. Retribution will fall on those who have not responded in faith to the gospel.

12. Those without Christ will pay the penalty of eternal destruction. They will be banished from the presence of God forever.

 2 Thessalonians 1:8–9

 [8] dealing out retribution to those who do not know God and to those who do not obey the gospel of our Lord Jesus. [9] These will pay the penalty of eternal destruction, away from the presence of the Lord and from the glory of His power,

13. God desires all to be saved from eternal punishment, and this was the goal of Jesus' suffering, death, and resurrection. The opportunity to accept His free offer of salvation is available, but He will not force any to accept it.

14. A delayed judgment is not to be interpreted as an escape from His wrath but as a demonstration of God's patience.

 2 Peter 3:9–10

 [9] The Lord is not slow about His promise, as some count slowness, but is patient toward you, not wishing for any to perish but for all to come to repentance.

 [10] But the day of the Lord will come like a thief, in which the heavens will pass away with a roar and the elements will be destroyed with intense heat, and the earth and its works will be burned up.

15. Each one must come to repentance and trust in Christ in order to escape eternal retribution.

16. Some will stubbornly refuse God's offer of salvation and remain under the judgment of God.

 Romans 2:5–6

 [5] But because of your stubbornness and unrepentant heart you are storing up wrath for yourself in the day of wrath and revelation of the righteous judgment of God, [6] who WILL RENDER TO EACH PERSON ACCORDING TO HIS DEEDS:

John 3:17

> For God did not send the Son into the world to judge the world, but that the world might be saved through Him.

17. The event in Revelation 20 is known as the Great White Throne Judgment.

18. Those who appear before the Judge are those who rejected the truth and God's free offer of salvation in Christ.

19. Jesus himself is the Judge seated on the throne.

20. There will be no Christians judged at the Great White Throne Judgment, because they were judged at Calvary when Christ took their place and paid for their sin. Judgment has already occurred for those in Christ. Their judgment occurred at Calvary when Christ was condemned to death in our place for our sin. Romans 8:1 says, "Therefore there is now no condemnation for those who are in Christ Jesus."

21. All those who are resurrected at this time stand before the Great White Throne and are cast into the lake of fire.

22. The lake of fire is a place of intense, conscious suffering, and the second death is an eternally fixed condition.

23. There is no indication in these verses that any unsaved person escapes this outcome.

24. The "second death" is final and eternal separation from God. It is an eternal death.

Revelation 20:11–14

> [11] Then I saw a great white throne and Him who sat upon it, from whose presence earth and heaven fled away, and no place was found for them. [12] And I saw the dead, the great and the small, standing before the throne, and books were opened; and another book was opened, which is *the book* of life; and the dead were judged from the things which were written in the books, according to their deeds. [13] And the sea gave up the dead which were in it, and death and Hades gave up the dead which were in them; and they were judged, every one *of them* according to their deeds. [14] Then death and Hades were thrown into the lake of fire. This is the second death, the lake of fire.

25. The Great White Throne Judgment is such a fearful scene that no one, either in heaven or earth, desires to stay.

26. Though many may try to flee from the presence of the Judge, there will be no place for them to hide from Him.

27. The dead mentioned here are those who died without Christ. Christians will have already been resurrected and safely taken home to heaven before this judgment occurs. (See 1 Thessalonians 4:13–18 below.)

28. Judgment is based on the careful records in the books.

29. The Book of Life will play an important role in this judgment.

30. All will be judged according to their deeds.

Revelation 21:8

> "But for the cowardly and unbelieving and abominable and murderers and immoral persons and sorcerers and idolaters and all liars, their part *will be* in the lake that burns with fire and brimstone, which is the second death."

Romans 8:1

> Therefore there is now no condemnation for those who are in Christ Jesus.

1 Thessalonians 4:13–18

> [13] But we do not want you to be uninformed, brethren, about those who are asleep, so that you will not grieve as do the rest who have no hope. [14] For if we believe that Jesus died and rose again, even so God will bring with Him those who have fallen asleep in Jesus. [15] For this we say to you by the word of the Lord, that we who are alive and remain until the coming of the Lord, will not precede those who have fallen asleep. [16] For the Lord Himself will descend from heaven with a shout, with the voice of *the* archangel and with the trumpet of God, and the dead in Christ will rise first. [17] Then we who are alive and remain will be caught up together with them in the clouds to meet the Lord in the air, and so we shall always be with the Lord. [18] Therefore comfort one another with these words.

Revelation 20:6

> Blessed and holy is the one who has a part in the first resurrection; over these the second death has no power, but they will be priests of God and of Christ and will reign with Him for a thousand years.

31. Those who receive the mark of the beast are those who join his company and worship him during the tribulation period.

32. Satan and his wicked leaders will be judged.

Revelation 20:10

> And the devil who deceived them was thrown into the lake of fire and brimstone, where the beast and the false prophet are also; and they will be tormented day and night forever and ever.

33. The unbelieving will also be thrown into the lake of fire.

34. Punishment in the lake of fire will be a conscious punishment.

35. This judgment is identified as "the second death."

36. It is a final and eternally fixed separation from God.

Revelation 19:20

> And the beast was seized, and with him the false prophet who performed the signs in his presence, by which he deceived those who had received the mark of the beast and those who worshiped his image; these two were thrown alive into the lake of fire which burns with brimstone.

37. Jesus teaches of the horrors and suffering of the second death.

Luke 16:19–31

> [19] "Now there was a rich man, and he habitually dressed in purple and fine linen, joyously living in splendor every day. [20] And a poor man named Lazarus was laid at his gate, covered with sores, [21] and longing to be fed with the *crumbs* which were falling from the rich man's table; besides, even the dogs were coming and licking his sores. [22] Now the poor man died and was carried away by the angels to Abraham's bosom; and the rich man also died and was buried. [23] In Hades he lifted up his eyes, being in torment, and saw Abraham far away and Lazarus in his bosom. [24] And he cried out and said, 'Father Abraham, have mercy on me, and send Lazarus so that he may dip the tip of his finger in water and cool off my tongue, for I am in agony in this flame.' [25] But Abraham said, 'Child, remember that during your life you received your good things, and likewise Lazarus bad things; but now he is being comforted here, and you are in agony. [26] And besides all this, between us and you there is a great chasm fixed,

> so that those who wish to come over from here to you will not be able, and *that* none may cross over from there to us.' [27] And he said, 'Then I beg you, father, that you send him to my father's house— [28] for I have five brothers—in order that he may warn them, so that they will not also come to this place of torment.' [29] But Abraham said, 'They have Moses and the Prophets; let them hear them.' [30] But he said, 'No, father Abraham, but if someone goes to them from the dead, they will repent!' [31] But he said to him, 'If they do not listen to Moses and the Prophets, they will not be persuaded even if someone rises from the dead.'"

38. The Bible does not call this story a parable. There is no reason to believe that this is anything but an account of actual events. (In other New Testament passages, Jesus identifies his stories as parables.)

39. The following seven conclusions can be drawn about this rich man:

    - He went to hell after he died. (vv. 22–23)
    - He was in constant torment. (v. 23)
    - He was conscious and aware of his condition. (vv. 23–31)
    - He was aware of the blessing of Lazarus. (vv. 23–24)
    - He had memory and could recall his life on earth. (vv. 25–31)
    - His condition was fixed. (v. 26)
    - He had no relief from his suffering. (v 24)
    - He had concern for those still living. (vv. 28–31)

Conclusion:

1. There is a resurrection of all men. (John 5:28–29)

2. There is a coming day of judgment. (Acts 17:31)

3. Those who reject Christ will be separated from God for eternity. (2 Thessalonians 1:8–9)

4. The wicked, after physical death, are in a state of conscious torment. (Luke 16:19–31)

5. Such terms as destruction (Revelation 17:11), the lake of fire (Revelation 20:14), and the second death (Revelation 20:14) all refer to the same thing – eternal banishment from God in hell.

B. Annihilation and eternal death are not the same thing.

The word *annihilated* means "to cease to exist." Some (The Seventh Day Adventist, for example) teach that to die in your sin means to cease to exist. This is not taught in the Bible.

1. Destruction – the Greek word is *apoleia*. This New Testament word translated "destroy or destruction" does not mean that the object is annihilated or ceases to exist. It means that the object is ruined, as far as its original purpose is concerned.

    a. Two examples of this definition

    Matthew 9:17

    "Nor do *people* put new wine into old wineskins; otherwise the wineskins burst, and the wine pours out and the wineskins are ruined *(apoleia); but they put new wine into fresh wineskins, and both are preserved."

    Matthew 26:8

    But the disciples were indignant when they saw *this*, and said, "Why this waste?"

    (The word *apoleia* is used here to describe the disciple's reaction to the use of the costly perfume the woman used to anoint Jesus' feet.)

    *Note: The parenthetical words have been added by author.

    b. The wicked perish in the same way. They are ruined for use, as far as the original purpose of their creation is concerned. (The wicked are not annihilated.)

2. Death – the Greek word is *thanatos* and means "separation." The term *second death* is synonymous with the lake of fire and eternal destruction.

    Isaiah 59:2

    But your iniquities have made a separation between you and your God,
    And your sins have hidden *His* face from you so that He does not hear.

    Revelation 20:10

    And the devil who deceived them was thrown into the lake of fire and brimstone, where the beast and the false prophet are also; and they will be tormented day and night forever and ever.

3. The phrase "day and night forever and ever," as described in these verses, obviously does not refer to a time of limited duration.

4. This phrase is a reference to eternity future.

C. The purpose of eternal punishment is to vindicate the righteousness of God.

Penalties in this life are largely corrective. Penalties in God's eternal judgment are not corrective. God's penalties have a primarily purpose – the vindication of the righteousness of God.

Romans 6:23

> For the wages of sin is death, but the free gift of God is eternal life in Christ Jesus our Lord.

Three factors that make punishment essential:

1. The appalling nature of sin

2. The impeccable (perfect) righteousness of God

3. The defiant rejection of God's mercy, love, and grace

D. There are two kinds of penalties for sin.

1. The *natural* consequences of sin. (For example, an alcoholic can expect the natural consequences of sickness, a broken home, and financial ruin.)

2. The *eternal* consequences of sin. (This is the ultimate judgment of God. If a person dies in his sin having never accepted God's free offer of salvation, he will be eternally separated from God in hell.)

   Many are inclined to think that because they have suffered the *natural* consequence of their sin, (for example, many years in prison) that this is the only punishment for their offence.

   The criminal may believe that if his crime is not discovered or if he is not convicted, he has avoided retribution for his crime. The Bible makes it clear. What he or she has done has not escaped the attentive, all-seeing eye of the all-knowing God. We may not face human courts in this life, but it is certain that if we fail to trust Christ for salvation and forgiveness of sin, we will assuredly stand at God's Great White Throne Judgment. The righteous Judge will one day "balance the books."

Ecclesiastes 11:9

> Rejoice, young man, during your childhood, and let your heart be pleasant during the days of young manhood. And follow the impulses of your heart and the desires of your eyes. Yet know that God will bring you to judgment for all these things.

E. Eternal punishment is logical.

Apart from the convincing biblical testimony, rational thought also leads us to the same conclusion. Eternal punishment is reasonable because:

1. There are wrongs upon this earth that have never been made right.
2. The wicked *must* be separated from the righteous, otherwise, heaven would not be any different than what we experience in this life.
3. It has been necessary for governments to affix penalties for crimes committed to produce an organized community. The same logic applies to the rule of God.
4. People need restraining factors to deter them in their crusade to do evil. It helps them control their actions.

F. Eternal punishment is an important biblical teaching.

1. It is extremely necessary for individuals to make their decision for Christ in this life. The Bible makes it clear that after physical death occurs there will never be a second chance.
2. The judgment of God exposes the awful nature of sin.
3. The judgment of God brings to light the dreadful results of rejecting God's gracious gift of salvation.
4. The judgment of God provides a stimulus for Christians to labor diligently to win the lost to Christ.

G. Eternal judgment of God is a sobering truth.

1. It will not help to blind our eyes to the eternal judgment of God.
2. We need to warn the lost of God eternal judgment.

Ezekiel 33:1–9

[1] And the word of the Lord came to me, saying, [2] "Son of man, speak to the sons of your people and say to them, 'If I bring a sword upon a land, and the people of the land take one man from among them and make him their watchman, [3] and he sees the sword coming upon the land and blows on the trumpet and warns the people, [4] then he who hears the sound of the trumpet and does not take warning, and a sword comes and takes him away, his blood will be on his *own* head. [5] He heard the sound of the trumpet but did not take warning; his blood will be on himself. But had he taken warning, he would have delivered his life. [6] But if the watchman sees the sword coming and does not blow the trumpet and the people are not warned, and a sword comes and takes a person from them, he is taken away in his iniquity; but his blood I will require from the watchman's hand.'

[7] "Now as for you, son of man, I have appointed you a watchman for the house of Israel; so you will hear a message from My mouth and give them warning from Me. [8] When I say to the wicked, 'O wicked man, you will surely die,' and you do not speak to warn the wicked from his way, that wicked man shall die in his iniquity, but his blood I will require from your hand. [9] But if you on your part warn a wicked man to turn from his way and he does not turn from his way, he will die in his iniquity, but you have delivered your life."

3. Those without Christ hate and spurn the thought of an eternal and final judgment of God. It is not a popular truth, but the sinner needs to be warned. God has used this truth to bring many to Christ.

4. We must declare the truth of the coming judgment with love and grace rather than using it as a hammer or a whip.

5. We must keep in mind that as the local church loses its love for the Word of God and for the lost, it also drops its emphasis on the truth of eternal judgment.

6. As churches stray from the scriptures, it is easier for them to believe that sin is not *so* bad, and that future punishment may not be so severe.

VII. Sin Affects our Relationship with God and Others

A. A clear or blameless conscience defined

Acts 24:16 (In his defense before the Governor in Jerusalem, Paul made this statement.)

> In view of this, I also do my best to maintain always a blameless conscience *both* before God and before men.

1 Timothy 1:18–19

> [18] This command I entrust to you, Timothy, *my* son, in accordance with the prophecies previously made concerning you, that by them you fight the good fight, [19] keeping faith and a good conscience, which some have rejected and suffered shipwreck in regard to their faith.

1. In these verses, Paul is *not* saying that he is blameless and that he has never done anything wrong.
2. Paul maintains that he has no reason to feel guilty before God or others.
3. Notice the word *maintain*. Paul was careful to confess and receive forgiveness for any wrong toward God or others.
4. Paul also tells Timothy that a good conscience is one of the weapons used in fighting a good fight in the ministry.
5. Contrary to what we may say, feel, or believe, we are responsible for our actions.
6. We often excuse guilt by blaming others or our circumstances for our offensive actions.
7. Clearing our conscience involves taking responsibility for our sin before God and before others.
8. A clear or blameless conscience is gained when we know that our offensive actions or attitudes against God and others have been fully confessed and forgiven.

B. Maintaining a clear conscience before our Heavenly Father

1 John 1:5–2:2

> [5] This is the message we have heard from Him and announce to you, that God is Light, and in Him there is no darkness at all. [6] If we say that we have fellowship with Him and *yet* walk in the darkness, we lie and do not practice the truth; [7] but if we walk in the Light as He Himself is in the Light, we have fellowship with one another, and the blood of Jesus His Son cleanses us from all sin. [8] If we say that we have no sin, we are deceiving ourselves and the truth is not in us. [9] If we confess our sins, He is faithful and righteous to forgive us our sins and to cleanse us from all unrighteousness. [10] If we say that we have not sinned, we make Him a liar and His word is not in us.

> [1] My little children, I am writing these things to you so that you may not sin. And if anyone sins, we have an Advocate with the Father, Jesus Christ the righteous; [2] and He Himself is the propitiation for our sins; and not for ours only, but also for *those of* the whole world.

Note that this passage is not about salvation.

1. As a child of God, we must maintain fellowship with God through confession of our sin. (v. 9)

2. This passage teaches us how to deal with sin in our lives.

3. The word *confess* literally means to agree with. God knows our sin and when we confess, we agree with Him about our sin.

4. This passage teaches that if we confess our sins to our God, He will forgive our sins and cleanse us from all unrighteousness. (God's forgiveness is the removal of sin from our relationship with God.)

5. If we try to cover up our sin, rationalize it away, or pretend it does not exist, we will not be able to maintain true fellowship with God.

6. This is not a license to sin, but a way to maintain constant communion with God. (v. 2:1–2)

C. Maintaining a clear conscience with others

This can be accomplished by confessing and asking for forgiveness for the wrong part we played in a personal conflict or offensive behavior.

Matthew 5:23–24

> [23] Therefore if you are presenting your offering at the altar, and there remember that your brother has something against you, [24] leave your offering there before the altar and go; first be reconciled to your brother, and then come and present your offering.

Ephesians 4:30–32

> [30] Do not grieve the Holy Spirit of God, by whom you were sealed for the day of redemption. [31] Let all bitterness and wrath and anger and clamor and slander be put away from you, along with all malice. [32] Be kind to one another, tender-hearted, forgiving each other, just as God in Christ also has forgiven you.

1. If we are to maintain a good fellowship with our Heavenly Father, we must also deal with our offenses toward others.

2. To maintain a clear conscience with others, we must face our wrongs.

3. In the same way we clear our conscience before God by confessing our sin and seeking His forgiveness, we should deal with people whom we have wronged and seek their forgiveness.

D. Hindrances of failing to maintain a clear conscience with others

1. We are unable to maintain a good relationship with God.

   Matthew 5:23–24

   > [23] Therefore if you are presenting your offering at the altar, and there remember that your brother has something against you, [24] leave your offering there before the altar and go; first be reconciled to your brother, and then come and present your offering.

2. Failing to maintain a clear conscience with others will adversely affect our witness for Christ.

3. We will have difficulty maintaining lasting relationships with family and friends.

   - We tend to justify our wrongs by accusing others of our offensive reactions.
   - If we take no responsibility for our sinful actions, we will alienate those around us.

E. The advantages of maintaining a clear conscience

1. We will develop a greater self-control to overcome new temptations.

2. We will develop a greater ability to build deep and lasting friendships.

3. We will strengthen our bridge of communication with family members (husbands, wives, children, parents, brothers, and sisters).

   - Offenses cause numerous wedges between family members and friends.
   - Real communication becomes difficult at first and ultimately becomes almost impossible if these offenses are not dealt with.
   - Confession and forgiveness open the door for future communication.
   - It is important to make no accusations or place blame when asking to be forgiven.

REVIEW QUESTIONS

1. Does the Bible, in any one verse, give a complete definition of sin?
2. The most translated word for *sin* in the Old Testament and New Testament literally means ___.
3. Name and describe four false ideas people have about sin.
4. What are sins of commission?
5. What are sins of omission?
6. Name three sinful attitudes.
7. What is a sinful nature?
8. What is the unpardonable sin? Explain your answer.
9. Does the Bible teach eternal punishment for the wicked?
10. Explain Revelation 21:8.
11. List seven features taught in connection with Luke 16:19–31.
12. Is there a resurrection for the wicked? Explain your answer.
13. Does the term *second death* mean "to cease to exist?"
14. Define the term *annihilation*.
15. What is the true significance of the word translated *perish*?
16. What is the meaning of the word *death*?
17. Name and explain two kinds of penalties for sin.
18. Does the Bible tell us that people will have a second chance to repent after they die?
19. What kind of an attitude should we have when we teach the unsaved about eternal punishment?
20. What is a *clear conscience*?
21. Name and explain five advantages of gaining a clear conscience.

CHAPTER 8

Anthropology
(What the Bible Teaches About Humankind)

I. The Creation of the Human Race

A. Humankind was created by God.

Genesis 1:27

> God created man in His own image, in the image of God He created him; male and female He created them.

Genesis 2:7

> Then the LORD God formed man of dust from the ground, and breathed into his nostrils the breath of life; and man became a living being.

1. The creation of Adam was an immediate and personal act of God, not by secondary agencies or processes.

2. The following characteristics exist in connection with the creation of all living things:

    a. God called Adam into being through an act of creation. (Genesis 1:27 – God created him in His own image.)

    b. Adam became a physical being by an act of formation. (Genesis 2:7 – The Lord God formed Adam out of the dust of the ground.)

    c. Adam became a complete living personal being by a final action. (Genesis 2:7 – God breathed into his nostrils the breath of life and the man became a living being.)

d. God created male and female. He created no other genders. This is true of all living things. Even plants need to be cross pollinated to produce fruit. God did not create any neutral gendered people.

e. This gender issue is true of all animals, plants, fish, birds, and insects. God created only male and female. He created no chaos of genders or confusion of sexualities.

3. God uses all three of the following Hebrew terms to describe the creation of people.

a. *Bara* means "created out of nothing."

b. *Asah* means "made the final dispositions and arrangements."

c. *Yatzar* means "formed to exist in a shape or appointed form."

Genesis 1:27

> God created *(bara) man in His own image, in the image of God He created *(bara) him; male and female He created *(bara) them.

Genesis 1:31

> God saw all that He had made (asah), and behold, it was very good. And there was evening and there was morning, the sixth day.

Genesis 2:7

> Then the LORD God formed (yatzar) man of dust from the ground, and breathed into his nostrils the breath of life; and man became a living being.

Isaiah 43:7

> "Everyone who is called by My name,
> And whom I have created (bara) for My glory,
> Whom I have formed (yatzar), even whom I have made (asah)."

*Note: The parenthetical words have been added by author.

4. Isaiah 43:7 illustrates the meaning of these three verbs:

a. I have created (bara) people for My glory. (This means that God made them out of nothing.)

b. I have formed (yatzar) people. (This means that God caused them to exist in a shape or an appointed form.)

c. I have made (asah) people. (This means that God made the final dispositions and arrangements respecting them.)

B. The Bible does not teach evolution in any form.

Genesis 1:24–28

> [24] Then God said, "Let the earth bring forth living creatures after their kind: cattle and creeping things and beasts of the earth after their kind"; and it was so. [25] God made the beasts of the earth after their kind, and the cattle after their kind, and everything that creeps on the ground after its kind; and God saw that it was good.
>
> [26] Then God said, "Let Us make man in Our image, according to Our likeness; and let them rule over the fish of the sea and over the birds of the sky and over the cattle and over all the earth, and over every creeping thing that creeps on the earth." [27] God created man in His own image, in the image of God He created him; male and female He created them. [28] God blessed them; and God said to them, "Be fruitful and multiply, and fill the earth, and subdue it; and rule over the fish of the sea and over the birds of the sky and over every living thing that moves on the earth."

Evolution Teaches	The Bible Teaches
Humankind rose from lower forms of life. Evolution starts with simple living organisms and moves to a more complex form of life.	Humankind was the result of the direct creative act of God; People were created separate from and made to have dominion over lower forms of life.
Humankind came into being through lower forms of animal life and is the climax of development.	God created humankind as a distinct, complex, and intelligent being. People were created separate and unique from the animal kingdom.
Through adaptation to their environment, animals changed from one species to another, and humankind finally emerged.	God created each after his or her own kind (species) without crossover. Though any given species can develop various breeds and pedigrees, there is no scientific evidence of a crossover from one species to another.

Note: In the book *Beginning of the World* published by the Creation-Science Research Center it says (p. 28), "Many scientists today are creationists and there is no scientific justification for anyone any longer to teach that evolution is the only satisfactory theory of origins. The actual facts of science can be understood much better in terms of an original creation than in terms of a continuing evolution." There are many resources available for students, prepared and published by the Institute for Creation Research, San Diego, California (https://www.icr.org). The Institute for Creation Research also maintains a learning facility called the Discovery Center in Dallas, Texas.

Genesis 3:20

> Now the man called his wife's name Eve, because she was the mother of all *the* living.

1. The whole human race descended from Adam and Eve.

2. Eve is the mother of all human beings.

3. Adam is the father of all human beings.

C. The date of Adam's creation is uncertain.

There is no biblical reason for assigning Adam's creation earlier than ten thousand years ago. The evolutionists need hundreds of millions of years to explain their view.

II. Humanity's Original State

A. Humankind was created in the image and likeness of God.

Genesis 1:26–27

> [26] Then God said, "Let Us make man in Our image, according to Our likeness; and let them rule over the fish of the sea and over the birds of the sky and over the cattle and over all the earth, and over every creeping thing that creeps on the earth." [27] God created man in His own image, in the image of God He created him; male and female He created them.

Genesis 2:7

> Then the LORD God formed man of dust from the ground, and breathed into his nostrils the breath of life; and man became a living being.

1. The two Hebrew words *image* and *likeness* are almost synonymous.

    a. *Image* signifies shadow.

    b. *Likeness* signifies resemblance.

2. These verses do not refer to a physical likeness since God does not have a body. God is spirit.

    a. People were created with a two-fold likeness: *natural* and *moral.*

    b. The *natural* likeness focuses on the fact that both individuals and God have personality traits. These three characteristics can never be lost:

        - An intellect – a mind, the ability to think
        - Sensibility – emotions, the ability to feel
        - A will – the ability to make decisions and carry out those decisions or plans

    c. People are both material and immaterial beings. Their physical bodies are material. The soul and spirit are immaterial.

    d. Moral likeness means Adam and Eve were innocent before God. They were created morally pure, upright, and without sin. They had a sinless nature. This moral characteristic could be lost and, in fact, was lost when Adam and Eve sinned.

Genesis 2:7

> Then the LORD God formed man of dust from the ground, and breathed into his nostrils the breath of life; and man became a living being.

Ecclesiastes 12:6–7

> [6] *Remember Him* before the silver cord is broken and the golden bowl is crushed, the pitcher by the well is shattered and the wheel at the cistern is crushed; [7] then the dust will return to the earth as it was, and the spirit will return to God who gave it.

3. The material part of people was formed by God out of the dust of the ground.

B. The immaterial part was breathed into humankind by God.

There are two views held in connection with the immaterial part of people:

1. Trichotomy – A person is composed of three parts: body, soul, and spirit.

2. Dichotomy – A person is composed of two parts: material and immaterial. In this view, the soul and spirit are not regarded as two distinct parts. They simply combine the soul and spirit as the same immaterial part of a person.

Though we would not view the difference between these two positions as a major doctrinal issue, we believe the scripture best reflects the trichotomy position because of the text of Hebrews 4:12.

Hebrews 4:12

> For the word of God is living and active and sharper than any two-edged sword, and piercing as far as the division of soul and spirit, of both joints and marrow, and able to judge the thoughts and intentions of the heart.

III. The Origin of The Soul of Humankind

A. After God created the body (the physical part) from dirt, the soul was created by God's own breath.

Genesis 2:7

> Then the LORD God formed man of dust from the ground, and breathed into his nostrils the breath of life; and man became a living being.

B. Both body (material) and soul (immaterial) are propagated from parent to child by natural generation.

Psalms 51:5

> Behold, I was brought forth in iniquity,
> And in sin my mother conceived me.

1. In Genesis 2:7 "breath of life" could be translated breath of lives (plural).

2. This view best explains the sinful nature which is passed on to all children.

3. Children are like their parents spiritually, morally, and physically.

C. The sinful action of Adam and Eve continues to be passed on from parent to child. Likewise, the sacrificial death of Jesus and the gift of grace is passed on to all who experience the new birth by trusting Christ for salvation.

Romans 5:15

> But the free gift is not like the transgression. For if by the transgression of the one the many died, much more did the grace of God and the gift by the grace of the one Man, Jesus Christ, abound to the many.

IV. The Creation of Woman

A. Adam was incomplete without the companionship of a woman, even though he was living in a perfect environment.

Genesis 2:20–22

> [20] The man gave names to all the cattle, and to the birds of the sky, and to every beast of the field, but for Adam there was not found a helper suitable for him. [21] So the LORD God caused a deep sleep to fall upon the man, and he slept; then He took one of his ribs and closed up the flesh at that place. [22] The LORD God fashioned into a woman the rib which He had taken from the man, and brought her to the man.

B. God created the woman to be a helper for the man.

Ephesians 5:22–33

> [22] Wives, *be subject* to your own husbands, as to the Lord. [23] For the husband is the head of the wife, as Christ also is the head of the church, He Himself *being* the Savior of the body. [24] But as the church is subject to Christ, so also the wives *ought to be* to their husbands in everything.
>
> [25] Husbands, love your wives, just as Christ also loved the church and gave Himself up for her, [26] so that He might sanctify her, having cleansed her by the washing of water with the word, [27] that He might present to Himself the church in all her glory, having no spot or wrinkle or any such thing; but that she would be holy and blameless. [28] So husbands ought also to love their own wives as their own bodies. He who loves his own wife loves himself; [29] for no one ever hated his own flesh, but nourishes and cherishes it, just as Christ also *does* the church, [30] because we are members of His body. [31] FOR THIS REASON A MAN SHALL LEAVE HIS FATHER AND MOTHER AND SHALL BE JOINED TO HIS WIFE, AND THE TWO SHALL BECOME ONE FLESH. [32] This mystery is great; but I am

> speaking with reference to Christ and the church. [33] Nevertheless, each individual among you also is to love his own wife even as himself, and the wife must *see to it* that she respects her husband.

1. This verse does not mean that women are to serve men as a slave but to serve *alongside* men as companions and supporters.

2. Some cultures view women in a demeaning and servitude position, but there is no support for this viewpoint in scripture.

3. God's plan is that a man, at a certain point in his life, leaves the authority and provision of his father and mother. He then forms a new family, wherein he provides and cares for his wife and children.

4. The wife is to be a helper, working alongside of her husband, not a ruler in the home.

5. In this newly formed family, the wife is to be in subjection to her husband, respecting and supporting his leadership.

6. The husband is to supply care and loving leadership for his wife and family. In this way, husbands are to earn the respect of their wives. He is not to demand his authority over his wife and treat her as one of his subjects.

7. Husbands are to treat their wives in the same way Jesus treats His church.

8. Jesus is head of the church (the Body of Christ) providing loving leadership, and the church is called upon to willingly follow the head with respectful obedience.

V. The Authority Given to Humankind

A. God gave people dominion over the lower creation.

Genesis 1:26

> Then God said, "Let Us make man in Our image, according to Our likeness; and let them rule over the fish of the sea and over the birds of the sky and over the cattle and over all the earth, and over every creeping thing that creeps on the earth."

1. People are clearly and uniquely different from the animal and vegetable kingdoms.

2. The human race is separated from the animal kingdom in origin, association, and destiny.

3. A beast cannot ascend to the level of people, but people, with their sinful nature, can easily descend to the level of a beast.

B. Adam was given authority to name the animals.

Genesis 2:19–20

> [19] Out of the ground the LORD God formed every beast of the field and every bird of the sky, and brought *them* to the man to see what he would call them; and whatever the man called a living creature, that was its name. [20] The man gave names to all the cattle, and to the birds of the sky, and to every beast of the field, but for Adam there was not found a helper suitable for him.

Genesis 1:26–28

> [26] Then God said, "Let Us make man in Our image, according to Our likeness; and let them rule over the fish of the sea and over the birds of the sky and over the cattle and over all the earth, and over every creeping thing that creeps on the earth." [27] God created man in His own image, in the image of God He created him; male and female He created them. [28] God blessed them; and God said to them, "Be fruitful and multiply, and fill the earth, and subdue it; and rule over the fish of the sea and over the birds of the sky and over every living thing that moves on the earth."

Psalms 8:5–9

> [5] Yet You have made him a little lower than God,
> And You crown him with glory and majesty!
> [6] You make him to rule over the works of Your hands;
> You have put all things under his feet,
> [7] All sheep and oxen,
> And also the beasts of the field,
> [8] The birds of the heavens and the fish of the sea,
> Whatever passes through the paths of the seas.
>
> [9] O LORD, our Lord,
> How majestic is Your name in all the earth!

1. God did not give the animals a soul. Animals are made only of the dust of the ground and were not created with the immaterial and eternal qualities that God breathed into humans.

2. Genesis 2:19–20 shows aptitude in the first man. Adam was intelligent enough to evaluate and name all the animals.

VI. The Fall of Humankind

A. Humankind's probation (time of testing)

Genesis 2:15–17

> [15] Then the LORD God took the man and put him into the garden of Eden to cultivate it and keep it. [16] The LORD God commanded the man, saying, "From any tree of the garden you may eat freely; [17] but from the tree of the knowledge of good and evil you shall not eat, for in the day that you eat from it you will surely die."

Genesis 3:1–13

> [1] Now the serpent was more crafty than any beast of the field which the LORD God had made. And he said to the woman, "Indeed, has God said, 'You shall not eat from any tree of the garden'?" [2] The woman said to the serpent, "From the fruit of the trees of the garden we may eat; [3] but from the fruit of the tree which is in the middle of the garden, God has said, 'You shall not eat from it or touch it, or you will die.'" [4] The serpent said to the woman, "You surely will not die! [5] For God knows that in the day you eat from it your eyes will be opened, and you will be like God, knowing good and evil." [6] When the woman saw that the tree was good for food, and that it was a delight to the eyes, and that the tree was desirable to make *one* wise, she took from its fruit and ate; and she gave also to her husband with her, and he ate. [7] Then the eyes of both of them were opened, and they knew that they were naked; and they sewed fig leaves together and made themselves loin coverings.
>
> [8] They heard the sound of the LORD God walking in the garden in the cool of the day, and the man and his wife hid themselves from the presence of the LORD God among the trees of the garden. [9] Then the LORD God called to the man, and said to him, "Where are you?" [10] He said, "I heard the sound of You in the garden, and I was afraid because I was naked; so I hid myself." [11] And He said, "Who told you that you were naked? Have you eaten from the tree of which I commanded you not to eat?" [12] The man said, "The woman whom You gave *to be* with me, she gave me from the tree, and I ate." [13] Then the LORD God said to the woman, "What is this you have done?" And the woman said, "The serpent deceived me, and I ate."

God placed Adam in the Garden of Eden to care for and maintain it (Genesis 2:15). The word *Eden* means pleasure or delight. God gave only one limitation to Adam and Eve. They could freely eat the fruit of any tree in this bountiful garden except for one. Adam and Eve were given a choice; obey or disobey God (Genesis 2:8–17). We do not know the exact location of the Garden of Eden, but our best guess is that it must have been somewhere in the Mesopotamian Valley near the headwaters of the Tigris and Euphrates Rivers. After the Fall, Adam and Eve were driven out of this wonderful place, and an angel was placed at the entrance to guard against re-entry. Obviously, this earthly "paradise" had to have been destroyed during the Flood of Noah's day.

1. Adam and Eve were created with sinless natures.

2. Adam and Eve were innocent before God.

3. A sinless *character* comes as the result of testing and resisting the temptation by making the right choice. This sinless disposition could either be retained or lost depending on the results of the moral test.

4. Adam and Eve's sinless *natures* were tested, and it is likely that if they had resisted the temptation and passed the test, they could have been transformed into sinless *characters.*

5. Adam and Eve were placed in the garden for a period of probation or testing.

6. They were given one simple test.

7. When the temptation came, they failed. (Genesis 3)

B. Humankind's temptation

Genesis 3:1–7

> [1] Now the serpent was more crafty than any beast of the field which the LORD God had made. And he said to the woman, "Indeed, has God said, 'You shall not eat from any tree of the garden'?" [2] The woman said to the serpent, "From the fruit of the trees of the garden we may eat; [3] but from the fruit of the tree which is in the middle of the garden, God has said, 'You shall not eat from it or touch it, or you will die.'" [4] The serpent said to the woman, "You surely will not die! [5] For God knows that in the day you eat from it your eyes will be opened, and you will be like God, knowing good and evil." [6] When the woman saw that the tree was good for food, and that it was a delight to the eyes, and that the tree was desirable to make *one* wise, she took

> from its fruit and ate; and she gave also to her husband with her, and he ate. [7] Then the eyes of both of them were opened, and they knew that they were naked; and they sewed fig leaves together and made themselves loin coverings.

2 Corinthians 11:3

> But I am afraid that, as the serpent deceived Eve by his craftiness, your minds will be led astray from the simplicity and purity *of devotion* to Christ.

Revelation 12:9

> And the great dragon was thrown down, the serpent of old who is called the devil and Satan, who deceives the whole world; he was thrown down to the earth, and his angels were thrown down with him.

1. The tempter was Satan, but he used the serpent to introduce the temptation.

2. The serpent evidently was originally incredibly beautiful and must have had some type of legs which gave him the power of upright motion.

3. Satan's seven-fold method of approach was used in the temptation of Eve.

   a. Satan made a statement in the form of a question.

   Genesis 3:1

   > Now the serpent was more crafty than any beast of the field which the LORD God had made. And he said to the woman, "Indeed, has God said, 'You shall not eat from any tree of the garden'?"

   b. Satan planted a seed of doubt in Eve's mind by asking this question. His claim was that God was withholding a great deal from her. When Satan said "any tree," he was encouraging Eve to focus on the restriction. He magnified the one prohibition and minimized the many, many blessings from God that she possessed. Satan tempts us in the same way today by making the Christian life seem like many prohibitions and few blessings.

   c. Satan made a flat contradiction to the Word of God.

   Genesis 3:4

   > The serpent said to the woman, "You surely will not die!"

d. Satan quickly moved to a lie once a glimmer of doubt was created.

John 8:44

> You are of *your* father the devil, and you want to do the desires of your father. He was a murderer from the beginning, and does not stand in the truth because there is no truth in him. Whenever he speaks a lie, he speaks from his own *nature*, for he is a liar and the father of lies.

e. Satan told Eve that God was withholding something good from her. This is at the core of selfish rebellion against God.

Genesis 3:5

> "For God knows that in the day you eat from it your eyes will be opened, and you will be like God, knowing good and evil."

f. Satan accused God of trying to keep Eve from something good. Today Satan still makes the worldly life (the pleasures of sin) look good. He makes us feel like God is robbing us of these pleasures. Christian beware!

g. Satan drew Eve's attention to the forbidden fruit and implemented his three-fold attraction to disobedience.

1 John 2:16

> For all that is in the world, the lust of the flesh and the lust of the eyes and the boastful pride of life, is not from the Father, but is from the world.

- The lust of the flesh – "good for food"
  Satan's attack came through the body's desire.
- The lust of the eyes – "a delight to the eyes"
  This is the so-called thrill and attractiveness of sin. It is the accumulation of things outside of God's plan and will. Satan makes them appear as enticing to the eye. He makes evil look good.
- The pride of life – "desirable to make one wise"
  This is what the Bible calls "vain glory." It is the worldly ambition to attract the attention of others and to acquire power and glory outside of the plan of God. It is imagining yourself to be something or someone great. It is a seeking of glory that only belongs to God.

4. Satan pursued this same three-fold attack on Christ, but his assault was unsuccessful. (Read Luke 4:1–13.)

    a. To turn stones into bread (lust of flesh)

    b. To view of a worldly kingdom (lust of the eyes)

    c. To cast Himself down from the pinnacle of the temple (pride of life – flaunting His power)

C. The disobedience of Adam and Eve

Genesis 3:6

> When the woman saw that the tree was good for food, and that it was a delight to the eyes, and that the tree was desirable to make *one* wise, she took from its fruit and ate; and she gave also to her husband with her, and he ate.

James 1:13–15

> [13] Let no one say when he is tempted, "I am being tempted by God"; for God cannot be tempted by evil, and He Himself does not tempt anyone. [14] But each one is tempted when he is carried away and enticed by his own lust. [15] Then when lust has conceived, it gives birth to sin; and when sin is accomplished, it brings forth death.

1. As a result of the cunning temptation of Satan, Eve and then Adam disobeyed God's command.

2. They knowingly and consciously exercised their own will.

3. It was not a case of being the victim of circumstances.

4. They made the decision to defy God's authority and regulation.

5. Their act was an act of rebellion against God.

6. Their choice was to walk away from a loving God, who had provided everything they needed. They did this to feed their own selfish desires.

VII. The Conscience of Humankind

A. The conscience gives a person an awareness of the good of one's conduct or motives, or it causes feelings of remorse for evil doing.

1 Samuel 24:4–5

> [4] The men of David said to him, "Behold, *this is* the day of which the LORD said to you, 'Behold; I am about to give your enemy into your hand, and you shall do to him as it seems good to you.'" Then David arose and cut off the edge of Saul's robe secretly. [5] It came about afterward that David's conscience bothered him because he had cut off the edge of Saul's *robe*.

B. A clear conscience is one which has no feeling of reproach. A blameless conscience does not accuse a person of willfully doing wrong.

In Acts 24:16, Paul defends himself before Felix, governor of Judea and Samaria.

Acts 24:16

> In view of this, I also do my best to maintain always a blameless conscience *both* before God and before men.

C. The conscience is that sense within us, which decides as to the moral quality of our thoughts, words, and actions.

Romans 2:14–16

> [14] For when Gentiles who do not have the Law do instinctively the things of the Law, these, not having the Law, are a law to themselves, [15] in that they show the work of the Law written in their hearts, their conscience bearing witness and their thoughts alternately accusing or else defending them, [16] on the day when, according to my gospel, God will judge the secrets of men through Christ Jesus.

D. A conscience can be educated or trained to recognize good and evil, but its action is involuntary.

E. The conscience may be defiled by continually being violated.

1 Timothy 4:2

> by means of the hypocrisy of liars seared in their own conscience as with a branding iron,

Titus 1:15

> To the pure, all things are pure; but to those who are defiled and unbelieving, nothing is pure, but both their mind and their conscience are defiled.

F. It is possible to train or modify your conscience by your response to it.

1. A good conscience (1 Timothy 1:5)

2. A clear conscience (1 Timothy 3:9)

3. A conscience void of offense (Acts 24:16)

4. An evil conscience (Hebrews 10:22)

5. A seared conscience – This is an individual who constantly resists the truth, violating his or her conscience until it becomes numb to evil. (1 Timothy 4:2)

6. A conscience void of offense is a conscience that is pleasing to God, not because it belongs to a Christian who never sins, but because confession is practiced, and forgiveness is obtained. (1 John 1:7–9)

1 Timothy 1:5

> But the goal of our instruction is love from a pure heart and a good conscience and a sincere faith.

1 Timothy 3:8–10

> [8] Deacons likewise *must be* men of dignity, not double-tongued, or addicted to much wine or fond of sordid gain, [9] *but* holding to the mystery of the faith with a clear conscience. [10] These men must also first be tested; then let them serve as deacons if they are beyond reproach.

Hebrews 10:22

> let us draw near with a sincere heart in full assurance of faith, having our hearts sprinkled *clean* from an evil conscience and our bodies washed with pure water.

John 8:7–10

> [7] But when they persisted in asking Him, He straightened up, and said to them, "He who is without sin among you, let him *be the* first to throw a stone at her." [8] Again He stooped down and wrote on the ground. [9] When they heard it, they *began* to go out one by one, beginning with the older ones, and He was left alone, and the woman, where she was, in the center *of the court.* [10] Straightening up, Jesus said to her, "Woman, where are they? Did no one condemn you?"

G. A clear conscience before God deals with sin by confession.

1 John 1:7–9

> [7] but if we walk in the Light as He Himself is in the Light, we have fellowship with one another, and the blood of Jesus His Son cleanses us from all sin. [8] If we say that we have no sin, we are deceiving ourselves and the truth is not in us. [9] If we confess our sins, He is faithful and righteous to forgive us our sins and to cleanse us from all unrighteousness.

We have already seen that God created people with a free will, the ability to make choices. After Adam and Eve chose to disobey God, we see the activity of their conscience. They became aware of their nakedness before one another and hid from God.

Note: Some consider the conscience to be the direct voice of God in an individual. Often, cartoonist personify the conscience as a cute little elf-like creature that whispers naughty things in our ears when we are tempted. There is nothing in the Bible that supports either of these views.

Conclusions:

1. The conscience is an in-born faculty.
2. It is triggered when we sin against God or someone else.
3. It is felt by a sense of guilt.
4. It is not the direct voice of God. If it were the voice of God, it would always be perfect in its conclusions.
5. God places a conscience in us to sit in judgment over our moral actions and attitudes.
6. It is subject to education, culture, and environment and, to a certain extent, may be rendered unreliable.

7. The conscience is active not passive. (Romans 2:15 and John 8:9)

8. The conscience may be weakened and defiled by our response to it. (In 1 Corinthians 8:7, Paul speaks to the Corinthian church concerning eating meat that has been offered to idols and sold in the market.)

1 Corinthians 8:7

> However not all men have this knowledge; but some, being accustomed to the idol until now, eat *food* as if it were sacrificed to an idol; and their conscience being weak is defiled.

VIII. The Disastrous Results of the Fall of the Human Race

A. People were alienated from God.

Genesis 3:7–10

> [7] Then the eyes of both of them were opened, and they knew that they were naked; and they sewed fig leaves together and made themselves loin coverings.
>
> [8] They heard the sound of the LORD God walking in the garden in the cool of the day, and the man and his wife hid themselves from the presence of the LORD God among the trees of the garden. [9] Then the LORD God called to the man, and said to him, "Where are you?" [10] He said, "I heard the sound of You in the garden, and I was afraid because I was naked; so I hid myself."

Genesis 3:16–19

> [16] To the woman He said,
> "I will greatly multiply
> Your pain in childbirth,
> In pain you will bring forth children;
> Yet your desire will be for your husband,
> And he will rule over you."
>
> [17] Then to Adam He said, "Because you have listened to the voice of your wife, and have eaten from the tree about which I commanded you, saying, 'You shall not eat from it';
>
> Cursed is the ground because of you;
> In toil you will eat of it
> All the days of your life.

> [18] "Both thorns and thistles it shall grow for you;
> And you will eat the plants of the field;
> [19] By the sweat of your face
> You will eat bread,
> Till you return to the ground,
> Because from it you were taken;
> For you are dust,
> And to dust you shall return."

1. There was an immediate personal loss to Adam and Eve.

    a. They were conscious of their nakedness and had a sense of shame.

    b. They had a dreadful fear of God. They tried to hide from God.

    c. They attempted to provide their own remedy for their sin. These are the same tactics people use today.

    - Seeking to cover the nakedness of sin with good deeds.
    - Hiding from God and hoping He would not notice our evil.
    - Blaming others rather than confessing our disobedience.

2. The immediate and far-reaching results of their disobedience were linked together.

B. People experienced death. (The word *death* means "separation.")

1 Corinthians 15:22

> For as in Adam all die, so also in Christ all will be made alive.

1. Physical death is the separation of the body from the soul and spirit. Adam and Eve were separated from the tree of life and began to die physically. (Genesis 3:24)

2. Spiritual death is the separation of the individual from God. This was immediate. Adam and Eve were cut off from God, and they knew it.

3. Eternal death is separation from God for all eternity. The Bible describes this death as hell. Apart from salvation through the shed blood of Christ, this eternal death is the destiny for the whole human race. (1 Corinthians 15:22) If a person does not trust Christ as Savior in this life, spiritual death becomes eternal death.

C. There were additional consequences brought on by Adam and Eve's sin.

Genesis 3:14–24

[14] The LORD God said to the serpent,

"Because you have done this,
Cursed are you more than all cattle,
And more than every beast of the field;
On your belly you will go,
And dust you will eat
All the days of your life;
[15] And I will put enmity
Between you and the woman,
And between your seed and her seed;
He shall bruise you on the head,
And you shall bruise him on the heel."
[16] To the woman He said,
"I will greatly multiply
Your pain in childbirth,
In pain you will bring forth children;
Yet your desire will be for your husband,
And he will rule over you."

[17] Then to Adam He said, "Because you have listened to the voice of your wife, and have eaten from the tree about which I commanded you, saying, 'You shall not eat from it';

Cursed is the ground because of you;
In toil you will eat of it
All the days of your life.
[18] "Both thorns and thistles it shall grow for you;
And you will eat the plants of the field;
[19] By the sweat of your face
You will eat bread,
Till you return to the ground,
Because from it you were taken;
For you are dust,
And to dust you shall return."

[20] Now the man called his wife's name Eve, because she was the mother of all *the* living. [21] The LORD God made garments of skin for Adam and his wife, and clothed them.

> [22] Then the LORD God said, "Behold, the man has become like one of Us, knowing good and evil; and now, he might stretch out his hand, and take also from the tree of life, and eat, and live forever"— [23] therefore the LORD God sent him out from the garden of Eden, to cultivate the ground from which he was taken. [24] So He drove the man out; and at the east of the garden of Eden He stationed the cherubim and the flaming sword which turned every direction to guard the way to the tree of life.

1. The serpent was cursed. It was limited to crawl upon its belly. (Genesis 3:14)

2. Satan's judgment was assured. (Genesis 3:15)

3. Jesus Christ (the seed of the woman) would (at Calvary) receive a bruise on his heal (a relatively slight wound). (Genesis 3:15)

4. Satan would receive a bruise to his head (a death blow). (Genesis 3:15)

5. The woman would experience sorrow and pain in childbirth. (Genesis 3:16)

6. The man would experience sorrow and would have to toil during his life on earth. (Genesis 3:17–19)

7. The ground was cursed. (Genesis 3:17–19)

8. Adam's future generations were affected.

Romans 5:12

> Therefore, just as through one man sin entered into the world, and death through sin, and so death spread to all men, because all sinned—

Romans 5:16–19

> [16] The gift is not like *that which came* through the one who sinned; for on the one hand the judgment *arose* from one *transgression* resulting in condemnation, but on the other hand the free gift *arose* from many transgressions resulting in justification. [17] For if by the transgression of the one, death reigned through the one, much more those who receive the abundance of grace and of the gift of righteousness will reign in life through the One, Jesus Christ.
>
> [18] So then as through one transgression there resulted condemnation to all men, even so through one act of righteousness there resulted justification of life to all men. [19] For as through the one man's disobedience the many were made sinners, even so through the obedience of the One the many will be made righteous.

Conclusions:

1. All humankind became sinners before God. (Romans 3:9–10, 23; Psalms 14; Isaiah 53:6)

2. This universal sinful condition was the direct result of the sin of Adam. (Romans 5:12, 16, 19)

3. All humankind came under condemnation, wrath, and the curse. (Romans 3:19; Ephesians 2:1)

4. All those who have rejected Christ as Savior are regarded as children of the devil and not children of God. (1 John 3:8–10; John 8:44; 1 John 5:19)

5. The whole human race became hopelessly enslaved to sin and Satan. (Romans 7:14–25; John 8:31–36; Ephesians 2:2)

6. The whole nature of humanity (mentally, morally, spiritually, and physically) is sadly altered by sin.

   a. Humankind's understanding is darkened. (Ephesians 4:18; 1 Corinthians 2:14)

   b. Humankind's heart is deceitful and wicked. (Jeremiah 17:9–10)

   c. Humankind's mind and conscience are defiled. (2 Corinthians 7:1)

   d. The will of all humans is weakened. (Romans 7:18)

7. The sad separations, as a result of sin:

   a. Humankind was separated from the Tree of Life. Access to the Tree of Life was the way to keep their bodies alive. (Genesis 3:22)

   b. Humankind was separated from the Garden of Eden. (Genesis 3:23–24)

   c. Humankind was separated from the presence of God. (Genesis 3:24; Isaiah 59:2)

Note: People have tried desperately to discredit the account of Adam and Eve in the book of Genesis. One of the reasons for this is that people do not like the sad record of the Fall. Here are two of the positions taken toward the Genesis account:

- Some call the Genesis account an allegory. They see it as a figurative story.
- Some call the Genesis account a myth. They perceive it as folklore.

There is no logical or biblical reason to deny the Genesis account as a factual account. We believe the Genesis description is accurately recorded and has truly occurred as the scripture states.

IX. Sin's Effect on Our View of Who We Are

God created you, loves you, and has a remarkable plan for your life. This plan includes your salvation, your Christian growth, and your service for the Lord Jesus Christ. God's plan for you is specially designed for you by your Creator. God never makes a mistake. Failure to see yourself as God's unique creation will rob you of the fullness of life in Christ.

A. Two basic standards by which we may determine our personal worth

1. God's Standard – He made you just the way He wanted you, and what you see in the mirror is exactly what He intended. He has known you from before the beginning of time. He created you for His glory, and you will be completely fulfilled when you live and serve for His glory. Remember, Jesus loves the real you! He uniquely designed you and equipped you. He managed your family tree. He has exactly positioned you into your family and into your culture.

Psalms 139:13–16

[13] For You formed my inward parts;
You wove me in my mother's womb.
[14] I will give thanks to You, for I am fearfully and wonderfully made;
Wonderful are Your works,
And my soul knows it very well.
[15] My frame was not hidden from You,
When I was made in secret,
And skillfully wrought in the depths of the earth;
[16] Your eyes have seen my unformed substance;
And in Your book were all written
The days that were ordained *for me*,
When as yet there was not one of them.

Jeremiah 29:11

'For I know the plans that I have for you,' declares the Lord, 'plans for welfare and not for calamity to give you a future and a hope.'

a. You are a unique creation of God.

b. God knew what you would look like before you were formed in your mother's womb.

c. God created your appearance, abilities, and strengths. He wisely placed you in your family and positioned you in your present culture and situation.

d. God ordained certain things to be a part of His plan for you.

2. Human Standard – We often measure ourselves with others. In comparing ourselves with those around us, we might use such terms as normal, average, ugly, beautiful, handicapped, gifted, privileged, unfortunate, etc.

Human standard focuses on:

a. Our physical appearance (the way we look).

b. Our abilities (physical and/or mental).

c. Our heritage (our parents and family).

d. Our environment (culture, surroundings, and circumstances).

The way we view these issues will play a major role in the development of our personalities. God warns us in the Bible about our attitude concerning these things. Read and meditate on the following warnings and instructions:

B. Warning against being dissatisfied about our self-worth

Isaiah 64:8

> But now, O LORD, You are our Father,
> We are the clay, and You our potter;
> And all of us are the work of Your hand.

Isaiah 45:9–10

> [9] "Woe to *the one* who quarrels with his Maker—
> An earthenware vessel among the vessels of earth!
> Will the clay say to the potter, 'What are you doing?'
> Or the thing you are making *say*, 'He has no hands'?
> [10] "Woe to him who says to a father, 'What are you begetting?'
> Or to a woman, 'To what are you giving birth?'"

Romans 9:20–21

> [20] On the contrary, who are you, O man, who answers back to God? The thing molded will not say to the molder, "Why did you make me like this," will it? [21] Or does not the potter have a right over the clay, to make from the same lump one vessel for honorable use and another for common use?

2 Corinthians 10:12–13

> [12] For we are not bold to class or compare ourselves with some of those who commend themselves; but when they measure themselves by themselves and compare themselves with themselves, they are without understanding. [13] But we will not boast beyond *our* measure, but within the measure of the sphere which God apportioned to us as a measure, to reach even as far as you.

1. We are instructed not to compare ourselves with others.
2. We are not to elevate ourselves above others nor diminish ourselves below others.
3. Those who measure themselves by others are "without understanding." (2 Corinthians 10:12–13)
4. We are to measure ourselves by God's measuring stick, which "God apportioned to us as a measure."
5. Woe is pronounced against: (Isaiah 45:9–10)
    - Those who argue with their Maker.
    - Those who question the work of the Potter.
    - Those who are unhappy with the product of their own birth.

    Note: When God uses the word *woe*, it is a severe warning of a great consequence.

C. The high costs of low self-worth

1. An inability to trust God – This negative reasoning follows this path:
    a. God is the Creator. God is love.
    b. God created me, loves me, and mapped out a plan for my life.
    c. If God created what I see in the mirror (or in the events of my life), then I cannot trust Him with the rest of my life.

   d. God must have made some drastic mistakes.

   e. Conclusion: I will have to take charge of my own life and see what I can do to compensate for God's mistake.

2. A resistance and rebellion against authority – This negative reasoning follows this path:

   a. God is the sovereign and source of all authority.

   b. The authorities over me (including my parents) have been unfair and are flawed.

   c. God cheated me in the past, as He placed me under this line-of-authority.

   d. If God cheated me before, then He may cheat me again.

   e. Conclusion: I live with a bitter attitude towards all authority, and I form a basic attitude of rebellion.

3. A hindrance in making lasting friendships – This negative reasoning follows this path:

   a. God created me.

   b. As I compare myself with others, it is apparent that I cannot measure up. God must have made a mistake when He created me.

   c. Others must see the obvious fact that I am inferior.

   d. If I criticize myself in their presence, maybe they will see that I understand I am inferior and will accept me. If I act superior to them, maybe they will not notice my weaknesses.

   e. Conclusion: I do not measure up to others, which reinforces in my mind what I already knew. I cannot measure up, therefore do not make lasting relationships.

   Note: Neither an inferior attitude nor a superior attitude is appealing to others. Both attitudes create difficulty in making and deepening friendships.

4. A failure to reach our true potential – This negative reasoning follows this path:

   a. God has created me with certain strengths and talents.

   b. As I compare myself to others, I begin to think that I am inferior and that others have better strengths and capabilities.

c. I am obviously not as talented as those around me. God must have failed to give me any good abilities.

d. I cannot be expected to achieve anything of worthiness or lasting value. I may as well not try.

e. Conclusion: Because of this poor attitude and a failure to do my best, schoolwork suffers, and employment opportunities pass me by. All this only reinforces my conclusions about my weaknesses and the cycle begins all over again. I begin to see myself as a "loser."

5. An over-emphasis on materialism – This negative reasoning follows this path:

   a. God created me and designed me.

   b. As I compare myself with others, it is apparent that I am mediocre.

   c. Others must see the obvious fact that I am of lesser value. God must have made a mistake in my design.

   d. Maybe if I "fix up" (or dress up) what I have or who I am, I can attract friends by impressing them. I will accumulate possessions (trendy clothes, an awesome computer, a fancy car, lots of cash, etc.), then others will be impressed, and my inferiority will be less noticeable.

   e. Conclusion: Because my attitude only attracts superficial friends, and deep friendships are never formulated, I am often left feeling lonely with shallow friendships.

X. The Development of Our True Self-Image and Worth (God's Standard)

The reasoning of poor self-worth leads to under-achievement, manipulation, disappointment, frustration, failure, loneliness, unhappiness, bitterness, and often despair. Among the things that can define and lower our opinion of ourselves are parental criticism and childhood teasing. Comparison of academic abilities, physical attributes, or mental aptitudes are other things that lead to this struggle of poor self-worth, but individuals who take this path begin their journey by making the mistake of comparing themselves to others in one or more of the following areas:

- Our physical appearance
- Our abilities
- Our heritage
- Our environment

Psalms 139:15–16

> [15] My frame was not hidden from You,
> When I was made in secret,
> *And* skillfully wrought in the depths of the earth;
> [16] Your eyes have seen my unformed substance;
> And in Your book were all written
> The days that were ordained *for me*,
> When as yet there was not one of them.

A. Accepting God's view of who we are will lead to a life of fulfillment.

God's view of our worth leads to a life of fulfillment, happiness, self-confidence, satisfaction, contentment, and achievement. It will give us the freedom to be ourselves. It will lead us to an ability to trust God with the details of our lives. It is based on the foundation that God is the sovereign Creator and Lord who never makes mistakes. Every individual is unique. Looking to our Creator and viewing ourselves as He sees us is a matter of being grounded in the truth of God's Word. God views everyone as uniquely created and fashioned for His glory. When we see ourselves as God sees us, it has the potential to significantly change our lives.

Remember, God loves the real you, not the one you may pretend to be.

Jeremiah 29:11

> 'For I know the plans that I have for you,' declares the LORD, 'plans for welfare and not for calamity to give you a future and a hope.'

1 Thessalonians 5:18

> in everything give thanks; for this is God's will for you in Christ Jesus.

2 Corinthians 12:7–10

> [7] Because of the surpassing greatness of the revelations, for this reason, to keep me from exalting myself, there was given me a thorn in the flesh, a messenger of Satan to torment me—to keep me from exalting myself! [8] Concerning this I implored the Lord three times that it might leave me. [9] And He has said to me, "My grace is sufficient for you, for power is perfected in weakness." Most gladly, therefore, I will rather boast about my weaknesses, so that the power of Christ may dwell in me. [10] Therefore I am well content with weaknesses, with insults, with distresses, with persecutions, with difficulties, for Christ's sake; for when I am weak, then I am strong.

Approaching our worth from God's viewpoint will lead to the following conclusions:

1. I acknowledge and accept the value God places on me and my life.
2. I see myself as uniquely created by a sovereign God and as part of His great blueprint for my life.
3. I develop an attitude of thanksgiving, even for those things that others might view as challenges. (1 Thessalonians 5:18)
4. I welcome these challenges as special gifts from God, and I understand that, with my cooperation, He can work out His glorious plan for my life. I seek to reach out to others as I develop a Christ-like life. (2 Corinthians 12:10)
5. I acknowledge a sense of God's special design for my life.
6. I anticipate His working in and through my life.
7. I am free from the feelings of inadequacy and uneasiness.
8. I seek to be what God wants me to be and daily depend on Him.
9. My life is ever expanding and becoming more and more fulfilling and exciting.
10. I see every personal contact as a "divine appointment," and I make friends effortlessly.
11. My life is full and free. God is daily working in and through my life for His glory.
12. I do not need to pretend to be someone I am not or impress anyone with my efforts or abilities.
13. I am always myself, and Christ can shine through me.

Remember, God loves the *real* you and desires to use the *real* you.

B. Steps to allowing God to heal a low self-image:

1. Begin to see yourself as God sees you.
2. Before the Lord, confess the sin of having a poor view of your worth. Your dissatisfaction of self is *actually* a discontentment toward God, the Potter.

Romans 9:20–21

> [20] On the contrary, who are you, O man, who answers back to God? The thing molded will not say to the molder, "Why did you make me like this," will it? [21] Or does not the potter have a right over the clay, to make from the same lump one vessel for honorable use and another for common use?

Isaiah 45:9–10

> [9] "Woe to *the one* who quarrels with his Maker—
> An earthenware vessel among the vessels of earth!
> Will the clay say to the potter, 'What are you doing?'
> Or the thing you are making *say*, 'He has no hands'?
> [10] "Woe to him who says to a father, 'What are you begetting?'
> Or to a woman, 'To what are you giving birth?'"

3. Acknowledge that God designed you and your life even before you were formed in your mother's womb.

Psalms 139:13–16

> [13] For You formed my inward parts;
> You wove me in my mother's womb.
> [14] I will give thanks to You, for I am fearfully and wonderfully made;
> Wonderful are Your works,
> And my soul knows it very well.
> [15] My frame was not hidden from You,
> When I was made in secret,
> *And* skillfully wrought in the depths of the earth;
> [16] Your eyes have seen my unformed substance;
> And in Your book were all written
> The days that were ordained *for me*,
> When as yet there was not one of them.

4. Accept the fact that your appearance, abilities, parentage, and environment are all a part of God's wonderful plan for your life to achieve His good goals in and through you.

2 Corinthians 12:9

> And He has said to me, "My grace is sufficient for you, for power is perfected in weakness." Most gladly, therefore, I will rather boast about my weaknesses, so that the power of Christ may dwell in me.

5. Accept that God is not finished molding you yet.

    Ephesians 2:10

    > For we are His workmanship, created in Christ Jesus for good works, which God prepared beforehand so that we would walk in them.

6. Think of your appearance, abilities, parentage, and environment as only a frame around the picture of the qualities the Holy Spirit wants to build into your life.

    Galatians 5:22–23

    > [22] But the fruit of the Spirit is love, joy, peace, patience, kindness, goodness, faithfulness, [23] gentleness, self-control; against such things there is no law.

    1 Peter 3:3–4

    > [3] Your adornment must not be *merely* external—braiding the hair, and wearing gold jewelry, or putting on dresses; [4] but *let it be* the hidden person of the heart, with the imperishable quality of a gentle and quiet spirit, which is precious in the sight of God.

    Proverbs 15:13

    > A joyful heart makes a cheerful face,
    > But when the heart is sad, the spirit is broken.

7. Recognize that it is the Artist's (God's) reputation that is at stake, not yours. He should not be criticized until the picture is completed.

8. Thank God for His workmanship so far and move forward with true confidence in His ability to finish what He has begun.

9. In prayer, give the Holy Spirit permission to produce the qualities listed in Galatians 5:22–23. As you daily yield to Him, He will build into your life these character traits.

    Galatians 5:22–23

    > [22] But the fruit of the Spirit is love, joy, peace, patience, kindness, goodness, faithfulness, [23] gentleness, self-control; against such things there is no law.

God has never made
a mistake and
never will.

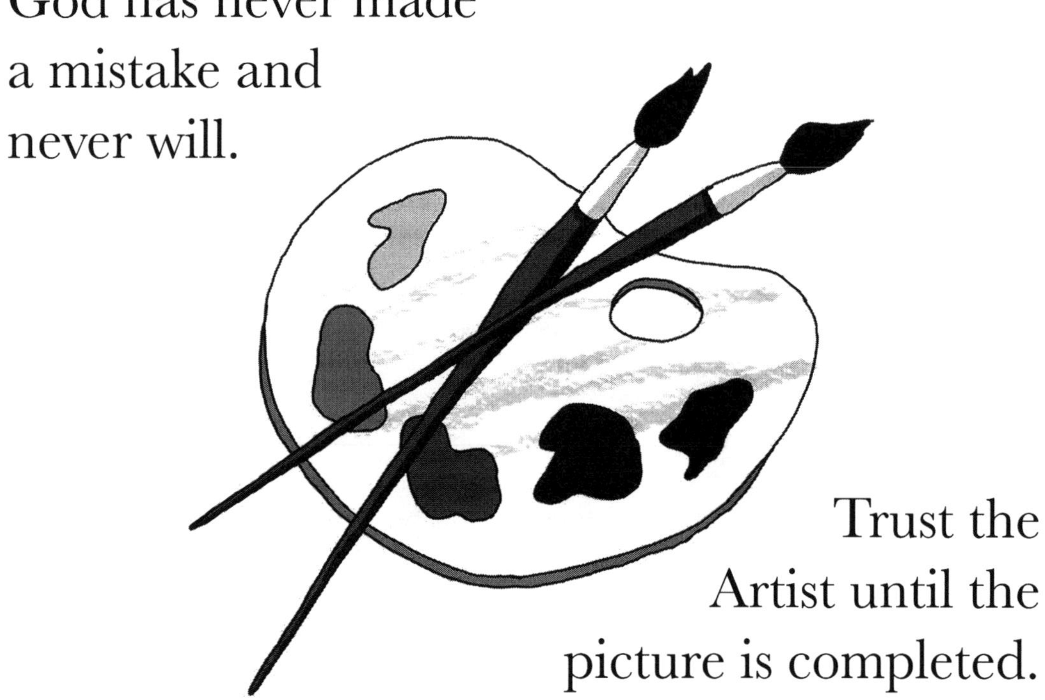

Trust the
Artist until the
picture is completed.

REVIEW QUESTIONS

1. Write out Genesis 2:7.
2. What does it mean to say that the creation of Adam was an immediate act of God?
3. What is the theory of evolution?
4. What has evolution failed to produce as evidence to prove its theory?
5. Explain what is known about the date of Adam's creation.
6. Name two ways that humankind was made in the likeness of God.
7. Explain the meaning of the theological term *trichotomy*.
8. Name the three parts of a person.
9. Name the two immaterial parts of people.
10. If we get our body through our parents, where does our soul come from?
11. Name the main responsibility given to Adam concerning God's creation.
12. What is the conscience?
13. Is the conscience the direct voice of God?
14. Is the conscience at all subject to education?
15. Who was the tempter of Eve?
16. Name four things Satan did in his method of approach in tempting Eve.
17. What was the three-fold attack of Satan, as he focused Eve's attention on the forbidden fruit?
18. Has Satan ever used this attack on anyone else? If so, who?
19. What was the immediate personal loss after the Fall?
20. Name and explain the three types of death.
21. From what three things were Adam and Eve separated after their sin?

22. Give three views people have toward the book of Genesis (particularly toward the account of the fall of humankind).

23. Name two standards by which we may measure ourselves.

24. In what four areas are we likely to measure ourselves?

25. Name and explain the four consequences of a low self-image.

26. Name the steps in removing an attitude of poor self-worth.

CHAPTER 9

Angelology
(What the Bible Teaches About Angels)

There is a class of beings mentioned often in the Bible who are called angels. The word *angel* literally means "messenger" in both Hebrew (Old Testament) and Greek (New Testament). They were created to serve God as His messengers. Angels are always referred to in the masculine gender. They are not to be confused with the pre-incarnate appearances of Christ, who is sometimes referred to as the Angel of Jehovah in the Old Testament.

Psalms 103:20

> Bless the LORD, you His angels,
> Mighty in strength, who perform His word,
> Obeying the voice of His word!

I. The Biblical Definition of the Origin and Character of Angels

A. Angels are spirit beings, though at times, God gives them the power to appear in human form.

Genesis 19:1

> Now the two angels came to Sodom in the evening as Lot was sitting in the gate of Sodom. When Lot saw *them*, he rose to meet them and bowed down *with his* face to the ground.

B. Angels are heavenly beings created by God, having access to heaven.

Colossians 1:16

> For by Him all things were created, *both* in the heavens and on earth, visible and invisible, whether thrones or dominions or rulers or authorities—all things have been created through Him and for Him.

Nehemiah 9:6

"You alone are the Lord.
You have made the heavens,
The heaven of heavens with all their host,
The earth and all that is on it,
The seas and all that is in them.
You give life to all of them
And the heavenly host bows down before You."

Matthew 18:10

"See that you do not despise one of these little ones, for I say to you that their angels in heaven continually see the face of My Father who is in heaven."

C. In general, angels are currently in a higher position than humankind.

Hebrews 2:6–7

But one has testified somewhere, saying,

"What is man, that You remember him?
Or the son of man, that You are concerned about him?
[7] "You have made him for a little while lower than the angels;
You have crowned him with glory and honor,
And have appointed him over the works of Your hands;"

D. Angels are an innumerable company.

Hebrews 12:22

But you have come to Mount Zion and to the city of the living God, the heavenly Jerusalem, and to myriads of angels,

2 Kings 6:15–17

[15] Now when the attendant of the man of God had risen early and gone out, behold, an army with horses and chariots was circling the city. And his servant said to him, "Alas, my master! What shall we do?" [16] So he answered, "Do not fear, for those who are with us are more than those who are with them." [17] Then Elisha prayed and said, "O Lord, I pray, open his eyes that he may see." And the Lord opened the servant's eyes and he saw; and behold, the mountain was full of horses and chariots of fire all around Elisha.

E. Angels are finite beings.

Matthew 24:36

"But of that day and hour no one knows, not even the angels of heaven, nor the Son, but the Father alone."

There are two kinds of angels defined in scripture – unfallen and fallen angels.

II. Unfallen Angels

These are the holy angels who kept their original state. They did not participate in the rebellion that was led by Lucifer (Satan). These angels are involved in ministering to the people of God. They are obedient to the voice of God.

Hebrews 1:14

Are they not all ministering spirits, sent out to render service for the sake of those who will inherit salvation?

Psalms 103:20

Bless the LORD, you His angels,
Mighty in strength, who perform His word,
Obeying the voice of His word!

A. Some of these unfallen angels are mentioned by name.

1. Michael, the archangel

His name means "who is like unto God."

Jude 9

But Michael the archangel, when he disputed with the devil and argued about the body of Moses, did not dare pronounce against him a railing judgment, but said, "The Lord rebuke you!"

2. Gabriel

His name means "the mighty one." Gabriel announces the birth of Jesus. (See also Luke 1:19.)

Luke 1:26–27

> [26] Now in the sixth month the angel Gabriel was sent from God to a city in Galilee called Nazareth, [27] to a virgin engaged to a man whose name was Joseph, of the descendants of David; and the virgin's name was Mary.
>
> (See also Daniel 8:16 and Daniel 9:21.)

B. Unfallen angels are sometimes mentioned by classification.

1. Cherubim – meaning is unknown. (See also Exodus 25:17–20.)

Genesis 3:24

> So He drove the man out; and at the east of the garden of Eden He stationed the cherubim and the flaming sword which turned every direction to guard the way to the tree of life.

2. Seraphim – meaning "fiery, burning ones."

Isaiah 6:2

> Seraphim stood above Him, each having six wings: with two he covered his face, and with two he covered his feet, and with two he flew.

3. The Angel of Jehovah

This is God Himself. Christ is the Angel of Jehovah. Genesis 22:11–12 describes one of the pre-incarnate manifestations of Christ in the Old Testament. (See also Genesis 16:1–13; Judges 13:3–21; Isaiah 63:9; Zechariah 1:12.)

Genesis 22:11–12

> [11] But the angel of the LORD called to him from heaven and said, "Abraham, Abraham!" And he said, "Here I am." [12] He said, "Do not stretch out your hand against the lad, and do nothing to him; for now I know that you fear God, since you have not withheld your son, your only son, from Me."

C. Unfallen angels have a ministry and presence.

1. Some unfallen angels were standing guard at the entrance of the Garden of Eden, following the sin of Adam and Eve.

Genesis 3:24

So He drove the man out; and at the east of the garden of Eden He stationed the cherubim and the flaming sword which turned every direction to guard the way to the tree of life.

2. These unfallen angels minister to the needs of the people of God.

Hebrews 1:14

Are they not all ministering spirits, sent out to render service for the sake of those who will inherit salvation?

3. Some unfallen angels ministered to the needs of Christ while He was here on earth.

   a. After Christ's temptation, the angels came and ministered to Him.

   Matthew 4:11

   Then the devil left Him; and behold, angels came and *began* to minister to Him.

   b. At the cross, an angel from heaven appeared to Jesus and strengthened Him.

   Luke 22:43

   Now an angel from heaven appeared to Him, strengthening Him.

4. Unfallen angels are active worshippers of God.

Psalms 148:2

Praise Him, all His angels;
Praise Him, all His hosts!

5. Unfallen angels will participate in God's judgment.

Matthew 13:41–42

[41] The Son of Man will send forth His angels, and they will gather out of His kingdom all stumbling blocks, and those who commit lawlessness, [42] and will throw them into the furnace of fire; in that place there will be weeping and gnashing of teeth.

6. Unfallen angels watch over little children.

Matthew 18:10

> "See that you do not despise one of these little ones, for I say to you that their angels in heaven continually see the face of My Father who is in heaven."

7. Unfallen angels are constantly at the disposal of God.

Matthew 26:53

> Or do you think that I cannot appeal to My Father, and He will at once put at My disposal more than twelve legions of angels?

Note: A Roman legion at that time was about 5,000 men. Twelve legions would amount to about 60,000 angels.

8. Unfallen angels rejoice when someone comes to Christ in repentance.

Luke 15:10

> "In the same way, I tell you, there is joy in the presence of the angels of God over one sinner who repents."

III. Fallen Angels

A. Fallen angels are the angels who chose to join the rebellion of Lucifer.

1. Some fallen angels are free.

Luke 8:30–33

> [30] And Jesus asked him, "What is your name?" And he said, "Legion"; for many demons had entered him. [31] They were imploring Him not to command them to go away into the abyss.
>
> [32] Now there was a herd of many swine feeding there on the mountain; and *the demons* implored Him to permit them to enter the swine. And He gave them permission. [33] And the demons came out of the man and entered the swine; and the herd rushed down the steep bank into the lake and was drowned.

Matthew 12:43–45

> [43] "Now when the unclean spirit goes out of a man, it passes through waterless places seeking rest, and does not find *it*. [44] Then it says, 'I will return to my house from which I came'; and when it comes, it finds *it* unoccupied, swept, and put in order. [45] Then it goes and takes along with it seven other spirits more wicked than itself, and they go in and live there; and the last state of that man becomes worse than the first. That is the way it will also be with this evil generation."

2. Some fallen angels are bound.

2 Peter 2:4

> For if God did not spare angels when they sinned, but cast them into hell and committed them to pits of darkness, reserved for judgment;

Jude 6

> And angels who did not keep their own domain, but abandoned their proper abode, He has kept in eternal bonds under darkness for the judgment of the great day,

3. Satan is among those that are free to roam the earth and do evil.

Job 1:7

> The LORD said to Satan, "From where do you come?" Then Satan answered the LORD and said, "From roaming about on the earth and walking around on it."

1 Peter 5:8

> Be of sober *spirit*, be on the alert. Your adversary, the devil, prowls around like a roaring lion, seeking someone to devour.

Revelation 12:9

> And the great dragon was thrown down, the serpent of old who is called the devil and Satan, who deceives the whole world; he was thrown down to the earth, and his angels were thrown down with him.

(Also see Matthew 25:41.)

4. Though scripture does not actually define demons as fallen angels, there is quite conclusive evidence that they are angels who rebelled against the authority of the triune God and placed themselves under the leadership of Satan.

    Revelation 12:7–9

    > [7] And there was war in heaven, Michael and his angels waging war with the dragon. The dragon and his angels waged war, [8] and they were not strong enough, and there was no longer a place found for them in heaven. [9] And the great dragon was thrown down, the serpent of old who is called the devil and Satan, who deceives the whole world; he was thrown down to the earth, and his angels were thrown down with him.

5. There are many references of demons indwelling both the bodies of people and of beasts. Some examples include Matthew 8:29–31 (swine), Mark 5:4–5 (the demon possessed man cured), Matthew 10:8 (man), Matthew 9:33 (man), Matthew 12:22 (the blind and mute man), Luke 8:26–33 (man and swine).

6. Demon possession, demonic influence, and satanic activity is very prevalent today. Police acknowledge the existence of many crimes connected with the occult. The occult is an intricate part of the illegal drug scene.

7. Undoubtedly men and women are demon possessed today in many instances. It may manifest itself in various ways. (For example, murderous acts of violence are carried out for no apparent reason.)

8. There is a difference between demon possession and demon influence. A Christian can certainly be influenced by demons, but since the believer is already indwelled by the Holy Spirit, it does not make sense that he or she could also be indwelled by an evil spirit.

B. Biblical terms used in connection with satanic activity.

1. Occult – having to do with the involvement, service, and worship of Satan

2. Magic – pretended effects by the supernatural

3. Astrology – foretelling the future by reading the stars

4. Charmers – power over serpents

5. Enchantments – incantations to enlist the aid of evil spirits, including Ouija board activity

6. Ventriloquism – throwing the voice by satanic power

7. Witchcraft – the practice of consorting with evil spirits

8. Divination – obtaining hidden knowledge and foretelling the future (fortune telling)

9. Sorcery – the use of power gained from evil spirits

10. Necromancy – revealing the future by contacting the spirits of the dead

11. Prognostication – indicating the future by signs and omens

C. God's Word makes it *clear* that we are to avoid all occult activities.

Deuteronomy 18:9–14

> [9] "When you enter the land which the LORD your God gives you, you shall not learn to imitate the detestable things of those nations. [10] There shall not be found among you anyone who makes his son or his daughter pass through the fire, one who uses divination, one who practices witchcraft, or one who interprets omens, or a sorcerer, [11] or one who casts a spell, or a medium, or a spiritist, or one who calls up the dead. [12] For whoever does these things is detestable to the LORD; and because of these detestable things the LORD your God will drive them out before you. [13] You shall be blameless before the LORD your God. [14] For those nations, which you shall dispossess, listen to those who practice witchcraft and to diviners, but as for you, the LORD your God has not allowed you *to do* so."

Leviticus 20:6

> "As for the person who turns to mediums and to spiritists, to play the harlot after them, I will also set My face against that person and will cut him off from among his people."

Leviticus 20:27

> "Now a man or a woman who is a medium or a spiritist shall surely be put to death. They shall be stoned with stones, their bloodguiltiness is upon them."

D. Occult practices are described in the Bible.

Occult practices, such as fortune-telling and witchcraft, were regularly practiced among the pagan nations of the ancient world. Such attempts to control evil spirits were expressly forbidden to the Hebrew people. Not only were these occult practices forbidden among

God's people, but these practices were one of the reasons God used Joshua and the people of Israel to destroy and drive out the nations from the land of Canaan.

Deuteronomy 18:9–12

> [9] "When you enter the land which the LORD your God gives you, you shall not learn to imitate the detestable things of those nations. [10] There shall not be found among you anyone who makes his son or his daughter pass through the fire, one who uses divination, one who practices witchcraft, or one who interprets omens, or a sorcerer, [11] or one who casts a spell, or a medium, or a spiritist, or one who calls up the dead. [12] For whoever does these things is detestable to the LORD; and because of these detestable things the LORD your God will drive them out before you."

1. Passing a son or daughter "through the fire"

This phrase refers to the practice of child sacrifice. This seems inconceivable to us today, but the fact that it was outlawed by God, indicates it must have been practiced in those days. Deuteronomy 18:10 and 2 Kings 16:3 record that King Ahaz sacrificed his son in this way. No doubt, wicked King Ahaz thought that such a sacrifice would appease some pagan god. His grandson, King Manasseh, sacrificed his sons two generations later. 2 Kings 21:6, 2 Chronicles 33:6, and 2 Kings 23:10 reveal that it was mainly the pagan god, Molech, who demanded this awful practice. But obviously Satan is behind this practice, for he is the destroyer. (Also see 2 Kings 17:31 and Jeremiah 19:5.)

2. Witchcraft

The practice of witchcraft, or divination, was a means for extracting information or guidance from a pagan god. Witchcraft describes the activity of Balaam, the soothsayer, who was hired to curse Israel (Numbers 22–23; Joshua 13:22). 1 Samuel 28 describes the woman medium at En-Dor who brought up the spirit of Samuel. All the major prophets condemned divination. (Also see Isaiah 44:25; Jeremiah 27:9; Jeremiah 29:8; Ezekiel 13:9.)

3. Soothsaying

Soothsaying is a relatively rare word in the Bible. The New American Standard version of the Bible uses the word only once. It describes some form of divination. Because it sounds like a Hebrew word for *cloud*, some scholars believe it refers to cloud reading. This may have been similar to tea leaf reading (reading the structure of a tea leaf) or astrology (reading of the stars). God forbids the practice in Deuteronomy 18:10–14 and Leviticus 19:26.

The wicked King Manasseh was also guilty of this sin (2 Kings 21:6; 2 Chronicles 33:6). The prophets of the Old Testament condemned this occult practice (Isaiah 2:6; Isaiah 57:3; Jeremiah 27:9, and Micah 5:12).

4. Interpreting Omens (enchantments)

   Behind this phrase lies four different Hebrew words. The most common of the four occurs in Genesis 30:27 and is a reference to Laban's "experience" and is translated "divined." Genesis 44:5,15 refers to Joseph's cup. Numbers 23:23 and 24:1 describe Balaam's activity. Leviticus 19:26 and Deuteronomy 18:10 specifically outlawed this practice. Another word used for this practice means "to hiss, whisper," and it may indicate the way the enchanter lowered his voice. In Ecclesiastes 10:11, interpreting omens relates to snake charming.

5. Sorcery

   Sorcery, or witchcraft, is forbidden in the law of Moses (Exodus 22:18; Deuteronomy 18:10). Sorcery was apparently practiced by the worst of the kings of Israel and Judah, but it was denounced by the prophets (2 Kings 9:22; 2 Chronicles 33:6; Nahum 3:4).

6. Conjuring Spells

   This phrase appears in Deuteronomy 18:11, Psalms 58:5, and Isaiah 47:9,12. It is sometimes translated "enchantments."

7. Consulting Mediums

   This phrase may refer to the same thing as practicing wizardry. The word describes the witch at En Dor, whom Saul engaged to conduct a seance and bring up the spirit of Samuel (1 Samuel 28:3,9).

8. Spiritism

   The word for *spiritist* always appears with a witch. The root of the word in Hebrew is the verb "to know." In modern English, wizard means someone very wise or inventive, a very clever or skillful person. However, in the Bible it is always a forbidden thing, a kind of black magic. Therefore, most modern versions translate the word as spiritist, fortune-teller, or sorcerer.

9. Calling Up the Dead or Necromancy

   These terms are both used to describe the same practice. The phrase *calls up the dead* occurs only in Deuteronomy 18:11, although this is exactly what an Old Testament witch did for King Saul.

10. Magic

The Hebrew word *magic* appears only in connection with Egyptian and Babylonian magicians. The first cluster of verses relates to Joseph in Egypt in Genesis 41:8,24. The second cluster of verses appears in connection with the plagues called up by Moses in Exodus 7:11– 9:11. The third cluster of verses deals with Daniel and the various government supported magicians of Babylon. This is not the same as the slight-of-hand of magician entertainers we might see on stage. This magic is the work of Satan and is evil at its core.

Conclusions:

1. It is because of these occult practices that God used the children of Israel to drive out the nations from the land of Canaan.

2. Whoever is involved with these activities is "detestable to the Lord."

3. The penalty God specified for such practices gives you a good indicator of what God thinks of the occult.

4. Beware: These passages and others stand as a warning to all people concerning the occult. (Also see 1 Chronicles 10:13; Revelation 21:8; Zechariah 10:2; Isaiah 47:13–14; 1 Samuel 15:23.)

IV. Satan

A. Satan's original situation

Ezekiel 28:11–19

[11] Again the word of the LORD came to me saying, [12] "Son of man, take up a lamentation over the king of Tyre and say to him, 'Thus says the Lord GOD,

"You had the seal of perfection,
Full of wisdom and perfect in beauty.
[13] "You were in Eden, the garden of God;
Every precious stone was your covering:
The ruby, the topaz and the diamond;
The beryl, the onyx and the jasper;
The lapis lazuli, the turquoise and the emerald;
And the gold, the workmanship of your settings and sockets,
Was in you.
On the day that you were created

They were prepared.
[14] "You were the anointed cherub who covers,
And I placed you *there*.
You were on the holy mountain of God;
You walked in the midst of the stones of fire.
[15] "You were blameless in your ways
From the day you were created
Until unrighteousness was found in you.
[16] "By the abundance of your trade
You were internally filled with violence,
And you sinned;
Therefore I have cast you as profane
From the mountain of God.
And I have destroyed you, O covering cherub,
From the midst of the stones of fire.
[17] "Your heart was lifted up because of your beauty;
You corrupted your wisdom by reason of your splendor.
I cast you to the ground;
I put you before kings,
That they may see you.

[18] "By the multitude of your iniquities,
In the unrighteousness of your trade
You profaned your sanctuaries.
Therefore I have brought fire from the midst of you;
It has consumed you,
And I have turned you to ashes on the earth
In the eyes of all who see you.
[19] "All who know you among the peoples
Are appalled at you;
You have become terrified
And you will cease to be forever."

1. Though Ezekiel 28:11–19 is addressed to the King of Tyre, the wording of this prophecy is such that it obviously refers to Satan's original position, his sin, and his judgment.

2. Satan was created by God as an angel with great beauty and position.

3. Satan rebelled against God because of his pride and self-centeredness.

4. Satan was cast out of the presence of God and destined for eternal judgment.

B. Satan's rebellious challenge and his desire to become God

Isaiah 14:12–14

[12] "How you have fallen from heaven,
O star of the morning, son of the dawn!
You have been cut down to the earth,
You who have weakened the nations!
[13] "But you said in your heart,
'I will ascend to heaven;
I will raise my throne above the stars of God,
And I will sit on the mount of assembly
In the recesses of the north.
[14] 'I will ascend above the heights of the clouds;
I will make myself like the Most High.'"

Notice the five "I will" statements of Satan:

1. I will ascend to heaven.

2. I will raise my throne above the stars of God.

3. I will sit on the mount of assembly in the recesses of the north.

4. I will ascend above the heights of the clouds.

5. I will make myself like the Most High. (There can be *only one* Most High.)

C. Biblical names and descriptions of Satan

1. Satan – This name means "adversary; the one who opposes or is an enemy of God and man." Satan is the personal name of the devil.

2. Devil – This name means "slanderer or false accuser."

3. The tempter – This name means "entices to do evil." (1 Thessalonians 3:5)

4. Beelzebub – This is the name of a heathen god, who was considered the chief evil spirit by the Jews. Beelzebub was the deemed ruler of demons. (Matthew 12:24–27)

5. The evil one – This name means "naturally evil." (Matthew 13:19,38)

6. The ruler of this world (John 12:31)

7. The god of this world (2 Corinthians 4:4)

8. Belial – This is a Hebrew term designating a person as godless or lawless. (2 Corinthians 6:15)

9. The prince of the power of the air – This is a reference to the fact that Satan has access to this world and freely roams the earth. (Ephesians 2:2)

10. The accuser of our brethren (Revelation 12:10)

11. Serpent (Revelation 12:9)

12. Apollyon – This name means "destroyer." (Revelation 9:11)

13. Liar – This name means "to pervert the truth." (John 8:44)

14. Enemy – This name means "opponent." (Matthew 13:28)

15. Dragon – This name refers to a "destructive creature." (Revelation 12:3,7,9)

D. Satan's personal existence

Satan is not merely an influence or a force. He is not a cute little cartoon character, who scrambles around whispering naughty things in people's ears and making a nuisance of himself. The descriptive names God uses in His Word tell us Satan opposes all that is good and godly in this world.

1. Satan is the enemy of your soul. He is the enemy of everything that is good and God honoring.

2. Satan is a liar and the inventor of lies. Jesus labels him the "father of lies." (John 8:44)

3. Satan is a destroyer of lives. He is an evil manipulator, who enslaves many with false promises of great things. He offers the "good" life but produces only death and destruction.

4. Satan is a person. Personal names and personal pronouns are used in connection with Satan.

Job 1:6–12

> [6] Now there was a day when the sons of God came to present themselves before the LORD, and Satan also came among them. [7] The LORD said to Satan, "From where do you come?" Then Satan answered the LORD and said, "From roaming about on the earth and walking around on it." [8] The LORD said to Satan, "Have you considered My servant Job? For there is no one like him on the earth, a blameless and upright man, fearing God and turning away from evil." [9] Then Satan answered the LORD, "Does Job fear God for nothing? [10] Have You not made a hedge about him and his house and all that he has, on every side? You have blessed the work of his hands, and his possessions have increased in the land. [11] But put forth Your hand now and touch all that he has; he will surely curse You to Your face." [12] Then the LORD said to Satan, "Behold, all that he has is in your power, only do not put forth your hand on him." So Satan departed from the presence of the LORD.

Revelation 20:1–3

> [1] Then I saw an angel coming down from heaven, holding the key of the abyss and a great chain in his hand. [2] And he laid hold of the dragon, the serpent of old, who is the devil and Satan, and bound him for a thousand years; [3] and he threw him into the abyss, and shut *it* and sealed *it* over him, so that he would not deceive the nations any longer, until the thousand years were completed; after these things he must be released for a short time.

1 Peter 5:8

> Be of sober *spirit*, be on the alert. Your adversary, the devil, prowls around like a roaring lion, seeking someone to devour.

John 8:44

> You are of *your* father the devil, and you want to do the desires of your father. He was a murderer from the beginning, and does not stand in the truth because there is no truth in him. Whenever he speaks a lie, he speaks from his own *nature*, for he is a liar and the father of lies.

E. Satan's powers

Satan's power must always be measured as operable only under the permissive will of God. Satan cannot do anything unless God permits him. (See story of Job.)

1. Satan has the power to appear in the heavens – probably in the presence of God. (Job 1:6)

2. Satan has the power to roam the earth. (Job 1:7)

3. Satan has the power to influence people. (Job 1:15)

4. Satan has the power to send destructive fire. (Job 1:16)

5. Satan has the power to cause a great wind. (Job 1:19)

6. Satan has the power to bring sickness upon human beings. (Job 2:6–7; Luke 13:11,16) Note that this does not mean that we can conclude that Satan is the originator of all sickness.

7. Satan has the "power of death." (Hebrews 2:14–15)

8. Satan has the power to ensnare. (1 Timothy 3:7)

9. Satan has the power to inflict spiritual blindness on the unbelieving. (2 Corinthians 4:3–4)

10. Satan has the power to tempt and test. (Matthew 4:1–11)

11. Satan has the power to deceive. (John 8:44)

    a. By making himself appear as an angel of light (2 Corinthians 11:13–15)

    b. By making his ministers appear as angels of light (2 Corinthians 11:14–15)

    c. By sowing false Christians in the church (Matthew 13:25)

    d. By raising up counterfeit prophets (2 Thessalonians 2:9–10)

    e. By substituting a form of godliness for reality (2 Timothy 3:5)

    f. By substituting truth with false doctrine (1 Timothy 4:1–3)

12. Satan has power to afflict God's servants (under the permissive will of God).

    a. By resisting God's servants (Zechariah 3:1)

    b. By harassing God's servants (2 Corinthians 12:7–10)

    c. By hindering God's servants (1 Thessalonians 2:18)

d. By testing (sifting) God's servants (Luke 22:31)

e. By accusing God's servants (Revelation 12:9)

13. Satan has power to hold the wicked in his snare. (1 John 5:19; 2 Timothy 2:26)

F. Important facts every believer should know about Satan and his methods

1. Our ignorance of Satan and his methods are all in Satan's favor.

2 Corinthians 2:11

> so that no advantage would be taken of us by Satan, for we are not ignorant of his schemes.

2. Satan's attacks vary.

1 Peter 5:8

> Be of sober *spirit*, be on the alert. Your adversary, the devil, prowls around like a roaring lion, seeking someone to devour.

2 Corinthians 11:3

> But I am afraid that, as the serpent deceived Eve by his craftiness, your minds will be led astray from the simplicity and purity *of devotion* to Christ.

Matthew 10:28

> Do not fear those who kill the body but are unable to kill the soul; but rather fear Him who is able to destroy both soul and body in hell.

G. The believer's response to Satan's tactics

1. Sometimes we must change our location to escape Satan's attempts to lure us to sinful actions.

2 Timothy 2:22

> Now flee from youthful lusts and pursue righteousness, faith, love *and* peace, with those who call on the Lord from a pure heart.

2. We are to be alert.

1 Thessalonians 5:6

> so then let us not sleep as others do, but let us be alert and sober.

3. We are to be prayerful.

1 Thessalonians 5:17

> pray without ceasing;

4. We are to be obedient.

1 Thessalonians 5:22

> abstain from every form of evil.

5. We are to be on guard.

Ephesians 4:27

> and do not give the devil an opportunity.

6. We are to resist Satan's temptations.

James 4:7

> Submit therefore to God. Resist the devil and he will flee from you.

7. We are to be knowledgeable and employ our offensive and defensive spiritual weapons.

Ephesians 6:11–13

> [11] Put on the full armor of God, so that you will be able to stand firm against the schemes of the devil. [12] For our struggle is not against flesh and blood, but against the rulers, against the powers, against the world forces of this darkness, against the spiritual *forces* of wickedness in the heavenly *places*. [13] Therefore, take up the full armor of God, so that you will be able to resist in the evil day, and having done everything, to stand firm.

8. We are to be discerning of his devices.

2 Corinthians 2:11

> so that no advantage would be taken of us by Satan, for we are not ignorant of his schemes.

9. We are to be dependent on the Holy Spirit for victory.

1 John 4:4

> You are from God, little children, and have overcome them; because greater is He who is in you than he who is in the world.

Ephesians 6:9

> And masters, do the same things to them, and give up threatening, knowing that both their Master and yours is in heaven, and there is no partiality with Him.

Galatians 5:16

> But I say, walk by the Spirit, and you will not carry out the desire of the flesh.

H. God's judgment of Satan

There are several steps recorded in the Bible that track Satan's path from his original rebellion to his final judgment.

1. Because of his original sin, Satan was cast out of heaven with limited access to God.

Ezekiel 28:16–17

> [16] "By the abundance of your trade
> You were internally filled with violence,
> And you sinned;
> Therefore I have cast you as profane
> From the mountain of God.
> And I have destroyed you, O covering cherub,
> From the midst of the stones of fire.
> [17] "Your heart was lifted up because of your beauty;
> You corrupted your wisdom by reason of your splendor.
> I cast you to the ground;
> I put you before kings,
> That they may see you."

2. Satan was judged at the cross in that his power over death was broken.

Hebrews 2:14

> Therefore, since the children share in flesh and blood, He Himself likewise also partook of the same, that through death He might render powerless him who had the power of death, that is, the devil,

1 Corinthians 15:55–57

> [55] "O DEATH, WHERE IS YOUR VICTORY? O DEATH, WHERE IS YOUR STING?" [56] The sting of death is sin, and the power of sin is the law; [57] but thanks be to God, who gives us the victory through our Lord Jesus Christ.

3. During this present age he is somewhat restrained by the Holy Spirit's work through believers.

    2 Thessalonians 2:6–7

    > [6] And you know what restrains him now, so that in his time he will be revealed. [7] For the mystery of lawlessness is already at work; only he who now restrains *will do so* until he is taken out of the way.

4. At the end of the tribulation period, Satan is battled, defeated, and confined to the earth.

    Revelation 12:7–11

    > [7] And there was war in heaven, Michael and his angels waging war with the dragon. The dragon and his angels waged war, [8] and they were not strong enough, and there was no longer a place found for them in heaven. [9] And the great dragon was thrown down, the serpent of old who is called the devil and Satan, who deceives the whole world; he was thrown down to the earth, and his angels were thrown down with him. [10] Then I heard a loud voice in heaven, saying,
    >
    > "Now the salvation, and the power, and the kingdom of our God and the authority of His Christ have come, for the accuser of our brethren has been thrown down, he who accuses them before our God day and night. [11] And they overcame him because of the blood of the Lamb and because of the word of their testimony, and they did not love their life even when faced with death."

5. During the Millennial Kingdom, Satan will be bound and confined to the bottomless pit.

Revelation 20:1–3

[1] Then I saw an angel coming down from heaven, holding the key of the abyss and a great chain in his hand. [2] And he laid hold of the dragon, the serpent of old, who is the devil and Satan, and bound him for a thousand years; [3] and he threw him into the abyss, and shut *it* and sealed *it* over him, so that he would not deceive the nations any longer, until the thousand years were completed; after these things he must be released for a short time.

6. Following the Millennium, Satan will be loosed for a short period of time, and then he will be defeated once for all by God and cast into the lake of fire, where he will remain powerless for all eternity.

Revelation 20:10

And the devil who deceived them was thrown into the lake of fire and brimstone, where the beast and the false prophet are also; and they will be tormented day and night forever and ever.

Revelation 20:7–9

[7] When the thousand years are completed, Satan will be released from his prison, [8] and will come out to deceive the nations which are in the four corners of the earth, Gog and Magog, to gather them together for the war; the number of them is like the sand of the seashore. [9] And they came up on the broad plain of the earth and surrounded the camp of the saints and the beloved city, and fire came down from heaven and devoured them.

Revelation 21:1–5

[1] Then I saw a new heaven and a new earth; for the first heaven and the first earth passed away, and there is no longer *any* sea. [2] And I saw the holy city, new Jerusalem, coming down out of heaven from God, made ready as a bride adorned for her husband. [3] And I heard a loud voice from the throne, saying, "Behold, the tabernacle of God is among men, and He will dwell among them, and they shall be His people, and God Himself will be among them, [4] and He will wipe away every tear from their eyes; and there will no longer be *any* death; there will no longer be *any* mourning, or crying, or pain; the first things have passed away."

[5] And He who sits on the throne said, "Behold, I am making all things new." And He said, "Write, for these words are faithful and true."

REVIEW QUESTIONS

1. Name two classifications of angels.
2. Name two angels mentioned in the Bible that kept their original state.
3. What is the difference between fallen angels and demons?
4. Who is the Angel of Jehovah?
5. How many devils are there?
6. Is Satan a person or an influence?
7. Is demon possession of a person possible today?
8. What is the difference between demon possession and demon influence?
9. What does the Bible say about consulting fortune tellers, astrologists, spiritualist, etc.?
10. What portion of scripture expressly forbids contact with evil spirits?
11. Can Satan do anything he wants? Explain your answer.
12. List the steps in Satan's judgment.

CHAPTER 10

Ecclesiology
(What the Bible Teaches About the Church)

There is little information concerning the church in the Old Testament. It is the mystery about which Paul writes.

> Ephesians 3:8–10
>
> > [8] To me, the very least of all saints, this grace was given, to preach to the Gentiles the unfathomable riches of Christ, [9] and to bring to light what is the administration of the mystery which for ages has been hidden in God who created all things; [10] so that the manifold wisdom of God might now be made known through the church to the rulers and the authorities in the heavenly *places*.
>
> Ephesians 5:32
>
> > This mystery is great; but I am speaking with reference to Christ and the church.
>
> Matthew 16:18
>
> > I also say to you that you are Peter, and upon this rock I will build My church; and the gates of Hades will not overpower it.

The word *church* means a called-out assembly or community. The New Testament also refers to the church as the Body of Christ (Ephesians 1:22–23; Colossians 1:24) and the bride of Christ (Revelation 21:9). The church officially began on the Day of Pentecost with the initial baptism of the Holy Spirit (Acts 2). It was anticipated, however, by Christ in the gospels. John 17 records Jesus' intercessory prayer for the church.

I. The Basic Concept of the Word "Church"

A. The meaning of the Greek word for *church*

1. The Greek word translated *church* comes from two Greek words

   - *ek* means "out"
   - *kalein* means "to call"

2. Together we get the word *ecclesia* or *ekklesia.*

   The word *ekklesia* is used over 100 times in the New Testament. It is used often in the book of Acts, in the letters of the apostle Paul, and in some of the general epistles. Most of the time this word refers to a local congregation.

3. The word *ekklesia* literally means "a called-out assembly." The church is a called-out assembly.

4. The church is made up of people, who by faith in Christ, are called out from the world and placed into the Body of Christ.

5. This "calling out and assembling in Christ" is the result of the baptism of the Holy Spirit. (See chapter 6 of this book.)

B. Two uses of the word *church* in the New Testament

1. The church as a living organism

   As a result of the baptism of the Holy Spirit, all those who put their faith in Christ from the Day of Pentecost (Acts 2) until the Rapture are united into one body and Christ is the head of that body. The Bible uses these terms to describe this organism:

   - The church
   - The Body of Christ
   - The Bride of Christ
   - The saints

   1 Corinthians 12:12–14

   > [12] For even as the body is one and *yet* has many members, and all the members of the body, though they are many, are one body, so also is Christ. [13] For by one Spirit we were all baptized into one body, whether Jews or Greeks, whether slaves or free, and we were all made to drink of one Spirit.
   >
   > [14] For the body is not one member, but many.

Ephesians 5:25–27

> [25] Husbands, love your wives, just as Christ also loved the church and gave Himself up for her, [26] so that He might sanctify her, having cleansed her by the washing of water with the word, [27] that He might present to Himself the church in all her glory, having no spot or wrinkle or any such thing; but that she would be holy and blameless.

The apostle uses two illustrations in these passages to describe the relationship within the church.

- The one flesh relationship of the husband and wife. Though they retain their individuality they are, nevertheless one in the union of marriage.
- The relationship of the various members of the human body, yet the oneness of the body.

2. The church as an organization

This describes a local gathering of people with no assurance that all are true believers. Some of Paul's epistles in the New Testament were addressed to local congregations in Ephesus, Philippi, Corinth, Colossi, and Thessalonica.

C. The word *church* in the gospels

The word *church* is used in the gospels on only two occasions.

Matthew 18:17

> If he refuses to listen to them, tell it to the church; and if he refuses to listen even to the church, let him be to you as a Gentile and a tax collector.

Matthew 16:17–18

> [17] And Jesus said to him, "Blessed are you, Simon Barjona, because flesh and blood did not reveal *this* to you, but My Father who is in heaven. [18] I also say to you that you are Peter, and upon this rock I will build My church; and the gates of Hades will not overpower it."

The New Testament church did not exist until after the death, resurrection, and ascension of Christ because its members are only redeemed by His shed blood and finished work on the cross.

II. General Clarifications Regarding the Church

A. The time span of the church

1. The church, as the Body of Christ, includes all who have trusted Christ for salvation between the Day of Pentecost (Acts 2) and the Rapture. (The Rapture is the moment when Jesus returns, and all believers will be taken out of this world to be with Him forever.)

    1 Corinthians 15:51–58

    > [51] Behold, I tell you a mystery; we will not all sleep, but we will all be changed, [52] in a moment, in the twinkling of an eye, at the last trumpet; for the trumpet will sound, and the dead will be raised imperishable, and we will be changed. [53] For this perishable must put on the imperishable, and this mortal must put on immortality. [54] But when this perishable will have put on the imperishable, and this mortal will have put on immortality, then will come about the saying that is written, "DEATH IS SWALLOWED UP in victory. [55] O DEATH, WHERE IS YOUR VICTORY? O DEATH, WHERE IS YOUR STING?" [56] The sting of death is sin, and the power of sin is the law; [57] but thanks be to God, who gives us the victory through our Lord Jesus Christ.
    >
    > [58] Therefore, my beloved brethren, be steadfast, immovable, always abounding in the work of the Lord, knowing that your toil is not *in* vain in the Lord.

    1 Thessalonians 4:13–18

    > [13] But we do not want you to be uninformed, brethren, about those who are asleep, so that you will not grieve as do the rest who have no hope. [14] For if we believe that Jesus died and rose again, even so God will bring with Him those who have fallen asleep in Jesus. [15] For this we say to you by the word of the Lord, that we who are alive and remain until the coming of the Lord, will not precede those who have fallen asleep. [16] For the Lord Himself will descend from heaven with a shout, with the voice of *the* archangel and with the trumpet of God, and the dead in Christ will rise first. [17] Then we who are alive and remain will be caught up together with them in the clouds to meet the Lord in the air, and so we shall always be with the Lord. [18] Therefore comfort one another with these words.

2. At the time of salvation, believers are removed from the classification the Bible calls "the world" and, being born again by the Holy Spirit, they become included in the church, the Body of Christ.

B. The uniqueness of the church

1. The church is unique because it is destined to be conformed to the image of Christ.

   Romans 8:29

   > For those whom He foreknew, He also predestined *to become* conformed to the image of His Son, so that He would be the firstborn among many brethren;

   1 John 3:2

   > Beloved, now we are children of God, and it has not appeared as yet what we will be. We know that when He appears, we will be like Him, because we will see Him just as He is.

2. The church is unique because all the members are a "new creation."

   2 Corinthians 5:17–18

   > [17] Therefore if anyone is in Christ, *he is* a new creature; the old things passed away; behold, new things have come. [18] Now all *these* things are from God, who reconciled us to Himself through Christ and gave us the ministry of reconciliation,

3. The church is unique because it includes people from all nations.

   Colossians 3:11

   > *a renewal* in which there is no *distinction between* Greek and Jew, circumcised and uncircumcised, barbarian, Scythian, slave and freeman, but Christ is all, and in all.

4. The church is unique because all its members are citizens of heaven.

   Philippians 3:20

   > For our citizenship is in heaven, from which also we eagerly wait for a Savior, the Lord Jesus Christ;

   Colossians 3:3

   > For you have died and your life is hidden with Christ in God.

Ephesians 1:3

Blessed *be* the God and Father of our Lord Jesus Christ, who has blessed us with every spiritual blessing in the heavenly *places* in Christ,

C. Simple biblical definitions of the local church

Matthew 18:20

"For where two or three have gathered together in My name, I am there in their midst."

Ephesians 4:1–4

[1] Therefore I, the prisoner of the Lord, implore you to walk in a manner worthy of the calling with which you have been called, [2] with all humility and gentleness, with patience, showing tolerance for one another in love, [3] being diligent to preserve the unity of the Spirit in the bond of peace. [4] *There is* one body and one Spirit, just as also you were called in one hope of your calling;

Colossians 3:12–14

[12] So, as those who have been chosen of God, holy and beloved, put on a heart of compassion, kindness, humility, gentleness and patience; [13] bearing with one another, and forgiving each other, whoever has a complaint against anyone; just as the Lord forgave you, so also should you. [14] Beyond all these things *put on* love, which is the perfect bond of unity.

D. Jesus' directive to the local church

John 13:34–35

[34] "A new commandment I give to you, that you love one another, even as I have loved you, that you also love one another. [35] By this all men will know that you are My disciples, if you have love for one another."

1. Loving one another in the church is one of the major themes of the New Testament.

2. Most of the epistles often teach about loving one another.

3. Loving others is difficult to maintain in a close community because we are all fundamentally selfish and proud.

4. The awful truth is that many churches have lost their witness and effectiveness in the local community because of needless divisions over trivial issues.

III. The Mission of the Church

A. To build one another up in spiritual maturity and equip each other for effective service for Christ

Ephesians 4:11–16

> [11] And He gave some *as* apostles, and some *as* prophets, and some *as* evangelists, and some *as* pastors and teachers, [12] for the equipping of the saints for the work of service, to the building up of the body of Christ; [13] until we all attain to the unity of the faith, and of the knowledge of the Son of God, to a mature man, to the measure of the stature which belongs to the fullness of Christ. [14] As a result, we are no longer to be children, tossed here and there by waves and carried about by every wind of doctrine, by the trickery of men, by craftiness in deceitful scheming; [15] but speaking the truth in love, we are to grow up in all *aspects* into Him who is the head, *even* Christ, [16] from whom the whole body, being fitted and held together by what every joint supplies, according to the proper working of each individual part, causes the growth of the body for the building up of itself in love.

B. To share the good news of salvation in Christ with the world

Acts 1:8

> "but you will receive power when the Holy Spirit has come upon you; and you shall be My witnesses both in Jerusalem, and in all Judea and Samaria, and even to the remotest part of the earth."

Matthew 28:18–20

> [18] And Jesus came up and spoke to them, saying, "All authority has been given to Me in heaven and on earth. [19] Go therefore and make disciples of all the nations, baptizing them in the name of the Father and the Son and the Holy Spirit, [20] teaching them to observe all that I commanded you; and lo, I am with you always, even to the end of the age."

Mark 16:15

> And He said to them, "Go into all the world and preach the gospel to all creation."

IV. The Personal Responsibility of Everyone in the Body of Christ

A. We are to love one another.

John 13:34–35

> [34] "A new commandment I give to you, that you love one another, even as I have loved you, that you also love one another. [35] By this all men will know that you are My disciples, if you have love for one another."

B. We are to present ourselves to God for His use.

Romans 12:1–2

> [1] Therefore I urge you, brethren, by the mercies of God, to present your bodies a living and holy sacrifice, acceptable to God, *which is* your spiritual service of worship. [2] And do not be conformed to this world, but be transformed by the renewing of your mind, so that you may prove what the will of God is, that which is good and acceptable and perfect.

C. We are to lay aside all that hinders us from becoming like Jesus.

Hebrews 12:1–2

> [1] Therefore, since we have so great a cloud of witnesses surrounding us, let us also lay aside every encumbrance and the sin which so easily entangles us, and let us run with endurance the race that is set before us, [2] fixing our eyes on Jesus, the author and perfecter of faith, who for the joy set before Him endured the cross, despising the shame, and has sat down at the right hand of the throne of God.

D. We are to be ambassadors for Christ.

2 Corinthians 5:19–20

> [19] namely, that God was in Christ reconciling the world to Himself, not counting their trespasses against them, and He has committed to us the word of reconciliation.
>
> [20] Therefore, we are ambassadors for Christ, as though God were making an appeal through us; we beg you on behalf of Christ, be reconciled to God.

E. We are to pray regularly.

Philippians 4:6

> Be anxious for nothing, but in everything by prayer and supplication with thanksgiving let your requests be made known to God.

1 Thessalonians 5:17

> pray without ceasing;

F. We are to support the local and world-wide ministry of the church through financial giving.

1. We are to give systematically.

   1 Corinthians 16:2

   > On the first day of every week each one of you is to put aside and save, as he may prosper, so that no collections be made when I come.

2. We are to give proportionately.

   1 Corinthians 16:2

   > On the first day of every week each one of you is to put aside and save, as he may prosper, so that no collections be made when I come.

3. We are to give cheerfully.

   2 Corinthians 9:7

   > Each one *must do* just as he has purposed in his heart, not grudgingly or under compulsion, for God loves a cheerful giver.

4. We are to give purposefully.

   1 Corinthians 16:2

   > On the first day of every week each one of you is to put aside and save, as he may prosper, so that no collections be made when I come.

   2 Corinthians 9:7

   > Each one *must do* just as he has purposed in his heart, not grudgingly or under compulsion, for God loves a cheerful giver.

5. We are not to give to impress others.

Matthew 6:1–4

> [1] "Beware of practicing your righteousness before men to be noticed by them; otherwise you have no reward with your Father who is in heaven.
>
> [2] "So when you give to the poor, do not sound a trumpet before you, as the hypocrites do in the synagogues and in the streets, so that they may be honored by men. Truly I say to you, they have their reward in full. [3] But when you give to the poor, do not let your left hand know what your right hand is doing, [4] so that your giving will be in secret; and your Father who sees *what is done* in secret will reward you."
>
> Note: The underlined words have been added by author.

God's plan is that God's work should be supported by God's people. This system has been in operation since early in the Old Testament.

V. The Character of the New Testament Church

A. Because the New Testament church had no church buildings, believers often met in homes.

1 Corinthians 16:19

> The churches of Asia greet you. Aquila and Prisca greet you heartily in the Lord, with the church that is in their house.

Colossians 4:15

> Greet the brethren who are in Laodicea and also Nympha and the church that is in her house.

B. The New Testament church had meetings wherever it was convenient or fitting.

Acts 2:46

> Day by day continuing with one mind in the temple, and breaking bread from house to house, they were taking their meals together with gladness and sincerity of heart,

C. The local New Testament church met on the first day of the week. This was the weekly anniversary of Jesus' Resurrection.

Acts 20:7

> On the first day of the week, when we were gathered together to break bread, Paul *began* talking to them, intending to leave the next day, and he prolonged his message until midnight.

1 Corinthians 16:2

> On the first day of every week each one of you is to put aside and save, as he may prosper, so that no collections be made when I come.

D. There were established leaders in the local New Testament church.

1 Timothy 3:1

> It is a trustworthy statement: if any man aspires to the office of overseer, it is a fine work he desires *to do.*

Titus 1:5

> For this reason I left you in Crete, that you would set in order what remains and appoint elders in every city as I directed you,

1 Timothy 3:8

> Deacons likewise *must be* men of dignity, not double-tongued, or addicted to much wine or fond of sordid gain,

E. Qualifications for leadership were instituted.

1 Timothy 3:1–13

> [1] It is a trustworthy statement: if any man aspires to the office of overseer, it is a fine work he desires *to do.* [2] An overseer, then, must be above reproach, the husband of one wife, temperate, prudent, respectable, hospitable, able to teach, [3] not addicted to wine or pugnacious, but gentle, peaceable, free from the love of money. [4] *He must be* one who manages his own household well, keeping his children under control with all dignity [5] (but if a man does not know how to manage his own household, how will he take care of the church of God?), [6] *and* not a new convert, so that he will not become conceited and fall into the condemnation incurred by the devil. [7] And he must have a good reputation with those outside *the church,* so that he will not fall into reproach and the snare of the devil.

> [8] Deacons likewise *must be* men of dignity, not double-tongued, or addicted to much wine or fond of sordid gain, [9] *but* holding to the mystery of the faith with a clear conscience. [10] These men must also first be tested; then let them serve as deacons if they are beyond reproach. [11] Women *must* likewise *be* dignified, not malicious gossips, but temperate, faithful in all things. [12] Deacons must be husbands of *only* one wife, *and* good managers of *their* children and their own households. [13] For those who have served well as deacons obtain for themselves a high standing and great confidence in the faith that is in Christ Jesus.

Titus 1:5–9

> [5] For this reason I left you in Crete, that you would set in order what remains and appoint elders in every city as I directed you, [6] *namely*, if any man is above reproach, the husband of one wife, having children who believe, not accused of dissipation or rebellion. [7] For the overseer must be above reproach as God's steward, not self-willed, not quick-tempered, not addicted to wine, not pugnacious, not fond of sordid gain, [8] but hospitable, loving what is good, sensible, just, devout, self-controlled, [9] holding fast the faithful word which is in accordance with the teaching, so that he will be able both to exhort in sound doctrine and to refute those who contradict.

F. Congregations exercised discipline and moral standards in the church.

1 Corinthians 5:1–13

> [1] It is actually reported that there is immorality among you, and immorality of such a kind as does not exist even among the Gentiles, that someone has his father's wife. [2] You have become arrogant and have not mourned instead, so that the one who had done this deed would be removed from your midst.
>
> [3] For I, on my part, though absent in body but present in spirit, have already judged him who has so committed this, as though I were present. [4] In the name of our Lord Jesus, when you are assembled, and I with you in spirit, with the power of our Lord Jesus, [5] *I have decided* to deliver such a one to Satan for the destruction of his flesh, so that his spirit may be saved in the day of the Lord Jesus.

> [6] Your boasting is not good. Do you not know that a little leaven leavens the whole lump *of dough*? [7] Clean out the old leaven so that you may be a new lump, just as you are *in fact* unleavened. For Christ our Passover also has been sacrificed. [8] Therefore let us celebrate the feast, not with old leaven, nor with the leaven of malice and wickedness, but with the unleavened bread of sincerity and truth.
>
> [9] I wrote you in my letter not to associate with immoral people; [10] I *did* not at all *mean* with the immoral people of this world, or with the covetous and swindlers, or with idolaters, for then you would have to go out of the world. [11] But actually, I wrote to you not to associate with any so-called brother if he is an immoral person, or covetous, or an idolater, or a reviler, or a drunkard, or a swindler—not even to eat with such a one. [12] For what have I to do with judging outsiders? Do you not judge those who are within *the church*? [13] But those who are outside, God judges. REMOVE THE WICKED MAN FROM AMONG YOURSELVES.

2 Thessalonians 3:6

> Now we command you, brethren, in the name of our Lord Jesus Christ, that you keep away from every brother who leads an unruly life and not according to the tradition which you received from us.

2 Corinthians 2:6–8

> [6] Sufficient for such a one is this punishment which *was inflicted* by the majority, [7] so that on the contrary you should rather forgive and comfort *him*, otherwise such a one might be overwhelmed by excessive sorrow. [8] Wherefore I urge you to reaffirm *your* love for him.

VI. The Ordinances of the Church

A. Baptism

There are four kinds of baptism mentioned in the New Testament.

1. John the Baptist's baptism

This was a baptism of repentance as a preparation for the arrival of the King (Jesus). John's baptism was primarily Jewish in character. John's purpose was to make it known that the promised King was about to arrive. His message was simple. Repent, because the King and kingdom is about to appear on the scene. Be baptized as a public declaration of your repentance.

Matthew 3:1–8

[1] Now in those days John the Baptist came, preaching in the wilderness of Judea, saying, [2] "Repent, for the kingdom of heaven is at hand." [3] For this is the one referred to by Isaiah the prophet when he said,

"The voice of one crying in the wilderness,
'Make ready the way of the Lord,
Make His paths straight!'"

[4] Now John himself had a garment of camel's hair and a leather belt around his waist; and his food was locusts and wild honey. [5] Then Jerusalem was going out to him, and all Judea and all the district around the Jordan; [6] and they were being baptized by him in the Jordan River, as they confessed their sins.

[7] But when he saw many of the Pharisees and Sadducees coming for baptism, he said to them, "You brood of vipers, who warned you to flee from the wrath to come? [8] Therefore bear fruit in keeping with repentance;"

Mark 1:1–7

[1] The beginning of the gospel of Jesus Christ, the Son of God.

[2] As it is written in Isaiah the prophet:

"Behold, I send My messenger ahead of You,
Who will prepare Your way;
[3] The voice of one crying in the wilderness,
'Make ready the way of the Lord,
Make His paths straight.'"

[4] John the Baptist appeared in the wilderness preaching a baptism of repentance for the forgiveness of sins. [5] And all the country of Judea was going out to him, and all the people of Jerusalem; and they were being baptized by him in the Jordan River, confessing their sins. [6] John was clothed with camel's hair and *wore* a leather belt around his waist, and his diet was locusts and wild honey. [7] And he was preaching, and saying, "After me One is coming who is mightier than I, and I am not fit to stoop down and untie the thong of His sandals."

Luke 3:1–4

[1] Now in the fifteenth year of the reign of Tiberius Caesar, when Pontius Pilate was governor of Judea, and Herod was tetrarch of Galilee, and his brother Philip was tetrarch of the region of Ituraea and Trachonitis, and Lysanias was tetrarch of Abilene, [2] in the high priesthood of Annas and Caiaphas, the word of God came to John, the son of Zacharias, in the wilderness. [3] And he came into all the district around the Jordan, preaching a baptism of repentance for the forgiveness of sins; [4] as it is written in the book of the words of Isaiah the prophet,

"The voice of one crying in the wilderness,
'Make ready the way of the Lord,
Make His paths straight."

John 1:19–34

[19] This is the testimony of John, when the Jews sent to him priests and Levites from Jerusalem to ask him, "Who are you?" [20] And he confessed and did not deny, but confessed, "I am not the Christ." [21] They asked him, "What then? Are you Elijah?" And he said, "I am not." "Are you the Prophet?" And he answered, "No." [22] Then they said to him, "Who are you, so that we may give an answer to those who sent us? What do you say about yourself?" [23] He said, "I am a voice of one crying in the wilderness, 'Make straight the way of the Lord,' as Isaiah the prophet said."

[24] Now they had been sent from the Pharisees. [25] They asked him, and said to him, "Why then are you baptizing, if you are not the Christ, nor Elijah, nor the Prophet?" [26] John answered them saying, "I baptize in water, *but* among you stands One whom you do not know. [27] *It is* He who comes after me, the thong of whose sandal I am not worthy to untie." [28] These things took place in Bethany beyond the Jordan, where John was baptizing.

[29] The next day he saw Jesus coming to him and said, "Behold, the Lamb of God who takes away the sin of the world! [30] This is He on behalf of whom I said, 'After me comes a Man who has a higher rank than I, for He existed before me.' [31] I did not recognize Him, but so that He might be manifested to Israel, I came baptizing in water." [32] John testified saying, "I have seen the Spirit descending as a dove out of heaven, and He remained upon Him. [33] I did not recognize Him, but He who sent me to baptize in water said to me, 'He upon whom you see the Spirit descending and remaining upon Him, this is the One who baptizes in the Holy Spirit.' [34] I myself have seen, and have testified that this is the Son of God."

2. Baptism of Jesus Christ

This baptism was an anointing, as Jesus began His public ministry as Prophet, Priest, and King. In a sense we can follow the Lord in baptism, in that we would be baptized in the same way, but not for the same reasons. Jesus was not baptized to give believers an incentive to be baptized, but to fulfill the requirements of the Law as He began His public ministry.

Mark 1:9–11

> [9] In those days Jesus came from Nazareth in Galilee and was baptized by John in the Jordan. [10] Immediately coming up out of the water, He saw the heavens opening, and the Spirit like a dove descending upon Him; [11] and a voice came out of the heavens: "You are My beloved Son, in You I am well-pleased."

Luke 3:21–22

> [21] Now when all the people were baptized, Jesus was also baptized, and while He was praying, heaven was opened, [22] and the Holy Spirit descended upon Him in bodily form like a dove, and a voice came out of heaven, "You are My beloved Son, in You I am well-pleased."

John 1:25–33

> [25] They asked him, and said to him, "Why then are you baptizing, if you are not the Christ, nor Elijah, nor the Prophet?" [26] John answered them saying, "I baptize in water, *but* among you stands One whom you do not know. [27] *It is* He who comes after me, the thong of whose sandal I am not worthy to untie." [28] These things took place in Bethany beyond the Jordan, where John was baptizing.
>
> [29] The next day he saw Jesus coming to him and said, "Behold, the Lamb of God who takes away the sin of the world! [30] This is He on behalf of whom I said, 'After me comes a Man who has a higher rank than I, for He existed before me.' [31] I did not recognize Him, but so that He might be manifested to Israel, I came baptizing in water." [32] John testified saying, "I have seen the Spirit descending as a dove out of heaven, and He remained upon Him. [33] I did not recognize Him, but He who sent me to baptize in water said to me, 'He upon whom you see the Spirit descending and remaining upon Him, this is the One who baptizes in the Holy Spirit.'"

Jesus' baptism was not the same as John's baptism of repentance because Jesus was the sinless Messiah. It was not believer's baptism but a unique baptism in fulfillment of the Old Testament law as He entered His public ministry as Prophet, Priest, and King.

a. A prophet was to be anointed.

Psalms 105:15

> "Do not touch My anointed ones,
> And do My prophets no harm."

b. A priest was to be anointed.

Exodus 40:12–16

> [12] "Then you shall bring Aaron and his sons to the doorway of the tent of meeting and wash them with water. [13] You shall put the holy garments on Aaron and anoint him and consecrate him, that he may minister as a priest to Me. [14] You shall bring his sons and put tunics on them; [15] and you shall anoint them even as you have anointed their father, that they may minister as priests to Me; and their anointing will qualify them for a perpetual priesthood throughout their generations." [16] Thus Moses did; according to all that the Lord had commanded him, so he did.

c. A king was to be anointed.

1 Samuel 10:1

> Then Samuel took the flask of oil, poured it on his head, kissed him and said, "Has not the Lord anointed you a ruler over His inheritance?"

3. Baptism of the Holy Spirit (This is not a water baptism.)

a. The baptism of the Holy Spirit achieves union with Christ, the head of the church.

b. The baptism of the Holy Spirit brings about union with the Body of Christ, the church.

c. The baptism of the Holy Spirit cannot be earned or self-generated.

d. The baptism of the Holy Spirit takes place the moment we accept Christ for salvation.

e. The baptism of the Holy Spirit was initially accomplished on the Day of Pentecost. (Acts 2)

(For clarity on the Baptism of the Holy Spirit, refer to chapter 6 on Pneumatology.)

4. Believer's water baptism

   a. Believer's baptism is a public declaration of our salvation and commitment to Christ.

   b. Believer's baptism is for believers only.

   c. Believer's baptism is not to be considered as a way of salvation, nor a component that completes our salvation.

5. General observations regarding believer's baptism recorded in the book of Acts

   The Holy Spirit did not choose to record every occasion of water baptism during the days of the early church. As you read the book of Acts, it becomes clear that the Holy Spirit recorded only those water baptisms that show God moving in a new direction and expanding the scope of the church. The baptisms recorded in the book of Acts were designed to make a statement to the church that these new converts were also to be accepted as part of the family of God. Notice the pattern of the accounts of various water baptisms in the book of Acts.

   a. The first water baptisms (after Peter's sermon on the Day of Pentecost)

Acts 2:37–38

> [37] Now when they heard *this*, they were pierced to the heart, and said to Peter and the rest of the apostles, "Brethren, what shall we do?" [38] Peter *said* to them, "Repent, and each of you be baptized in the name of Jesus Christ for the forgiveness of your sins; and you will receive the gift of the Holy Spirit."

Acts 2:41

> So then, those who had received his word were baptized; and that day there were added about three thousand souls.

b. The first Samaritans to be saved (the result of Philip's ministry in Samaria)

Acts 8:12–16

> [12] But when they believed Philip preaching the good news about the kingdom of God and the name of Jesus Christ, they were being baptized, men and women alike. [13] Even Simon himself believed; and after being baptized, he continued on with Philip, and as he observed signs and great miracles taking place, he was constantly amazed.
>
> [14] Now when the apostles in Jerusalem heard that Samaria had received the word of God, they sent them Peter and John, [15] who came down and prayed for them that they might receive the Holy Spirit. [16] For He had not yet fallen upon any of them; they had simply been baptized in the name of the Lord Jesus.

c. The first Jewish proselyte to be saved (Philip and the Ethiopian Eunuch)

Acts 8:35–38

> [35] Then Philip opened his mouth, and beginning from this Scripture he preached Jesus to him. [36] As they went along the road they came to some water; and the eunuch said, "Look! Water! What prevents me from being baptized?" [37] [And Philip said, "If you believe with all your heart, you may." And he answered and said, "I believe that Jesus Christ is the Son of God."] [38] And he ordered the chariot to stop; and they both went down into the water, Philip as well as the eunuch, and he baptized him.

d. The baptism of Saul (later named Paul and previously an intimidating enemy of Christians)

Acts 9:18

> And immediately there fell from his eyes something like scales, and he regained his sight, and he got up and was baptized;

e. The first Gentiles to be saved (Acts 10 – Cornelius and those with him believed)

Note the reaction of the Christian Jews at this news. (Acts 11)

Acts 10:47–48

> [47] "Surely no one can refuse the water for these to be baptized who have received the Holy Spirit just as we *did*, can he?" [48] And he ordered them to be baptized in the name of Jesus Christ. Then they asked him to stay on for a few days.

f. The first convert in Europe (Lydia)

Acts 16:14–15

> [14] A woman named Lydia, from the city of Thyatira, a seller of purple fabrics, a worshiper of God, was listening; and the Lord opened her heart to respond to the things spoken by Paul. [15] And when she and her household had been baptized, she urged us, saying, "If you have judged me to be faithful to the Lord, come into my house and stay." And she prevailed upon us.

g. The Philippian jailer and his family (under the authority of the cruel Roman government)

Acts 16:31–33

> [31] They said, "Believe in the Lord Jesus, and you will be saved, you and your household." [32] And they spoke the word of the Lord to him together with all who were in his house. [33] And he took them that *very* hour of the night and washed their wounds, and immediately he was baptized, he and all his *household.*

h. The synagogue leader and his family in Corinth (Crispus and his family believed)

Acts 18:8

> Crispus, the leader of the synagogue, believed in the Lord with all his household, and many of the Corinthians when they heard were believing and being baptized.

i. John the Baptist's converts, baptized a second time as believers (baptized again as members of the Body of Christ)

Acts 19:1–7

[1] It happened that while Apollos was at Corinth, Paul passed through the upper country and came to Ephesus, and found some disciples. [2] He said to them, "Did you receive the Holy Spirit when you believed?" And they *said* to him, "No, we have not even heard whether there is a Holy Spirit." [3] And he said, "Into what then were you baptized?" And they said, "Into John's baptism." [4] Paul said, "John baptized with the baptism of repentance, telling the people to believe in Him who was coming after him, that is, in Jesus." [5] When they heard this, they were baptized in the name of the Lord Jesus. [6] And when Paul had laid his hands upon them, the Holy Spirit came on them, and they *began* speaking with tongues and prophesying. [7] There were in all about twelve men.

B. The Lord's Supper (Communion)

1. Jesus Himself established the Lord's Supper with His disciples.

Matthew 26:26–30

[26] While they were eating, Jesus took *some* bread, and after a blessing, He broke *it* and gave *it* to the disciples, and said, "Take, eat; this is My body." [27] And when He had taken a cup and given thanks, He gave *it* to them, saying, "Drink from it, all of you; [28] for this is My blood of the covenant, which is poured out for many for forgiveness of sins. [29] But I say to you, I will not drink of this fruit of the vine from now on until that day when I drink it new with you in My Father's kingdom."

[30] After singing a hymn, they went out to the Mount of Olives.

1 Corinthians 11:23–28

[23] For I received from the Lord that which I also delivered to you, that the Lord Jesus in the night in which He was betrayed took bread; [24] and when He had given thanks, He broke it and said, "This is My body, which is for you; do this in remembrance of Me." [25] In the same way *He took* the cup also after supper, saying, "This cup is the new covenant in My blood; do this, as often as you drink *it*, in remembrance of Me." [26] For as often as you eat this bread and drink the cup, you proclaim the Lord's death until He comes.

> [27] Therefore whoever eats the bread or drinks the cup of the Lord in an unworthy manner, shall be guilty of the body and the blood of the Lord. [28] But a man must examine himself, and in so doing he is to eat of the bread and drink of the cup.

a. The Lord's Supper was instituted by the Lord as He met with His disciples just before His betrayal and crucifixion.

b. The Lord's Supper is to be done on a regular basis by believers until Christ returns for His church.

c. The Lord's Supper was instituted as a reminder to believers that their salvation is founded in the broken body and shed blood of Christ Jesus.

d. The Lord's Supper is meant to be a time for self-examination for Christians.

e. The Lord's Supper is to be observed during a gathering of believers.

f. There are no biblical criteria as to how often the Lord's Supper is to be practiced, but that it be observed regularly by believers only.

2. The Bible does *not* teach the following about the Lord's Supper:

a. Upon eating and drinking the elements of the Lord's Supper, the elements are transformed into the actual physical body and blood of Jesus Christ. This is called transubstantiation and is held by the Roman Catholic Church. This concept is *not* taught in scripture.

b. Christ is present in the elements by His omnipotent power and gives special blessing to believers. This is called consubstantiation. The concept was first held by Martin Luther. Luther's conclusions were more of a reaction to the Roman Catholic teaching of transubstantiation than based on the teaching of Jesus or the apostles in the New Testament. This also has *no* foundation in scripture.

c. The ordinance of the Lord's Supper secures favor with God resulting in salvation. Participating in the Lord's Supper is *not a* part of our salvation.

VII. The Following Methods are Used in Governing the Church Organizations

A. Three patterns of church government (simple definitions based on history)

1. Episcopal – this form of church government leaves the decision making in the hands of men, known as bishops. Though some decisions are made by the local church leadership, the denominational leaders make all the major decisions.

2. Presbyterian – this form of church government allows the congregation to elect local leadership and empowers them with the decision-making authority.

3. Congregational – this form of church government places the congregation as the highest authority in the local church, and major decisions are determined with a vote of the church membership.

B. Church membership

1. Since attending church gatherings was not a popular activity in the early church, and often attendees risked their lives by meeting in person, there was no need to maintain church membership rolls as is more common today.

2. The church ultimately followed the procedure of church membership mainly for four reasons:

   a. Church membership is a practical way to properly handle legal and business matters.

   b. Church membership is important in maintaining the identity of true believers.

   c. Church membership is necessary to maintain doctrinal purity. Churches today maintain a written doctrinal statement to which each member must agree.

   d. Church membership establishes a framework for church discipline in accordance with scripture. (1 Corinthians 5)

REVIEW QUESTIONS

1. What is the basic definition of the word *church*?

2. Define two New Testament uses of the term *church*.

3. Name the two ordinances of the church.

4. Name and describe the three views of the Lord's Supper (the Communion service).

5. When did the New Testament church begin?

6. Was the church anticipated in the gospels? Explain.

7. Was the concept of the church clearly taught in the Old Testament?

8. Define and explain the following words and phrases?

    - citizenship in heaven

    - ambassadors

9. Explain the importance of the unity of the Body of Christ.

10. What is the mission of the church?

11. Does every believer or only the pastor(s) have the responsibility to share the gospel of Christ?

12. Name and explain the four biblical principles for financially supporting the ministry of the church?

CHAPTER 11

Eschatology – Part 1
(Bible Prophecy)

INTRODUCTION

With some exceptions, this chapter is dedicated to prophecy which has already been fulfilled. This material is included to demonstrate how graphically and literally our sovereign and all-knowing God has predicted events in the past so that we will see how vividly He will fulfill prophetic passages in the future.

1 Kings 8:56

> "Blessed be the LORD, who has given rest to His people Israel, according to all that He promised; not one word has failed of all His good promise, which He promised through Moses His servant."

The subject of prophecy has been sadly neglected in recent years. This is because of several misconceptions.

1. Some associate prophecy with fanaticism. This, of course, is unfair and stems from ignorance of the subject. Almost every doctrine of scripture has been mistreated at the hands of some fanatical group. Prophecy is no exception. In fact, many have been carried away with heretical teachings of misguided predictions of the end of the world.

2. Some have taken the attitude that prophetic portions cannot be understood and, therefore, have adopted a policy of leaving those passages alone.

3. Some have considered prophetic scripture as unimportant.

4. Some bypass prophecy because they lack the faith to believe that God means what He says. Prophecy challenges our faith.

The subject of prophecy is very important in the Bible. It includes everything that was future at the time the prophecy was given. It considers both fulfilled and unfulfilled prophecy. It is estimated that approximately thirty percent of scripture was prophetic at the time it was written. This is no small matter and shows us that almost every message preached from the pulpit will be affected in some way by prophecy. In John 16:13, Christ, anticipating the coming of the Holy Spirit to indwell believers, specifically mentioned that He (the Holy Spirit) would show them things to come. It is for this reason that we are spending two chapters on prophecy. As the student of the Bible gives attention to this subject, the believer will be able to understand prophetic passages. This understanding is the result of the teaching ministry of the Holy Spirit.

I. Several Reasons Why the Study of Prophecy is Important

A. It provides comfort and assurance to the believer who sees the faithfulness of God in keeping His word.

When we see the plan of God unfolding down through the ages, it brings a great sense of encouragement to see His power and sovereignty displayed before our very eyes. God's plan reveals that all things ultimately work out for His glory.

B. A knowledge of God's prophetic program helps us to direct our efforts in keeping with His will.

Many sincere people are laboring apart from the program of God, simply because they are ignorant of God's master plan and purpose for the ages.

C. Prophecy has a purifying effect on the life of the believer.

If we understand the imminency of Christ's return, we will likely choose to live our lives in harmony with His Word.

1 John 3:2–3

[2] Beloved, now we are children of God, and it has not appeared as yet what we will be. We know that when He appears, we will be like Him, because we will see Him just as He is. [3] And everyone who has this hope *fixed* on Him purifies himself, just as He is pure.

II. Fundamental Issues to Consider and Apply as We Study Prophetic Scripture

A. We must accept the literal interpretation of a passage whenever possible, unless the context indicates that symbolism is utilized.

2 Peter 1:20–21

[20] But know this first of all, that no prophecy of Scripture is *a matter* of one's own interpretation, [21] for no prophecy was ever made by an act of human will, but men moved by the Holy Spirit spoke from God.

B. We must keep in mind that individual messages of scripture may catalog events without necessarily enumerating other incidents or events that may lie in between.

For example, an Old Testament author in a single verse may write about the First Advent and the Second Advent of Christ, without commenting on the hidden events in the "valley period" that lie between the two events.

C. We must approach prophecy in the context of the entire plan of God revealed in the Bible.

It is imperative that we have a good working knowledge of the whole Bible, so we can properly understand isolated portions.

Revelation 22:18–19

> [18] I testify to everyone who hears the words of the prophecy of this book: if anyone adds to them, God will add to him the plagues which are written in this book; [19] and if anyone takes away from the words of the book of this prophecy, God will take away his part from the tree of life and from the holy city, which are written in this book.

D. We must understand that most prophecy centers around the Jewish Messiah and the nation of Israel.

To fully understand prophecy, we must be prepared to accept the promises of God concerning Israel and the Messiah. When we see that God has been faithful in keeping His promises in the past, we can be sure that God will be faithful in keeping His promises in the future.

Revelation 19:10

> Then I fell at his feet to worship him. But he said to me, "Do not do that; I am a fellow servant of yours and your brethren who hold the testimony of Jesus; worship God. For the testimony of Jesus is the spirit of prophecy."

E. We must understand that most prophecy centers around God's covenants with Israel concerning the land, the King, and the kingdom.

As the New Testament opens, there is a spirit of expectancy concerning a King and a kingdom. The forerunner, John the Baptist, announces the "kingdom is near." The King was rejected and crucified, but He rose again and one day will return "in power and great glory" to take His rightful place on the throne of David.

F. An understanding of God's program during various historical times gives us a more accurate understanding of prophecy.

1. A dispensation is a period of time during which a particular revelation of God's mind and will is operative.

   Usually during these periods people are tested as to their obedience to that specific manifestation of God's will. The dispensations cover the time from creation to the New Heaven and New Earth. Most of these time periods begin with instruction and end with God's judgment.

2. Scripture describes seven of these dispensations

   Innocence .... Creation to the Fall of Humankind

   Conscience .... The Fall of Humankind to the Flood

   Human Government .... The Flood to the Tower of Babel

   Promise .... The Tower of Babel to the giving of the Law

   Law .... The giving of the Law to the death, burial, and resurrection of Christ

   Church .... The Day of Pentecost to the Rapture of the Church

   Millennial Kingdom .... The one thousand-year earthly reign of Christ

G. Much prophecy revolves around the three major covenants God made with Israel.

Without a clear understanding of these three covenants and God's intentions in connection with their implementation and fulfillment, the student of the prophetic word will have difficulty accurately understanding the majority of the prophecies of the Old and New Testament. A covenant is God's carefully worded and binding contract with humanity.

1. The Abrahamic Covenant

Genesis 12:1–3

[1] Now the LORD said to Abram,

"Go forth from your country,
And from your relatives
And from your father's house,
To the land which I will show you;
[2] And I will make you a great nation,
And I will bless you,
And make your name great;
And so you shall be a blessing;
[3] And I will bless those who bless you,
And the one who curses you I will curse.
And in you all the families of the earth will be blessed."

Genesis 13:14–18

[14] The LORD said to Abram, after Lot had separated from him, "Now lift up your eyes and look from the place where you are, northward and southward and eastward and westward; [15] for all the land which you see, I will give it to you and to your descendants forever. [16] I will make your descendants as the dust of the earth, so that if anyone can number the dust of the earth, then your descendants can also be numbered. [17] Arise, walk about the land through its length and breadth; for I will give it to you." [18] Then Abram moved his tent and came and dwelt by the oaks of Mamre, which are in Hebron, and there he built an altar to the LORD.

Genesis 15:18–21

> [18] On that day the LORD made a covenant with Abram, saying,
>
> "To your descendants I have given this land,
> From the river of Egypt as far as the great river, the river Euphrates:
>
> [19] the Kenite and the Kenizzite and the Kadmonite [20] and the Hittite and the Perizzite and the Rephaim [21] and the Amorite and the Canaanite and the Girgashite and the Jebusite."

a. The Abrahamic Covenant has three applications.

1) Individual – Abraham is to be blessed

- Land, servants, cattle, silver, and gold
- Spiritual blessings
- Abraham's name is to be great

2) National – Abraham was to become a great nation

- Given a land
- Promised a large offspring
- Treatment of Israel will become a standard of God's judgment

3) Universal – Abraham was to be an avenue of blessing (Genesis 12:3)

- "I will bless those who bless you"
- "I will curse those who curse you"
- "all peoples on earth will be blessed through you." (This is being fulfilled in this age through the salvation that is offered through the sacrificial death and resurrection of the Jewish Messiah, Jesus Christ.)

b. The Abrahamic Covenant is unconditional.

1) It was renewed to Isaac (Genesis 26:1–5)

2) It was renewed to Jacob (Genesis 28:12–17; 35:9–15; 49:10)

2. The Palestinian Covenant (the enjoyment and custody of the land)

Genesis 13:14–16

> [14] The LORD said to Abram, after Lot had separated from him, "Now lift up your eyes and look from the place where you are, northward and southward and eastward and westward; [15] for all the land which you see, I will give it to you and to your descendants forever. [16] I will make your descendants as the dust of the earth, so that if anyone can number the dust of the earth, then your descendants can also be numbered."

Deuteronomy 29:9–27

> [9] So keep the words of this covenant to do them, that you may prosper in all that you do.
>
> [10] "You stand today, all of you, before the LORD your God: your chiefs, your tribes, your elders and your officers, *even* all the men of Israel, [11] your little ones, your wives, and the alien who is within your camps, from the one who chops your wood to the one who draws your water, [12] that you may enter into the covenant with the LORD your God, and into His oath which the LORD your God is making with you today, [13] in order that He may establish you today as His people and that He may be your God, just as He spoke to you and as He swore to your fathers, to Abraham, Isaac, and Jacob.
>
> [14] "Now not with you alone am I making this covenant and this oath, [15] but both with those who stand here with us today in the presence of the LORD our God and with those who are not with us here today [16] (for you know how we lived in the land of Egypt, and how we came through the midst of the nations through which you passed; [17] moreover, you have seen their abominations and their idols *of* wood, stone, silver, and gold, which *they had* with them); [18] so that there will not be among you a man or woman, or family or tribe, whose heart turns away today from the LORD our God, to go and serve the gods of those nations; that there will not be among you a root bearing poisonous fruit and wormwood. [19] It shall be when he hears the words of this curse, that he will boast, saying, 'I have peace though I walk in the stubbornness of my heart in order to destroy the watered *land* with the dry.' [20] The LORD shall never be willing to forgive him, but rather the anger of the LORD and His jealousy will burn against that man, and every curse which is written in this book will rest on him, and the LORD will blot out his name from under heaven. [21] Then the LORD will single him out for adversity from all the tribes of Israel, according to all the curses of the covenant which are written in this book of the law.

> [22] "Now the generation to come, your sons who rise up after you and the foreigner who comes from a distant land, when they see the plagues of the land and the diseases with which the LORD has afflicted it, will say, [23] 'All its land is brimstone and salt, a burning waste, unsown and unproductive, and no grass grows in it, like the overthrow of Sodom and Gomorrah, Admah and Zeboiim, which the LORD overthrew in His anger and in His wrath.' [24] All the nations will say, 'Why has the LORD done thus to this land? Why this great outburst of anger?' [25] Then *men* will say, 'Because they forsook the covenant of the LORD, the God of their fathers, which He made with them when He brought them out of the land of Egypt. [26] They went and served other gods and worshiped them, gods whom they have not known and whom He had not allotted to them. [27] Therefore, the anger of the LORD burned against that land, to bring upon it every curse which is written in this book;"

Deuteronomy 30:15–20

> [15] "See, I have set before you today life and prosperity, and death and adversity; [16] in that I command you today to love the LORD your God, to walk in His ways and to keep His commandments and His statutes and His judgments, that you may live and multiply, and that the LORD your God may bless you in the land where you are entering to possess it. [17] But if your heart turns away and you will not obey, but are drawn away and worship other gods and serve them, [18] I declare to you today that you shall surely perish. You will not prolong *your* days in the land where you are crossing the Jordan to enter and possess it. [19] I call heaven and earth to witness against you today, that I have set before you life and death, the blessing and the curse. So choose life in order that you may live, you and your descendants, [20] by loving the LORD your God, by obeying His voice, and by holding fast to Him; for this is your life and the length of your days, that you may live in the land which the LORD swore to your fathers, to Abraham, Isaac, and Jacob, to give them."

Note: This covenant was given to Israel in the land of Moab, and it was delivered through Moses. The terms of the covenant are spelled out in detail in Deuteronomy chapters 28, 29, and 30.

a. The Abrahamic Covenant provided Israel with the land of Palestine as an everlasting possession. The ownership of the land was unconditional.

b. Israel's relationship to the land is set forth in the Palestinian Covenant.

c. The Palestinian Covenant addresses Israel's occupation and enjoyment of the land.

d. The Palestinian Covenant is conditional.

1) If the people of Israel were obedient and worshipped and served God, they would be able to live in the land and enjoy its fruit.

2) If the people of Israel were disobedient and turned away from God, they would not be able to live in and enjoy the land.

e. The Old Testament predicts three removals and three restorations of Israel in relationship to the Palestinian Covenant.

1) The Egyptian Exile (400 years)

- Dispersion (removal from the land)

Genesis 15:13

> *God* said to Abram, "Know for certain that your descendants will be strangers in a land that is not theirs, where they will be enslaved and oppressed four hundred years."

- Restoration (return to the land)

Genesis 15:14–21

> [14] "But I will also judge the nation whom they will serve, and afterward they will come out with many possessions. [15] As for you, you shall go to your fathers in peace; you will be buried at a good old age. [16] Then in the fourth generation they will return here, for the iniquity of the Amorite is not yet complete."
>
> [17] It came about when the sun had set, that it was very dark, and behold, *there appeared* a smoking oven and a flaming torch which passed between these pieces. [18] On that day the LORD made a covenant with Abram, saying,
>
> "To your descendants I have given this land, From the river of Egypt as far as the great river, the river Euphrates:
>
> [19] the Kenite and the Kenizzite and the Kadmonite [20] and the Hittite and the Perizzite and the Rephaim [21] and the Amorite and the Canaanite and the Girgashite and the Jebusite."

2) The Babylonian / Persian / Assyrian Captivity (70 years)

- Dispersion (removal from the land)

Jeremiah 25:11

> This whole land will be a desolation and a horror, and these nations will serve the king of Babylon seventy years.

- Restoration (return to the land)

Jeremiah 25:12

> 'Then it will be when seventy years are completed I will punish the king of Babylon and that nation,' declares the LORD, 'for their iniquity, and the land of the Chaldeans; and I will make it an everlasting desolation.'

3) The final dispersion and restoration (into all the nations of the world)

- Dispersion (removal from land and dispersed into many nations)

Deuteronomy 28:63–67

> [63] It shall come about that as the LORD delighted over you to prosper you, and multiply you, so the LORD will delight over you to make you perish and destroy you; and you will be torn from the land where you are entering to possess it. [64] Moreover, the LORD will scatter you among all peoples, from one end of the earth to the other end of the earth; and there you shall serve other gods, wood and stone, which you or your fathers have not known. [65] Among those nations you shall find no rest, and there will be no resting place for the sole of your foot; but there the LORD will give you a trembling heart, failing of eyes, and despair of soul. [66] So your life shall hang in doubt before you; and you will be in dread night and day, and shall have no assurance of your life. [67] In the morning you shall say, 'Would that it were evening!' And at evening you shall say, 'Would that it were morning!' because of the dread of your heart which you dread, and for the sight of your eyes which you will see."

- Restoration (Since the reestablishment of Israel in 1948, the stage is already set for this event.)

Deuteronomy 30:1–7

> [1] "So it shall be when all of these things have come upon you, the blessing and the curse which I have set before you, and you call *them* to mind in all nations where the LORD your God has banished you, [2] and you return to the LORD your God and obey Him with all your heart and soul according to all that I command you today, you and your sons, [3] then the LORD your God will restore you from captivity, and have compassion on you, and will gather you again from all the peoples where the LORD your God has scattered you. [4] If your outcasts are at the ends of the earth, from there the LORD your God will gather you, and from there He will bring you back. [5] The LORD your God will bring you into the land which your fathers possessed, and you shall possess it; and He will prosper you and multiply you more than your fathers.
>
> [6] "Moreover the LORD your God will circumcise your heart and the heart of your descendants, to love the LORD your God with all your heart and with all your soul, so that you may live. [7] The LORD your God will inflict all these curses on your enemies and on those who hate you, who persecuted you."

f. Jesus prophesied concerning the possession of the land.

1) The destruction of Jerusalem (fulfilled in 70 AD)

This is phase one of the final dispersion of the Jewish nation.

Luke 21:20–24

> [20] "But when you see Jerusalem surrounded by armies, then recognize that her desolation is near. [21] Then those who are in Judea must flee to the mountains, and those who are in the midst of the city must leave, and those who are in the country must not enter the city; [22] because these are days of vengeance, so that all things which are written will be fulfilled. [23] Woe to those who are pregnant and to those who are nursing babies in those days; for there will be great distress upon the land and wrath to this people; [24] and they will fall by the edge of the sword, and will be led captive into all the nations; and Jerusalem will be trampled under foot by the Gentiles until the times of the Gentiles are fulfilled."

Note: The Romans, under Hadrian, finished the job of dispersing the Jewish people from their land when he crushed a second Jewish rebellion for independence in a 3-year war ending in 135 AD. The rebellion was led by Simon bar Kochba, who was declared to be the messiah. Bar Kochba's rebellion had disastrous results. Cassius Dio, a second century Roman historian, claimed that the Romans killed 580,000 Jews during this war. The Romans completely destroyed Jerusalem and are believed to have run a plow over part or all of the city. The surviving Jews were expelled and were banned from returning to Jerusalem.

2) The restoration of Israel to the land with Christ as King (will be fulfilled at Jesus Christ's Second Advent)

Luke 21:25–31

> [25] "There will be signs in sun and moon and stars, and on the earth dismay among nations, in perplexity at the roaring of the sea and the waves, [26] men fainting from fear and the expectation of the things which are coming upon the world; for the powers of the heavens will be shaken. [27] Then they will see THE SON OF MAN COMING IN A CLOUD with power and great glory. [28] But when these things begin to take place, straighten up and lift up your heads, because your redemption is drawing near."
>
> [29] Then He told them a parable: "Behold the fig tree and all the trees; [30] as soon as they put forth *leaves*, you see it and know for yourselves that summer is now near. [31] So you also, when you see these things happening, recognize that the kingdom of God is near."

Note: With the establishment of the modern state of Israel in 1947–48, the stage was set for this restoration. God is by no means done with Israel. As you can see, He has made promises to Israel that He fully intends to keep. If God does not keep His covenant promises to Israel, there is no reason to believe He will keep His promises to us. (See Ezekiel 37.)

1 Kings 8:56

> "Blessed be the LORD, who has given rest to His people Israel, according to all that He promised; not one word has failed of all His good promise, which He promised through Moses His servant."

3. The Davidic Covenant (the promise of a King in David's lineage to rule forever)

2 Samuel 7:12–16

> [12] "When your days are complete and you lie down with your fathers, I will raise up your descendant after you, who will come forth from you, and I will establish his kingdom. [13] He shall build a house for My name, and I will establish the throne of his kingdom forever. [14] I will be a father to him and he will be a son to Me; when he commits iniquity, I will correct him with the rod of men and the strokes of the sons of men, [15] but My lovingkindness shall not depart from him, as I took *it* away from Saul, whom I removed from before you. [16] Your house and your kingdom shall endure before Me forever; your throne shall be established forever."

a. The Davidic Covenant was delivered to David through Nathan the prophet.

b. The Davidic Covenant secured three things for David and his posterity:

   1) An eternal house – Family successors to his dynasty

   2) An eternal throne – Not a physical throne but a position as king of Israel from his offspring

   3) An eternal kingdom – The nation of Israel over which to rule

c. The Davidic Covenant is unconditional and eternal.

d. The Davidic Covenant finds its complete fulfillment in the person of Christ as King.

e. If the Davidic Covenant is kept in mind, it will not be difficult to understand the purpose of the book of Matthew, the lineage that is listed in Matthew 1, and the circumstances surrounding the birth of Christ.

Psalms 89:28–37

> [28] "My lovingkindness I will keep for him forever,
> And My covenant shall be confirmed to him.
> [29] "So I will establish his descendants forever
> And his throne as the days of heaven.

[30] "If his sons forsake My law
And do not walk in My judgments,
[31] If they violate My statutes
And do not keep My commandments,
[32] Then I will punish their transgression with the rod
And their iniquity with stripes.
[33] "But I will not break off My lovingkindness from him,
Nor deal falsely in My faithfulness.
[34] "My covenant I will not violate,
Nor will I alter the utterance of My lips.
[35] "Once I have sworn by My holiness;
I will not lie to David.
[36] "His descendants shall endure forever
And his throne as the sun before Me.
[37] "It shall be established forever like the moon,
And the witness in the sky is faithful." *Selah.*

Psalms 132:11–12

[11] The LORD has sworn to David
A truth from which He will not turn back:
"Of the fruit of your body I will set upon your throne.
[12] "If your sons will keep My covenant
And My testimony which I will teach them,
Their sons also shall sit upon your throne forever."

1 Kings 8:25

Now therefore, O LORD, the God of Israel, keep with Your servant David my father that which You have promised him, saying, 'You shall not lack a man to sit on the throne of Israel, if only your sons take heed to their way to walk before Me as you have walked.'

1 Kings 9:5

then I will establish the throne of your kingdom over Israel forever, just as I promised to your father David, saying, 'You shall not lack a man on the throne of Israel.'

H. The church age was not seen by the Old Testament prophets.

Romans 16:25–27

> [25] Now to Him who is able to establish you according to my gospel and the preaching of Jesus Christ, according to the revelation of the mystery which has been kept secret for long ages past, [26] but now is manifested, and by the Scriptures of the prophets, according to the commandment of the eternal God, has been made known to all the nations, *leading* to obedience of faith; [27] to the only wise God, through Jesus Christ, be the glory forever. Amen.

Ephesians 3:1–11

> [1] For this reason I, Paul, the prisoner of Christ Jesus for the sake of you Gentiles— [2] if indeed you have heard of the stewardship of God's grace which was given to me for you; [3] that by revelation there was made known to me the mystery, as I wrote before in brief. [4] By referring to this, when you read you can understand my insight into the mystery of Christ, [5] which in other generations was not made known to the sons of men, as it has now been revealed to His holy apostles and prophets in the Spirit; [6] *to be specific*, that the Gentiles are fellow heirs and fellow members of the body, and fellow partakers of the promise in Christ Jesus through the gospel, [7] of which I was made a minister, according to the gift of God's grace which was given to me according to the working of His power. [8] To me, the very least of all saints, this grace was given, to preach to the Gentiles the unfathomable riches of Christ, [9] and to bring to light what is the administration of the mystery which for ages has been hidden in God who created all things; [10] so that the manifold wisdom of God might now be made known through the church to the rulers and the authorities in the heavenly *places*. [11] *This was* in accordance with the eternal purpose which He carried out in Christ Jesus our Lord,

Colossians 1:25–27

> [25] Of *this church* I was made a minister according to the stewardship from God bestowed on me for your benefit, so that I might fully carry out the *preaching of* the word of God, [26] *that is*, the mystery which has been hidden from the *past* ages and generations, but has now been manifested to His saints, [27] to whom God willed to make known what is the riches of the glory of this mystery among the Gentiles, which is Christ in you, the hope of glory.

1 Peter 1:10–12

> [10] As to this salvation, the prophets who prophesied of the grace that *would come* to you made careful searches and inquiries, [11] seeking to know what person or time the Spirit of Christ within them was indicating as He predicted the sufferings of Christ and the glories to follow. [12] It was revealed to them that they were not serving themselves, but you, in these things which now have been announced to you through those who preached the gospel to you by the Holy Spirit sent from heaven—things into which angels long to look.

III. Daniel's Prophecy of the Image in Nebuchadnezzar's Dream (Daniel 2:31–45)

Background:

Daniel was deported in the first group of exiles by King Nebuchadnezzar in 605 BC. Immediately after Nebuchadnezzar had taken Jerusalem and following the death of his father, Nabopolassar returned to Babylon to claim the throne. He took captive King Jehoiachin, along with the princes, noblemen, and choice young men of Judah. Among those deported to Babylon was Daniel. Nebuchadnezzar placed Jehoahaz as governor of Judea, while he returned to Babylon to claim his throne after the death of his father. The story of Daniel's dedication and courage is found in Daniel chapter 1. Daniel 2:1–30 records the events leading to Daniel's interpretation of Nebuchadnezzar's dream. Daniel 2:31–46 records the content of the dream and its interpretation.

A. The content of the dream

Daniel 2:31–35

> [31] "You, O king, were looking and behold, there was a single great statue; that statue, which was large and of extraordinary splendor, was standing in front of you, and its appearance was awesome. [32] The head of that statue *was made* of fine gold, its breast and its arms of silver, its belly and its thighs of bronze, [33] its legs of iron, its feet partly of iron and partly of clay. [34] You continued looking until a stone was cut out without hands, and it struck the statue on its feet of iron and clay and crushed them. [35] Then the iron, the clay, the bronze, the silver and the gold were crushed all at the same time and became like chaff from the summer threshing floors; and the wind carried them away so that not a trace of them was found. But the stone that struck the statue became a great mountain and filled the whole earth."

1. Awesome statue (v. 31)
    a. Single statue
    b. Large in size
    c. Great in impressiveness
    d. Extraordinary splendor in brightness
    e. Awesome in appearance (fearful, dreadful)
2. Head of fine gold (v. 32)
3. Breast and arms of silver (v. 32)
4. Belly and thighs of bronze (v. 32)
5. Legs of iron (v. 33)
6. Feet partly iron and partly clay (v. 33)
7. A Stone cut without hands (v. 34)
8. The Stone struck the statue on the weakened feet and crushed them. (v. 34)
9. The entire statue was crushed into a fine powder, and the wind subsequently blew it all away so that there was no trace of the image to be found. (v. 35)
10. The Stone became a great mountain and filled the whole earth. (v. 35)

B. The interpretation of the dream

Daniel 2:36–45

> [36] "This *was* the dream; now we will tell its interpretation before the king. [37] You, O king, are the king of kings, to whom the God of heaven has given the kingdom, the power, the strength and the glory; [38] and wherever the sons of men dwell, *or* the beasts of the field, or the birds of the sky, He has given *them* into your hand and has caused you to rule over them all. You are the head of gold.
>
> [39] After you there will arise another kingdom inferior to you, then another third kingdom of bronze, which will rule over all the earth.

> [40] Then there will be a fourth kingdom as strong as iron; inasmuch as iron crushes and shatters all things, so, like iron that breaks in pieces, it will crush and break all these in pieces. [41] In that you saw the feet and toes, partly of potter's clay and partly of iron, it will be a divided kingdom; but it will have in it the toughness of iron, inasmuch as you saw the iron mixed with common clay. [42] *As* the toes of the feet *were* partly of iron and partly of pottery, *so* some of the kingdom will be strong and part of it will be brittle. [43] And in that you saw the iron mixed with common clay, they will combine with one another in the seed of men; but they will not adhere to one another, even as iron does not combine with pottery.
>
> [44] In the days of those kings the God of heaven will set up a kingdom which will never be destroyed, and *that* kingdom will not be left for another people; it will crush and put an end to all these kingdoms, but it will itself endure forever. [45] Inasmuch as you saw that a stone was cut out of the mountain without hands and that it crushed the iron, the bronze, the clay, the silver and the gold, the great God has made known to the king what will take place in the future; so the dream is true and its interpretation is trustworthy."

1. The awesome statue (v. 31)

The text is clear that this image represents the four great world empires, beginning with Nebuchadnezzar's Babylonian Empire. The four empires are the Babylonian, Medo-Persian, Greek, and Roman. These world empires are characterized by the four materials. The splendor and awesome character of the image speaks of the great power, splendor, and sovereignty of these empires. Each of the empires ruled over all the nations and peoples of the world and were organized into a single state. Each were to be feared by all men. To each of these empires, God, who is the only real Sovereign One, granted this power. However, with each subsequent empire, there was a definite loss of wealth and centralized power from the preceding empire, even though the land mass incorporated was *increased* with each of them. This image is used to prophesy concerning the period of time referred to by Christ as "the times of the Gentiles" in Luke 21:24, which records, "and they will fall by the edge of the sword and will be led captive into all the nations; and Jerusalem will be trampled underfoot by the Gentiles until the times of the Gentiles are fulfilled."

2. Head made of fine gold (v. 36–38)

The head made of fine gold characterized the wealth and power of the Babylonian Empire. The Babylonian Empire lasted about seventy years.

3. Breast and arms made of silver (v. 39)

   The breast and arms of silver characterized the Medo-Persian Empire. Darius the Mede conquered Babylon on October 26, 539 BC. Inferior in wealth and centralized power, the Medo-Persian Empire increased the conquered territory over the Babylonian Empire. The Medo-Persian Empire lasted about 200 years.

4. Belly and thighs made of bronze (v. 39)

   The belly and thighs made of bronze is a characterization of the Greek Empire. Alexander was twenty years old when he became king of Macedonia. He quickly conquered the other Greek states and united them under his rule. In 330 BC, he took Persia, having already conquered Gaza and Egypt. He then went on to conquer India. At the height of his power, his empire stretched from Macedonia to Northern India. He died on June 13, 323 BC at the age of thirty-two. After his death, his empire was divided into four parts and given to his four generals. Fighting among these generals brought chaos and anarchy. The Greek Empire retained its significant power only about 130 years.

5. Legs made of iron (v. 40)

   The legs made of iron is a characterization of the Roman Empire. The Roman Empire expanded with their strong armies like a steam roller, crushing everything and everyone who was in its path. At the height of its power, the Roman Empire extended from Britannia (Britain) to India. Its armies were fierce, and their methods were cruel. The Roman period began about 60 BC and extended for about five hundred years.

6. Feet made of partly iron and partly clay (v. 41–44a)

   The feet made of partly iron and partly clay is a characterization of the *revived* Roman Empire. This is yet in the future and is not necessarily a revival of the Roman Empire, as such, but an alliance of ten kings that includes the land area of Europe. The ten toes represent the fragile alliance that will be crushed by the Stone cut without hands. (More about this in later chapters of Daniel.)

7. The Stone cut without hands is none other than the Lord Jesus Christ, Israel's Messiah. (v. 44)

8. The Stone striking and crushing the weakened feet on the statue is a picture of Christ's Second Advent when He will come in "power and great glory." (v. 44–45)

9. The entire statue was crushed into a fine powder and the wind subsequently blew it all away so that there was no trace of the image to be found. This shows that Christ will end the Gentile rule when He is seated on the throne of David to rule all nations. (v. 45)

10. The Stone became a great mountain and filled the whole earth. This event looks past the church age to the Second Advent of Christ, when He will return to the earth in "power and great glory." Jesus Christ will take His place on the throne of David, thus completely fulfilling the Davidic Covenant. He will put an end to "the times of the Gentiles." All Gentile rule will end (v. 35 and 44), and Jesus' kingdom will fill the whole earth and will be a kingdom of righteousness and peace. Finally, the Prince of Peace will rule all! (v. 45)

C. Christ's own prophecy concerning these events

Matthew 24:15–30

> [15] "Therefore when you see the ABOMINATION OF DESOLATION which was spoken of through Daniel the prophet, standing in the holy place (let the reader understand), [16] then those who are in Judea must flee to the mountains. [17] Whoever is on the housetop must not go down to get the things out that are in his house. [18] Whoever is in the field must not turn back to get his cloak. [19] But woe to those who are pregnant and to those who are nursing babies in those days! [20] But pray that your flight will not be in the winter, or on a Sabbath. [21] For then there will be a great tribulation, such as has not occurred since the beginning of the world until now, nor ever will. [22] Unless those days had been cut short, no life would have been saved; but for the sake of the elect those days will be cut short. [23] Then if anyone says to you, 'Behold, here is the Christ,' or 'There *He is*,' do not believe *him*. [24] For false Christs and false prophets will arise and will show great signs and wonders, so as to mislead, if possible, even the elect. [25] Behold, I have told you in advance. [26] So if they say to you, 'Behold, He is in the wilderness,' do not go out, *or*, 'Behold, He is in the inner rooms,' do not believe *them*. [27] For just as the lightning comes from the east and flashes even to the west, so will the coming of the Son of Man be. [28] Wherever the corpse is, there the vultures will gather.
>
> [29] "But immediately after the tribulation of those days THE SUN WILL BE DARKENED, AND THE MOON WILL NOT GIVE ITS LIGHT, AND THE STARS WILL FALL from the sky, and the powers of the heavens will be shaken. [30] And then the sign of the Son of Man will appear in the sky, and then all the tribes of the earth will mourn, and they will see the SON OF MAN COMING ON THE CLOUDS OF THE SKY with power and great glory."

Mark 13:18–32

> [18] But pray that it may not happen in the winter. [19] For those days will be a *time of* tribulation such as has not occurred since the beginning of the creation which God created until now, and never will. [20] Unless the Lord had shortened *those* days, no life would have been saved; but for the sake of the elect, whom He chose, He shortened the days. [21] And then if anyone says to you, 'Behold, here is the Christ'; or, 'Behold, *He is* there'; do not believe *him*; [22] for false Christs and false prophets will arise, and will show signs and wonders, in order to lead astray, if possible, the elect. [23] But take heed; behold, I have told you everything in advance.
>
> [24] "But in those days, after that tribulation, THE SUN WILL BE DARKENED AND THE MOON WILL NOT GIVE ITS LIGHT, [25] AND THE STARS WILL BE FALLING from heaven, and the powers that are in the heavens will be shaken. [26] Then they will see THE SON OF MAN COMING IN CLOUDS with great power and glory. [27] And then He will send forth the angels, and will gather together His elect from the four winds, from the farthest end of the earth to the farthest end of heaven.
>
> [28] "Now learn the parable from the fig tree: when its branch has already become tender and puts forth its leaves, you know that summer is near. [29] Even so, you too, when you see these things happening, recognize that He is near, *right* at the door. [30] Truly I say to you, this generation will not pass away until all these things take place. [31] Heaven and earth will pass away, but My words will not pass away. [32] But of that day or hour no one knows, not even the angels in heaven, nor the Son, but the Father *alone*."

Luke 21:20–28

> [20] "But when you see Jerusalem surrounded by armies, then recognize that her desolation is near. [21] Then those who are in Judea must flee to the mountains, and those who are in the midst of the city must leave, and those who are in the country must not enter the city; [22] because these are days of vengeance, so that all things which are written will be fulfilled. [23] Woe to those who are pregnant and to those who are nursing babies in those days; for there will be great distress upon the land and wrath to this people; [24] and they will fall by the edge of the sword, and will be led captive into all the nations; and Jerusalem will be trampled under foot by the Gentiles until the times of the Gentiles are fulfilled.

> [25] "There will be signs in sun and moon and stars, and on the earth dismay among nations, in perplexity at the roaring of the sea and the waves, [26] men fainting from fear and the expectation of the things which are coming upon the world; for the powers of the heavens will be shaken. [27] Then they will see THE SON OF MAN COMING IN A CLOUD with power and great glory. [28] But when these things begin to take place, straighten up and lift up your heads, because your redemption is drawing near."

IV. Daniel's Vision of the Four Beasts

Background:

It should be noted that these visions and dreams, through which God revealed the future to Daniel, are built one upon another. It is exceedingly difficult to understand the full scope of the individual visions, without taking into consideration the other visions in Daniel's book.

We begin by clearly establishing what Daniel saw in the vision. As we study this vision, we should note that this prophecy was given in 562 BC, during the first year King Belshazzar was king in Babylon. (See Daniel 7:1.) This prophecy was given twenty-three years before the Medo-Persian Empire overthrew Babylon. This prophecy was given two hundred thirty years before Alexander the Great appeared on the scene. This prophecy was given almost five hundred years before the arrival of the Roman Empire.

A. Content of the vision

Daniel 7:1–3

> [1] In the first year of Belshazzar king of Babylon Daniel saw a dream and visions in his mind *as he lay* on his bed; then he wrote the dream down *and* related the *following* summary of it. [2] Daniel said, "I was looking in my vision by night, and behold, the four winds of heaven were stirring up the great sea. [3] And four great beasts were coming up from the sea, different from one another."

1. The First Beast

Daniel 7:4

> "The first *was* like a lion and had *the* wings of an eagle. I kept looking until its wings were plucked, and it was lifted up from the ground and made to stand on two feet like a man; a human mind also was given to it."

a. It was like a lion.

b. It had wings of an eagle.

c. In time, its wings were torn off.

d. In time, it was made to stand on two of its feet like a man.

e. A human mind was given to it.

2. The Second Beast

Daniel 7:5

> "And behold, another beast, a second one, resembling a bear. And it was raised up on one side, and three ribs *were* in its mouth between its teeth; and thus they said to it, 'Arise, devour much meat!'"

a. It was like a bear.

b. It was raised up on one side.

c. It had three ribs between its teeth.

d. It was told, "Get up and eat your fill of flesh."

3. The Third Beast

Daniel 7:6

> "After this I kept looking, and behold, another one, like a leopard, which had on its back four wings of a bird; the beast also had four heads, and dominion was given to it."

a. It was like a leopard.

b. It has four wings of a bird on its back.

c. It had four heads.

d. Authority to rule was given to it.

4. The Fourth Beast

Daniel 7:7

> "After this I kept looking in the night visions, and behold, a fourth beast, dreadful and terrifying and extremely strong; and it had large iron teeth. It devoured and crushed and trampled down the remainder with its feet; and it was different from all the beasts that were before it, and it had ten horns."

a. This beast was dreadful and to be feared.

b. It was terrifying.

c. It was exceedingly strong, stronger than all the other beasts.

d. It was armed with large iron teeth.

e. It was so strong that it completely destroyed all that remained of the previous beasts.

f. It was unlike any of the beasts that preceded it.

g. It had ten horns.

5. The Ten Horns and the Little Horn

Daniel 7:8

> "While I was contemplating the horns, behold, another horn, a little one, came up among them, and three of the first horns were pulled out by the roots before it; and behold, this horn possessed eyes like the eyes of a man and a mouth uttering great *boasts*."

a. After a time, a little horn sprouted among the ten horns.

b. It uprooted and replaced three of the ten horns.

c. It had eyes like the eyes of a man.

d. It had a mouth and boasted great, dictatorial things.

6. The Ancient of Days

Daniel 7:9–11

> [9] "I kept looking
> Until thrones were set up,
> And the Ancient of Days took *His* seat;
> His vesture *was* like white snow
> And the hair of His head like pure wool.
> His throne *was* ablaze with flames,
> Its wheels *were* a burning fire.
> [10] "A river of fire was flowing
> And coming out from before Him;
> Thousands upon thousands were attending Him,
> And myriads upon myriads were standing before Him;
> The court sat,
> And the books were opened.
>
> [11] Then I kept looking because of the sound of the boastful words which the horn was speaking; I kept looking until the beast was slain, and its body was destroyed and given to the burning fire."

a. His clothing was like white snow.

b. His hair was like pure wool.

c. He sat on a throne that was ablaze with flames and wheels of fire.

d. A river of fire was flowing from His throne.

e. Huge multitudes were attending Him.

f. He set up His judgment court and opened the books upon which His judgment would be based.

7. The Judgment of the Beasts

Daniel 7:11–12

> [11] "Then I kept looking because of the sound of the boastful words which the horn was speaking; I kept looking until the beast was slain, and its body was destroyed and given to the burning fire. [12] As for the rest of the beasts, their dominion was taken away, but an extension of life was granted to them for an appointed period of time."

a. The boasting of the little horn continued for a time.

b. The fourth beast, along with the little horn, was slain and cast into the burning fire.

c. The other beasts' lives were extended for a designated period of time; however, they were not allowed any power to rule over any territory or peoples.

8. The Coming of the Son of Man

Daniel 7:13–14

[13] "I kept looking in the night visions,
And behold, with the clouds of heaven
One like a Son of Man was coming,
And He came up to the Ancient of Days
And was presented before Him.
[14] "And to Him was given dominion,
Glory and a kingdom,
That all the peoples, nations and *men of every* language
Might serve Him.
His dominion is an everlasting dominion
Which will not pass away;
And His kingdom is one
Which will not be destroyed."

a. The Son of Man was presented to the Ancient of Days.

b. The Ancient of Days granted to the Son of Man the glory and power to rule over the people of all nations and all language groups covering the face of the earth. All were to serve Him. (v. 14)

c. His kingdom united all the earth into one.

d. His kingdom would last for all eternity and would never be destroyed.

B. The interpretation of the vision (Read Daniel 7:15–28)

The four beasts represent the four great world empires, beginning with Nebuchadnezzar's Babylonian Empire. The empires were the Babylonian, the Medo-Persian, the Greek, and the Roman.

1. The First Beast (The Lion – The Babylonian Empire)

Daniel 7:4

> "The first *was* like a lion and had *the* wings of an eagle. I kept looking until its wings were plucked, and it was lifted up from the ground and made to stand on two feet like a man; a human mind also was given to it."

a. The lion, king of the beasts, pictures the grandeur and power of the Babylonian Empire.

b. Jeremiah refers to Nebuchadnezzar when he warns of the destruction coming to Judah in Jeremiah 4:6–7.

Jeremiah 4:6–7

> [6] "Lift up a standard toward Zion!
> Seek refuge, do not stand *still*,
> For I am bringing evil from the north,
> And great destruction.
> [7] "A lion has gone up from his thicket,
> And a destroyer of nations has set out;
> He has gone out from his place
> To make your land a waste.
> Your cities will be ruins
> Without inhabitant."

c. As time passed, the power and glory once owned by king Nebuchadnezzar was vastly diminished after his death in 562 BC.

d. In the next twenty-three years, the power and glory of the once powerful "lion" was squandered and misused.

e. Toward the end of the Babylon rule, it was more like a "paper tiger" than a powerful lion.

f. Daniel 5 describes the excesses and sensuality of the last days of the Babylonian rule. Babylon fell to the Persians in 539 BC.

2. The Second Beast (The Bear – The Medo-Persian Empire)

Daniel 7:5

> "And behold, another beast, a second one, resembling a bear. And it was raised up on one side, and three ribs *were* in its mouth between its teeth; and thus they said to it, 'Arise, devour much meat!'"

a. The bear pictures the Medo-Persian Empire.

b. Raised up on one side refers to the Persian element of the Medo-Persian Empire which was the stronger of the two.

c. The three ribs in between its teeth pictures the three major territories they conquered in establishing their empire.

d. The bear was told to arise and devour much meat. The Medo-Persian Empire increased the conquered territory over the Babylonian Empire.

3. The Third Beast (The Leopard – The Greek Empire)

Daniel 7:6

> "After this I kept looking, and behold, another one, like a leopard, which had on its back four wings of a bird; the beast also had four heads, and dominion was given to it."

a. The leopard is a characterization of the Greek Empire and corresponds to the belly and thighs of bronze on Nebuchadnezzar's image.

b. The leopard is one of the fastest creatures of the animal world and, when equipped with four wings, would make it even faster. Pictured in this third beast is the swiftness with which Alexander the Great conquered.

c. The four heads are a picture of the four divisions into which the Greek Empire was divided, following the death of Alexander. The four parts were divided among four of his generals, each of which ruled his own sovereign state.

d. The phrase *dominion was given to it* simply refers to the power of the empire.

4. The Fourth Beast (The non-descript Beast – The Roman Empire) Daniel 7:7 and 7:19–20

Daniel 7:7

> "After this I kept looking in the night visions, and behold, a fourth beast, dreadful and terrifying and extremely strong; and it had large iron teeth. It devoured and crushed and trampled down the remainder with its feet; and it was different from all the beasts that were before it, and it had ten horns."

Daniel 7:19–20

> [19] "Then I desired to know the exact meaning of the fourth beast, which was different from all the others, exceedingly dreadful, with its teeth of iron and its claws of bronze, *and which* devoured, crushed and trampled down the remainder with its feet, [20] and *the meaning* of the ten horns that *were* on its head and the other *horn* which came up, and before which three *of them* fell, namely, that horn which had eyes and a mouth uttering great *boasts* and which was larger in appearance than its associates."

a. The fourth beast is a characterization of the Roman Empire.

b. This beast corresponds with the legs of iron in Nebuchadnezzar's image.

c. The Roman Empire conquered with its strong armies, crushing everything and everyone in its path. The Roman armies were fierce, and their methods were cruel. The Roman Empire was dreadful and to be feared.

d. This empire was terrifyingly strong and burly. It was extremely strong, stronger than all the others. It was like no other empire that had preceded it.

e. The large iron teeth refer to the ability of the Roman Empire to devour, crush, and trample down all other peoples.

5. The Ten Horns and the Little Horn

Daniel 7:8

> "While I was contemplating the horns, behold, another horn, a little one, came up among them, and three of the first horns were pulled out by the roots before it; and behold, this horn possessed eyes like the eyes of a man and a mouth uttering great *boasts*."

Daniel 7:20–25

> [20] and *the meaning* of the ten horns that *were* on its head and the other *horn* which came up, and before which three *of them* fell, namely, that horn which had eyes and a mouth uttering great *boasts* and which was larger in appearance than its associates. [21] I kept looking, and that horn was waging war with the saints and overpowering them [22] until the Ancient of Days came and judgment was passed in favor of the saints of the Highest One, and the time arrived when the saints took possession of the kingdom.

[23] "Thus he said: 'The fourth beast will be a fourth kingdom on the earth, which will be different from all the *other* kingdoms and will devour the whole earth and tread it down and crush it. [24] As for the ten horns, out of this kingdom ten kings will arise; and another will arise after them, and he will be different from the previous ones and will subdue three kings. [25] He will speak out against the Most High and wear down the saints of the Highest One, and he will intend to make alterations in times and in law; and they will be given into his hand for a time, times, and half a time."

a. The ten horns are a ten-nation alliance that will arise in the last days.

b. After a time, a little horn will sprout among the ten horns. This little horn that emerges from the ten-nation alliance is none other than the "man of sin" (the Antichrist), who will appear on the scene at the beginning of the tribulation period. He will subdue three of the kingdoms, so that only seven are left.

c. The little horn will uproot and replace three of the ten horns. It had eyes like the eyes of a man. It had a mouth and made great (domineering) boasts. The corresponding descriptions of the little horn are found here in Daniel and in the book of Revelation. (This illustrates the continuity of the Word of God.)

Parallels Between Daniel 7 and Revelation 13	
Daniel 7:8 While I was contemplating the horns, behold, another horn, a little one, came up among them, and three of the first horns were pulled out by the roots before it; and behold, this horn possessed eyes like the eyes of a man and a mouth uttering great *boasts.*	Revelation 13:1 And the dragon stood on the sand of the seashore. Then I saw a beast coming up out of the sea, having ten horns and seven heads, and on his horns *were* ten diadems, and on his heads *were* blasphemous names.
Daniel 7:25 He will speak out against the Most High and wear down the saints of the Highest One, and he will intend to make alterations in times and in law; and they will be given into his hand for a time, times, and half a time.	Revelation 13:5 There was given to him a mouth speaking arrogant words and blasphemies, and authority to act for forty-two months was given to him.

Daniel 7:25	Revelation 13:6
He will speak out against the Most High and wear down the saints of the Highest One, and he will intend to make alterations in times and in law; and they will be given into his hand for a time, times, and half a time.	And he opened his mouth in blasphemies against God, to blaspheme His name and His tabernacle, *that is*, those who dwell in heaven.
Daniel 7:21	Revelation 13:7
I kept looking, and that horn was waging war with the saints and overpowering them	It was also given to him to make war with the saints and to overcome them, and authority over every tribe and people and tongue and nation was given to him.

6. The Ancient of Days

Daniel 7:9–10

[9] "I kept looking
Until thrones were set up,
And the Ancient of Days took *His* seat;
His vesture *was* like white snow
And the hair of His head like pure wool.
His throne *was* ablaze with flames,
Its wheels *were* a burning fire.
[10] "A river of fire was flowing
And coming out from before Him;
Thousands upon thousands were attending Him,
And myriads upon myriads were standing before Him;
The court sat,
And the books were opened."

a. The Ancient of Days is a reference to God seated in judgment.

b. His clothing, white like snow, is a picture of His righteousness.

c. The hair of His head like pure wool is a reference to His eternal character.

d. He sat on a throne that was ablaze with flames and wheels of fire. The river of fire flowing from His throne speaks of His judgment.

e. The thousands upon thousands attending Him is a reference to the worshipping saints in His presence.

f. He set up His judgment court and opened the books, upon which His judgments would be based.

7. The Judgment

Daniel 7:26–27

> [26] 'But the court will sit *for judgment*, and his dominion will be taken away, annihilated and destroyed forever. [27] Then the sovereignty, the dominion and the greatness of *all* the kingdoms under the whole heaven will be given to the people of the saints of the Highest One; His kingdom *will be* an everlasting kingdom, and all the dominions will serve and obey Him.'

The boasting of the little horn continued for a time. This is obviously challenging the authority of the Judge. (See Daniel 7:8)

8. The Battle of Armageddon

Revelation 19:11–20

> [11] And I saw heaven opened, and behold, a white horse, and He who sat on it *is* called Faithful and True, and in righteousness He judges and wages war. [12] His eyes *are* a flame of fire, and on His head *are* many diadems; and He has a name written *on Him* which no one knows except Himself. [13] *He is* clothed with a robe dipped in blood, and His name is called The Word of God. [14] And the armies which are in heaven, clothed in fine linen, white *and* clean, were following Him on white horses. [15] From His mouth comes a sharp sword, so that with it He may strike down the nations, and He will rule them with a rod of iron; and He treads the wine press of the fierce wrath of God, the Almighty. [16] And on His robe and on His thigh He has a name written, "KING OF KINGS, AND LORD OF LORDS."
>
> [17] Then I saw an angel standing in the sun, and he cried out with a loud voice, saying to all the birds which fly in midheaven, "Come, assemble for the great supper of God, [18] so that you may eat the flesh of kings and the flesh of commanders and the flesh of mighty men and the flesh of horses and of those who sit on them and the flesh of all men, both free men and slaves, and small and great."
>
> [19] And I saw the beast and the kings of the earth and their armies assembled to make war against Him who sat on the horse and against His army.

> [20] And the beast was seized, and with him the false prophet who performed the signs in his presence, by which he deceived those who had received the mark of the beast and those who worshiped his image; these two were thrown alive into the lake of fire which burns with brimstone.

The little horn (the Antichrist) was slain and cast into the burning fire.

9. Jesus' teaching about the Judgment of the Nations

Matthew 25:31–41

> [31] "But when the Son of Man comes in His glory, and all the angels with Him, then He will sit on His glorious throne. [32] All the nations will be gathered before Him; and He will separate them from one another, as the shepherd separates the sheep from the goats; [33] and He will put the sheep on His right, and the goats on the left.
>
> [34] "Then the King will say to those on His right, 'Come, you who are blessed of My Father, inherit the kingdom prepared for you from the foundation of the world. [35] For I was hungry, and you gave Me *something* to eat; I was thirsty, and you gave Me *something* to drink; I was a stranger, and you invited Me in; [36] naked, and you clothed Me; I was sick, and you visited Me; I was in prison, and you came to Me.' [37] Then the righteous will answer Him, 'Lord, when did we see You hungry, and feed You, or thirsty, and give You *something* to drink? [38] And when did we see You a stranger, and invite You in, or naked, and clothe You? [39] When did we see You sick, or in prison, and come to You?' [40] The King will answer and say to them, 'Truly I say to you, to the extent that you did it to one of these brothers of Mine, *even* the least *of them*, you did it to Me.'
>
> [41] "Then He will also say to those on His left, 'Depart from Me, accursed ones, into the eternal fire which has been prepared for the devil and his angels;"

a. These verses provide a description of the judgment of the nations, which will probably take place immediately following the Battle of Armageddon.

b. The principle issue in this judgment is how the nations of the world treated Israel, especially during the Tribulation. The seven-year Tribulation is referred to by Jeremiah as a time of Jacob's (Israel's) trouble. (Jeremiah 30:7)

c. This issue is in keeping with the Abrahamic Covenant.

10. The Coming of the Son of Man

Daniel 7:13–14

[13] "I kept looking in the night visions,
And behold, with the clouds of heaven
One like a Son of Man was coming,
And He came up to the Ancient of Days
And was presented before Him.
[14] "And to Him was given dominion,
Glory and a kingdom,
That all the peoples, nations and *men of every* language
Might serve Him.
His dominion is an everlasting dominion
Which will not pass away;
And His kingdom is one
Which will not be destroyed."

a. The Son of Man (Jesus) was presented to the Ancient of Days (God, the Judge).

b. The Ancient of Days granted to the Son of Man the glory and power to rule over the people of all nations and all language groups covering the face of the earth. All were to serve Him. (v. 14)

c. His kingdom united all the earth into one.

d. His kingdom will last for all eternity and will never be destroyed.

Revelation 20:4–6

[4] Then I saw thrones, and they sat on them, and judgment was given to them. And I *saw* the souls of those who had been beheaded because of their testimony of Jesus and because of the word of God, and those who had not worshiped the beast or his image, and had not received the mark on their forehead and on their hand; and they came to life and reigned with Christ for a thousand years. [5] The rest of the dead did not come to life until the thousand years were completed. This is the first resurrection. [6] Blessed and holy is the one who has a part in the first resurrection; over these the second death has no power, but they will be priests of God and of Christ and will reign with Him for a thousand years.

Note: The coming of the Son of Man corresponds with the "Stone cut without hands" in Nebuchadnezzar's dream (Daniel 2:44). The "saints" here would not only include those who accepted Christ during the church age who will reign with Him and will have already been raptured, but also those, both Jews and Gentiles, who recognize Jesus Christ as Israel's Messiah and turned to Him during the Tribulation. These tribulation saints are referred to in Revelation 20:4–6.

Jeremiah 30:7–18

[7] 'Alas! for that day is great,
There is none like it;
And it is the time of Jacob's distress,
But he will be saved from it.

[8] 'It shall come about on that day,' declares the LORD of hosts, 'that I will break his yoke from off their neck and will tear off their bonds; and strangers will no longer make them their slaves. [9] But they shall serve the LORD their God and David their king, whom I will raise up for them.

[10] 'Fear not, O Jacob My servant,' declares the LORD,
'And do not be dismayed, O Israel;
For behold, I will save you from afar
And your offspring from the land of their captivity.
And Jacob will return and will be quiet and at ease,
And no one will make him afraid.
[11] 'For I am with you,' declares the LORD, 'to save you;
For I will destroy completely all the nations where I have scattered you,
Only I will not destroy you completely.
But I will chasten you justly
And will by no means leave you unpunished.'

[12] "For thus says the LORD,
'Your wound is incurable
And your injury is serious.
[13] 'There is no one to plead your cause;
No healing for *your* sore,
No recovery for you.
[14] 'All your lovers have forgotten you,
They do not seek you;
For I have wounded you with the wound of an enemy,
With the punishment of a cruel one,
Because your iniquity is great
And your sins are numerous.

[15] 'Why do you cry out over your injury?
Your pain is incurable.
Because your iniquity is great
And your sins are numerous,
I have done these things to you.
[16] 'Therefore all who devour you will be devoured;
And all your adversaries, every one of them, will go into captivity;
And those who plunder you will be for plunder,
And all who prey upon you I will give for prey.
[17] 'For I will restore you to health
And I will heal you of your wounds,' declares the LORD,
'Because they have called you an outcast, saying:
"It is Zion; no one cares for her."'

[18] "Thus says the LORD,
'Behold, I will restore the fortunes of the tents of Jacob
And have compassion on his dwelling places;
And the city will be rebuilt on its ruin,
And the palace will stand on its rightful place."

e. How awful that day will be! None will be like it. It will be a time of trouble for Jacob, but he (Israel) will be saved out of it.

f. It will seem like there is no hope for Israel.

g. Instead, they will serve the LORD their God and David their King (Jesus).

h. Even though it will look hopeless, God will ultimately restore Jacob (Israel).

V. Daniel's Vision of the Ram, Goat, and Little Horn

Background:

Two years after Daniel's vision of the four beasts (recorded in Daniel 7), God spoke to Daniel through another vision. With the introduction of each vision, there are more details given than in the preceding revelation. This vision focuses on the Greek Empire and, more specifically, on the reign of Antiochus Epiphanes. Antiochus Epiphanes ruled over Syria, Babylon, and Asia Minor from 175–164 BC. We should note that this prophecy was given in 550 BC during the third year of King Belshazzar's reign over the Babylonian Empire (Daniel 8:1).

A. The content of the vision

Daniel 8:1–14

> [1] In the third year of the reign of Belshazzar the king a vision appeared to me, Daniel, subsequent to the one which appeared to me previously. [2] I looked in the vision, and while I was looking I was in the citadel of Susa, which is in the province of Elam; and I looked in the vision and I myself was beside the Ulai Canal. [3] Then I lifted my eyes and looked, and behold, a ram which had two horns was standing in front of the canal. Now the two horns *were* long, but one *was* longer than the other, with the longer one coming up last. [4] I saw the ram butting westward, northward, and southward, and no *other* beasts could stand before him nor was there anyone to rescue from his power, but he did as he pleased and magnified *himself.*
>
> [5] While I was observing, behold, a male goat was coming from the west over the surface of the whole earth without touching the ground; and the goat *had* a conspicuous horn between his eyes. [6] He came up to the ram that had the two horns, which I had seen standing in front of the canal, and rushed at him in his mighty wrath. [7] I saw him come beside the ram, and he was enraged at him; and he struck the ram and shattered his two horns, and the ram had no strength to withstand him. So he hurled him to the ground and trampled on him, and there was none to rescue the ram from his power. [8] Then the male goat magnified *himself* exceedingly. But as soon as he was mighty, the large horn was broken; and in its place there came up four conspicuous *horns* toward the four winds of heaven.
>
> [9] Out of one of them came forth a rather small horn which grew exceedingly great toward the south, toward the east, and toward the Beautiful *Land.* [10] It grew up to the host of heaven and caused some of the host and some of the stars to fall to the earth, and it trampled them down. [11] It even magnified *itself* to be equal with the Commander of the host; and it removed the regular sacrifice from Him, and the place of His sanctuary was thrown down. [12] And on account of transgression the host will be given over *to the horn* along with the regular sacrifice; and it will fling truth to the ground and perform *its will* and prosper. [13] Then I heard a holy one speaking, and another holy one said to that particular one who was speaking, "How long will the vision *about* the regular sacrifice apply, while the transgression causes horror, so as to allow both the holy place and the host to be trampled?" [14] He said to me, "For 2,300 evenings *and* mornings; then the holy place will be properly restored."

1. Daniel's Location (Daniel 8:1–2)

    a. In his vision, Daniel is placed in Susa, the city which would later become the capital of the Medo-Persian Empire.

    b. Susa was located about two hundred miles east of Babylon where Daniel served in the court of Belshazzar, the last king of Babylon.

    c. Belshazzar would reign as king for 11 more years before Babylon would fall to the Medes and the Persians. (Daniel 5)

    d. This vision focuses on the second and third empires.

2. The Ram (Daniel 8:3–4)

    a. The ram was standing in front of the Aiel River.

    b. The ram had two horns. Both horns were long, but the longer horn came up last.

    c. The ram was butting towards the west, north, and south.

    d. The ram was so powerful that no one could oppose it.

3. The Male Goat (Daniel 8:5–8)

    a. The goat came from the west.

    b. The goat moved so quickly over the surface of the earth that his feet did not touch the ground.

    c. The goat had a pronounced horn between his eyes.

    d. The goat faced off with the ram and overwhelmingly destroyed the ram.

    e. The male goat heightened his power greatly, but soon after he attained this power, the horn between his eyes broke off.

    f. Four horns, pointing toward the east, west, north, and south, replaced the one great horn.

4. The Small Horn (Daniel 8:9–14)

    a. The small horn grew out of one of the four horns of the male goat.

    b. This horn was small at first but grew more powerful.

c. The small horn's power was expanded to the south, the east, and the Beautiful Land.

d. The small horn magnified himself and caused some of the stars of the heavens to fall, and he trampled them down.

e. The small horn magnified himself and turned his hostility to opposing the Lord of Hosts.

f. The small horn magnified himself, removed the daily sacrifice, opposed the truth, and threw down the sanctuary of the Lord of Hosts.

5. Daniel overhears the angels' discussion (Daniel 8:13–14)

a. Daniel overhears the angels discussing the duration of the suspension of the daily sacrifice.

b. The suspension of the daily sacrifice was to last for 2,300 days (6.3 years).

c. The holy place will be restored after the 2,300 days are completed.

B. The interpretation of vision

Daniel 8:15–25

> [15] When I, Daniel, had seen the vision, I sought to understand it; and behold, standing before me was one who looked like a man. [16] And I heard the voice of a man between *the banks of* Ulai, and he called out and said, "Gabriel, give this *man* an understanding of the vision." [17] So he came near to where I was standing, and when he came I was frightened and fell on my face; but he said to me, "Son of man, understand that the vision pertains to the time of the end."
>
> [18] Now while he was talking with me, I sank into a deep sleep with my face to the ground; but he touched me and made me stand upright. [19] He said, "Behold, I am going to let you know what will occur at the final period of the indignation, for *it* pertains to the appointed time of the end.
>
> [20] The ram which you saw with the two horns represents the kings of Media and Persia.
>
> [21] The shaggy goat *represents* the kingdom of Greece, and the large horn that is between his eyes is the first king. [22] The broken *horn* and the four *horns that* arose in its place *represent* four kingdoms *which* will arise from *his* nation, although not with his power.

> [23] "In the latter period of their rule,
> When the transgressors have run *their course*,
> A king will arise,
> Insolent and skilled in intrigue.
> [24] "His power will be mighty, but not by his *own* power,
> And he will destroy to an extraordinary degree
> And prosper and perform *his will*;
> He will destroy mighty men and the holy people.
> [25] "And through his shrewdness
> He will cause deceit to succeed by his influence;
> And he will magnify *himself* in his heart,
> And he will destroy many while *they are* at ease.
> He will even oppose the Prince of princes,
> But he will be broken without human agency."

Daniel 8:16 is the first recorded appearance of the angel, Gabriel. He appears a second time to Daniel and teaches him concerning the seventy weeks of years (Daniel 9:21). In Daniel 9, Gabriel reveals to Daniel the time of the Messiah's death. The next time Gabriel appears is to announce the birth of John the Baptist to Zechariah (Luke 1:19). The only other recorded appearance of Gabriel is to Mary announcing the conception of Jesus. One could easily conclude that the happy privilege of heralding the coming of the Messiah and our Savior was delegated to Gabriel, whose name means "man of God."

1. The Ram (Daniel 8:20)

    a. The ram had two long horns. The two horns represent the two kingdoms that were combined to make up the Medo-Persian Empire.

    b. The ram was standing in front of the Aiel River, in the city of Susa, which was the capital of the Medo-Persian Empire.

    c. Both of the ram's horns were long but the longer horn came up last. The Media kingdom was established first, but when Persia arose, it became by far the stronger of the two and dominated the Medo-Persian Empire.

    d. The ram was butting towards the west, north, and south. These are the directions in which the Medo-Persian Empire pushed to expand its domain.

    e. The ram was so powerful that no one could oppose him. No kingdom was a match for the Medo-Persian Empire, not even Babylon, who fell to the Medo-Persian Empire 11 years after this prophecy was given.

2. The Male Goat (Daniel 8:21–22)

    a. The male goat represents Greece.

    b. The goat advanced from the west. He moved so quickly over the surface of the earth, that his feet did not touch the ground. He came from the west and pushed quickly to the east to conquer all nations and kingdoms in his path. In 331 BC, Alexander the Great eliminated the Medo-Persian Empire with his swift conquering force.

    c. The male goat had a pronounced horn between his eyes. Alexander the Great is the notable horn between the eyes of the goat.

    d. The male goat faced off with the ram and overwhelmingly destroyed the ram. The Grecian Empire heightened its power greatly, but soon after attaining this power, the "horn between its eyes was broken off." At age thirty-two, Alexander the Great died at the height of his power.

    e. The four horns, pointing toward the east, west, north, and south, replaced the one great horn. Following Alexander's death, the Greek Empire was divided into four parts and given to four of his generals. Each general ruled his territory as a sovereign dominion. Those four divisions were:

        - East – Syria, Babylon was ruled by Antigonus
        - West – Macedonia was ruled by Cassander
        - North – Asia Minor (including Palestine) was ruled by Lysimachus
        - South – Egypt was ruled by Ptolemy

3. The Small Horn (Daniel 8:23–25)

    a. The small horn grew out of one of the four horns of the male goat. In the years following the division of the Greek Empire in 323 BC, infighting, confusion, and anarchy prevailed among the territories.

    b. The small horn was small at first but grew more powerful. Territories changed, alliances were made, and power shifted.

    c. The small horn's power was expanded to the south, the east, and the Beautiful Land (Israel). In 175 BC, Antiochus IV Epiphanes ruled Syria but expanded his kingdom to the east, south, and toward the Beautiful Land (Israel). In 169 BC, Antiochus IV Epiphanes captured Jerusalem.

    d. The small horn magnified himself and caused some of the stars of the heavens to fall and he trampled them down. Nicknamed the Madman, Antiochus IV Epiphanes was a tyrant and a persecutor of the Jews. His evil deeds oppressed the Jews, blasphemed God, and desecrated the temple, as described in the Apocryphal books of the Maccabaeus. The stars, which he cast to the ground and stomped upon, are a picture of the people of Israel. Antiochus IV Epiphanes executed an estimated 100,000+ Jews, the first of which were those who held positions of authority and responsibility in Israel (princes, priests, and rabbis). Thousands more were taken captive.

e. Antiochus IV Epiphanes turned his hostility to opposing the Prince of Princes (God). He removed the daily sacrifice. He was not satisfied with simply causing havoc in Israel. In December of 168 BC, a year after he had conquered Jerusalem, he sacrificed a pig on the altar at the temple site and sprinkled its blood over the entire temple building. He suspended the daily sacrifices. He corrupted the Jewish young people by introducing lewd and immoral practices. He changed the Jewish feasts to celebrations of pagan gods and offered the high priesthood to the highest bidder.

4. Daniel's overhearing of the angels' discussion

Daniel 8:12–14

> [12] And on account of transgression the host will be given over *to the horn* along with the regular sacrifice; and it will fling truth to the ground and perform *its will* and prosper. [13] Then I heard a holy one speaking, and another holy one said to that particular one who was speaking, "How long will the vision *about* the regular sacrifice apply, while the transgression causes horror, so as to allow both the holy place and the host to be trampled?" [14] He said to me, "For 2,300 evenings *and* mornings; then the holy place will be properly restored."

a. Daniel overhears angels discussing the duration of the suspension of the daily sacrifice. The suspension of the daily sacrifice was to last for 2,300 days (6.3 years). The holy place was to be restored after the 2,300 days were completed.

b. In 166 BC, the Jews revolted under the leadership of Mattathias.

c. The temple was reconsecrated by Judas Maccabaeus on approximately December 25, 165 BC. The daily sacrifices were then resumed. We do not have the exact dates of the duration of this period but, going back 2,300 days from the reconsecration of the temple, takes us back to 171 BC. This was when Antiochus IV Epiphanes began his crusade against the Jews by taking a bribe from Menelaus, making him the high priest while murdering his predecessor, Onaias III. We believe the 2,300 days were literal days.

d. Antiochus IV Epiphanes and his treacherous deeds are also prophesied in Daniel 11:21–35.

Daniel 11:21–35

[21] "In his place a despicable person will arise, on whom the honor of kingship has not been conferred, but he will come in a time of tranquility and seize the kingdom by intrigue. [22] The overflowing forces will be flooded away before him and shattered, and also the prince of the covenant. [23] After an alliance is made with him he will practice deception, and he will go up and gain power with a small *force of* people. [24] In a time of tranquility he will enter the richest *parts* of the realm, and he will accomplish what his fathers never did, nor his ancestors; he will distribute plunder, booty and possessions among them, and he will devise his schemes against strongholds, but *only* for a time. [25] He will stir up his strength and courage against the king of the South with a large army; so the king of the South will mobilize an extremely large and mighty army for war; but he will not stand, for schemes will be devised against him. [26] Those who eat his choice food will destroy him, and his army will overflow, but many will fall down slain. [27] As for both kings, their hearts will be *intent* on evil, and they will speak lies *to each other* at the same table; but it will not succeed, for the end is still *to come* at the appointed time. [28] Then he will return to his land with much plunder; but his heart will be *set* against the holy covenant, and he will take action and *then* return to his *own* land.

[29] "At the appointed time he will return and come into the South, but this last time it will not turn out the way it did before. [30] For ships of Kittim will come against him; therefore he will be disheartened and will return and become enraged at the holy covenant and take action; so he will come back and show regard for those who forsake the holy covenant. [31] Forces from him will arise, desecrate the sanctuary fortress, and do away with the regular sacrifice. And they will set up the abomination of desolation. [32] By smooth *words* he will turn to godlessness those who act wickedly toward the covenant, but the people who know their God will display strength and take action. [33] Those who have insight among the people will give understanding to the many; yet they will fall by sword and by flame, by captivity and by plunder for *many* days. [34] Now when they fall they will be granted a little help, and many will join with them in hypocrisy. [35] Some of those who have insight will fall, in order to refine, purge and make them pure until the end time; because *it is* still *to come* at the appointed time."

Deuteronomy 18:21–22

> [21] You may say in your heart, 'How will we know the word which the LORD has not spoken?' [22] When a prophet speaks in the name of the LORD, if the thing does not come about or come true, that is the thing which the LORD has not spoken. The prophet has spoken it presumptuously; you shall not be afraid of him.

VI. Daniel's Prophecy of Seventy Weeks of Years

Background:

As we introduce this prophetic portion, it is noteworthy that we focus on the occasion of this revelation to Daniel. (Daniel 9:1) Foremost on Daniel's mind is the prophecy of Jeremiah found in Jeremiah 25:11–12.

Jeremiah 25:11–12 (Speaking of Jerusalem and Judea)

> [11] This whole land will be a desolation and a horror, and these nations will serve the king of Babylon seventy years.
>
> [12] 'Then it will be when seventy years are completed I will punish the king of Babylon and that nation,' declares the LORD, 'for their iniquity, and the land of the Chaldeans; and I will make it an everlasting desolation.'

Though Jeremiah began his prophetic ministry twenty-two years before Daniel, he was a contemporary of Daniel. In Jeremiah 25:11–12, he prophesies concerning the duration of the captivity as being seventy years. This seventy-year captivity was to give the land the required rest for the 490 years Israel refused to honor the sabbath rest of the land. The law called for them to give the land a rest every seventh year. Just as the law required a sabbath rest on the seventh day of the week, so the law also required the land have a sabbath rest every seventh year. When the 490 years is divided by seven, it equals seventy years. This is the amount of time that the land should have been given its sabbath rest.

Leviticus 25:1–4

> [1] The LORD then spoke to Moses at Mount Sinai, saying, [2] "Speak to the sons of Israel and say to them, 'When you come into the land which I shall give you, then the land shall have a sabbath to the LORD. [3] Six years you shall sow your field, and six years you shall prune your vineyard and gather in its crop, [4] but during the seventh year the land shall have a sabbath rest, a sabbath to the LORD; you shall not sow your field nor prune your vineyard.'"

Leviticus 26:32–35

> [32] I will make the land desolate so that your enemies who settle in it will be appalled over it. [33] You, however, I will scatter among the nations and will draw out a sword after you, as your land becomes desolate and your cities become waste.
>
> [34] 'Then the land will enjoy its sabbaths all the days of the desolation, while you are in your enemies' land; then the land will rest and enjoy its sabbaths. [35] All the days of *its* desolation it will observe the rest which it did not observe on your sabbaths, while you were living on it.

If we count back 490 years from 605 BC, when Jerusalem was destroyed, it takes us to the days when Eli's wicked sons judged in Israel. This was just prior to the appointment of Saul, the first king of Israel. In the closing verses of 2 Chronicles 36, the author describes Nebuchadnezzar's destruction of Jerusalem and King Cyrus' edict that gave Ezra permission for the Jews to return to Jerusalem and rebuild the temple. The author specifically refers to Jeremiah's prophecy of the seventy-year captivity in fulfillment of the sabbath rest for the land.

Daniel 9:1–27

> [1] In the first year of Darius the son of Ahasuerus, of Median descent, who was made king over the kingdom of the Chaldeans— [2] in the first year of his reign, I, Daniel, observed in the books the number of the years which was *revealed as* the word of the LORD to Jeremiah the prophet for the completion of the desolations of Jerusalem, *namely*, seventy years. [3] So I gave my attention to the Lord God to seek *Him by* prayer and supplications, with fasting, sackcloth and ashes. [4] I prayed to the LORD my God and confessed and said, "Alas, O Lord, the great and awesome God, who keeps His covenant and lovingkindness for those who love Him and keep His commandments, [5] we have sinned, committed iniquity, acted wickedly and rebelled, even turning aside from Your commandments and ordinances. [6] Moreover, we have not listened to Your servants the prophets, who spoke in Your name to our kings, our princes, our fathers and all the people of the land.
>
> [7] "Righteousness belongs to You, O Lord, but to us open shame, as it is this day—to the men of Judah, the inhabitants of Jerusalem and all Israel, those who are nearby and those who are far away in all the countries to which You have driven them, because of their unfaithful deeds which they have committed against You. [8] Open shame belongs to us, O Lord, to our kings, our princes and our fathers, because we have sinned against You. [9] To the Lord our God *belong* compassion and

forgiveness, for we have rebelled against Him; [10] nor have we obeyed the voice of the LORD our God, to walk in His teachings which He set before us through His servants the prophets. [11] Indeed all Israel has transgressed Your law and turned aside, not obeying Your voice; so the curse has been poured out on us, along with the oath which is written in the law of Moses the servant of God, for we have sinned against Him. [12] Thus He has confirmed His words which He had spoken against us and against our rulers who ruled us, to bring on us great calamity; for under the whole heaven there has not been done *anything* like what was done to Jerusalem. [13] As it is written in the law of Moses, all this calamity has come on us; yet we have not sought the favor of the LORD our God by turning from our iniquity and giving attention to Your truth. [14] Therefore the LORD has kept the calamity in store and brought it on us; for the LORD our God is righteous with respect to all His deeds which He has done, but we have not obeyed His voice.

[15] "And now, O Lord our God, who have brought Your people out of the land of Egypt with a mighty hand and have made a name for Yourself, as it is this day—we have sinned, we have been wicked. [16] O Lord, in accordance with all Your righteous acts, let now Your anger and Your wrath turn away from Your city Jerusalem, Your holy mountain; for because of our sins and the iniquities of our fathers, Jerusalem and Your people *have become* a reproach to all those around us. [17] So now, our God, listen to the prayer of Your servant and to his supplications, and for Your sake, O Lord, let Your face shine on Your desolate sanctuary. [18] O my God, incline Your ear and hear! Open Your eyes and see our desolations and the city which is called by Your name; for we are not presenting our supplications before You on account of any merits of our own, but on account of Your great compassion. [19] O Lord, hear! O Lord, forgive! O Lord, listen and take action! For Your own sake, O my God, do not delay, because Your city and Your people are called by Your name."

[20] Now while I was speaking and praying, and confessing my sin and the sin of my people Israel, and presenting my supplication before the LORD my God in behalf of the holy mountain of my God, [21] while I was still speaking in prayer, then the man Gabriel, whom I had seen in the vision previously, came to me in *my* extreme weariness about the time of the evening offering. [22] He gave *me* instruction and talked with me and said, "O Daniel, I have now come forth to give you insight with understanding. [23] At the beginning of your supplications the command was issued, and I have come to tell *you*, for you are highly esteemed; so give heed to the message and gain understanding of the vision.

> [24] "Seventy weeks have been decreed for your people and your holy city, to finish the transgression, to make an end of sin, to make atonement for iniquity, to bring in everlasting righteousness, to seal up vision and prophecy and to anoint the most holy *place.* [25] So you are to know and discern *that* from the issuing of a decree to restore and rebuild Jerusalem until Messiah the Prince *there will be* seven weeks and sixty-two weeks; it will be built again, with plaza and moat, even in times of distress. [26] Then after the sixty-two weeks the Messiah will be cut off and have nothing, and the people of the prince who is to come will destroy the city and the sanctuary. And its end *will come* with a flood; even to the end there will be war; desolations are determined. [27] And he will make a firm covenant with the many for one week, but in the middle of the week he will put a stop to sacrifice and grain offering; and on the wing of abominations *will come* one who makes desolate, even until a complete destruction, one that is decreed, is poured out on the one who makes desolate."

2 Chronicles 36:19–23

> [19] Then they burned the house of God and broke down the wall of Jerusalem, and burned all its fortified buildings with fire and destroyed all its valuable articles. [20] Those who had escaped from the sword he carried away to Babylon; and they were servants to him and to his sons until the rule of the kingdom of Persia, [21] to fulfill the word of the LORD by the mouth of Jeremiah, until the land had enjoyed its sabbaths. All the days of its desolation it kept sabbath until seventy years were complete.
>
> [22] Now in the first year of Cyrus king of Persia—in order to fulfill the word of the LORD by the mouth of Jeremiah—the LORD stirred up the spirit of Cyrus king of Persia, so that he sent a proclamation throughout his kingdom, and also *put it* in writing, saying, [23] "Thus says Cyrus king of Persia, 'The LORD, the God of heaven, has given me all the kingdoms of the earth, and He has appointed me to build Him a house in Jerusalem, which is in Judah. Whoever there is among you of all His people, may the LORD his God be with him, and let him go up!'"

Daniel prophesied during the seventy-year captivity. It is with this on his mind that Daniel prays this moving prayer of national confession and repentance on behalf of disobedient Israel (Daniel 9:3–19). God responds by sending the angel, Gabriel, with a revelation of the seventy weeks of years (490 years) decreed in lots of seven (Daniel 9:23). The revelation of the seventy weeks of years was given to Daniel as a message of hope and encouragement.

This passage (Daniel 9:24–27) predicts the following:

- The end of the sinful rule of humankind (v. 24)

- The atoning sacrifice of Christ (v. 24–26)
- The ushering in of the righteous reign of the Messiah (v. 24)
- The end of the seventy-year Babylonian captivity (v. 25)
- The restoration of Jerusalem during distressing times (v. 25)
- The coming of the Messiah (v. 25–26)
- The destruction of Jerusalem by the Romans in 70 AD (v. 26)
- The time of world-wide turmoil and conflict (v. 26)
- The Antichrist's behavior during the seven-year Tribulation (v. 27)

Note: Christ is obviously aware of Daniel's 70 weeks of years (Daniel 9:26) when He refers to the destruction of Jerusalem by the Romans in Luke 21:24.

Luke 21:24

> and they will fall by the edge of the sword, and will be led captive into all the nations; and Jerusalem will be trampled under foot by the Gentiles until the times of the Gentiles are fulfilled.

A. Definition of the seventy weeks of years

1. The Hebrew word for *week* is the "seven."

2. The literal translation of the phrase is "seventy sevens."

3. While the Hebrew word *seven* could refer to seven days, based on historical events, it is obvious that the word *seven* in Daniel 9 refers to years rather than days.

4. The prophecy includes seventy units of seven years each, which is equal to 490 years.

B. Gabriel's overview of what will happen during these seventy weeks of years

Daniel 9:24

> "Seventy weeks have been decreed for your people and your holy city, to finish the transgression, to make an end of sin, to make atonement for iniquity, to bring in everlasting righteousness, to seal up vision and prophecy and to anoint the most holy *place*."

1. The seventy weeks of years will involve Israel's relationship to the Holy City (Jerusalem).

2. Sin will rule during these days.

3. Christ will make an atonement for sin.

4. The seventy weeks of years will be followed by a reign of righteousness ("to bring in everlasting righteousness").

5. The vision and the prophecy will be sealed up.

   Note: The Hebrew word here is *chatham* (haw-tham') and means "to close up; to make an end, to mark or seal (up), to stop." The idea here is not to keep the vision hidden but to see it through to the end or to its completion. Daniel's vision and prophecy pertains almost exclusively to "the times of the Gentiles."

6. The "most holy place" is obviously a reference to Christ. (The word *place* in the NASB has been added to the text but does not appear in the original.)

C. The 490-year time clock of Daniel 9:25–27

1. The first "tic" of the clock (v. 25) – The clock started ticking the day the decree was issued for the Jews to return to rebuild Jerusalem.

2. It should be noted that there were four decrees given by Persian kings which allowed the Jews to return to the land.

   a. The decree of Cyrus was to rebuild the temple given in 539 BC. (Ezra 1:1–4)

   b. The decree of Darius was to resume the work of rebuilding the temple given in 519 BC. (Ezra 5:3–7)

   c. The decree of Artaxerxes gave permission to Ezra and any Jew to return with Ezra to beautify the temple. This decree was given in 457 BC. (Ezra 7:11–16)

   d. The decree of Artaxerxes gave permission to Nehemiah to return to rebuild the walls of Jerusalem. This decree was given in 444 BC. (Nehemiah 2:1–8)

      Nehemiah 2:1–8

      > [1] And it came about in the month Nisan, in the twentieth year of King Artaxerxes, that wine *was* before him, and I took up the wine and gave it to the king. Now I had not been sad in his presence. [2] So the king said to me, "Why is your face sad though you are not sick? This is nothing but sadness of heart." Then I was very much afraid. [3] I said to the king, "Let the king live forever. Why should my face not be sad when the city, the place of my fathers' tombs, lies desolate and its gates have been consumed by fire?" [4] Then the king said to me, "What would you request?" So I prayed to the God of heaven. [5] I said to the king, "If it please the king, and if your servant has found favor before you, send me to Judah, to the

city of my fathers' tombs, that I may rebuild it." [6] Then the king said to me, the queen sitting beside him, "How long will your journey be, and when will you return?" So it pleased the king to send me, and I gave him a definite time. [7] And I said to the king, "If it please the king, let letters be given me for the governors *of the provinces* beyond the River, that they may allow me to pass through until I come to Judah, [8] and a letter to Asaph the keeper of the king's forest, that he may give me timber to make beams for the gates of the fortress which is by the temple, for the wall of the city and for the house to which I will go." And the king granted *them* to me because the good hand of my God *was* on me.

D. The 69 weeks of years (Daniel 9:25–26)

1. The 69 weeks of years are stated in three segments.

Seven weeks of years	(7 x 7)	49 years
Sixty-two weeks of years	(62 x 7)	334 years
	subtotal	483 years
One week of years	7 years	+7 years
	TOTAL	490 years

Note: Some have suggested that the first segment of 49 years is the time it took to completely rebuild the city of Jerusalem. Nehemiah rebuilt the walls in a phenomenal 52 days (Nehemiah 6:15). The remainder of the project, however, including the streets and the moats, mentioned in the latter part of Daniel 9:25, took some time longer. While it is difficult to establish a date for the restoration of the entire city, the 49 years should be about right.

2. Daniel 9:26 dates the time of the Messiah.

3. Following the segment of sixty-two weeks of years (334 years) the Messiah will be "cut off." The sixty-two weeks of years (334 years) plus the first segment of seven weeks of years (forty-nine years) makes a total of 483 years from the time the edict was given.

4. The phrase *cut off* is a Jewish idiom referring to death.

5. Daniel's prophecy makes more sense when you make your calculations using the Jewish calendar of a 360-day year.

6. What is not seen in this prophecy, is the church age, which began at Pentecost and will extend until the rapture of the church.

7. The destruction of Jerusalem was also prophesied by Christ and recorded in Luke 21:20–24.

Luke 21:20–24

> [20] "But when you see Jerusalem surrounded by armies, then recognize that her desolation is near. [21] Then those who are in Judea must flee to the mountains, and those who are in the midst of the city must leave, and those who are in the country must not enter the city; [22] because these are days of vengeance, so that all things which are written will be fulfilled. [23] Woe to those who are pregnant and to those who are nursing babies in those days; for there will be great distress upon the land and wrath to this people; [24] and they will fall by the edge of the sword, and will be led captive into all the nations; and Jerusalem will be trampled under foot by the Gentiles until the times of the Gentiles are fulfilled."

E. The seventieth week

Daniel 9:27

> "And he will make a firm covenant with the many for one week, but in the middle of the week he will put a stop to sacrifice and grain offering; and on the wing of abominations *will come* one who makes desolate, even until a complete destruction, one that is decreed, is poured out on the one who makes desolate."

1. This seven-year period is the tribulation period, referred to by Jeremiah as "the time of Jacob's trouble." (Jeremiah 30:7)

2. The covenant making and covenant breaking is the program of the Antichrist.

    a. He is the little/big horn that emerges from the ten-kingdom alliance pictured in Daniel's vision and recorded in Daniel 7.

    b. He is the beast that arises out of the sea in Revelation 13.

    c. He will appear as a messenger of peace and promise to bring order to a chaotic and war-torn world.

    d. He will allow Israel to rebuild the temple and resume the sacrificial ceremonies.

    e. He will make a covenant with Israel that promises the Jews can live in peace in their land without fear. This is what Israel longs for today.

f. After three and a half years, he will show his true colors and rally as many nations that will follow him in breaking the covenant and turning against Israel.

g. The last three and a half years are referred to as "the Great Tribulation." It focuses on Israel and will culminate in the Battle of Armageddon.

h. This wicked world leader will bring many under his wing of protection and lead them into idolatry.

3. Revelation 13:11–18 tells us the false prophet (another beast) will deceive many with signs, wonders, and miracles, and he will compel all to worship the image of the first beast.

Revelation 13:11–18

> [11] Then I saw another beast coming up out of the earth; and he had two horns like a lamb and he spoke as a dragon. [12] He exercises all the authority of the first beast in his presence. And he makes the earth and those who dwell in it to worship the first beast, whose fatal wound was healed. [13] He performs great signs, so that he even makes fire come down out of heaven to the earth in the presence of men. [14] And he deceives those who dwell on the earth because of the signs which it was given him to perform in the presence of the beast, telling those who dwell on the earth to make an image to the beast who had the wound of the sword and has come to life. [15] And it was given to him to give breath to the image of the beast, so that the image of the beast would even speak and cause as many as do not worship the image of the beast to be killed. [16] And he causes all, the small and the great, and the rich and the poor, and the free men and the slaves, to be given a mark on their right hand or on their forehead, [17] and *he provides* that no one will be able to buy or to sell, except the one who has the mark, *either* the name of the beast or the number of his name. [18] Here is wisdom. Let him who has understanding calculate the number of the beast, for the number is that of a man; and his number is six hundred and sixty-six.

CHAPTER 12

Eschatology – Part 2
(Prophecy Yet to be Fulfilled)

I. Definitions

In order to fully understand the content of this chapter, it is beneficial to define the following terms and events:

A. **The First Advent of Christ** – The first time Jesus came to earth. This took place in Bethlehem when the eternal Son of God was born to the virgin Mary.

B. **The Second Advent of Christ** – This describes the second time Jesus will physically come to earth to sit on the throne of David to rule for 1,000 years (the Millennium).

C. **The Church Age** – This is the period of time beginning at Pentecost and ending when the church is raptured.

D. **The Rapture of the Church** – This is the event in which all believers (both physically dead and alive) are taken up to meet Jesus Christ in the air and live with Him forever. At that time all believers will receive a new glorified body, like the body of Jesus. (1 Thessalonians 4:13–18; 1 Corinthians 15:50–58)

E. **The Tribulation** – This word is used to describe the seven-year rule of the Antichrist. (Scripture also portrays this as Daniel's seventieth week of years.)

F. **The Great Tribulation** – This term describes the turbulent final three and a half years of the seven-year Tribulation. The Bible refers to this as the time of Jacob's (Israel's) trouble.

G. **The Millennium** – The 1,000-year peaceful reign of Christ on earth, during which Satan is bound and has no influence.

H. Two great days

In this study we want to turn our attention to two great days. They are major days in the prophetic word.

- The Day of the Lord (sometimes referred to as *the Day of Jehovah*)
- The Day of Christ (sometimes referred to as *the Day of the Lord Jesus*)

A careful study of these two days is necessary to fully understand the coming events that will mark the fulfillment of all biblical prophecy. As we examine the texts, we will see that the phrase *the Day of the Lord* is a broad term that the Holy Spirit used to refer to the closing days of this world as we know it. This day incorporates the rapture of the church, the tribulation period, the Second Advent of Christ, the 1,000-year reign of Christ, all of God's end-time judgments, and all the events of the last days.

We will also see that the references to *the Day of Christ* and *the Day of the Lord Jesus* are terms which refer only to the rapture of the church.

1. The Day of the Lord (sometimes referred to as *the Day of Jehovah*)

    This day is one of the major themes of the Old Testament.

    a. The Day of the Lord and the Day of Jehovah are one and the same.

    b. The following are Old Testament references to this day:

        Isaiah 13:6–9

            [6] Wail, for the day of the LORD is near!
            It will come as destruction from the Almighty.
            [7] Therefore all hands will fall limp,
            And every man's heart will melt.
            [8] They will be terrified,
            Pains and anguish will take hold of *them*;
            They will writhe like a woman in labor,
            They will look at one another in astonishment,
            Their faces aflame.
            [9] Behold, the day of the LORD is coming,
            Cruel, with fury and burning anger,
            To make the land a desolation;
            And He will exterminate its sinners from it.

Ezekiel 30:3 (Read within the context)

> "For the day is near,
> Even the day of the LORD is near;
> It will be a day of clouds,
> A time *of doom* for the nations."

Joel 1:15

> Alas for the day!
> For the day of the LORD is near,
> And it will come as destruction from the Almighty.

Joel 2:1–3

> [1] Blow a trumpet in Zion,
> And sound an alarm on My holy mountain!
> Let all the inhabitants of the land tremble,
> For the day of the LORD is coming;
> Surely it is near,
> [2] A day of darkness and gloom,
> A day of clouds and thick darkness.
> As the dawn is spread over the mountains,
> *So* there is a great and mighty people;
> There has never been *anything* like it,
> Nor will there be again after it
> To the years of many generations.
> [3] A fire consumes before them
> And behind them a flame burns.
> The land is like the garden of Eden before them
> But a desolate wilderness behind them,
> And nothing at all escapes them.

Joel 2:19–32

> [19] The LORD will answer and say to His people,
> "Behold, I am going to send you grain, new wine and oil,
> And you will be satisfied *in full* with them;
> And I will never again make you a reproach among the nations.
> [20] "But I will remove the northern *army* far from you,
> And I will drive it into a parched and desolate land,
> And its vanguard into the eastern sea,
> And its rear guard into the western sea.

And its stench will arise and its foul smell will come up,
For it has done great things."

[21] Do not fear, O land, rejoice and be glad,
For the LORD has done great things.
[22] Do not fear, beasts of the field,
For the pastures of the wilderness have turned green,
For the tree has borne its fruit,
The fig tree and the vine have yielded in full.
[23] So rejoice, O sons of Zion,
And be glad in the LORD your God;
For He has given you the early rain for *your* vindication.
And He has poured down for you the rain,
The early and latter rain as before.
[24] The threshing floors will be full of grain,
And the vats will overflow with the new wine and oil.
[25] "Then I will make up to you for the years
That the swarming locust has eaten,
The creeping locust, the stripping locust and the gnawing locust,
My great army which I sent among you.
[26] "You will have plenty to eat and be satisfied
And praise the name of the LORD your God,
Who has dealt wondrously with you;
Then My people will never be put to shame.
[27] "Thus you will know that I am in the midst of Israel,
And that I am the LORD your God,
And there is no other;
And My people will never be put to shame.

[28] "It will come about after this
That I will pour out My Spirit on all mankind;
And your sons and daughters will prophesy,
Your old men will dream dreams,
Your young men will see visions.
[29] "Even on the male and female servants
I will pour out My Spirit in those days.

[30] "I will display wonders in the sky and on the earth,
Blood, fire and columns of smoke.
[31] "The sun will be turned into darkness
And the moon into blood
Before the great and awesome day of the LORD comes.
[32] "And it will come about that whoever calls on the name of the LORD

Will be delivered;
For on Mount Zion and in Jerusalem
There will be those who escape,
As the LORD has said,
Even among the survivors whom the LORD calls."

Amos 5:18

Alas, you who are longing for the day of the LORD,
For what purpose *will* the day of the LORD *be* to you?
It *will be* darkness and not light;

The entire book of Zephaniah is focused on *the Day of the Lord.*

c. The following are New Testament references to *the Day of the Lord*:

Peter makes mention to *the Day of the Lord* as he quotes the prophet Joel (Joel 2:28–32) in a reference to the last days. He includes the whole church age in Joel's prophecy.

2 Peter 3:3–14

[3] Know this first of all, that in the last days mockers will come with *their* mocking, following after their own lusts, [4] and saying, "Where is the promise of His coming? For *ever* since the fathers fell asleep, all continues just as it was from the beginning of creation." [5] For when they maintain this, it escapes their notice that by the word of God *the* heavens existed long ago and *the* earth was formed out of water and by water, [6] through which the world at that time was destroyed, being flooded with water. [7] But by His word the present heavens and earth are being reserved for fire, kept for the day of judgment and destruction of ungodly men.

[8] But do not let this one *fact* escape your notice, beloved, that with the Lord one day is like a thousand years, and a thousand years like one day. [9] The Lord is not slow about His promise, as some count slowness, but is patient toward you, not wishing for any to perish but for all to come to repentance.

[10] But the day of the Lord will come like a thief, in which the heavens will pass away with a roar and the elements will be destroyed with intense heat, and the earth and its works will be burned up.

> [11] Since all these things are to be destroyed in this way, what sort of people ought you to be in holy conduct and godliness, [12] looking for and hastening the coming of the day of God, because of which the heavens will be destroyed by burning, and the elements will melt with intense heat! [13] But according to His promise we are looking for new heavens and a new earth, in which righteousness dwells.
>
> [14] Therefore, beloved, since you look for these things, be diligent to be found by Him in peace, spotless and blameless,

Acts 2:20

> 'THE SUN WILL BE TURNED INTO DARKNESS
> AND THE MOON INTO BLOOD,
> BEFORE THE GREAT AND GLORIOUS DAY OF THE LORD SHALL COME.'

In essence, the Day of the Lord includes everything that is a part of the end times, including God's judgment.

2. The Day of Christ (sometimes referred to as *the Day of the Lord Jesus*)

   This term is not found in the Old Testament.

   a. While *the Day of the Lord* refers to a series of events, *the Day of Christ* refers to the rapture of the church.

   b. Because the church is the "mystery" revealed only in the New Testament, *the Day of Christ* is not seen in the Old Testament.

   c. There are many references to this day in the teachings of the New Testament.

1 Corinthians 1:7–8

> [7] so that you are not lacking in any gift, awaiting eagerly the revelation of our Lord Jesus Christ, [8] who will also confirm you to the end, blameless in the day of our Lord Jesus Christ.

Philippians 1:6

> *For I am* confident of this very thing, that He who began a good work in you will perfect it until the day of Christ Jesus.

Philippians 1:10

> so that you may approve the things that are excellent, in order to be sincere and blameless until the day of Christ;

Philippians 2:16

> holding fast the word of life, so that in the day of Christ I will have reason to glory because I did not run in vain nor toil in vain.

d. The Day of the Lord includes the Day of Christ.

- Note the opening statement in 1 Thessalonians 5:1–6.
- Paul writes that they should not be ignorant of these truths, because these things are taught throughout the Old Testament, as well as in the teachings of Jesus. (See also Matthew 24 and 25.)

1 Thessalonians 5:1–6

> [1] Now as to the times and the epochs, brethren, you have no need of anything to be written to you. [2] For you yourselves know full well that the day of the Lord will come just like a thief in the night. [3] While they are saying, "Peace and safety!" then destruction will come upon them suddenly like labor pains upon a woman with child, and they will not escape. [4] But you, brethren, are not in darkness, that the day would overtake you like a thief; [5] for you are all sons of light and sons of day. We are not of night nor of darkness; [6] so then let us not sleep as others do, but let us be alert and sober.

3. These two important days contrasted

a. The Day of Christ specifically refers to the rapture of the church.

- Note the opening statement in 1 Thessalonians 4:13–18.
- Paul wrote to correct the erroneous teaching in the church at Thessalonica. They were teaching that the Christians who had died missed the rapture.
- He proceeded to correct this error with the true sequence of the last days.

1 Thessalonians 4:13–18

> [13] But we do not want you to be uninformed, brethren, about those who are asleep, so that you will not grieve as do the rest who have no hope. [14] For if we believe that Jesus died and rose again, even so God will bring with Him those who have fallen asleep in Jesus. [15] For this we say to you by the word of the Lord, that we who are alive and remain until the coming of the Lord, will not precede those who have fallen asleep. [16] For the Lord Himself will descend from heaven with a shout, with the voice of *the* archangel and with the trumpet of God, and the dead in Christ will rise first. [17] Then we who are alive and remain will be caught up together with them in the clouds to meet the Lord in the air, and so we shall always be with the Lord. [18] Therefore comfort one another with these words.

b. The Day of the Lord includes everything that is to transpire during the end times, including the rapture. (See 1 Thessalonians 5:1-6.)

I. Three future judgments

1. The Judgment Seat of Christ

2 Corinthians 5:10

> For we must all appear before the judgment seat of Christ, so that each one may be recompensed for his deeds in the body, according to what he has done, whether good or bad.

1 Corinthians 3:10–15

> [10] According to the grace of God which was given to me, like a wise master builder I laid a foundation, and another is building on it. But each man must be careful how he builds on it. [11] For no man can lay a foundation other than the one which is laid, which is Jesus Christ. [12] Now if any man builds on the foundation with gold, silver, precious stones, wood, hay, straw, [13] each man's work will become evident; for the day will show it because it is *to be* revealed with fire, and the fire itself will test the quality of each man's work. [14] If any man's work which he has built on it remains, he will receive a reward. [15] If any man's work is burned up, he will suffer loss; but he himself will be saved, yet so as through fire.

a. This is a judgment of the believer's works and service done after salvation.

b. This judgment is not for sin, but for rewards or loss of rewards.

c. This occurs sometime after the rapture of the church.

2. The judgment of the nations

Matthew 25:31–46

> [31] "But when the Son of Man comes in His glory, and all the angels with Him, then He will sit on His glorious throne. [32] All the nations will be gathered before Him; and He will separate them from one another, as the shepherd separates the sheep from the goats; [33] and He will put the sheep on His right, and the goats on the left.
>
> [34] "Then the King will say to those on His right, 'Come, you who are blessed of My Father, inherit the kingdom prepared for you from the foundation of the world. [35] For I was hungry, and you gave Me *something* to eat; I was thirsty, and you gave Me *something* to drink; I was a stranger, and you invited Me in; [36] naked, and you clothed Me; I was sick, and you visited Me; I was in prison, and you came to Me.' [37] Then the righteous will answer Him, 'Lord, when did we see You hungry, and feed You, or thirsty, and give You *something* to drink? [38] And when did we see You a stranger, and invite You in, or naked, and clothe You? [39] When did we see You sick, or in prison, and come to You?' [40] The King will answer and say to them, 'Truly I say to you, to the extent that you did it to one of these brothers of Mine, *even* the least *of them*, you did it to Me.'
>
> [41] "Then He will also say to those on His left, 'Depart from Me, accursed ones, into the eternal fire which has been prepared for the devil and his angels; [42] for I was hungry, and you gave Me *nothing* to eat; I was thirsty, and you gave Me nothing to drink; [43] I was a stranger, and you did not invite Me in; naked, and you did not clothe Me; sick, and in prison, and you did not visit Me.' [44] Then they themselves also will answer, 'Lord, when did we see You hungry, or thirsty, or a stranger, or naked, or sick, or in prison, and did not take care of You?' [45] Then He will answer them, 'Truly I say to you, to the extent that you did not do it to one of the least of these, you did not do it to Me.' [46] These will go away into eternal punishment, but the righteous into eternal life."

a. Here Jesus teaches concerning the judgment of the nations, which will take place when He comes to earth "in power and great glory" (His Second Advent).

b. As the text indicates, the issue in this judgment will be how the nations treated Israel, especially during the tribulation period.

c. Again, we are reminded of the Abrahamic Covenant which called for a blessing on those who blessed Israel and a curse on those who cursed Israel.

Genesis 12:3

> "And I will bless those who bless you,
> And the one who curses you I will curse.
> And in you all the families of the earth will be blessed."

d. Scripture is not very clear on the timing of this judgment, but the most logical time is for it to occur at the end of the tribulation period.

e. Following the Tribulation, God will address the issue of how the nations treated Israel during the "time of Jacob's trouble."

3. The Great White Throne Judgment

Revelation 20:11–15

> [11] Then I saw a great white throne and Him who sat upon it, from whose presence earth and heaven fled away, and no place was found for them. [12] And I saw the dead, the great and the small, standing before the throne, and books were opened; and another book was opened, which is *the book* of life; and the dead were judged from the things which were written in the books, according to their deeds. [13] And the sea gave up the dead which were in it, and death and Hades gave up the dead which were in them; and they were judged, every one *of them* according to their deeds. [14] Then death and Hades were thrown into the lake of fire. This is the second death, the lake of fire. [15] And if anyone's name was not found written in the book of life, he was thrown into the lake of fire.

a. This judgment will occur after the Millennium.

b. It is God's final judgment of those who have rejected Christ and died in their sin.

c. Everyone whose name is not found recorded in the Book of Life will experience the second death described in Revelation 20:15.

d. No Christians will appear before the Great White Throne Judgment. Christians are those who have accepted the blood of Christ in payment for their sin and their names are written in the Lamb's Book of Life.

J. Three future battles

1. The battle to plunder Israel (Ezekiel 38–39) The Bible is unclear about the timing of this battle.

2. The Battle of Armageddon (Joel 3, Zechariah 12 and 14, Revelation 16:13–16, Revelation 19:11–21)

3. The last great battle (Revelation 20:7–10) This battle takes place at the end of the Millennium.

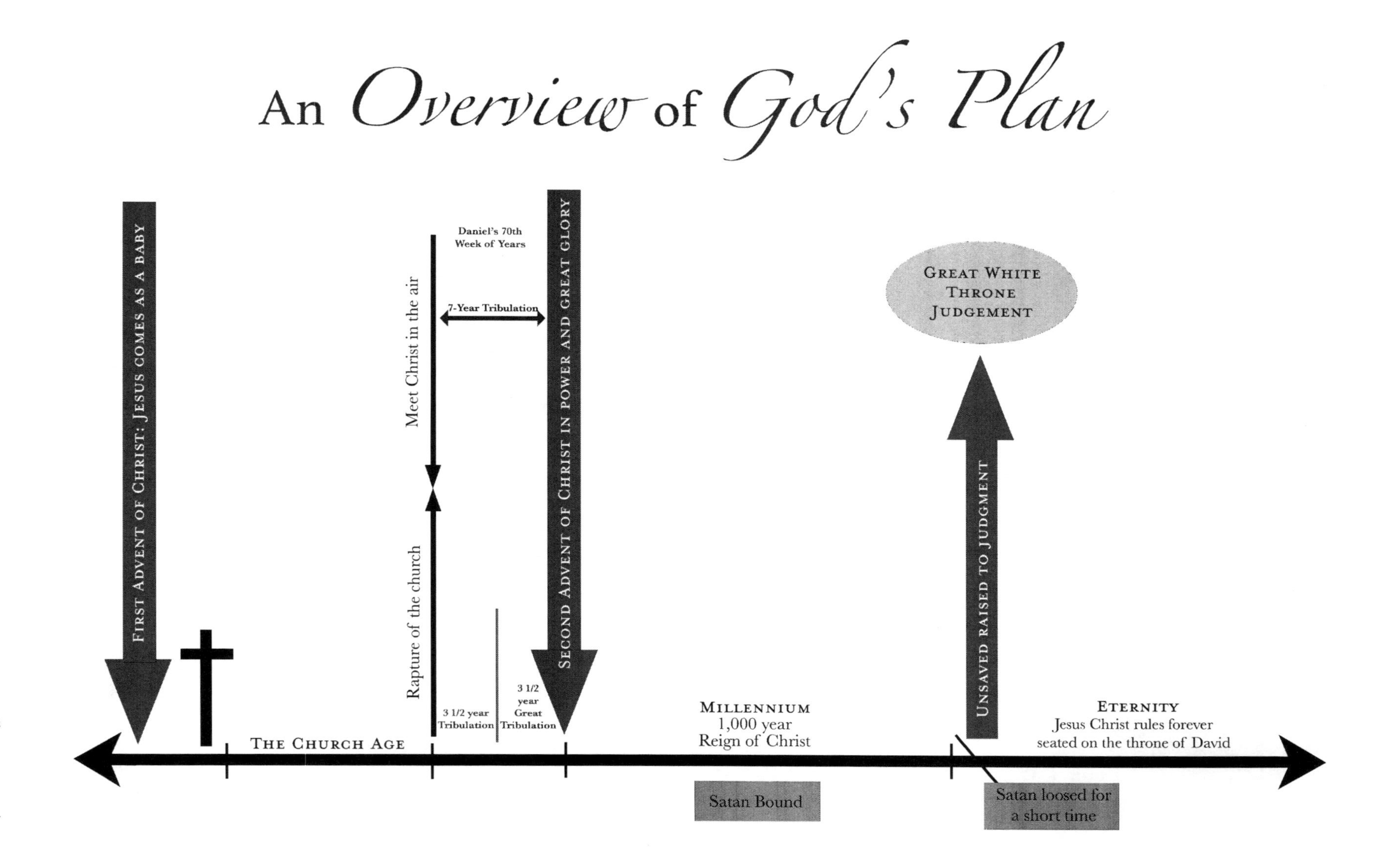
An Overview of God's Plan
First Advent of Christ: Jesus comes as a baby
The Church Age
Rapture of the church
Meet Christ in the air
Daniel's 70th Week of Years
7-Year Tribulation
3 1/2 year Tribulation
3 1/2 year Great Tribulation
Second Advent of Christ in power and great glory
Millennium
1,000 year
Reign of Christ
Satan Bound
Great White Throne Judgement
Unsaved raised to judgment
Eternity
Jesus Christ rules forever
seated on the throne of David
Satan loosed for a short time

II. A Chronological List of Events That Are Yet to Be Fulfilled

A. The apostasy in the church

1 Timothy 4:1–3

> [1] But the Spirit explicitly says that in later times some will fall away from the faith, paying attention to deceitful spirits and doctrines of demons, [2] by means of the hypocrisy of liars seared in their own conscience as with a branding iron, [3] *men* who forbid marriage *and advocate* abstaining from foods which God has created to be gratefully shared in by those who believe and know the truth.

2 Timothy 3:1–7

> [1] But realize this, that in the last days difficult times will come. [2] For men will be lovers of self, lovers of money, boastful, arrogant, revilers, disobedient to parents, ungrateful, unholy, [3] unloving, irreconcilable, malicious gossips, without self-control, brutal, haters of good, [4] treacherous, reckless, conceited, lovers of pleasure rather than lovers of God, [5] holding to a form of godliness, although they have denied its power; Avoid such men as these. [6] For among them are those who enter into households and captivate weak women weighed down with sins, led on by various impulses, [7] always learning and never able to come to the knowledge of the truth.

2 Timothy 4:3–4

> [3] For the time will come when they will not endure sound doctrine; but *wanting* to have their ears tickled, they will accumulate for themselves teachers in accordance to their own desires, [4] and will turn away their ears from the truth and will turn aside to myths.

2 Thessalonians 2:1–12

> [1] Now we request you, brethren, with regard to the coming of our Lord Jesus Christ and our gathering together to Him, [2] that you not be quickly shaken from your composure or be disturbed either by a spirit or a message or a letter as if from us, to the effect that the day of the Lord has come. [3] Let no one in any way deceive you, for *it will not come* unless the apostasy comes first, and the man of lawlessness is revealed, the son of destruction, [4] who opposes and exalts himself above every so-called god or object of worship, so that he takes his seat in the temple of God, displaying himself as being God. [5] Do you not remember that

> while I was still with you, I was telling you these things? [6] And you know what restrains him now, so that in his time he will be revealed. [7] For the mystery of lawlessness is already at work; only he who now restrains *will do so* until he is taken out of the way. [8] Then that lawless one will be revealed whom the Lord will slay with the breath of His mouth and bring to an end by the appearance of His coming; [9] *that is*, the one whose coming is in accord with the activity of Satan, with all power and signs and false wonders, [10] and with all the deception of wickedness for those who perish, because they did not receive the love of the truth so as to be saved. [11] For this reason God will send upon them a deluding influence so that they will believe what is false, [12] in order that they all may be judged who did not believe the truth, but took pleasure in wickedness.

1 John 2:18

> Children, it is the last hour; and just as you heard that antichrist is coming, even now many antichrists have appeared; from this we know that it is the last hour.

Note: These scriptures above describe the very days in which we are living.

B. The Rapture of the church

Though the English word *rapture* is not found in the Bible, the Greek word is translated "caught up" in most English Bible versions. The word *rapture* comes from the Latin Vulgate Bible, which was translated from the Greek word *harpázō*, meaning to "catch (away, up), pluck, pull, take (by force)."

1 Corinthians 15:50–58

> [50] Now I say this, brethren, that flesh and blood cannot inherit the kingdom of God; nor does the perishable inherit the imperishable. [51] Behold, I tell you a mystery; we will not all sleep, but we will all be changed, [52] in a moment, in the twinkling of an eye, at the last trumpet; for the trumpet will sound, and the dead will be raised imperishable, and we will be changed. [53] For this perishable must put on the imperishable, and this mortal must put on immortality. [54] But when this perishable will have put on the imperishable, and this mortal will have put on immortality, then will come about the saying that is written, "Death is swallowed up in victory. [55] O death, where is your victory? O death, where is your sting?" [56] The sting of death is sin, and the power of sin is the law; [57] but thanks be to God, who gives us the victory through our Lord Jesus Christ.

> [58] Therefore, my beloved brethren, be steadfast, immovable, always abounding in the work of the Lord, knowing that your toil is not *in* vain in the Lord.

1 Thessalonians 4:13–18

> [13] But we do not want you to be uninformed, brethren, about those who are asleep, so that you will not grieve as do the rest who have no hope. [14] For if we believe that Jesus died and rose again, even so God will bring with Him those who have fallen asleep in Jesus. [15] For this we say to you by the word of the Lord, that we who are alive and remain until the coming of the Lord, will not precede those who have fallen asleep. [16] For the Lord Himself will descend from heaven with a shout, with the voice of *the* archangel and with the trumpet of God, and the dead in Christ will rise first. [17] Then we who are alive and remain will be <u>caught up</u> together with them in the clouds to meet the Lord in the air, and so we shall always be with the Lord. [18] Therefore comfort one another with these words.
>
> Note: The underlined words have been added by author.

C. The seven-year Tribulation

This tribulation period is Daniel's seventieth week. It is divided into two periods of three and a half years each. The first three and a half-year period will be one of relative peace for Israel and the world, as the "man of sin" (the Antichrist) rallies the world to his cause. The second three and a half years is called The Great Tribulation because of the increased troublesome times, especially for Israel. Some of the major passages where the seven years of tribulation are described are Matthew 24:15–28, Mark 13:14–27, Luke 21:20–28, and Revelation 6–19.

The following events occur during this seven-year tribulation period:

1. The Antichrist is revealed.

    a. Daniel's vision includes a description of the Antichrist.

    Speculations continue to surface concerning the identity of this satanic leader. Some of those have included Adolf Hitler, Benito Mussolini, and the Pope. These speculations are no doubt futile and a waste of energy. There is nothing in scripture that gives the slightest indication that we will know who the Antichrist is before he makes his powerful move. The general thrust of scripture indicates that in the beginning of his leadership, he will appear and act like the world's greatest all time "good guy." He will appear as the angel of peace and a messenger of hope for the world. His agenda will be one of deception, in which he keeps his true purposes secret until after he has taken the world into his confidence.

Daniel 11:36–45

> [36] "Then the king will do as he pleases, and he will exalt and magnify himself above every god and will speak monstrous things against the God of gods; and he will prosper until the indignation is finished, for that which is decreed will be done. [37] He will show no regard for the gods of his fathers or for the desire of women, nor will he show regard for any *other* god; for he will magnify himself above *them* all. [38] But instead he will honor a god of fortresses, a god whom his fathers did not know; he will honor *him* with gold, silver, costly stones and treasures. [39] He will take action against the strongest of fortresses with *the help of* a foreign god; he will give great honor to those who acknowledge *him* and will cause them to rule over the many, and will parcel out land for a price.
>
> [40] "At the end time the king of the South will collide with him, and the king of the North will storm against him with chariots, with horsemen and with many ships; and he will enter countries, overflow *them* and pass through. [41] He will also enter the Beautiful Land, and many *countries* will fall; but these will be rescued out of his hand: Edom, Moab and the foremost of the sons of Ammon. [42] Then he will stretch out his hand against *other* countries, and the land of Egypt will not escape. [43] But he will gain control over the hidden treasures of gold and silver and over all the precious things of Egypt; and Libyans and Ethiopians *will follow* at his heels. [44] But rumors from the East and from the North will disturb him, and he will go forth with great wrath to destroy and annihilate many. [45] He will pitch the tents of his royal pavilion between the seas and the beautiful Holy Mountain; yet he will come to his end, and no one will help him."

2 John 7

> For many deceivers have gone out into the world, those who do not acknowledge Jesus Christ *as* coming in the flesh. This is the deceiver and the antichrist.

b. These New Testament passages give us further details of both the spirit of the antichrist (1 John 2:18–23) and the physical appearance of the Antichrist (2 Thessalonians 2:3–12). He will be revealed after the church and the Holy Spirit are removed.

1 John 2:18–23

> [18] Children, it is the last hour; and just as you heard that antichrist is coming, even now many antichrists have appeared; from this we know that it is the last hour. [19] They went out from us, but they were not *really* of us; for if they had been of us, they would have remained with us; but *they went out*, so that it would be shown that they all are not of us. [20] But you have an anointing from the Holy One, and you all know. [21] I have not written to you because you do not know the truth, but because you do know it, and because no lie is of the truth. [22] Who is the liar but the one who denies that Jesus is the Christ? This is the antichrist, the one who denies the Father and the Son. [23] Whoever denies the Son does not have the Father; the one who confesses the Son has the Father also.

2 Thessalonians 2:3–12

> [3] Let no one in any way deceive you, for *it will not come* unless the apostasy comes first, and the man of lawlessness is revealed, the son of destruction, [4] who opposes and exalts himself above every so-called god or object of worship, so that he takes his seat in the temple of God, displaying himself as being God. [5] Do you not remember that while I was still with you, I was telling you these things? [6] And you know what restrains him now, so that in his time he will be revealed. [7] For the mystery of lawlessness is already at work; only he who now restrains *will do so* until he is taken out of the way. [8] Then that lawless one will be revealed whom the Lord will slay with the breath of His mouth and bring to an end by the appearance of His coming; [9] *that is*, the one whose coming is in accord with the activity of Satan, with all power and signs and false wonders, [10] and with all the deception of wickedness for those who perish, because they did not receive the love of the truth so as to be saved. [11] For this reason God will send upon them a deluding influence so that they will believe what is false, [12] in order that they all may be judged who did not believe the truth, but took pleasure in wickedness.

2. The Antichrist signs a seven-year treaty with Israel. In the middle of the Tribulation, the Antichrist breaks the treaty.

Daniel 9:27

> "And he will make a firm covenant with the many for one week, but in the middle of the week he will put a stop to sacrifice and grain offering; and on the wing of abominations *will come* one who makes desolate, even until a complete destruction, one that is decreed, is poured out on the one who makes desolate."

2 Thessalonians 2:4

> who opposes and exalts himself above every so-called god or object of worship, so that he takes his seat in the temple of God, displaying himself as being God.

3. The three and a half-year Great Tribulation is the second half of the Tribulation and the "time of Jacob's trouble." There will be severe persecution towards Israel.

Jeremiah 30:7

> 'Alas! for that day is great,
> There is none like it;
> And it is the time of Jacob's distress,
> But he will be saved from it.'

4. The nations gather to annihilate Israel at the Battle of Armageddon.

Revelation 16:12–16

> [12] The sixth *angel* poured out his bowl on the great river, the Euphrates; and its water was dried up, so that the way would be prepared for the kings from the east.
>
> [13] And I saw *coming* out of the mouth of the dragon and out of the mouth of the beast and out of the mouth of the false prophet, three unclean spirits like frogs; [14] for they are spirits of demons, performing signs, which go out to the kings of the whole world, to gather them together for the war of the great day of God, the Almighty. [15] ("Behold, I am coming like a thief. Blessed is the one who stays awake and keeps his clothes, so that he will not walk about naked and men will not see his shame.") [16] And they gathered them together to the place which in Hebrew is called Har-Magedon.

Joel 3:9–13

> [9] Proclaim this among the nations:
> Prepare a war; rouse the mighty men!
> Let all the soldiers draw near, let them come up!
> [10] Beat your plowshares into swords And your pruning hooks into spears;
> Let the weak say, "I am a mighty man."
> [11] Hasten and come, all you surrounding nations,
> And gather yourselves there.
> Bring down, O Lord, Your mighty ones.

[12] Let the nations be aroused
And come up to the valley of Jehoshaphat,
For there I will sit to judge
All the surrounding nations.
[13] Put in the sickle, for the harvest is ripe.
Come, tread, for the wine press is full;
The vats overflow, for their wickedness is great.

Revelation 14:14–20

[14] Then I looked, and behold, a white cloud, and sitting on the cloud *was* one like a son of man, having a golden crown on His head and a sharp sickle in His hand. [15] And another angel came out of the temple, crying out with a loud voice to Him who sat on the cloud, "Put in your sickle and reap, for the hour to reap has come, because the harvest of the earth is ripe." [16] Then He who sat on the cloud swung His sickle over the earth, and the earth was reaped.

[17] And another angel came out of the temple which is in heaven, and he also had a sharp sickle. [18] Then another angel, the one who has power over fire, came out from the altar; and he called with a loud voice to him who had the sharp sickle, saying, "Put in your sharp sickle and gather the clusters from the vine of the earth, because her grapes are ripe." [19] So the angel swung his sickle to the earth and gathered *the clusters from* the vine of the earth, and threw them into the great wine press of the wrath of God. [20] And the wine press was trodden outside the city, and blood came out from the wine press, up to the horses' bridles, for a distance of two hundred miles.

Revelation 19:11–15

[11] And I saw heaven opened, and behold, a white horse, and He who sat on it *is* called Faithful and True, and in righteousness He judges and wages war. [12] His eyes *are* a flame of fire, and on His head *are* many diadems; and He has a name written *on Him* which no one knows except Himself. [13] *He is* clothed with a robe dipped in blood, and His name is called The Word of God. [14] And the armies which are in heaven, clothed in fine linen, white *and* clean, were following Him on white horses. [15] From His mouth comes a sharp sword, so that with it He may strike down the nations, and He will rule them with a rod of iron; and He treads the wine press of the fierce wrath of God, the Almighty.

Further details that happen during the Tribulation:

a. There will be wars.

Revelation 6:3–4

> [3] When He broke the second seal, I heard the second living creature saying, "Come." [4] And another, a red horse, went out; and to him who sat on it, it was granted to take peace from the earth, and that *men* would slay one another; and a great sword was given to him.

b. There will be famines.

Revelation 6:5–6

> [5] When He broke the third seal, I heard the third living creature saying, "Come." I looked, and behold, a black horse; and he who sat on it had a pair of scales in his hand. [6] And I heard *something* like a voice in the center of the four living creatures saying, "A quart of wheat for a denarius, and three quarts of barley for a denarius; and do not damage the oil and the wine."

c. There will be much loss of life.

Revelation 6:7–8

> [7] When the Lamb broke the fourth seal, I heard the voice of the fourth living creature saying, "Come." [8] I looked, and behold, an ashen horse; and he who sat on it had the name Death; and Hades was following with him. Authority was given to them over a fourth of the earth, to kill with sword and with famine and with pestilence and by the wild beasts of the earth.

d. There will be great hostility toward those who stand with Christ. These people become followers of Jesus during the Tribulation.

Revelation 6:9–11

> [9] When the Lamb broke the fifth seal, I saw underneath the altar the souls of those who had been slain because of the word of God, and because of the testimony which they had maintained; [10] and they cried out with a loud voice, saying, "How long, O Lord, holy and true, will You refrain from judging and avenging our blood on those who dwell on the earth?" [11] And there was given to each of them a white robe; and they were told that they should rest for a little while longer, until *the number of* their fellow servants and their brethren who were to be killed even as they had been, would be completed also.

e. Great natural disasters will come upon the earth.

Revelation 6:12–14

> [12] I looked when He broke the sixth seal, and there was a great earthquake; and the sun became black as sackcloth *made* of hair, and the whole moon became like blood; [13] and the stars of the sky fell to the earth, as a fig tree casts its unripe figs when shaken by a great wind. [14] The sky was split apart like a scroll when it is rolled up, and every mountain and island were moved out of their places.

f. In response to God's wrath, those on earth will be in terror.

Revelation 6:12–17

> [12] I looked when He broke the sixth seal, and there was a great earthquake; and the sun became black as sackcloth *made* of hair, and the whole moon became like blood; [13] and the stars of the sky fell to the earth, as a fig tree casts its unripe figs when shaken by a great wind. [14] The sky was split apart like a scroll when it is rolled up, and every mountain and island were moved out of their places. [15] Then the kings of the earth and the great men and the commanders and the rich and the strong and every slave and free man hid themselves in the caves and among the rocks of the mountains; [16] and they said to the mountains and to the rocks, "Fall on us and hide us from the presence of Him who sits on the throne, and from the wrath of the Lamb; [17] for the great day of their wrath has come, and who is able to stand?"

g. All heaven will stand in silent awe when the unspeakable results of God's fury is unleashed.

Revelation 8:1

> When the Lamb broke the seventh seal, there was silence in heaven for about half an hour.

D. The Millennium

The Second Advent of Christ is when Jesus comes in power and great glory as victor to set up His 1,000-year earthly kingdom. During this 1,000-year peaceful reign, Satan will be bound.

Revelation 20:1–3

> [1] Then I saw an angel coming down from heaven, holding the key of the abyss and a great chain in his hand. [2] And he laid hold of the dragon, the serpent of old, who is the devil and Satan, and bound him for a thousand years; [3] and he threw him into the abyss, and shut *it* and sealed *it* over him, so that he would not deceive the nations any longer, until the thousand years were completed; after these things he must be released for a short time.

E. Satan loosed for a short time

Revelation 20:3

> and he threw him into the abyss, and shut *it* and sealed *it* over him, so that he would not deceive the nations any longer, until the thousand years were completed; after these things he must be released for a short time.

Revelation 20:7–9

> [7] When the thousand years are completed, Satan will be released from his prison, [8] and will come out to deceive the nations which are in the four corners of the earth, Gog and Magog, to gather them together for the war; the number of them is like the sand of the seashore. [9] And they came up on the broad plain of the earth and surrounded the camp of the saints and the beloved city, and fire came down from heaven and devoured them.

F. The last great battle (Revelation 20:7–10) Revelation is very clear that when Satan is loosed, he will make one last effort to war against Christ.

G. Satan ultimately defeated

Revelation 20:10

> And the devil who deceived them was thrown into the lake of fire and brimstone, where the beast and the false prophet are also; and they will be tormented day and night forever and ever.

H. The Great White Throne Judgment

At this judgment Satan, his angels, and all those who have rejected Christ are judged and cast into the lake of fire.

Revelation 20:11–15

> [11] Then I saw a great white throne and Him who sat upon it, from whose presence earth and heaven fled away, and no place was found for them. [12] And I saw the dead, the great and the small, standing before the throne, and books were opened; and another book was opened, which is *the book* of life; and the dead were judged from the things which were written in the books, according to their deeds. [13] And the sea gave up the dead which were in it, and death and Hades gave up the dead which were in them; and they were judged, every one *of them* according to their deeds. [14] Then death and Hades were thrown into the lake of fire. This is the second death, the lake of fire. [15] And if anyone's name was not found written in the book of life, he was thrown into the lake of fire.

I. A new heaven and a new earth

This present heaven and earth will be replaced. Christ will take His place on the throne of David and reign for eternity.

Revelation 21:1–6

> [1] Then I saw a new heaven and a new earth; for the first heaven and the first earth passed away, and there is no longer *any* sea. [2] And I saw the holy city, new Jerusalem, coming down out of heaven from God, made ready as a bride adorned for her husband. [3] And I heard a loud voice from the throne, saying, "Behold, the tabernacle of God is among men, and He will dwell among them, and they shall be His people, and God Himself will be among them, [4] and He will wipe away every tear from their eyes; and there will no longer be *any* death; there will no longer be *any* mourning, or crying, or pain; the first things have passed away."
>
> [5] And He who sits on the throne said, "Behold, I am making all things new." And He said, "Write, for these words are faithful and true." [6] Then He said to me, "It is done. I am the Alpha and the Omega, the beginning and the end. I will give to the one who thirsts from the spring of the water of life without cost."

2 Peter 3:10–13

> [10] But the day of the Lord will come like a thief, in which the heavens will pass away with a roar and the elements will be destroyed with intense heat, and the earth and its works will be burned up.

> [11] Since all these things are to be destroyed in this way, what sort of people ought you to be in holy conduct and godliness, [12] looking for and hastening the coming of the day of God, because of which the heavens will be destroyed by burning, and the elements will melt with intense heat! [13] But according to His promise we are looking for new heavens and a new earth, in which righteousness dwells.

III. The Establishment of Christ's Eternal Kingdom

A. God's promises found in the covenants

1. The Abrahamic Covenant (Genesis 12,13,15)

   It is the universal application that is at the forefront as we look at the arrival of Christ. Jesus is the descendent of Abraham and the one through whom "all of the families of the earth will be blessed" (Genesis 12:3). This is the reason Matthew begins the genealogy of Jesus Christ with Abraham.

2. The Davidic Covenant (2 Samuel 7:4–17)

   This covenant guarantees that the Messiah will ultimately reign forever. This is summarized in 2 Samuel 7:16, "Your house and your kingdom shall endure before Me forever; your throne shall be established forever." This is the focus of the book of Matthew.

3. The major components of the Davidic Covenant:

   a. This covenant secured for David: (v. 11,13,16)

      - A house forever (Davidic heirs to the throne)
      - A throne forever (Kingly position for his heirs)
      - A kingdom forever (A nation over which to rule)

   b. This covenant is unconditional and eternal.

   c. This covenant finds its complete fulfillment in the person of Christ the King.

If the Abrahamic Covenant and the Davidic Covenant are kept in mind, it will not be difficult to understand the purpose of the book of Matthew. The book was written to present Christ as King of the Jews and their long-awaited Messiah.

The misconception that God is finished with Israel and that He has no intention of fulfilling His promises to them has no foundation in biblical truth and is a serious departure from His written Word. Matthew 24:35 records Jesus affirming God's promises when He says, "Heaven and earth will pass away, but my words will never pass away." Paul addresses this question in Romans 11:1, "I say then, God has not rejected His people, has He? May it never be! For I too am an Israelite, a descendant of Abraham, of the tribe of Benjamin." Also note Romans 11:11 which reads "I say then, they did not stumble so as to fall, did they? May it never be! But by their transgression, salvation has *come* to the Gentiles, to make them jealous." The fact is that there are just too many unfulfilled promises and prophecies for the God of justice and faithfulness to merely disregard. If God fails to keep His promises to Israel, there is no reason for us to believe that God will keep His promises to us.

B. God's promises to Israel fulfilled in the New Testament

After just over four hundred years of silence, the angel, Gabriel, who had announced the coming of the Messiah to Daniel, breaks into human history with the announcement of the birth of John the Baptist. Six months later Gabriel made the announcement of the birth of Christ, the Messiah.

As we approach the New Testament, we must move seamlessly to the arrival of Christ, His ministry, His death, His resurrection, and the church age. In fact, it is a continuation of God's plan, which has its foundation in the covenants God made with Israel in the Old Testament. The offering of Christ, the Messiah, is in complete harmony with the fulfillment of these covenants. The message of John the Baptist was a call for Israel to repent since Israel's King had arrived and was living among them. Israel rejected her King and Messiah, and, consequently, Christ's kingdom continues to be postponed. Israel was scattered throughout the nations, and a new purpose was launched: the church was established in order that the gospel be delivered to the rest of the world. All this is in harmony with the providence and plan of God.

2 Peter 3:9

> The Lord is not slow about His promise, as some count slowness, but is patient toward you, not wishing for any to perish but for all to come to repentance.

1. The book of Matthew opens by tracing the lineage of Christ from Abraham to David and from David to Christ. See Matthew 1.

2. The book of Matthew is characterized by many references to the messages of the Old Testament prophets, who wrote concerning the coming of the Messiah.

Matthew 1:23 (See Isaiah 7:14.)

> "Behold, the virgin shall be with child and shall bear a Son, and they shall call His name Immanuel," which translated means, "God with us."

Matthew 2:6 (See Micah 5:2.)

"'AND YOU, BETHLEHEM, LAND OF JUDAH,
ARE BY NO MEANS LEAST AMONG THE LEADERS OF JUDAH;
FOR OUT OF YOU SHALL COME FORTH A RULER
WHO WILL SHEPHERD MY PEOPLE ISRAEL.'"

Matthew 2:15 (See Hosea 11:1.)

He remained there until the death of Herod. *This was* to fulfill what had been spoken by the Lord through the prophet: "OUT OF EGYPT I CALLED MY SON."

Matthew 2:18 (See Jeremiah 31:15.)

"A VOICE WAS HEARD IN RAMAH,
WEEPING AND GREAT MOURNING,
RACHEL WEEPING FOR HER CHILDREN;
AND SHE REFUSED TO BE COMFORTED,
BECAUSE THEY WERE NO MORE."

Matthew 2:22–23 (Isaiah 53:2–4 – The Nazarene was one who was despised.)

[22] But when he heard that Archelaus was reigning over Judea in place of his father Herod, he was afraid to go there. Then after being warned *by God* in a dream, he left for the regions of Galilee, [23] and came and lived in a city called Nazareth. *This was* to fulfill what was spoken through the prophets: "He shall be called a Nazarene."

Matthew 3:3 (See Isaiah 40:3.)

For this is the one referred to by Isaiah the prophet when he said,

"THE VOICE OF ONE CRYING IN THE WILDERNESS,
'MAKE READY THE WAY OF THE LORD,
MAKE HIS PATHS STRAIGHT!'"

Matthew 4:14–16 (See Isaiah 9:1–2.)

[14] *This was* to fulfill what was spoken through Isaiah the prophet:

[15] "THE LAND OF ZEBULUN AND THE LAND OF NAPHTALI, BY THE WAY OF THE SEA, BEYOND THE JORDAN, GALILEE OF THE GENTILES— [16] "THE PEOPLE WHO WERE SITTING IN DARKNESS SAW A GREAT LIGHT, AND THOSE WHO WERE SITTING IN THE LAND AND SHADOW OF DEATH, UPON THEM A LIGHT DAWNED."

C. The ministry of John the Baptist

1. John the Baptist was a forerunner to announce the coming of the King.

Matthew 3:1–12

[1] Now in those days John the Baptist came, preaching in the wilderness of Judea, saying, [2] "Repent, for the kingdom of heaven is at hand." [3] For this is the one referred to by Isaiah the prophet when he said,

"THE VOICE OF ONE CRYING IN THE WILDERNESS,
'MAKE READY THE WAY OF THE LORD,
MAKE HIS PATHS STRAIGHT!'"

[4] Now John himself had a garment of camel's hair and a leather belt around his waist; and his food was locusts and wild honey. [5] Then Jerusalem was going out to him, and all Judea and all the district around the Jordan; [6] and they were being baptized by him in the Jordan River, as they confessed their sins.

[7] But when he saw many of the Pharisees and Sadducees coming for baptism, he said to them, "You brood of vipers, who warned you to flee from the wrath to come? [8] Therefore bear fruit in keeping with repentance; [9] and do not suppose that you can say to yourselves, 'We have Abraham for our father'; for I say to you that from these stones God is able to raise up children to Abraham. [10] The axe is already laid at the root of the trees; therefore every tree that does not bear good fruit is cut down and thrown into the fire.

[11] "As for me, I baptize you with water for repentance, but He who is coming after me is mightier than I, and I am not fit to remove His sandals; He will baptize you with the Holy Spirit and fire. [12] His winnowing fork is in His hand, and He will thoroughly clear His threshing floor; and He will gather His wheat into the barn, but He will burn up the chaff with unquenchable fire."

a. John the Baptist was born six months before Christ.

b. John the Baptist began his public ministry six months before Christ began His.

c. As Christ's public ministry begins, John the Baptist fades into the background.

d. John the Baptist is imprisoned and later beheaded just about three months after Christ began His public ministry.

2. John the Baptist was a preacher of righteousness.

3. John the Baptist's message was for all to repent in preparation for the entrance of the King of Righteousness.

D. Jesus' formal offer to the Jews to become their King

Matthew 21:1–9

> [1] When they had approached Jerusalem and had come to Bethphage, at the Mount of Olives, then Jesus sent two disciples, [2] saying to them, "Go into the village opposite you, and immediately you will find a donkey tied *there* and a colt with her; untie them and bring them to Me. [3] If anyone says anything to you, you shall say, 'The Lord has need of them,' and immediately he will send them." [4] This took place to fulfill what was spoken through the prophet:
>
> [5] "Say to the daughter of Zion,
> 'Behold your King is coming to you,
> Gentle, and mounted on a donkey,
> Even on a colt, the foal of a beast of burden.'"
>
> [6] The disciples went and did just as Jesus had instructed them, [7] and brought the donkey and the colt, and laid their coats on them; and He sat on the coats. [8] Most of the crowd spread their coats in the road, and others were cutting branches from the trees and spreading them in the road. [9] The crowds going ahead of Him, and those who followed, were shouting,
>
> "Hosanna to the Son of David;
> Blessed is He who comes in the name of the Lord;
> Hosanna in the highest!"

1. Notice the Jewish character of this event.

- It has to do with a king in the line of David.

- Christ meekly, but genuinely, offers himself to Israel to become their King in fulfillment of the Davidic Covenant.

2. Mark also announces the coming King.

Mark 11:9–10

[9] Those who went in front and those who followed were shouting:

"Hosanna!
Blessed is He who comes in the name of the Lord;
[10] Blessed *is* the coming kingdom of our father David;
Hosanna in the highest!"

3. John gives an account of this event.

John 12:13–15

[13] took the branches of the palm trees and went out to meet Him, and *began* to shout, "Hosanna! Blessed is He who comes in the name of the Lord, even the King of Israel." [14] Jesus, finding a young donkey, sat on it; as it is written, [15] "Fear not, daughter of Zion; behold, your King is coming, seated on a donkey's colt."

4. As Jesus approaches Jerusalem, the sincerity of Christ's offer is recorded in the book of Luke.

Luke 20:38–44

[38] "Now He is not the God of the dead but of the living; for all live to Him." [39] Some of the scribes answered and said, "Teacher, You have spoken well." [40] For they did not have courage to question Him any longer about anything.

[41] Then He said to them, "How *is it that* they say the Christ is David's son? [42] For David himself says in the book of Psalms,

'The Lord said to my Lord,
"Sit at My right hand,
[43] Until I make Your enemies a footstool for Your feet."'

[44] Therefore David calls Him 'Lord,' and how is He his son?"

E. The King rejected by Israel

The long-awaited Messiah presented Himself as Israel's King, and they did not accept Him as their King.

John 19:14b–16

> And he said to the Jews, "Behold, your King!" [15] So they cried out, "Away with *Him*, away with *Him*, crucify Him!" Pilate said to them, "Shall I crucify your King?" The chief priests answered, "We have no king but Caesar." [16] So he then handed Him over to them to be crucified.

F. The ushering in of Christ's earthly kingdom

Following the seven-year tribulation period, Jesus will make His Second Advent appearance. He will return to the earth and become the victor of the Battle of Armageddon. The Tribulation (Daniel's seventieth week of years) is part of God's judgment of Israel and the nations, as well as the ushering in of the righteous reign of Christ the King.

Revelation 16:16–17

> [16] And they gathered them together to the place which in Hebrew is called Har-Magedon.
>
> [17] Then the seventh *angel* poured out his bowl upon the air, and a loud voice came out of the temple from the throne, saying, "It is done."

Revelation 19:1–12

> [1] After these things I heard something like a loud voice of a great multitude in heaven, saying,
>
> "Hallelujah! Salvation and glory and power belong to our God; [2] BECAUSE HIS JUDGMENTS ARE TRUE AND RIGHTEOUS; for He has judged the great harlot who was corrupting the earth with her immorality, and HE HAS AVENGED THE BLOOD OF HIS BOND-SERVANTS ON HER." [3] And a second time they said, "Hallelujah! HER SMOKE RISES UP FOREVER AND EVER." [4] And the twenty-four elders and the four living creatures fell down and worshiped God who sits on the throne saying, "Amen. Hallelujah!" [5] And a voice came from the throne, saying,
>
> "Give praise to our God, all you His bond-servants, you who fear Him, the small and the great." [6] Then I heard *something* like the voice of a great multitude and like the sound of many waters and like the sound of mighty peals of thunder, saying,

> "Hallelujah! For the Lord our God, the Almighty, reigns.
>
> [7] Let us rejoice and be glad and give the glory to Him, for the marriage of the Lamb has come and His bride has made herself ready." [8] It was given to her to clothe herself in fine linen, bright *and* clean; for the fine linen is the righteous acts of the saints.
>
> [9] Then he said to me, "Write, 'Blessed are those who are invited to the marriage supper of the Lamb.'" And he said to me, "These are true words of God." [10] Then I fell at his feet to worship him. But he said to me, "Do not do that; I am a fellow servant of yours and your brethren who hold the testimony of Jesus; worship God. For the testimony of Jesus is the spirit of prophecy."
>
> [11] And I saw heaven opened, and behold, a white horse, and He who sat on it *is* called Faithful and True, and in righteousness He judges and wages war. [12] His eyes *are* a flame of fire, and on His head *are* many diadems; and He has a name written *on Him* which no one knows except Himself.

IV. Conditions that Will Define the End Times

Matthew 24:4–28 and Luke 21:20–36 record a major discourse by Christ Jesus concerning the end times. Note the questions Jesus is answering. They ask *when* and *what will be the signs* of His coming and of the end of the age?

These are not just random statements concerning conditions that will exist prior to and during the last days, but our Lord follows a definite sequence of events in answer to His disciples' questions. In a parallel passage found in Luke 21:20–36, Jesus refers to these events as the completion of "the times of the Gentiles," which we have seen is a reference to Daniel's seventy weeks of years. This prophecy focuses on the seventieth week of years (or the seven years of the Tribulation), which immediately precedes the Second Advent of Christ.

A. Destruction of the temple

In Matthew 24:1–2 Jesus tells of the destruction of the temple and surrounding buildings. This took place in 70 AD.

B. Beginning of the Tribulation

Matthew 24:4–14 describes the events of the first 3½ years of the Tribulation.

C. The Great Tribulation

Matthew 24:15–28 describes the events of the second 3½ years of the Tribulation as "the Great Tribulation."

D. The Second Advent of Christ

Matthew 24:29–31 describes the Second Advent of Christ that will take place at the end of the Tribulation when He comes "in power and great glory." (See Revelation 1:7.)

E. The judgment of the nations

In Matthew 25:31–46, Jesus teaches concerning the judgment of the nations, which will be carried out upon His Second Advent. As the text indicates, the issue in this judgment will be how the nations treated Israel during the tribulation years. Again, we are reminded of the Abrahamic Covenant that called for a blessing on those who blessed Israel and a curse on those who cursed Israel. (See Genesis 12:3.)

In Matthew 24:32 – 25:30, Jesus gives several parables and illustrations that focus on the answer to the disciples' original questions recorded in Matthew 24:3 concerning the "signs of His coming."

Matthew 25:31–46

> 31 "But when the Son of Man comes in His glory, and all the angels with Him, then He will sit on His glorious throne. 32 All the nations will be gathered before Him; and He will separate them from one another, as the shepherd separates the sheep from the goats; 33 and He will put the sheep on His right, and the goats on the left.
>
> 34 "Then the King will say to those on His right, 'Come, you who are blessed of My Father, inherit the kingdom prepared for you from the foundation of the world. 35 For I was hungry, and you gave Me *something* to eat; I was thirsty, and you gave Me *something* to drink; I was a stranger, and you invited Me in; 36 naked, and you clothed Me; I was sick, and you visited Me; I was in prison, and you came to Me.' 37 Then the righteous will answer Him, 'Lord, when did we see You hungry, and feed You, or thirsty, and give You *something* to drink? 38 And when did we see You a stranger, and invite You in, or naked, and clothe You? 39 When did we see You sick, or in prison, and come to You?' 40 The King will answer and say to them, 'Truly I say to you, to the extent that you did it to one of these brothers of Mine, *even* the least *of them*, you did it to Me.'

[41] "Then He will also say to those on His left, 'Depart from Me, accursed ones, into the eternal fire which has been prepared for the devil and his angels; [42] for I was hungry, and you gave Me *nothing* to eat; I was thirsty, and you gave Me nothing to drink; [43] I was a stranger, and you did not invite Me in; naked, and you did not clothe Me; sick, and in prison, and you did not visit Me.' [44] Then they themselves also will answer, 'Lord, when did we see You hungry, or thirsty, or a stranger, or naked, or sick, or in prison, and did not take care of You?' [45] Then He will answer them, 'Truly I say to you, to the extent that you did not do it to one of the least of these, you did not do it to Me.' [46] These will go away into eternal punishment, but the righteous into eternal life."

F. Recently fulfilled prophecy that sets the stage for the introduction of the Tribulation that begins after the Rapture of the church

1. On May 14, 1948, against all odds, Israel became a sovereign nation for the first time since Nebuchadnezzar conquered Jerusalem in 697 BC.

    - This door was opened in 1947 when the United Nations narrowly supported a resolution to establish a homeland for the Jewish people. The motion passed by only one vote.
    - If the Antichrist is going to make and break a covenant with Israel, Israel would have had to become a sovereign nation.

    Daniel 9:27

    "And he will make a firm covenant with the many for one week, but in the middle of the week he will put a stop to sacrifice and grain offering; and on the wing of abominations *will come* one who makes desolate, even until a complete destruction, one that is decreed, is poured out on the one who makes desolate."

2. Israel has won several major wars with most of its neighboring nations and against all odds remains a sovereign nation yet today.

    - The war of independence in 1948 began immediately after Ben Gurion declared Israel a sovereign nation. Israel had no organized army and very few weapons.
    - During the six-day war in 1967, Israel was attacked by most of its neighboring nations and pulled off a stunning victory.
    - The Yom Kipper War in October of 1973 started on the Jewish holiday of rest, fasting, and prayer. Israel was unprepared for this attack but was still victorious.

3. All the current talk of globalism is not surprising, since during the Tribulation, Satan will establish a one-world government (led by the Antichrist), with a unified financial system (controlled by the mark of the beast), and a universal religion (led by the false prophet).

Revelation 13:16–17

[16] And he causes all, the small and the great, and the rich and the poor, and the free men and the slaves, to be given a mark on their right hand or on their forehead, [17] and *he provides* that no one will be able to buy or to sell, except the one who has the mark, *either* the name of the beast or the number of his name.

Revelation 13:4

they worshiped the dragon because he gave his authority to the beast; and they worshiped the beast, saying, "Who is like the beast, and who is able to wage war with him?"

4. Jesus prophesied about the current condition of the world prior to the Tribulation and the Second Advent.

Matthew 24:3–12

[3] As He was sitting on the Mount of Olives, the disciples came to Him privately, saying, "Tell us, when will these things happen, and what *will be* the sign of Your coming, and of the end of the age?"

[4] And Jesus answered and said to them, "See to it that no one misleads you. [5] For many will come in My name, saying, 'I am the Christ,' and will mislead many. [6] You will be hearing of wars and rumors of wars. See that you are not frightened, for *those things* must take place, but *that* is not yet the end. [7] For nation will rise against nation, and kingdom against kingdom, and in various places there will be famines and earthquakes. [8] But all these things are *merely* the beginning of birth pangs.

[9] "Then they will deliver you to tribulation, and will kill you, and you will be hated by all nations because of My name. [10] At that time many will fall away and will betray one another and hate one another. [11] Many false prophets will arise and will mislead many. [12] Because lawlessness is increased, most people's love will grow cold."

(See also Mark 13:1–13.)

a. New heresies and false doctrines are being introduced at an increasing rate like never before. This is even the case within the church.

b. International conflicts often arise in this generation.

c. Global pandemics are on the rise.

d. Famine and earthquake activity in our world is increasing.

e. Christians are being persecuted and martyred every day.

f. Anarchy reigns in many of our streets and communities around the world.

g. Jesus calls these things "the beginning of birth pangs" of the end of the age.

We must remember that after the Rapture of the church occurs and when the Antichrist reveals himself, the seven-year Tribulation begins.

2 Thessalonians 2:1–3

> [1] Now we request you, brethren, with regard to the coming of our Lord Jesus Christ and our gathering together to Him, [2] that you not be quickly shaken from your composure or be disturbed either by a spirit or a message or a letter as if from us, to the effect that the day of the Lord has come. [3] Let no one in any way deceive you, for *it will not come* unless the apostasy comes first, and the man of lawlessness is revealed, the son of destruction

V. The Church and the Tribulation

A. In order to come to the right conclusions about the Tribulation we must start our study in the Old Testament.

1. If you begin your study of future events in the New Testament with the teachings of Christ, as many do, you will likely come to many wrong conclusions in your study of the prophetic word.

2. Remember, the Bible is a unit. The words and teachings of Christ are not *more* inspired than the writings of the Old Testament prophets. The Bible clearly teaches *all* scripture is *equally* inspired by God.

3. God's plan for the ages did not begin in the book of Matthew or Revelation, but in the book of beginnings (Genesis). This is the reason our study of prophecy began in Genesis 3, rather than Matthew 1.

B. Biblical reasons why we believe the church will not go through the Tribulation:

1. Because the seven-year Tribulation is Daniel's last week of years and is part of God's judgment on the nation of Israel for rejecting their King.

2. The church age is not a part of the seventy weeks of years found in Daniel 9.

3. Because the tribulation period is the "time of Jacob's (Israel's) trouble."

    a. The Tribulation is designed as a judgment on Israel for its unfaithfulness to God.

    b. The trouble that Israel faces during the last three and a half years will play a major role in drawing them back to God and recognizing Jesus Christ as their Messiah.

    c. Many of the events that will take place during the Tribulation are Jewish in character.

        1) Rebuilding of the temple

        2) Reestablishing the sacrifices

        3) Bringing God's judgment on Israel

4. Because the Holy Spirit (the Restrainer) will be removed from this world (Rapture of the church) prior to the appearance of the Antichrist and the beginning of the tribulation period.

    a. The Holy Spirit, who is present in the life of every believer, is the Great Restrainer.

    b. The Holy Spirit came on the Day of Pentecost to indwell those who trusted Christ. These early Christians then became the first members of the church, the Body of Christ.

    c. The Restrainer's presence in the world is through the life of believers, as they stand for righteousness, justice, and truth. (2 Thessalonians 2:6–7)

        1 John 4:3–4

        > [3] and every spirit that does not confess Jesus is not from God; this is the *spirit* of the antichrist, of which you have heard that it is coming, and now it is already in the world. [4] You are from God, little children, and have overcome them; because greater is He who is in you than he who is in the world.

    d. When the church is removed, so also the Holy Spirit and His godly influence will be removed.

e. With no one left on earth to speak on behalf of God's righteousness, the way for the Antichrist is paved for his evil work.

2 Thessalonians 2:1–7

[1] Now we request you, brethren, with regard to the coming of our Lord Jesus Christ and our gathering together to Him, [2] that you not be quickly shaken from your composure or be disturbed either by a spirit or a message or a letter as if from us, to the effect that the day of the Lord has come. [3] Let no one in any way deceive you, for *it will not come* unless the apostasy comes first, and the man of lawlessness is revealed, the son of destruction, [4] who opposes and exalts himself above every so-called god or object of worship, so that he takes his seat in the temple of God, displaying himself as being God. [5] Do you not remember that while I was still with you, I was telling you these things? [6] And you know what restrains him now, so that in his time he will be revealed. [7] For the mystery of lawlessness is already at work; only he who now restrains *will do so* until he is taken out of the way.

5. Because a spirit of expectancy in connection with the Rapture of the church is a prominent theme in almost every text referring to this event. (If the Rapture were to take place at the end or in the middle of the Tribulation, it would be easy to set a date for the Rapture.)

1 Corinthians 15:52

in a moment, in the twinkling of an eye, at the last trumpet; for the trumpet will sound, and the dead will be raised imperishable, and we will be changed.

1 Thessalonians 4:16

For the Lord Himself will descend from heaven with a shout, with the voice of *the* archangel and with the trumpet of God, and the dead in Christ will rise first.

Matthew 24:50

the master of that slave will come on a day when he does not expect *him* and at an hour which he does not know,

Matthew 25:13

Be on the alert then, for you do not know the day nor the hour.

Matthew 24:44

For this reason you also must be ready; for the Son of Man is coming at an hour when you do not think *He will.*

Mark 13:33

"Take heed, keep on the alert; for you do not know when the *appointed* time will come."

Mark 13:36–37

[36] "in case he should come suddenly and find you asleep. [37] What I say to you I say to all, 'Be on the alert!'"

1 John 2:28

Now, little children, abide in Him, so that when He appears, we may have confidence and not shrink away from Him in shame at His coming.

6. God has a pattern of removing the righteous before He sends judgment. God removed Lot before the judgment of Sodom and Gomorrah. God removed Noah and his family before He judged the world with a flood. God will remove His people before the judgment of the Tribulation. God differentiates between "us" and "them" in 1 Thessalonians 5:3–11. God's wrath is for them, the unbelievers.

1 Thessalonians 5:3–11

[3] While they are saying, "Peace and safety!" then destruction will come upon them suddenly like labor pains upon a woman with child, and they will not escape. [4] But you, brethren, are not in darkness, that the day would overtake you like a thief; [5] for you are all sons of light and sons of day. We are not of night nor of darkness; [6] so then let us not sleep as others do, but let us be alert and sober. [7] For those who sleep do their sleeping at night, and those who get drunk get drunk at night. [8] But since we are of *the* day, let us be sober, having put on the breastplate of faith and love, and as a helmet, the hope of salvation. [9] For God has not destined us for wrath, but for obtaining salvation through our Lord Jesus Christ, [10] who died for us, so that whether we are awake or asleep, we will live together with Him. [11] Therefore encourage one another and build up one another, just as you also are doing.

7. Because the Tribulation is God's judgment for Israel. God's judgment for the church already took place at the cross when Jesus took our place and paid the penalty for our sin.

Romans 8:1–2

> [1] Therefore there is now no condemnation for those who are in Christ Jesus. [2] For the law of the Spirit of life in Christ Jesus has set you free from the law of sin and of death.

John 3:18

> He who believes in Him is not judged; he who does not believe has been judged already, because he has not believed in the name of the only begotten Son of God.

John 5:24

> "Truly, truly, I say to you, he who hears My word, and believes Him who sent Me, has eternal life, and does not come into judgment, but has passed out of death into life."

Galatians 3:12–13

> [12] However, the Law is not of faith; on the contrary, "HE WHO PRACTICES THEM SHALL LIVE BY THEM." [13] Christ redeemed us from the curse of the Law, having become a curse for us—for it is written, "CURSED IS EVERYONE WHO HANGS ON A TREE"—

1 Thessalonians 5:9–11

> [9] For God has not destined us for wrath, but for obtaining salvation through our Lord Jesus Christ, [10] who died for us, so that whether we are awake or asleep, we will live together with Him. [11] Therefore encourage one another and build up one another, just as you also are doing.

In the end Jesus is the Victor!

REVIEW QUESTIONS

(Chapters 11 and 12)

1. Describe some of the attitudes people take toward prophecy.
2. Why is the study of prophecy important?
3. What are some of the rules we should keep in mind when studying prophecy?
4. What is a dispensation?
5. Name the three major covenants in the Old Testament.
6. Give the main features of each of these three covenants.
7. What are the three applications in the Abrahamic Covenant?
8. Which covenants are conditional, and which are unconditional?
9. Start at the present time and give a list of the events that will take place in the future.
10. What has happened to Israel's promised kingdom?
11. How will this present church age end?
12. Name some of the things that will take place during the Tribulation.
13. What is the difference between the Rapture and the Second Advent of Christ?
14. Are signs given for the church? Explain.
15. Name, describe, and distinguish between the three judgments listed in your notes.
16. When will the Battle of Armageddon take place?

DOCTRINAL POSITIONS REFLECTED IN THIS BOOK

GOD

There is one God, Creator of all things, holy, infinitely perfect, and eternally existing in unity as three equally divine Persons: The Father, the Son, and the Holy Spirit.

THE BIBLE

The Bible is the inspired word of God. God has spoken in the scriptures, both Old and New Testaments, through the words of human authors. As the verbally inspired Word of God, the Bible is without error in the original writings, the complete revelation of His person and will, and the ultimate authority by which every realm of human knowledge and endeavor should be judged.

THE HUMAN CONDITION

God created Adam and Eve in His own image, but they sinned when tempted by Satan. As the offspring of Adam, all human beings are sinners by nature and by choice, alienated from God, and under His wrath. Only through God's saving work in Jesus Christ can we be rescued and reconciled to God.

JESUS CHRIST

Jesus Christ is God incarnate, fully God and fully man, one Person in two natures. Jesus, Israel's promised Messiah, was conceived by the Holy Spirit and born of the virgin Mary. He lived a sinless life, was crucified under Pontius Pilate, arose bodily from the dead, ascended into heaven, and sits at the right hand of God the Father as our High Priest and Advocate.

THE WORK OF CHRIST

Jesus Christ, as our representative and substitute, shed His blood on the cross as the perfect, all-sufficient sacrifice for our sins. His death and victorious resurrection constitute the only grounds for salvation. His righteousness is accredited to every true believer.

THE HOLY SPIRIT

The Holy Spirit is fully God and was sent to indwell believers. He glorifies the Lord Jesus Christ in all He does. He also indwells, illuminates, guides, equips, and empowers believers for Christ-like living and service.

SPIRITUAL GIFTS

The gifts of the Spirit fall into two categories: *temporal gifts,* given to the apostles and the early church to authenticate their position and message until the New Testament was completed and *ministry gifts*, some of which are given to every believer for the edification and ministry of the church, the body of Christ.

THE CHURCH

The true church comprises all who have been justified by God's grace through faith alone in Christ alone. They are united by the Holy Spirit in the body of Christ, of which He is the Head.

THE RAPTURE OF THE CHURCH (1 Thessalonians 4:13–18)

The Rapture of the church will precede the seven-year tribulation period during which God will pour out His wrath upon the earth. The Bible calls this tribulation period "The time of Jacob's (Israel's) trouble" and is not for the church. At the Rapture, believers will meet Jesus in the air.

THE SECOND ADVENT OF CHRIST

Jesus will return with His saints to the earth, following the Tribulation, to set up His millennial kingdom and rule the world for 1,000 years.

Printed in the United States
by Baker & Taylor Publisher Services